Alexander Tzonis and Liane Lefaivre

Architecture in Europe

MEMORY AND INVENTION **since 1968**

Alexander Tzonis and Liane Lefaivre

Architecture in Europe

MEMORY AND INVENTION
since 1968

RIZZOLI
NEW YORK

To Peter Loerakker in memoriam (1959–1991)

Frontispiece: Alain Sarfati, detail of housing
unit in Savigny-Le-Temple (see pp. 166–7)

Jean-Louis Cohen's essay translated from
the French by Jacqueline Taylor

First published in the United States of America in 1992 by
Rizzoli International Publications, Inc.
300 Park Avenue South, New York, NY 10010

Library of Congress Cataloging-in-Publication Data

Tzonis, Alexander.
    Architecture in Europe since 1968 : memory and invention /
Alexander Tzonis and Liane Lefaivre.
        p.   cm.
    Includes bibliographical references and index.
    ISBN 0–8478–1624–9
    1. Architecture, Modern—20th century—Europe—Themes, motives.
2. Architecture—Europe—Themes, motives.   I. Lefaivre, Liane.
II. Title.
NA958.T96   1992
724'.6—dc20   92–11565
                                                          CIP

Printed and bound in Singapore

Contents

8   Preface and acknowledgments

10   **INTRODUCTION: BETWEEN UTOPIA AND REALITY: EIGHT TENDENCIES IN ARCHITECTURE SINCE 1968 IN EUROPE** **Alexander Tzonis and Liane Lefaivre**

24   **THE SECOND-HAND CITY: MODERN TECHNOLOGY AND CHANGING URBAN IDENTITY** **Fritz Neumeyer** Chair, History and Theory of Architecture, University of Dortmund

32   **NEW DIRECTIONS IN FRENCH ARCHITECTURE AND THE SHOWCASE OF THE PARIS CITY EDGE (1965–90)** **Jean-Louis Cohen** Professor, École d'Architecture, Paris-Villemin

36   **THE DILEMMA OF TECHNOLOGY** **Peter Rice** Director, Ove Arup & Partners, London

42   **ON ECOLOGICAL ARCHITECTURE: A MEMO** **Lucius Burckhardt** Chair, Architectural Theory, Technical University, Kassel

       THE PROJECTS

44   **Atelier d'urbanisme, d'architecture et d'informatique Lucien Kroll** **THE MEDICAL FACULTY AT WOLUWE-SAINT LAMBERT, 'LA MÉMÉ'**

48   **Architectenburo Herman Hertzberger b.v.** **CENTRAAL BEHEER OFFICE BUILDING**

52   **Ricardo Bofill Taller de Arquitectura** **LA MURALLA ROJA**

54   **Studio Arquitectos PER (Clotet & Tusquets)** **BELVEDERE GEORGINA**

56   **Aldo Rossi** **SAN CATALDO CEMETERY**

60   **Aldo Rossi** **GALLARATESE HOUSING PROJECT**

64   **Mario Botta Architetto** **HOUSE AT RIVA SAN VITALE**

68   **Ralph Erskine** **BYKER WALL**

72   **Hans Hollein** **SCHULLIN JEWELRY**

74   **Foster Associates Ltd** **WILLIS, FABER & DUMAS HEAD OFFICE**

78   **Estudio Rafael Moneo** **BANKINTER**

80   **Luigi Snozzi** **CASA KALMAN**

82   **Antonio Cruz Villalon   Antonio Ortiz Garcia** **HOUSING BLOCK ON DOÑA MARIA CORONEL STREET**

84   **Renzo Piano & Richard Rogers** **CENTRE CULTUREL D'ART GEORGES POMPIDOU**

90   **Alvaro Siza** **BOUÇA SOCIAL HOUSING**

92   **Atelier d'urbanisme, d'architecture et d'informatique Lucien Kroll** **ZUP PERSEIGNE**

96   **Neave Brown** **ALEXANDRA ROAD HOUSING**

100   **Francisco Javier Saenz de Oiza** **BANCO DE BILBAO**

104   **Nicholas Grimshaw and Partners Ltd** **SPORTS HALL FOR IBM**

106   **Oscar Niemeyer Office** **COMMUNIST PARTY HEADQUARTERS**

110   **Atelier Gustav Peichl** **ORF-STUDIO**

112   **Hans Hollein** **STÄDTISCHES MUSEUM**

114   **Antonio Barrionuevo Ferrer**
HOUSING BLOCK IN PINO MONTANO

116   **Foster Associates Ltd**
RENAULT PARTS DISTRIBUTION CENTRE

120   **Building Workshop Renzo Piano**
SCHLUMBERGER INDUSTRIAL SITE

124   **Michael Hopkins & Partners**
RESEARCH LABORATORIES FOR
SCHLUMBERGER

126   **James Stirling, Michael Wilford and**
Associates
NEW STATE GALLERY

132   **Clotet, Paricio & Assoc., S.A.**
BANCO DE ESPAÑA HEADQUARTERS

134   **Oswald Matthias Ungers Architekt**
ARCHITECTURAL MUSEUM

136   **Richard Meier & Partners**
MUSEUM FOR THE DECORATIVE ARTS

138   **Alejandro de la Sota**
POST OFFICE AND
TELECOMMUNICATIONS BUILDING

142   **Studio d'Architettura Aurelio Galfetti**
PUBLIC TENNIS CLUB

144   **Ricardo Bofill Taller de Arquitectura**
LES COLONNES DE SAINT CHRISTOPHE

148   **Estudio Rafael Moneo**
MUSEO NACIONAL DE ARTE ROMANO

152   **Raili and Reima Pietilä Architects**
TAMPERE MAIN LIBRARY

156   **Richard Rogers**
LLOYD'S OF LONDON

160   **Atelier Peter Zumthor**
PROTECTION SHED OVER ROMAN RUINS

164   **Philippe Chaix   Jean Paul Morel**
Architectes
ZENITH OF MONTPELLIER

166   **Alain Sarfati-AREA**
88 HOUSING UNITS IN SAVIGNY-LE-
TEMPLE

168   **Weber, Brandt and Partners**
NEW MEDICAL FACULTY, TECHNICAL
UNIVERSITY OF AACHEN

172   **Adrien Fainsilber**
CITÉ DES SCIENCES ET DE L'INDUSTRIE,
PARC DE LA VILLETTE

174   **Jean Nouvel, Gilbert Lezènes, Pierre**
Soria, Architecture Studio
INSTITUT DU MONDE ARABE

178   **Jean Nouvel et Associés**
NÉMAUSUS

182   **Rem Koolhaas (OMA)**
THE NETHERLANDS DANCE THEATRE

186   **Rob Krier**
SCHINKELPLATZ HOUSING PROJECT

188   **Dominique Perrault Architecte**
ÉSIÉÉ, ÉCOLE D'INGÉNIEURS EN
ÉLECTRONIQUE ET ÉLECTROTECHNIQUE

190   **Christian de Portzamparc**
CITÉ DE LA MUSIQUE

194   **Hans Hollein**
NEUES HAAS HAUS

196   **Aldo van Eyck**
HUBERTUS

198   **Giancarlo De Carlo Architetto**
MAZZORBO HOUSING PROJECT

202   **Erith & Terry**
RICHMOND RIVERSIDE

204   **Gregotti Associati International**
UNIVERSITY OF PALERMO SCIENCE
DEPARTMENTS

208   **Architekt Dipl. Ing. Klaus Kada**
GLASMUSEUM

210   **Hans Kollhoff**
LUISENPLATZ HOUSING PROJECT

214   **Myrto Vitart (for Jean Nouvel Associés)**
ONYX CULTURAL CENTRE

218   **Mario Bellini**
INDUSTRIAL AND OFFICE COMPLEX ON
THE VIA KULISCIOFF

220   **Coop Himmelblau**
ROOFTOP REMODELLING

224   **Otto von Spreckelsen**
LA GRANDE ARCHE DE LA DÉFENSE

226   **Pei Cobb Freed & Partners Architects**
GRAND LOUVRE

230   **Aldo and Hannie van Eyck**
ESTEC, EUROPEAN SPACE RESEARCH
AND TECHNOLOGY CENTRE

234 **Héctor Fernández Martín/Vetges tu i Mediterrània, Arquitectos**
PRODUCTION CENTRE FOR VALENCIAN TELEVISION

236 **Matthias Sauerbruch and Elias Zenghelis (OMA)**
APARTMENT HOUSE AT CHECKPOINT CHARLIE

238 **Amado-Domenech Arquitectos**
BARRIO DEL CANYERET

242 **Bouchez + Associés**
SOCIAL HOUSING ON THE BOULEVARD VINCENT AURIOL

244 **Chemetov & Huidobro Architectes**
MINISTRY OF ECONOMY, FINANCE AND BUDGET

246 **Building Workshop Renzo Piano**
S. NICOLA FOOTBALL STADIUM

248 **Building Workshop Renzo Piano**
BERCY II SHOPPING CENTRE

252 **Arata Isozaki & Associates**
PALAU D'ESPORTS SANT JORDI

254 **Santiago Calatrava Valls Architecte-Ingenieur S.A.**
STADELHOFEN RAILWAY STATION

258 **Foster Associates Ltd**
TERMINAL FOR STANSTED AIRPORT

260 **Miralles Pinós Arquitectos**
'LA PISTA' CIVIC CENTRE OF HOSTALETS

264 **Building Workshop Renzo Piano**
HOUSING, RUE DE MEAUX

268 **Frank Gehry and Associates**
VITRA DESIGN MUSEUM

272 **Venturi, Scott Brown and Associates, Inc.**
THE NATIONAL GALLERY, SAINSBURY WING

276 **Hans Hollein**
THE SALZBURG GUGGENHEIM MUSEUM

280 **Tadao Ando Architect & Associates**
JAPAN PAVILION EXPO '92

284 **Santiago Calatrava Valls Architecte-Ingenieur S.A.**
TGV RAILWAY STATION OF LYON-SATOLAS

286 **Zaha M. Hadid**
ZOLLHOF 3 MEDIA CENTRE

290 **Daniel Libeskind Architekturbüro**
EXTENSION OF THE BERLIN MUSEUM WITH THE DEPARTMENT JEWISH MUSEUM

291 Documentation: architects' biographies, project specifications and select bibliographies

310 Photographic acknowledgments

311 Index

Preface and acknowledgments

The 'Europe' of the title of this book, a designation inherited from post-war history, refers to the political entity of what up to now was called Western Europe, as distinct from Eastern Europe. To this political unity has corresponded an architectural one. Obviously, the particular and diverse conditions – cultural heritage, regional idiosyncrasies, geographical and environmental, not to mention political and economic factors – of each country where an architectural enterprise takes place and shape determine to a certain extent its ultimate character, regardless of the nationality of the architect. The reader should not, however, expect to find either a stylistic or a clearly identifiable cultural 'Europeanness' among the architectural projects presented here. As stylistic and cultural products, they share little in common. They reveal a plurality of points of view, a plurality which is heightened by the inclusion of architects from outside the Western European area – Oscar Niemeyer, I.M. Pei, Richard Meier, Frank Gehry, Robert Venturi and Denise Scott Brown, Arata Isozaki and Tadao Ando, to name only a few. This globality, together with the reciprocal contemporary practice of European architects operating around the world, is what architecture in Europe shares with the increasingly mobile practice in the rest of the so-called Western world.

If there is a uniqueness to the architecture created in Europe during the period covered by this book – our selection includes projects built or planned to be built – it derives from the nature of the client and the institutional context of the projects. The client is often the state and the architectural practice is carried out within a relatively unrestricted legal and economic framework. These aspects explain the distinct architectural quality of large-scale public institutional architecture and of social housing, and a more open approach to programmatic, morphological and technological experimentation evident in European buildings.

The period covered opens with the exuberant events of May 1968 and closes with European unification. Although these limits stand for cultural and political events, they express fundamental shifts in European life with unprecedented consequences in its architecture, as we hope to show. During this period, architecture was dominated by a discord between extremes of individualism and rules, tradition and invention, technophilia and technophobia, centripetal and centrifugal relations to urban centres. Our intention has been to map the most salient developments of the period, to create a framework for locating, describing and interpreting architecture, rather than offering an exhaustive historical account. In so doing, we employed three approaches: a comprehensive introductory essay on the period; a 'forum' presenting reflections by some of the most prominent European critics of the period; a critical essay on each of the architectural projects included – these essays are linked in order to develop a number of arguments. In composing this panorama of architectural development in Europe, we have identified salient tendencies and patterns, evolving what philosophers call 'reconstructed' categories rather than using concepts already 'in use'. Our hope is that this will open up the discussion about the architecture of the past two decades.

The 'forum' of invited critics brings together Jean-Louis Cohen, Fritz Neumeyer, Peter Rice and Lucius Burckhardt to discuss the issues of typology, urbanism, technology and ecology as they relate to the design of buildings during the period. We are grateful for their contribution, broadening and deepening the scope of the panorama we set out to explore.

The architectural projects which are presented in depth here were selected on the basis of their strong identity and the unique and paradigmatic role they have played in the development of European-based architecture, however subtle, controversial or unequal this role might be. Presented chronologically, according to their date of completion (if completed), these projects are encountered as if in a city without walls, to paraphrase André Malraux's description of art books as museums without walls. All the same, by removing a building from its actual, living context and presenting it in a book, we do not mean to imply that this is just as good a substitute experience as real life.

In assembling the documentation of these projects, we have worked in close collaboration with their creators and their offices. Without their assistance, our efforts would have been futile. Many others have contributed decisively in the generation of this work and we would like to express our gratitude here.

First we would like to acknowledge our indebtedness to the Technological University of Delft, whose one hundred and fiftieth anniversary falls this year. This book is our birthday offering.

We are also indebted to many of the university's members, above all Caterina Burge, who assisted in the development of the book in all its stages, Yu Li, who carried out bibliographical research, Nan Fang, Xiadong Li, Alexander Koutamanis, Catherine Visser, Leo Oorschot, Eric Offermans, Toos Schoenmakers and all the members of our research group, Architecture Knowledge Systems. Also included in our acknowledgments should be the first year students of the Harvard Graduate School of Design during the 1970s.

We would like to express our thanks to Luis Fernández Galiano, who introduced us to Spanish architecture, to Anthony Tischhauser who eagerly responded to all our calls for help, as well as to Aldo Castellano, Richard Ingersoll, Adrian Jolles, Claudia Jolles, Luca Molinari, Toshio Nakamura, Judy and Tician Papachristou, André Schimmerling, Giorgos Simioforidis, Giorgos Tsirtsilakis and Yushi Uehara, for their suggestions and advice. We are also grateful to Adelina von Fürstenberg for her help in documenting the Daniel Libeskind project.

We would like to express our special thanks to Deidi von Schaewen for her generous help without which the book would have been a less interesting one.

Over the years, Stathis Eust has supported our work by nurturing our archive on an almost weekly basis, which we gratefully acknowledge here.

It was proposed to us by our publishers that we should undertake this publication and we are grateful to all those who, at various stages, have guided us in this enterprise, from commissioning to publication.

As with most of our writings in the last six years, this book took shape under the jasmine bower in the shady garden of the Miranda, on the island of Hydra, in Greece.

Delft, 1992

Introduction
Between Utopia and Reality: Eight Tendencies in Architecture Since 1968 in Europe

Alexander Tzonis and Liane Lefaivre

Populism

1968, the year of 'the spring', of 'uncontrollable spontaneity', in Europe as in many parts of the world, when, in the words of Daniel Cohn-Bendit, 'imagination is revolution' was declared, had a significant impact on the development of architecture. In no other major social political upheaval had architecture occupied such a privileged position. Admittedly, in the 18th century Rousseau had expressed strong ideas about socio-therapeutic landscape and Condorcet about participatory design.[1] American and Russian radicals had also put forth clear concepts about architecture in response to revolutionary ideas of the time. These, however, were put into practice neither by the French, American or Russian revolutionaries. In the manifestos of Spring '68, from Berkeley to Berlin, from Paris to Prague, architecture became a central focus. In the varying degrees of sophistication or apocalyptic ecstasy typical of the period, architecture was used to attack the establishment in order to exemplify the poverty, pain and pollution of the modern machine civilization, or it was held up as the sensuous, visionary, utopian 'alternative' worth fighting for.

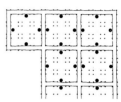

S. Woods, G. Candilis, A. Josic, Free University of Berlin (1963)

As with every revolution, such ideas and feelings were brooding quietly in the background for several years before suddenly bursting forth as explosive issues, among both professionals and the wider public. Critical writings which up to now were to be found only in esoteric, small-circulation magazines, such as *Le Carré Bleu* (Paris),[2] were suddenly the leading articles of new large-circulation magazines, such as *Architecture, Mouvement, Continuité*, the French magazine of the younger generation of architects.[3] The debt of the youth in revolt to the previous generation of intellectuals, such as Henri Lefebvre, C. Wright Mills, Herbert Marcuse, Theodor Adorno, has been much written about.[4] Their ideas about 'production', 'consumption', 'bureaucracy', 'alienation', 'reification', 'appropriation', 'community', 'direct democracy', 'survival', 'way of living', became an integral part of the new architectural proposals. Conversely, in order to demonstrate their ideas Henri Lefebvre and Herbert Marcuse referred to examples from architecture and urbanism.

This broadening and deepening of the horizon of architecture had both theoretical and institutional effects. It drew architectural thinking into discussions comparable in abstraction, and ambition, only to those which had taken place in the Renaissance and the 17th century. The difference now was that architecture was stripped of any claims to absolute and timeless principles or metaphysical eternal values. Design norms and their application became contextualized, relativized, politicized.

The earlier ideas of modern architecture and urbanism came under attack, especially when they made claims about truth, objectivity, process and social benevolence, notions which now came to be considered as arbitrary or suspect and as serving vested interests in much the same way as the traditional academic ideas of architecture they had replaced. Modern architecture and urbanism were now seen as expressing either a productivist ideology or an ideology of mass consumption. In other words, modern architecture was identified as serving a 'dominant class ideology'. As a whole, the doctrine of modern architecture was seen as being too reductive, too pragmatic, to satisfy deeper, even physical, human desires.[5]

From the point of view of cognition, this critique led to new ways of perceiving and understanding architecture. There was a shift away from spatial and aesthetic categories, away from terms which were supposed to describe shapes and feelings towards them. Buildings came to be seen as signs which carried mostly ideological messages expressing power and serving interests. In the new framework, such ideological messages were to be done away with and replaced by new ones. If buildings were to signify anything at all through image, it would be only on condition that they expressed 'liberation through imagination' or, in the manner of a billboard, a purely populist iconology. Buildings were now meant to be seen as networks where people moved and interacted, as platforms where they acted out their aspirations for emancipation.

Institutionally, the very presuppositions about the legitimacy of the architectural profession to impose its will on users through design were challenged. In scope, the assault recalled the challenging of fundamental institutional premises of the building guilds during the Renaissance and the *Ancien Régime* by the then young, upstart architectural profession. The authority of architects was seen as an anachronism in an era of 'consumer sovereignty'. Marxist, phenomenological, pro-consumerist, but also anti-consumerist, the new radical ideas about architecture all shared a radical liberationist approach to architecture,

Christian de Portzamparc, Château d'Eau, Marne-la-Vallée, France (1974)

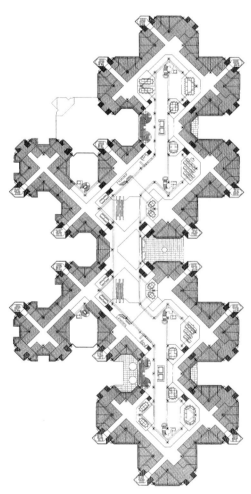

Herman Hertzberger, Ministry of Social Affairs, The Hague (1989)

expressed to some degree through unleashing the imagination of the individual and opening the way for a populist, 'user lib' approach to design.

Such ideas about architecture, which had originated mainly among students, young practitioners and young user groups, soon had an effect on the views of an older generation, the generation of the 'clients'. If 1968 was the year when such ideas were conceived, 1972 was when they first took physical form. This book, therefore, opens with works finished during this year.

The impact of populist ideas on buildings completed in 1972 is evident. And, although finished two years later, no other project captures the slogan 'imagination is revolution' better than the then 27-year-old Christian de Portzamparc's Château d'Eau in Marne-la-Vallée outside Paris (1971–74). His design consisted in dressing a pre-existing water tower – a utilitarian structure frequently 'littering' the traditional French landscape with its oppressive, severe 'rational functionality' – in a mantle of luxuriant verdure. The result was a dream-like ziggurat reminiscent of the fantastic architectural inventions found Francesco Colonna's *Hypnerotomachia Poliphili* (1499).[6] In the same vein, Tusquets and Clotet's Belvedere Georgina (Gerona, Spain, 1972, see pp. 54–55) was a poetic, playful, Buñuel-like critical metaphor, unthinkable in its irony when compared to post-war architecture.

So infectious was the youthful vernal spirit of 1968 in Europe that the Centre Pompidou (Paris, 1971–77, pp. 84–89), that gigantic, multi-functional complex of networks and platforms, was not only conceived but actually commissioned and built. The protagonist of the building was to be 'the people'. Filling up the transparent escalators attached to the front of the building, 'the people' became the building's facade, a dynamic proscenium overlooking an amphitheatre-like square. Open balconies fed the crowds onto the escalators at each level, where a columnless, unobstructed platform offered the maximum of flexibility for expression.

Lucien Kroll's La Mémé (Louvain, Belgium, 1968–72, pp. 44–47), making use of John Habraken's minimal support system, also offered a series of platforms on which the users with maximum freedom could divide internal spaces at will with subdivisions, and even determine the external covering of the building. Here everyone was free to exercise their imagination. Similar processes of participatory design took place in Ralph Erskine's Byker Wall (Newcastle upon Tyne, 1968–74, pp. 68–71) and in Giancarlo De Carlo's much later Mazzorbo housing project (Venice, 1980–85, pp. 198–201), although in these two cases the process was much more directed by the architect, whose intervention, however, was not biased by formalistic architectural presuppositions and taboos. With Herman Hertzberger's Centraal Beheer (Apeldoorn, Holland, 1968–72, pp. 48–51), these ideas entered the workplace, the white-collar workplace, traditionally a much more constrained area than housing. Hertzberger's space was cellular as opposed to most massive workplaces which were open plan. Its modularity was homogeneous without being regimented. Within it, employees enjoyed maximum freedom of choice. The minimally standardized cells accommodated alternative lifestyles while the total vista of the interior offered the image of a participatory democracy of the street. The same effect was tried again, twenty years later, by Hertzberger in the Ministry of Social Affairs in The Hague and by Ralph Erskine in his Sanska building in Gotenberg, Sweden. Here, as in Portzamparc's Château d'Eau, Kroll's Mémé, or Piano and Rogers' Centre Pompidou, the building emerges as a cultural object that implements Henri Lefebvre's vision of 'overcoming the conflict between everyday life and festivity' and 'everyday life becoming a work of art', the building 'a play'.[7]

Although populist architecture continued to be produced well into the 1980s, by the early 1970s it had already lost its leading role. It had emerged to a great extent as a critique and as an alternative to welfare-state architecture. When the welfare state began to collapse in the 1970s, not only under the weight of criticism but mainly because of the 'fiscal crisis' which occurred in that decade, it became obvious that the ideals of populism were no longer viable. First, as putting such ideals into practice presupposed an economic basis and a certain redistribution of wealth, as propounded by the welfare state, they were no longer affordable. And second, it was increasingly apparent that putting into practice proclaimed ideals frequently invited conflict and led to a fragmentation of individuals and groups. In fact, this bottom-up procedure, which was aimed at gradually combining individual preferences into a global, polymorphic, heteroclite, joyful whole, very often created a confrontational attitude and an adversarial spirit that displaced not only conciliation but also creative synthesis. Also made evident was the erosion of skills and professional know-how which, it soon became clear, were only rarely linked with power interests and most often with highly collective needs of environmental comfort and quality. Soon, populist architecture's invitation to participatory design was to be greeted if not with outright hostility then with apathy.[8]

Le rappel à l'ordre

Le rappel à l'ordre ('call to order') is an expression often applied to the movement in art and architecture that followed a few years after the First World War and was characterized by a return to conservative values. The expression, borrowed from the title of a minor essay by Jean Cocteau which appeared in 1926, referred to a reaction against the radical, anti-institutional ideas which had dominated culture during the first two decades of the 20th century. We apply here the same term to the movement which appeared in the 1970s as a reaction against populism in architecture, a reaction which was generalized against much earlier expressions of experimental, adversary, emancipatory avant-gardism.

As opposed to populism, which subjected architecture to political, social, economic and functional programmes, the *rappel à l'ordre* declared the independence or 'autonomy' of architectural forms. Autonomy was a term much used in many areas of culture in the 1970s following the arguments of the French philosopher of the left, Louis Althusser. As opposed to the so-called vulgar economicist Marxists, he advanced the view that certain products of society were relatively independent of their economic substructure. This position made the reorientation of many young architects towards a new kind of approach to formalism which was then taking place appear more acceptable from a political point of view. For them populism was politically naive, socially destructive, culturally catastrophic.

If for populists architecture was a political arena for acting out social struggle and cultural confrontation, for these opponents of populism architecture became once more a civil scenographic platform for people to perform politely their given, public roles. The accent was, once again, on architecture's rules and responsibilities, manners and masks. We can see this aspect of civic design in the almost theatrical decorum and the public face of the New State Gallery in Stuttgart by James Stirling (1977–84, pp. 126–31). Here, not only do the city fabric and the street pattern determine to a high degree the form of the building, but also the visitor, like the objects and architectural spaces of the buildings, has become part of a spectacle. A similar civic-theatrical quality characterizes Rob Krier's facades in his Schinkelplatz housing project in Berlin (1983–87, pp. 186–87).

Contrary to populism's 'spontaneous' design whose departing point was perceived as a *tabula rasa*, the *rappel à l'ordre* stressed the necessity of historical knowledge and the need to backtrack to tradition. This re-use of the past varied in degree from project to project. It is cautiously practised in the facade of Vittorio Mazzucconi in Paris (the 22, Avenue Matignon Building, 1972–76), where a small area of the front of the new building is made up of fragments from the demolished old facade, or, on a larger scale, the reweaving of fragments from the ruins of an earthquake into a new structural organization, as in the case of Francesco Venezia's project for Gibellina in Sicily (1981–89). It becomes a major concern in the Schinkelplatz housing of Krier (Berlin, 1983–87). In Erith & Terry's Richmond Riverside project (Richmond, England, 1985–88, pp. 202–03), historical precedents are indispensable in the design. In Terry Farrell's propylaeum at Clifton Nurseries (Covent Garden, London, 1980–81), the use of classical architectural historical elements is altogether different from the projects we have just mentioned. Although the gateway is classical in its entirety, the canon is applied only in bits and pieces. These are not fragments used in a nostalgic or even tragic sense, as above, but more in the jocular vein. Their light air, literally and metaphorically, alludes to garden follies of the past, appropriate to the context, but applied here in a more abstract, cerebral way – even though this cerebralism is not solemn but jocular.

The concept of 'typology' was central to the *rappel à l'ordre*. It linked its ideological commitments to autonomy, a civic design tradition with concrete architectural practice: a building type implied a thing in itself, an object apart from and prior to use, above and beyond social political and economic pragmatics. Furthermore, the belief in building types suggested the need for continuity rather than a break with the past. But as happens with many, in fact most, generic concepts that serve to reorient thinking, the meaning of type and typology was never defined precisely.

'Typology' meant many things to many people during the polemics of the mid- to late-1970s. It was at once a timeless metaphysical notion and a history-bound one. In applied design, moreover, typology was associated with borrowing very specific architectural forms from particular categories of buildings. Thus, the borrowings were not dictated by the specifics of the problem at hand. French Revolution, the Empire, the industrial complexes of the 19th century, the agricultural buildings of northern Italy, the light, ephemeral, seaside resort structures of the turn of the century, buildings of the Fascist regime of Italy and occasionally of the Nazi period in Germany, all these formed the canonical corpus of typological resources to be drawn upon.

Did these exemplars have anything in common? Although much has been said about their totalitarian origins, nothing seems to be ideologically consistent in the final analysis. What is totalitarian, for example, about the 19th century, or sea-cabins of the time? Neither is the theory that all these prototypes were of a consistent high quality valid as many have claimed, among them Vincent Scully in his text on Aldo Rossi,[9] the person who definitely contributed most to the idea of typology and its concrete visual expression. A closer inspection, however, will easily reveal that they all share the same 'visual denominator', to use Heinrich Wölfflin's expression, the same universe of forms, the same style.

The characteristics of the canonical body of typology are to be found in projects as diverse as Aldo Rossi's Gallaratese housing (1969–73, pp. 60–63) or his San Cataldo Cemetery (1971–73, pp. 56–59), the Student House in Chieti of Giorgio Grassi (Italy, under construction from 1979) – who was also, with Rossi, a proponent of 'typology' – or Stirling's New State Gallery in Stuttgart (1977–84, pp. 126–31), O.M. Unger's Architectural Museum in Frankfurt (1981–84, pp. 134–35), Chemetov and Huidobro's Ministry of Economy, Finance and Budget in Paris (1982–90, pp. 244–45) or the work of Leon and Rob Krier.

Vittorio Mazzucconi, 22 Avenue Matignon, Paris (1972–76)

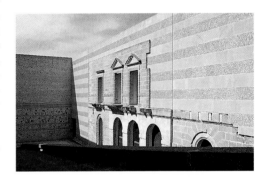

Francesco Venezia, Gibellina, Sicily (1981–89)

Terry Farrell, Clifton Nurseries, Covent Garden, London (1980–81)

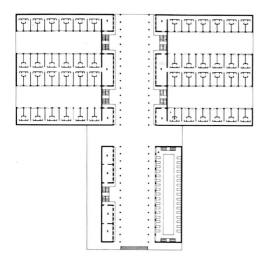

Giorgio Grassi, Student House, Chieti, Italy (under construction from 1979)

Without much effort one recognizes the compositional elements that make up this style: the square, the cube, the equilateral triangle, the circle, the right angle, the orthogonal grid, the tripartite composition, the long, linear, pilastered colonnade, the well-circumscribed space. This manifest affirmation of style as the unifier of all these projects and its widespread, wholehearted acceptance in the mid-1970s were in dramatic contrast to the flamboyant declarations of populism that visual order had come to an end.

Occasionally the notion of 'type' was used, in the framework of the *rappel à l'ordre*, for a semantic and narrative purpose rather than as a stylistic, compositional device. It was employed to give meaning to a building through visual metaphor. In this case, a building type was taken as a contextual framework out of which a fragment was borrowed to be assembled with other such fragments into a new amalgam. The new composite object obviously had at once a strange and even absurd appearance. At second glance, however, as in the case of all metaphors, a new meaning emerged. A remarkable example of this metaphorical use of typology is found in Aldo Rossi's San Cataldo Cemetery (1971–73) where analogies and constructs finally achieve the creation of a new framework for the various original meanings.

From the point of view of cognition, that is perceiving and understanding what a building is and what it does, the idea of typology made perfect sense. As we have already mentioned, the populist belief in the unlimited freedom of expression of the user, however noble, was naive psychologically and sociologically. The idea of the building type on the other hand, a kind of template, a spatial pattern stored in memory, or perhaps even deeper, a schema encoded in the mind, 'competent' to categorize natural objects or artifacts, could have led to a contribution in architectural theory. It could have brought it closer to theories of thinking and knowledge of our time as in the cases of the theory of music and poetry. A well-founded typology of buildings through such cognitive schemata could have brought some discipline into design, while allowing for variation. Building types would have served as frames, as cognitive scientists call them, to be instantiated when needed and as the specifics of a given situation required. A building type conceived as a frame could have helped link memory with invention.

This did not, however, occur. And neither did typology become a method, as happened with literary analysis. It did not become a means of abstraction and generalization for revealing a hidden structure underlying empirical reality in order to make people conscious of it, as, for instance, the literary critic Gyorgy Lukács did in his analysis of the heroes of the 19th-century realist novel in terms of 'social types'.[10] Aldo Rossi did, in fact, allude to this use, but without turning it into a genuine method.

In the end, as applied in the 1970s, typology was only a token which stood for a formal vocabulary implicitly expressing not so much a new visual sensitivity as new aspirations for security at that tumultuous moment. All the same, it succeeded in giving substance and direction to the *rappel à l'ordre* for over a decade.

But to call the *rappel à l'ordre* and the products of a period only a reaction to the failures of populism and the threat of chaos is an insufficient explanation for it. Other reasons account for it and for the peculiar choice of style that accompanied it. The *rappel à l'ordre* shifted attention towards financially less ambitious problems, away from the typical welfare-state projects of the post-war period. At a moment of mounting fiscal crises in Europe and around the world, it helped to focus attention on the revitalization of small-scale pockets of the historical centres of cities through private investment. But because of its strong preoccupation with autonomy of form, its relative indifference to the pragmatic context and practical content of buildings, its nostalgic rather than instrumental attitude to the past, it often proved ill equipped to cope in reality with the true problems of the historical centre of European cities, such as congestion, being unsuited to new programmatic demands and lifestyles, and physical obsolescence.

At a moment of economic difficulty, building in general was cut down and the contribution of the architect was seen as a superfluous luxury. This negative perception of architecture which the radical attacks of populism against the profession made even worse, the *rappel à l'ordre* tried to change, arguing for the indispensability of architectural knowledge, and thus of architects. The return to the values of professional specialization and elite craftsmanship certainly fitted in with the new *Zeitgeist*, occasionally referred to as neo-conservatism, which celebrated the individual. Thus 'excellence' became the slogan that replaced populist 'liberation'. Excellence, in turn, reinforced the neo-conservative goals of consumption and acquisition that populism had tried so hard to discredit.

Beyond such relatively short-term cycles of ideology, the *rappel à l'ordre* had a more long-term impact. It helped some aspects of architectural knowledge to be preserved at a highly destructive and confusing moment of cultural crisis at the end of the 1960s. But on the other hand, it very often turned its back not only on social and political questions, but also on those of technology and function.[11]

Neo-rigorism

The notion of a 'rigorist' architecture, that is to say one that intentionally represented 'only what has a true function', stripped down to its barest elements and eschewing all superfluous ornamentation, is often traced back to the early 1740s. This is when Carlo Lodoli,[12] a Venetian Franciscan friar, earned for himself the appellation of 'the Socrates of architecture' as a result of his immensely successful public diatribes against the Baroque architecture of his day, as passionate as they were learned. He preached that in order for architecture to renew itself and achieve 'eternal youth', it had to throw off the heavy shapes of the past, overloaded with formal conventions, and adapt itself to ever-advancing modern technology.

Of course, the origins of this radical, revolutionary idea – it was to imply no less than the complete overthrow of the classical canon and the creation of a wholly new one – go back at least a century earlier, to Galileo and the birth of mechanics,[13] to the time when the separation between the representation of structural strength and its reality – in the words of the time, between 'form' and 'matter' – was identified. There were two consequences of this realization for architecture: that for a building to be truly solid and truly functional, aspects related to the science of mechanics were more important than traditional conventions of architecture; but also, conversely, that to make a building represent solidity and functionality, it was not necessary to make it so in reality.

Despite the fact that the *rappel à l'ordre* movement did not pay much attention to these questions, they continued to preoccupy an important number of architects during the 1970s. Increasingly so as new materials and new techniques of scientific analysis of structures were produced, oblivious of the socio-cultural crisis which was so central a concern at the end of the 1960s.

The Centre Pompidou is, once more, a significant project in the framework of this neo-rigorist movement. In fact, its design made it evident that after decades of trials, modifications and improvements, Lodoli's rigorist vision of an architecture of 'eternal youth' was finally about to be realized. The project's success was due to:
(i) identifying and containing all the elements that make up the structural and functional elements of the building in discrete articulated channels (in this case functional is equated with service operations only);
(ii) segregating these channels from the rest of the building, packaging them into special zones, vertical as well as horizontal, and placing these zones in highly visible locations, either on the front and back of the building or in an exposed area under each ceiling.

The exposure of this piping service network gave the Centre Pompidou, in addition to the stripped skeletal look of earlier rigorist buildings, a special appearance. Many buildings were to adopt this look for over a decade: for instance, Ludwig Leo's Umlaufstank (Large Circulating Tunnel) in the heart of Berlin and Weber, Brandt and Partners' Teaching Hospital in Aachen (1968–86, pp. 168–71). Lodoli, the passionate morphologist of nature of the early Enlightenment, who was particularly fond of collecting embalmed animal carcasses and conserved organs, in addition to animal skeletons – hence the notorious smell of his collection room – would have been fascinated by the effect of this exposure.

However, the reasons behind this arrangement for the masterpiece of Piano and Rogers were not just visual, no matter how powerful the visual effect might be, or even an expression of the idea of architectural 'honesty' whereby nothing is hidden from the public. This representation of structural function was truly functional: it yielded a column-and-duct-free interior space offering maximum flexibility and possibilities of improvisation, and an ease of access to the servant[14] areas without disrupting the rest of the served spaces.

But there was another, deeper and more ambitious reason for this rigorism. It offered a new means of expanding one's understanding of the world. The building through its exposed structural and functional mechanisms was not intended to exhibit only its own devices, but to have these devices serve as a kind of map, a model of universal phenomena. More specifically, the tubular frames and piping hierarchies were a means of representation of the properties and structures of matter, their boundaries, their qualities and their relations. Furthermore, the implied model for ordering the building's space was not merely descriptive, it was also prescriptive. It showed not only how to look at the world, but how to make it. The topology of spaces as well as the iconology of the structures called for commitment to progress and to technology.

The building's bold geometry of articulated volumes, the clarity of the outline of their figures, the energy of their colour, the very icons of the truss scaffolding and the mechanical gadgetry, recall Fernand Léger's 'heightened appreciation' of the 'special strengths and imperatives . . . to be found in the new conditions that the modern age has brought us', to quote Hilton Kramer.[15] In fact, there are very few works in modern architecture, including those of Le Corbusier, that have succeeded in radiating the promise of beauty and 'the sense of joy in the very nature of modern life' as much as the Centre Pompidou. We have referred in some detail to this building because of its emblematic uniqueness, as well as the major impact it had on architects in Europe and around the world.

The same qualities are present in the work of Norman Foster, an equivalent celebration of the modern age and more than just 'high tech', as it is usually called. If one were to give preeminence to the Centre Pompidou rather than to the Renault Parts Distribution Centre (Swindon, England, 1980–83, pp. 116–19), which is probably more cognitively intriguing as an implicit representation of the world, of the properties of materials and the distribution of forces, this would be because of the programmatic dynamism of the Centre Pompidou in comparison to the mundane Renault Centre.

The rigorism of the 1970s, as we have already remarked, was concerned with visually expressing not only a building's structural aspects, but its functional aspects as well. The

Ludwig Leo, Large Circulating and Cavitation Tunnel, Berlin (1975–)

Peter Loerakker, house in Almere, Holland (1985)

Takis Zenetos, School of Hagios Dimitrios, Athens (1969–76)

rhythm and elegance that characterize the very best new rigorist buildings are the result of the intelligence of the warp and woof of their spatial structure. The rigorist buildings of that decade took the organization of the traditional functionalist plan one step further: they exemplified a new topology, accounting for 'servant' and 'served' organs.

This topological innovation was not invented at that moment. It bears traces of Rogers' and Foster's apprenticeship at Yale in the 1960s with Serge Chermayeff, when they were students at the school of architecture then housed in a building by Louis Kahn, the Yale Art Gallery. It was in Louis Kahn's conception of buildings in terms of spatial/functional categories of 'servant' and 'served' and in Serge Chermayeff's bi-zonal planning in terms of strips of 'mobility' versus 'tranquillity', 'community' versus 'privacy', 'flows' versus 'containers', that this new topology was first envisaged. It was Kahn and Chermayeff who gave the promise of a more intelligent design, beyond the simplified, so-called 'functionalist' buildings that Robert Venturi had dubbed 'ducks'.[16]

Very often, however, neo-rigorist ideas led to easy formulas and banal results. In these cases, neo-rigorism failed not only to convey a Léger-like, heroic message and to offer intellectual pleasure, but created exactly the opposite effect, dullness. It induced a feeling of hostility against modern life and its technology because they were perceived as leading to a boring world where imagination has no place.

An approach which departed from this seemingly exhausted area of supports and suspensions, while still remaining within the framework of structural rigorism, exploited the almost classical post-and-beam combinatorics, also inspired by Louis Kahn. This route was taken by Herman Hertzberger's Ministry of Social Affairs (The Hague, 1979–90) with its endless variety of well-formed structures.

Another path was tried by those who sought to find by empathy – reviving earlier efforts by architects such as Eero Saarinen – a sculptural quality in the individual elements of construction. In this tradition of experimentation are Renzo Piano's petal-like stands of the S. Nicola Football Stadium in Bari (1987–90, pp. 246–47) which almost mimetically emulate the structure of a flower. Equally biomorphic, as if the results of the slow process of growth or of evolution, are Calatrava's steel or concrete forms of the Stadelhofen Railway Station in Zürich (1985–90, pp. 254–57)) and his Satolas Station near Lyon (1989–92, pp. 284–85).

Neo-rigorism, whose emergence we have identified as being almost contemporary with the populist movement and which was developed further during the time of *rappel à l'ordre*, continued to produce alternative experiments with structure well into the 1980s. Renzo Piano at the Schlumberger Industrial Site in Montrouge, Paris (1981–84, pp. 120–23), and Michael Hopkins at Schlumberger's Research Laboratories in Cambridge, England (1984, pp. 124–25), used fibre membranes to invent new possibilities for revealing landscapes of the distribution of forces in space. Yet the mood of the 1980s in Europe appears to be directed towards more subtle means of representing structure and function than the exhibitionistic ways the 1970s. We see this in the appeal that the restrained, elegant rigorism of Alejandro de la Sota's masterpiece, the Post Office and Telecommunications Building of León (1985, pp. 138–41), has exerted on a much younger generation, as well as in products of this younger generation of the end of the 1980s in Europe, such as the houses in Almere, Holland, by Jan Bentham and Mels Crouwel (1982–84) and by Peter Loerakker (1983). We can see it in the strategy adopted at the Palau d'Esports Sant Jordi of Arata Isozaki (Barcelona, 1985–90, pp. 252–53), where the spectacular achievements of construction technology and the complex multi-functionality of the interior are kept under a low profile, submerged under a quiet roof.

A rigorist treatment of the outside of a building which avoids showing, if not actually covering up, function and structure, has been tried in the past in articulating environmental control conditions through shading devices, such as the famous invention of the *brise-soleil* by Le Corbusier, or Louis Kahn's wrapping of 'stone wall ruins' around glass walls. There have been a few interesting examples of this approach during the last twenty years, such as the neo-brutalist concrete *brises-soleil* of the School of Hagios Dimitrios by Takis Zenetos (Athens, 1969–76) and the metal ones by Jean Nouvel at Némausus (Nîmes, 1985–87, pp. 178–81), those of the Banco de Bilbao (Madrid, 1971–78, pp. 100–03) by Francisco Javier Saenz de Oiza, of La Pista by Miralles and Pinós (Els Hostalets de Balenya, 1987–91, pp. 260–63), and of the housing project for the Boulevard Vincent Auriol by Bouchez + Associés (Paris, 1987–90, pp. 242–43). These are, however, relatively isolated cases.

Skin rigorism

Traditionally, rigorists, including those of the 1970s, exposed what they thought to be the true essence of architecture by revealing the contents of a building's interior, making its structure and function manifest. Other recent descendants of Lodoli, paying particular attention to its covering, proclaimed that the true essence of architecture lies in its external envelope. To use an anatomical analogy, implied in the thinking of rigorists, theirs was not an architecture of the skeleton, or of the organs, or even of the intestines, but rather of the skin.

Vernacular buildings of all kinds have for centuries been designed in this manner. In the professional tradition of architecture, however, as opposed to the vernacular, there have only been a few cases of such skin architecture: 19th-century brick walls; walls covered in ceramics; and, more recently, curtain walls, like that of Prouvé-Niemeyer's French Communist Party Headquarters (Paris, 1965–80, pp. 106–09), which curves round to give the impression of fluttering in a truly curtain-like manner.

Contemporary precedents of skin rigorism include Buckminster Fuller's experiments with the Dymaxion Deployment Unit (1927). Resembling an onion dome sitting on the ground, it disguises behind its industrial bulbous skin its mysterious cupola structure. Frank Lloyd Wright's 'Streamlined Moderne' curved walls of the 1930s, undoubtedly inspired by the skin design of the American car, led to the glass-tubed, curved skin of the Johnson Wax Tower, a direct descendant of which is Francisco Javier Saenz de Oiza's Banco de Bilbao (Madrid, 1971–78).

Oscar Niemeyer, Maison de la Culture, Le Havre (1972–82)

Concrete too has had its use in skin rigorism. Structure and skin are combined in the curvaceous, biomorphic-streamlined walls by Oscar Niemeyer, particularly graceful in his Bobigny Bourse du Travail (1972–80) and in his Maison de la Culture in Le Havre (1972–82). Mario Bellini's Industrial and Office Complex on the Via Kuliscioff (Milan, 1982–88, pp. 218–19) and, certainly, Aurelio Galfetti's Public Tennis Club in Bellinzona (1982–85, pp. 142–43) also stand out as excellent examples of the exceptionally rigorous treatment of the building's skin.

The metaphor of a building's exterior as epidermis was carried further in the rippling profiles of the facades of Henri Gaudin's ceramic tile-covered housing project on the Rue Ménilmontant in Paris (1987). Rather than keeping the structure a complete unknown behind the skin, columns are permitted to emerge occasionally between sliced slots, giving the effect not of laceration but of playful hide-and-seek.

Henri Gaudin, housing block on the Rue Ménilmontant, Paris (1987)

Mies van der Rohe's Glass Skyscraper of 1922, although only a paper project, had for decades been an unchallenged example of skin architecture whose effects could only be imagined through the suggestive power of the drawing. Quite possibly it was Foster's precedent for his Willis, Faber & Dumas Head Office (Ipswich, 1970–75, pp. 74–77), perhaps the most eminent example of this trend up to now. The suspended glass skin, with its puzzling geometry and equivocal effects, now reflective, now revealing, put forth the new poetics of the skin most forcefully, which become the overriding element in the design of the whole building. In the tight urban context of Ipswich, the mirroring effect was both sympathetic to the old fabric, indeed almost sentimental, as well as surrealistic. A similar mirroring effect, but used in an open space and applied to a spherical shape and to a spherical scheme, as in the Géode of Adrien Fainsilber (Cité des Sciences et de l'Industrie, Paris, 1980–86, pp. 172–73), achieved a symbolic quality. It became an icon of the potential of cognition to map vast amounts of information about the universe onto highly compressed capsules of representation.

If the rigorist poetics of function had to rely on the expressiveness of the shape of inhabited volumes and their location, and if the rigorist poetics of structure relied on the sculptural effects of the skeleton, or on the proportion and rhythm of its elements, where perfection was measured at the scale of the metre, or at most the centimetre, then the poetics of the mirror-glass curtain depended on seamless detailing and the millimetre.

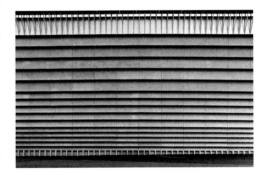

Jacques Herzog and Pierre de Meuron, Ricola Storage Building, Laufen, Switzerland (1986–87)

Not all skin rigorism relied on the mirroring effect or on the translucency and transparency of the glass covering. In fact, signs of fatigue quickly appeared. This invited the use of a completely different skin material together with a different poetics. Repetitive, uneventful, occasionally dull and quiet, but still carrying the sensitivity of crafted detailing and the intensity that large, obsessively well-ordered surfaces can evoke, building skins made of wood or metal began to be used. These also concealed structure and internal divisions and avoided the use of openings which would interrupt the uniformity, regularity or smoothness of the protective covering. The resulting lack of scale, on the one hand, magnifies the slightest detail, while on the other, it emphasizes the overall profile of the building.

There is a tension between these two extremes, the exaggerated contrast of large-size volume and small-size detail, interacting through mutual estrangement and mutually reinforcing each other's identity. The fragmented, analytical nature of most non-skin rigorist buildings, with openings yawning between solids, with vertical elements contrasted with horizontals, appears excessively bombastic and brutal in relation to the subtleties and delicacies of skin architecture, the qualities of which are brought forth with mastery in the skin of the external walls of, for instance, Peter Zumthor's protection shed in Chur (1985–86, pp. 160–63), or in Jacques Herzog and Pierre de Meuron's Ricola Storage Building (Laufen, Switzerland, 1986–87).

In contrast to the meticulous standardization of elements of the external walls in these two projects, the fishscale-like tiles which cover Renzo Piano's Bercy II Shopping Centre (Paris, 1987–90, pp. 248–51) have great individuality; almost every scale is different in size and shape. The result appears organic, the fishscale-like tiles bizarrely appropriate to the fish-like shape of the building. The tiles are, however, only superficially mimetic or organic: the intricate geometric arrangement of the roof tiles emerges as a cognitive map of a highly abstract and subtle system of spatial ordering, not periodic but variant, and thus more exciting than the repetitive tile patterns in, say, a Roman mosaic. The tiling on the roof is a representation of a rule system, a game, through which a unit is moved along a surface, a curved surface, and, along the way, its figure is translated and modified to adapt to the changing constraints of the surface without leaving any gaps, any imperfections, as it continues. Contemplating this kind of conceptual game can have a sublime effect.

Another type of skin rigorism, perceived especially if we look at the building from above, is that of Piano's teflon-coated fibreglass membrane used on the site of the old Schlumberger Industrial Plant on the periphery of Paris (pp. 120–23), as opposed to Frei Otto's tents of the 1960s, or Michael Hopkins' translucent, teflon-coated fibreglass membrane of the Schlumberger Laboratories in Cambridge (pp. 124–25), where the structure supporting the tent is loudly proclaimed. In Piano's Schlumberger structure the supports of the protruding curves of the membrane remain a mystery, very much like the bones behind the taut skin of a young torso.

Piano is not only a poet and mathematician of the built skin, he is also a great experimentalist. In Bercy II, at IRCAM and in the housing project of the Rue de Meaux (Paris, 1988–91, pp. 264–67), he has investigated the possibilities of layers of skin that enjoy relative independence from the external wall of which it is a part. In contrast to previous ways of pressing and gluing the two together, this multi-layer approach, which exploits new developments in ceramics, plastics and metal, will without question revolutionize not only economic, technical and ecological aspects of architecture as they relate to the exterior of buildings, but also the quality of the man-made environment as a work of art.

Critical regionalism

After a long period of disrepute, regionalism once again emerged as a dominant architectural tendency during the 1970s and '80s. It had little to do, however, with the means and aims of the sentimental, scenographic, nationalist regionalism of the past, nor was it chauvinistic, as in the case of the various expressions of regionalism of the last two centuries. Yet there was a common thread linking the two versions: both aimed to create an architecture of 'place', in relation to which the individual does not feel alone or alien: regionalism tried to create an architecture of belonging, of 'community'.[17]

As in the past, the regionalism of the 1970s and '80s identified particular and local determinants of design in opposition to general and universal norms. In conceiving the Mazzorbo housing project (pp. 198–201), for example, Giancarlo De Carlo proceeded to find shapes of windows, entrances, fireplaces and chromatic structures from houses of the Venetian Lagoon from which to develop the equivalent elements of his new project. As in the past, the new regionalism used the existing architectural attributes of a region to achieve regionalist aims, that is, to tag onto a building its 'place' and 'social' identity. Finally, as in the past, regionalism was used to express aspirations of liberation from the brute force of *a priori* dogmas imposed by a power perceived as foreign and illegitimate.

In his essay on German architecture, Goethe had set out to identify architectural elements from the Gothic cathedral of Strasbourg, an 'astonishing . . ., barbaric . . . mass of details', which he recognized, nevertheless, as 'German': 'our architecture'. He juxtaposed these elements with classical 'French' architecture which he considered to have been imposed from 'another region', producing a 'uniformity [which] presses upon the soul'.[18] The alien oppressor that the new regionalism in the 1970s and '80s opposed was not an occupying authority, but the expanding realm of bureaucracy and technocracy as well as the centrifugal commercial forces liquidating the urban realm and its accompanying urban life. In this spirit, Luis Marin de Terán and Aurelio del Pozo's La Corza housing in Seville (1984–85) borrowed architectural elements from the local working-class district of Triana and the yellow ochre ground from the park of Maria Luisa in Seville, rather than applying the standard, official, technocratic housing types.

The sense of the longed-for 'place' and community, however, in the new regionalism was meant to be open and broad, not confined to ethnic constraints. The form of the court house in the Barrio del Canyeret by Amado and Domenech (Lerida, 1982–90, pp. 238–41) repeats elements from the fortification above the new building which correspond to the wave-like shape of the citadel and result in a form reminiscent of a wall enclosing a coherent old town. The new building, however, is not in the least suggestive of a new, fortified, closed society. What it provides, in addition to an 'image' of community, is in fact a promenade, a *rambla* just like the existing citadel wall offers. Consequently, it creates a generous and highly gratifying public space with wonderful views and good for strolling, an architectural/urbanistic opportunity conducive to human encounters. Once again, the project contrasts with the technocratic, bureaucratic alternative of official public complexes, surrounded by its car park and efficiently aggregating services within a compact volume.

The roots of the regionalism of the past, which can be called romantic regionalism, can be traced back at least to 19th-century English picturesque and its search for a *genius loci*. Goethe's notion of an architecture 'true to the region', as opposed to a 'paternalistically' imposed one from 'another region', employed elements from the buildings of a nationalistically defined area whose identity it wanted to preserve. Romantic regionalism was the cultural counterpart of the 19th-century political movements of emancipation from a declining, absolutist and aristocratic world order. And in its effort to hammer home a sense of unity, romantic regionalism developed what is in fact an architecture of nostalgia and memory. In this architecture the viewer was meant to feel an almost hallucinatory sense of participation in a common ethnic past.

Long after traditional 19th-century regionalism based on ethnicity had gone, romantic regionalist architecture of remarkable technical ingenuity continued to be produced. It co-existed harmoniously with an advanced technological and socio-economic infrastructure, in countries such as Finland, well into the 20th century. One can find, even today, such examples in the work of Imre Mackovecz and Beno Taba in Hungary.

The distinctive character of contemporary regionalism is not only 'adversary', as with romantic regionalism; it is 'critical' as well. This sounds like a contradiction in terms, since 'regionalism' connotes positive if not conservative values, while 'critical' implies negativism if not radicalism. Critical, in the sense we use this term, is closer to the Kantian *critique*, and also to the agitated writings of the Frankfurt School; it challenges not only the actual world, but also the legitimacy of *possible* world views. In other words, it challenges, it critiques, habits of thinking and the role of clichés. In terms of architecture, this critical viewpoint is based cognitively, and aesthetically, on 'defamiliarization'.

Defamiliarization, a concept closely related to Brecht's *Verfremdung* ('estranging'), but also to the Aristotelian *xenicon*, was coined by the literary critic Victor Schklovsky in the 1920s. He defined it as aiming to 'prick consciousness' and destroy the hypnotic effect of contemporary consumer culture.[19] In the *manzana* patio of the Seville housing by Cruz and Ortiz (1974–76, pp. 82–83), the traditional regional rectilinear form is unexpectedly replaced by a kidney-shaped one. Consequently, while the spatial component remains the same, it reappears in an unexpected shape, thus precluding any sentimental and scenographic effects. By introducing such an architectural component traditionally associated with community, the intention of the architects is to remind its users of its meaning and warn of the potential loss of that community, which might occur in the process of technological advancement and the bureaucratic rationalization of the city. By using this element, the architects imply that they are trying to arrest this process. The same is the case with Luis Marin de Terán and Aurelio del Pozo's La Corza (Seville, 1985), where the regional elements are meshed with others reminiscent of Bruno Taut and Ernst May's social housing which create similar defamiliarization effects.

One of the most intricate uses of defamiliarization in the framework of critical regionalism is to be found in Rafael Moneo's Museo Nacional de Arte Romano in Merida (1980–86, pp. 148–51). The employment of regional elements is evident. The aura of *romanidad* is overpowering, created by the arched walls and naves which surround the visitor and which are constructed out of hand-crafted Seville bricks of the same dimensions as their Roman predecessors. But what is even more impressive is the deliberate conflict that is set up between the grid-system, on which these neo-Roman elements are laid, and the grid of the original Roman remains on which they rest. The two spatial schemata superimposed in confrontation not only prohibit a sentimental and scenographic identification with a chauvinistic past, as would have been the case in a romantic approach; they also elicit a chain of reflections about the continuity of urban life and community today.

In the first half of the 20th century, regionalism manifested itself, at times, in ways that were far from noble. This type of architecture was exploited by Nazis and Fascists with a view to neo-tribal, atavistic ends. Another exploitative form in which regionalism resurfaces in this century is tourism. While the ends of tourist-motivated regionalism are economic, as opposed to political, the means are the same – an architecture which is based on familiarization with the past. The products of tourist regionalism are ultimately as kitsch as those of political regionalism.

In the period after the Second World War, we encounter Stalinist neo-folkloristic regionalism, but also that of Lewis Mumford, which he proposed as an alternative to the creeping 'imperial order' of post-war 'technocracy' and 'despotism', to the 'mechanical order', indeed to the international style and modernism in general which, he thought, had lost by then much of its original emancipatory and rational character. Mumford also reflected an anxiety over the free-wheeling maximization of choice in the United States based on mobility, or rather automobility, and electronic communications, and the contempt of a new generation of planners for what was perceived as the 'deep seated doctrine that seeks order in simple, mappable patterns', as the prominent sociologist Melvin Webber put it. While very little was built in the United States, in Europe a regionalism following ideas close to Mumford's resulted in a few buildings which still stand today, such as the Torre Velasca in Milan by Ernesto Rogers, Lodovico Belgiojoso and Enrico Peressutti (1950–58), James Stirling's Preston Infill Housing (1957–59) and Giancarlo De Carlo's apartment house in Matera (mid-1950s). The critical regionalist tendency of the 1970s appears as a continuation and amplification of that brief moment of the 1950s, as expressed in Mumford's writings and in the buildings of Europe. Furthermore, the technique of estrangement practised by the critical regionalist architects, defamiliarizing familiar regional elements in order to represent on a higher cognitive level the idea of regionalism, parallels an approach suggested by Robert Venturi in his celebrated essay, *Complexity and Contradiction in Architecture* (1966). In it, Venturi gave predominance to the desirability of using 'conventional element(s)', but in place of strangemaking, Venturi proposed the concept of vividness and the employment of 'convention unconventionally'.[20]

Critical regionalism did not result in an identifiable architectural style. That would have contradicted its very definition. The most deeply rooted way of expressing the identity of a place is by resorting to local myth and iconology. This is the case in Raili and Reima Pietilä's Tampere Main Library (1978–86, pp. 152–55) with its bird-like form. In this building, the very traditional regionalist design does not succumb to merely romantic folklorism. A primordial icon is married to contemporary technology and a contemporary, open way of life.

Josep Martorell, Oriol Bohigas and David Mackay, Thau School, Barcelona (1972–74)

Although the design strategy used by the Pietiläs and others makes use of a particular region's unique topographical characteristic, this is done by reincorporating it into the design of the project in the way the building relates to the site. Antonio Follina's Sports Club in Nervesa della Battaglia (Italy, 1971–75), Roberto Gabetti and Aimaro Isola's Conca Bianca residential complex outside Turin (1976–89), Luigi Snozzi's Casa Kalman in Locarno, Switzerland (1974–76, pp. 80–81), and Josep Martorell, Oriol Bohigas and David Mackay's Thau School in Barcelona (1972–74) are excellent demonstrations of this technique. In Mario Botta's house at Riva San Vitale in Ticino, Switzerland (1971–73, pp. 64–67), the three-dimensional scheme of the building is extracted from the region, then transferred back to the new structure by using rustic constructions to be found locally. Once again, the result is far from being a form of nationalist or touristic romanticism, or commercial, consumerist degradation. Similarly, Aldo van Eyck in Hubertus (1982–87, pp. 196–97) introduces a more abstract attribute, extracted from traditional Dutch domestic architecture, that of transparency and spatial depth, so frequently pictured in 17th-century Dutch painting.

In the case of Spanish architecture, one of the most fascinating cases of critical regionalism, we find volumes of prismatic purity constructed in impeccable brick, in a relatively broad area from Rafael Moneo's Bankinter (Madrid, 1973–76, pp. 78–79) and Antonio Velez's housing cooperative in Madrid (1979–82, to Clotet and Paricio's Banco de España in Gerona, near Barcelona (1982–85, pp. 132–33); this widespread occurrence reflects the fact that the regional element of the brick prism was broadly diffused through the Iberian Peninsula. On the other hand, the vivid colour of Antonio Barrionuevo's housing block in Pino Montano, Seville (1981–83, pp. 114–15), is unique, the product of a Sevillian regional architectural attribute. Equally unique are the granite panels used in the Galician projects of José Bar Boo's subsidized housing in Vigo (1977), as well as the intriguing configuration of a humble communal wash-house and meeting place by Pascuala Campos Michelena (1984) in the relatively isolated village of Comparo near Pontevedra, also in Galicia, which is related to the regional *horreo*, a stone granary on stilts with a pitched roof.

Regional elements originating in local architecture are identified, isolated, schematized and finally made new when used in a new context in the above mentioned projects, a process left most often to the architect's intuition. However, in the Mazzorbo housing project of Giancarlo De Carlo, who is committed to participatory architecture, the use of regional elements is not left to the architect's personal intuitions (pp. 198–201). De Carlo's historical exploration is not a one-way street; the users also have their say. It is here that his method which superficially resembles that of Aldo Rossi in its use of memory radically diverges from it. According to De Carlo, to identify the collective meaning of an architectural element one has to carry out a transaction, an interactive process requiring the participation of the place's inhabitants. It is only in this way that the resulting information can be put to an effective, emancipatory use, De Carlo believes. In this respect the Mazzorbo project might be considered part of – indeed at the forefront of – the populist as well as the critical regionalist movements. The work of Lucien Kroll, especially ZUP Perseigne (1978, pp. 92–95), also often combines populist and critical regionalist characteristics.

In its efforts to appeal to a wider public, or by succumbing to the pressures of commercialism, critical regionalism walked a tightrope during the 1970s and '80s. The danger it faced was often a reversion to earlier forms of regionalism – sentimental, scenographic, ethnocentric. There was as well the equally grave danger of deteriorating into an architecture of tourist commercialism. It must also be admitted that critical regionalism has appeared ineffectual in identifying a *genius loci*, in establishing 'placeness', and in sustaining community in the highly hostile conditions of the contemporary no-man's-land that exists on the periphery of the post-industrial, post-agrarian, post-urban landscape, conditions of a seemingly uncontrollable chaos of form, meaning, function and human ties.

The call to disorder

In a very widely read book of the late 1980s by James Gleick entitled *Chaos, Making a New Science* (1987),[21] Heinz-Otto Peitgen, a physicist at the University of Bremen, is cited as observing that the attraction of the once very popular pure geometrical 'apartment blocks in the Bauhaus style . . . seems to have passed.' Peitgen noted that an 'enthusiasm [for a] new kind of geometry . . . a different perspective of looking at nature' was emerging in the mid-1980s, characterized by twisted shapes, by stretched, knotted and weird floating particles. These strange structures looked like parodies of Euclid in their application to 'intractable' problems, or they simply resembled celebrations of chaos itself.

In the design of the Schullin Jewelry Shop by Hans Hollein (Vienna, 1972–74, pp. 72–73), which is in all respects highly finished, polished and well formed, a major crack in the facade destroys the subtle classical coherence of the work. The spastic geometry of disintegration is not arbitrary. It is the product of a carefully studied design act, meticulously drawn and fastidiously executed. Hollein's example was one of the first rare cases of such a display of chaos during the early 1970s, despite the fact that the anarchic, polyarchic, anti-planning ideas of the period welcomed celebrations of what Richard Sennett called in a contemporary work, *The Uses of Disorder* (1970), 'the promise and the justification of disorder'. Peichl's ORF-Studio of 1981 is another early example. The radiant explosion of its plan also manifests the destruction of classical ideas of coherence, a concept which in fact dates back to the late-1960s. One has to remember that the populist movement was explicitly anti-classical, and so were expressions of lyrical individuality, such as Hundert-wasser's in the 1970s. But these cases of anti-classicism did not have the paradoxically systematic character of the chaotic structures of the 1980s.[22]

It is only since the mid-1980s that the ideas behind Hollein's cracked facade and Peichl's exploded plan are being understood on the level of principles, rules and system. An increasing number of projects, first on paper, then built, emerged which contradicted all the tendencies of the period: the populist striving for a politically engaged design; the *rappel à l'ordre* to re-establish an autonomous tradition based on architecture; the functional and structural rigorists' attempts to introduce a higher level of rationality in building; critical regionalism's attempts to maintain the shaping of places with a sense of community.

In the past, there have been periodic eruptions of love for disorder and a desire to escape from the ideas of coherence and system of the type observed by Peitgen, cited above. At such times, a whole world view emerges in science, in literature, in the arts and architecture, which tries to subvert the coherent systems for thinking and acting then predominant. Such was the period that Eugenio Battisti called the 'anti-rinascimento' (1989), embodied in the anti-classical, anti-Ciceronian prose style of Montaigne's essays (1571–92) and also in the anti-classical composition of Michelangelo's Laurentian Library.[23] Another such period was Constructivism in the 1920s. Yet in each of these recurring appeals to disorganization, there lies behind this seemingly negative attitude to order a highly consistent design thinking, a strong thematic continuity, and possibly even an equally rational scope of investigation. Thus, in the experiments of spatial composition by Gustav Peichl, Klaus Kada, or Michael Szyszkowitz and Karla Kowalski, Zaha Hadid, or Frank Gehry, we can discern an anti-methodical method: the high predictability with which unpredictable events occur in the work. This is why it is possible to recognize their projects and why we can sense intuitively their high quality in comparison with superficial imitations.

As with the other cases of apparently disordered architecture in the past, the rule behind the arbitrariness is that of canonically undoing the classical canon. Each architect, each project, takes its own approach to unmaking the coherence of the classical edifice, each arriving in the end at a consistent method and creating a work that manifests once more consistency, but of a different kind. To borrow Wittgenstein's famous metaphor of the city, it is like when one part of the city is built and 'circumscribed' with its own ideas of perfection, then another area suddenly draws people into it where they can build a sort of 'suburb' in an altogether different manner and with a different sense of perfection.[24]

Seemingly there is a destructive delight in this architectural exercise of shifting conceptions of order. It could be argued that there might even be a critical intention; that the architects of the 1980s are concerned with organizing anti-celebrations in opposition to those of mainstream architecture, or those of the architecture of other contemporary movements in praise of order. Yet these architects of the 1980s and '90s appear too positively predisposed to have the label 'critical' assigned to them. Their search for alternative spatial order does not seem to stem from their adversary stance so much as from their cognitive investigations.

At the same time, the hidden order of their works, their anti-classical 'chaotism', should be distinguished from the tradition of functionalist anti-classicism, a tradition which also created awkward geometries such as the angular, tortured shapes of bastions, the hornworks and hoardings of military architecture, or the utilitarian irregular configurations of our time in projects such as Claude Parent's Villa Drusch (Versailles, 1961–63) and Ivry Town Centre by Jean Renaudie (1970–78).

In the chaos-loving projects of the 1980s, their anti-classicism has a cognitive character. They suggest a process of undoing regularity which can tell us much about how the mind understands regularity. Coop Himmelblau's design for the Merz School in Stuttgart (1981 – never completed) or Rooftop Remodelling (Vienna, 1983–89, pp. 220–23) are two most striking examples; once one has contemplated these two structures, classical architecture will never be the same. The building is made to appear like an intricately assembled mechanism which can only be explained once it has been disassembled. This approach can therefore provide an understanding of cognitive structures of ordering space which are broader and deeper than those of the conventions of the classical canon. If artifacts are the outcome of thinking which takes place in time, and not only in space, then clearly this thinking process can be much more easily analysed if one's interpretation takes into account the aspect of time. But since buildings are space constructs, to convey time through their fabric is possible only symbolically – in other words, if the fabric of the building *represents* time implicitly. Thus, the time and process aspects of architectural conception are reconstructed in the mind of the viewers as they experience buildings as representations of time and process.

This collapsing of the four dimensions into the three-dimensions of buildings has precedents, of course. Sigfried Giedeon has made this point very clearly in his book *Space, Time and Architecture*, and as Peter Collins has observed in his *Changing Ideals of Modern Architecture*,[25] the 18th-century designers of picturesque landscapes very consciously integrated the dimension of time in their projects. This was achieved by forcing the viewer to move through the spatial complex. In the architecture of chaos of the 1980s, the same object is achieved without necessarily making the visitors walk around the building. Instead,

Hundertwasser, house, Vienna (1985)

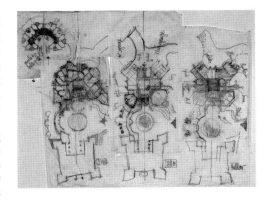

Michael Szyszkowitz and Karla Kowalski, addition to the Technical School for Forestry, Pichl Castle, near Graz, Austria (1982–85)

Günther Domenig, Nix-Nuz-Nix – 'Good-for-Nothing Bird', designed as a symbol for the Z-Bank, Graz, Austria (1983)

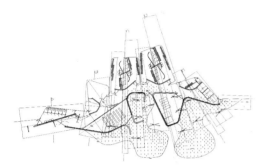

Miralles Pinós Arquitectos, Archery Range for the 1992 Olympics, Barcelona (1990–92)

they gaze at the static, disordered patterns of these complexes in the same way that they would contemplate a dynamic phenomenon in a disturbed, viscous fluid or, on a large scale, in the galaxy itself. And this experience is what makes cognitively intriguing the last decade's architectural explorations of disorder.

Despite their highly abstract character, these spatial compositions very often include iconic elements, mimetic images. Thus, the image of the bird forms a strange leitmotif of this architecture. The body of the bird appears, for instance, in Günther Domenig's Ornamental Birds (1980–83) and his Nix-Nuz-Nix ('good-for-nothing') Bird (Graz, Austria, July 1983). Although more sculpture than building, these birds serve as models for more complex buildings such as Domenig's Stone House (Steindorf, Carinthia, Austria, 1984–86). The bird-like geometry of his constructions implies time and process, not only because birds fly in time, but also because their very morphology results from a slow process through which the profile is carved and polished by evolution and time. This is why, in fact, in Domenig's designs the bird image echoes the image of craggy hills and rocks, and of broken tree trunks. These shapes are the outcome of natural processes of transformation, processes of destruction or growth, both dynamic phenomena occurring in time.

There is a strong zoomorphic character, picturing the formal explosion of a 'fractal dragon' rather than a bird in flight, which again implies movement as well as the natural process of evolution of form, in Aldo and Hannie van Eyck's ESTEC – European Space Research and Technology Centre (1986–89, pp. 230–33). Movement caused by the unleashing of the forces of nature is also suggested in the Archery Range of Miralles and Pinós (Barcelona, 1990–92). Its structures dug into their chthonic surroundings seem to wave and bend as if in the process of being rocked by an earthquake. The chaos wrought by Miralles and Pinós has a dynamic quality, each shed seeming to collide with the other in a mysterious propagation of movement.

Despite their apparent disorganization, the 'chaotism' of these projects was more obsessed with understanding in an abstract manner organization, construction and destruction, growth and decay. These buildings were not a comment on the distress and derangement of reality in the surrounding environment, either natural or artificial.

Realism

Architecture since the Second World War has come to be strongly associated with inhumanity, desolation and devastation. The mere mention of post-war urban design invokes images of asphalt deserts and mean streets, nightmares of bureaucratic and technocratic know-how, 'anomic', 'atopic' graveyards of urbanity. Although these apocalyptic generalizations are not wholly accurate, they capture the way many architects – and non-architects – of the post-1968 generation feel about post-war planning and construction in European cities, a devastation often judged worse than the war itself.

It was this devastation that the post-'68 generation of architects tried to arrest, by giving power to the users to decide their own architectural fate, by recourse to architectural tradition, or through the attempt to create an architecture of community. By the mid-1980s, however, none of these efforts seemed to be fulfilling their promise. Even worse, they had, occasionally, been used as fronts, alibis behind which technocratically and bureaucratically minded business was transacted as usual. The cult of the political as much as the cult of the cultural and the precious, the cult of fabulism as much as that of beautification, the cult of 'place', but also the cult of 'chaos', often seemed ineffectual, particularly in areas of urban obsolescence. It was in this context that an architecture of new vitality began to appear in the mid-1980s. It coincided with a number of projects of considerable scale emerging all over Europe after a period of relative economic recovery. They were located in a specific class of sites which suddenly became attractive because of their low land value and privileged location. These were mostly forgotten pockets of urban areas that had previously been occupied by industrial, transportation, distribution or institutional facilities of the pre-First-World-War industrial era. They were factories, railway stations, slaughterhouses for the mass food market, warehouses, control complexes, 'machines to govern', to use Foucault's expression, and occasionally military structures. Technological and socio-economic developments, combined with the ageing of the structures, had made such facilities obsolete. Similarly, many parts of inner cities, 'bombed out' through so-called urban renewal schemes of the post-war years, were also obsolete. Their obsolescence and their subsequent piecemeal cannibalization by opportunistic commercial developments had led to anomic, atopic, irredeemable no-man's-lands, what Lewis Mumford called the 'anti-city'. It seemed impossible that any planning intervention or architectural ordering could give such areas any aesthetic appearance in the traditional sense, any character of 'place'.

The character of these sites was negative: hardness of materials, harshness of texture, roughness of shape, industrial colour, fragmentation of space. The realist architects made a world which represented the very negative, 'dirty' attributes of these sites. Indeed, they made them appear even more intense in projects such as Rem Koolhaas's Netherlands Dance Theatre (The Hague, 1984–87, pp. 182–85), Myrto Vitart's ONYX Cultural Centre (Saint Herblain, 1987–88, pp. 214–17), Jean Nouvel's Némausus (Nîmes, 1986–87, pp. 178–81), Matthias Sauerbruch and Elias Zenghelis's Apartment House at Checkpoint Charlie (Berlin, 1983–90, pp. 236–37), Héctor Fernández and Vetges tu i Mediterrània's Production Centre for Valencian Television (Valencia, 1986–89, pp. 234–35), Miralles and

Pinós's La Pista at Hostalets (1987–91, pp. 260–63), Gilles Bouchez's social housing on the Boulevard Vincent Auriol (Paris, 1987–90, pp. 242–43). They implied that there was actually something intriguing in these negative qualities.

The selective representation in a project of characteristics drawn from the context of its site, even if these characteristics are considered 'negative' or 'lowly', has strong affinities, if not an underlying continuity, with the 'angry-young-man' brutalist architecture of the 1950s, such as James Stirling's Preston Infill working-class housing project (England, 1957–59) and with later buildings such as Alejandro de la Sota's masterpiece, the Colegio Maravillas (Madrid, 1961), not to mention Venturi and Scott Brown's pop realism of the late 1960s and early 1970s. There are further parallels with the 'adhocism' of the early 1970s, a term used by Charles Jencks and Nathan Silver with reference to architects working in a manner recalling the process of waste reclamation.[26]

But perhaps more than any other cultural tendency, these new architectural works bear similarities with a movement in American literature which in an issue of *Granta* magazine, its editor Bill Buford called the 'dirty realist' school of writing.[27] Like their architectural counterparts, this generation of writers, disenchanted with their seniors' 'post-modern', 'deconstructionist' stance, set out to take a hard, critical look at everyday life in a world cluttered by the 'oppressive details of modern consumerism'.[28] In a mood reminiscent of many of the post-war neo-realist writings and films, this fiction, 'informed by a discomforting and sometimes elusive irony', is 'so spare in manner that it takes some time before one realizes how completely a whole culture and a whole moral condition are being represented'.

What was the meaning of this return to realism in architecture? Was it created by an attraction to the negative qualities of hardness, harshness, roughness and incompleteness? Such an attraction can be found as early as the Renaissance in the notion of *non-finito*, and then later in that of the sublime, a concept that was perhaps associated with the beginnings of the crisis of confidence in the possibility of a perfect world of urbanity. Or was it because, to quote Kant's famous passage from *Observations on the Feeling of the Beautiful and the Sublime* (1764), this 'portrayal of the infernal kingdom arouse[s] enjoyment, but with horror'?[29]

To some architects, such as Hans Kollhoff, the answer is the latter. In his interview with film director Wim Wenders,[30] he appears to agree with Wenders, who – metaphorically, of course – calls Berlin 'a murderous city . . . but that's the way a city should be'. The 'excitement is really only created at the cracks, where suddenly everything goes wrong'. 'Where it all perfectly fits together, there is nothing left,' Wenders observes.

It seems, however, that a different reading can be made of the intensification of 'dirty real' characteristics in these new buildings. Once again, one can recognize in their architecture the technique of defamiliarization. But this use of 'strangemaking' is uniquely strange. It does not resemble defamiliarization as applied by critical regionalism or any of the other movements of the past twenty-five years. Instead of making the world appear unfamiliar by inserting within it highly contrasting elements, pricking consciousness by confronting geometries, as Rafael Moneo did in his Museo Nacional de Arte Romano (Merida, 1980–86, pp. 148–51), by confronting different spatial schemata as did Coop Himmelblau in Rooftop Remodelling (Vienna, 1983–89, pp. 220–23), or by confronting the rectangular with the biomorphic internal court in Cruz and Ortiz's housing block on Doña Maria Coronel Street (Seville, 1974–76, pp. 82–83), realists make strange the characteristics of an area by carrying them over into the building and intensifying them in a mirror-like way. They hold up a convex mirror whose lens emphasizes rather than covers up reality, or, to use the expression of Schklovsky writing about Tolstoy, they 'make the stone stony'. Thus, architecture seems once more, as in the 19th century, to be responding to what the art historian Linda Nochlin referred to as 'the call for truth, honesty and sincerity'.[31] These concepts, however, have lost their 19th-century foundation on claims of absolute objectivity. What realist architecture is doing is responding, again, to the demand for 'contemporaneity', to be 'of one's own time'. This does not necessarily imply only the use of industrial products, the colours, materials and images of industrially produced desolation. The conflicts of our time go much deeper. On the cognitive and on the moral level, this deeper realistic portrayal of the world recognizes and tries to represent what occurs when ideas about 'well-formedness' and 'worldmaking' lead to not one but multiple possible worlds. Thus, the representation of this reality might employ Corinthian motifs together with plain commercial brick walls as the context requires, as Venturi's multi-faceted Sainsbury Wing of the National Gallery in London demonstrates (1986–91, pp. 272–75). The building as a composition of incommensurable parts is not an endorsement of post-war urban disintegration, of the destruction of the sense of place or of belonging; it is rather a means of questioning them and an argument, if not always a means, for overcoming them.

The eighth tendency

Building in Europe since 1968, like building in many parts of the world, has witnessed an explosion of variety and individuality. Perhaps never before in history have so many alternative approaches to architecture been proposed and so quickly implemented simultaneously. There has been a plethora of morphologies, a cornucopia of typologies. For an era of proliferation of the technological means of production of buildings, for an epoch of triumph for the rights of the individual and freedom of expression, this should come as no surprise. The question still remains as to what, and how successfully, has been achieved in this architecture in the face of the new constraints that confront all people in their everyday lives in Europe today.

Undoubtedly architecture as a form of cognition has reached an extreme degree of sophistication: the buildings of the last two decades all over Europe implement intricate models of space organization in complex problem solving. They carry meanings, make statements about the world and about themselves in an unprecedentedly rich fashion. As we have seen, the endowment of memory and the competence of invention, apparently antagonistic, have reinforced each other and thus have soared in contemporary architecture. Parallel to this development runs the growing sophistication in discussing architecture as a cultural expression, as one can conclude from the essays which follow by Fritz Neumeyer and Jean-Louis Cohen, as well as from the architectural projects themselves which we have analysed.

On the other hand, what limits these dynamic tendencies of the last two decades, seven of which we have identified here, is their propensity to bypass existing questions in their anxious effort to respond to fresh ones. Moreover, in several instances, the new questions have not always measured up, in terms of challenge, to those left unanswered, a point that both Peter Rice and Lucius Burckhardt make in their contributions on the current situation with regard to technology and ecology respectively.

Certainly, this is how history has always worked: most conflicts are never resolved; they are simply transcended. Yet the conflict between individuality and efficiency that populism addressed, between tradition and change that the *rappel à l'ordre* struggled with, between true and apparent functionality that neo-rigorism confronted, between community and globality that critical regionalism tried to overcome, and between coherence and completeness that adherents of chaos in architecture and urbanism were engaged in, has proved particularly tenacious. It would seem that the 'end of history' is still a long way off in architecture. Thus the concern with reality by a younger generation of architects indicates the need to use the successful experiments of the last twenty years, but it also indicates the need to move beyond exclusive, insular, fragmented tendencies towards a more inclusive, coherent, global one. This is not to advocate a return to bygone totalistic simplicities in a world so clearly made up of a multiplicity of human beliefs, a world in which the integrity of each should be respected, in which the imperative of accepting the 'Other' – an imperative embodied in Daniel Libeskind's deeply moving design for the Department Jewish Museum in Berlin (1989–, pp. 290–93) – should be followed. It is rather to argue for a new tendency which recognizes the question of morality as central to an architecture which will have to grow rationally in a world made up of multiple worlds.

Notes

1. We are referring to Jean Jacques Rousseau's *Les rêveries d'un promeneur solitaire* (1776–78), so influential in creating a link between the new aesthetics of freedom associated with the picturesque landscape and criticism of the *Ancien Régime*, and also to the *Mémoire sur les hôpitaux* by the philosopher Nicolas Caritat, Marquis de Condorcet (written 1786, unpublished until 1977). This was the first instance of an argument for participation of the users grouped in districts and of a multi-disciplinary team of experts in architectural design. Both texts are contained in our documentary history of architecture from 1125–1810, *Origins of Modern Architecture* (Nijmegen, 1990, in Dutch).

2. *Le Carré Bleu* was founded in 1958 by André Schimmerling. It published texts of members of Team X and its disciples and members of the Union International des Architectes. Among its collaborators were Giancarlo De Carlo, Shadrach Woods, Alison and Peter Smithson, Arthur Glickson. A retrospective issue of the magazine was published in June 1989. It is still being published.

3. Founded in 1967 by Philippe Boudon, Alain Sarfati and Bernard Hamburger, among others. See our bibliography on Sarfati's housing project in Savigny-le-Temple (1982–86) for further reading.

4. See in particular Henri Lefebvre, *Everyday Life in the Modern World*, New York, 1971 (first published in French, 1968).

5. Particularly as influenced by the writings of the Frankfurt School, especially such works as Theodor Adorno's *Against Epistemology*, Cambridge, MA, 1982 (first published in German, 1952).

6. *Hypnerotomachia Poliphili*, Venice, 1499.

7. Henri Lefebvre, *op. cit.*

8. See L. Lefaivre and A. Tzonis, 'In the Name of the People, the Populist Movement in Architecture', *Forum*, 1975, no. 3, for further reading on the history of the populist movement.

9. Vincent Scully, 'Postscript: Ideology in Form', in A. Rossi's *A Scientific Autobiography*, Cambridge, MA, 1984.

10. Gyorgy Lukács, *The Historical Novel*, 1962 (first published 1955); also his *Studies in European Realism*, 1950 (first published 1947).

11. See our 'The narcissistic phase in architecture', *Harvard Architectural Review*, vol. 1, Spring 1980, pp. 52–61.

12. The doctrines of Carlo Lodoli, who never published, were set down by his disciples in Count Francesco Algarotti's *Saggio* (1756), Francesco Milizia's *Principi di Architettura Civile* (1781) and Andrea Memmo's *Elementi di Architettura Lodoliana* (1786).

13. Galileo Galilei, *Dialogues Concerning Two New Sciences*, New York, 1914 (first published in Leiden, 1638).

14. 'Servant' and 'served' are terms coined by Louis Kahn.

15. Hilton Kramer, *The Age of the Avant-Garde*, New York, 1973, pp. 244–46.

16. Robert Venturi, *Complexity and Contradiction in Architecture*, New York, 1966.

17. See A. Tzonis, L. Lefaivre and A. Alofsin's 'Die Frage des Regionalismus' in *Für eine andere Architektur* (M. Andritzky, L. Burckhardt and O. Hoffman, eds, Frankfurt, 1981); and 'The grid and the pathway' in *Architecture in Greece*, no. 5, 1981; and 'El regionalismo critico en la arquitectura española actual' in *A&V*, no. 3, 1985, pp. 4–19. Kenneth Frampton has written perceptively about the movement in many of his articles and in *Modern Architecture, a Critical History* (London, 1985, 2nd ed.). See also S. Amourgis (ed.), *Critical Regionalism, The Pomona Meeting Proceedings*, Pomona, CSP University, 1991.

18. See our 'Critical Regionalism' in S. Amourgis, *op. cit.*, for further reading on the historical origins of regionalism in architecture.

19. Victor Schklovsky, 'Art as Technique', in Lee T. Lemon and M. Reiss, *Russian Formalists*, Lincoln, Nebraska, 1965.

20. Robert Venturi, *op. cit.*, p. 48.

21. James Gleick, *Chaos, Making a New Science*, New York, 1987.

22. Richard Sennett, *The Uses of Disorder*, New York, 1970.

23. Eugenio Battisti, *L'anti-rinascimento*, Milan, 1989.

24. Ludwig Wittgenstein, *Philosophical Investigations*, New York, 1958.

25. Sigfried Giedeon, *Space, Time and Architecture*, Cambridge, MA, 1959; Peter Collins, *Changing Ideals in Modern Architecture*, London, 1965.

26. Charles Jencks and Nathan Silver, *Adhocism*, London, 1972.

27. L. Lefaivre has written about this aspect of contemporary architecture in 'Dirty Realism in European Architecture Today', *Design Book Review*, no. 17, pp. 17–20; and 'Dirty Realism', *Archithèse*, Zürich, Jan. 1990 (special issue ed. L. Lefaivre with contributions by Richard Ingersoll, Fritz Neumeyer, Rem Koolhaas, Enric Miralles and Carme Pinós, among others).

28. Bill Buford, 'Editorial', *Dirty Realism*, Granta 8, Cambridge, England, 1983.

29. Immanuel Kant, *Observations on the Feeling of the Beautiful and the Sublime*, Berkeley and Los Angeles, 1960 (first published 1764).

30. Hans Kollhoff, *Quaderns*, no. 177, 1989.

31. Linda Nochlin, *Realism*, Harmondsworth, 1971.

The Second-Hand City: Modern Technology and Changing Urban Identity

Fritz Neumeyer

Modern technology invades the city

I would like to begin with two key images that capture the essence of what I have to say, in that they represent two moments in the development of the urban phenomenon of the 19th century. Both images illustrate the impact of modern technology on the urban environment. In the first, a painting by Adolf Menzel of 1848 entitled *Berlin Landscape*, we find the city in the distance and the rural landscape in fore- and middleground virtually unchanged in their idyllic nature. Only the track of iron rails carrying a steaming locomotive gives evidence of the fact that modern times have arrived. But the train, a dark, horizontal object, appears quite well integrated into the picturesque landscape surrounding the city of Berlin. Menzel has depicted no unsettling overtones to disturb the peaceful ambience. The city, visible in the background of the painting, seems to live its life as ever, and the train crossing in the foreground looks no more threatening than any other carriage we might expect to find in a setting such as this one. In this case, however, it is not a horse-powered carriage, but instead one propelled by a black metallic creature, the machine.

In a painting by Hans Baluschek entitled *Railroad in the Cityscape*, painted almost fifty years after Menzel's, the scenery has undergone dramatic change: the black metallic object has left the urban periphery behind and has finally arrived downtown, now having gained a strange and shocking presence as the locomotive appears right in the middle of the city street. In Baluschek's painting from the last decade of the 19th century, the industrial era has already reached an advanced stage of development, bringing changes that drastically affect the urban environment. And, the way this painting makes its visual argument, modern reality stands in opposition to Menzel's view, and is figured in a moment of unexpected violation that seems to leave open no alternative or escape. The dynamic forces behind the process of modernization are no longer in harmony with the landscape of the city, and, in a foreboding way, their dramatic appearance at once suggests their inevitability and irreversibility. There is no doubt about what has happened. The train and the machine age have advanced towards the heart of the city, cutting through the urban space and, arriving at the front door of the city dweller, ambushing him the moment he steps out.

By the end of the 19th century, modern technology had deeply penetrated the cityscape, leaving in its wake the footprints of the modernist invasion. Wide-span girders and other modern construction work, no longer camouflaged or hidden behind architectural screens in historical style, irrupted into the traditional city, clashing with the space of monuments. Ironwork designed by engineers confronted the architecture of stone and the dignified language of classical forms spoken by architects. Like blades, the engineers' iron structures chopped up the body of the city, fragmenting the urban tissue and assaulting its 'beauty' by dissecting the homogeneous composition of blocks and squares. Bridges, elevated railway structures, gasometers and other modern objects of unfamiliar shape became significant new elements in the traditional cityscape, taking on a disturbingly powerful and threatening presence. Modernity was on the verge of erecting its own 'unpleasant' monuments and *points de vue*, which would disrupt the urban identity and ravage the urban scenery.

Artists, sensing these moments of provocative action and violation, visualized the radical changes taking place in the landscape or the city as the beginning of something new. Baluschek painted a compelling image of what his contemporaries decried as the 'brutish appearance' of iron within the city. Captured in a low-angle view of the locomotive roaring down the middle of the street is the shocking presence of modernity. The painting insistently portrays a dramatic juxtaposition that would give an appropriate compositional form to the collision between the functional and the symbolic. A new reality had sprung up, irreversible, frightening, powerful, but nevertheless imbued with its own immanent beauty, a kind of beauty whose inherent laws were only waiting to be discovered. The rupture between modern reality and historical context – which would eventually occur on all levels of society – was irreconcilable. Modern reality would take over the urban space as its own theatrical platform, instigating changes of far-reaching social and aesthetic dimensions. As Baluschek's painting

Adolf Menzel, *Berlin Landscape* (1848)

Hans Baluschek, *Railroad within Cityscape* (1890)

The Berlin Elevated Railway entering a building (*c.* 1900)

Gustave Caillebotte, *Pont l'Europe* (1878)

Andre Kertész, *Meudon* (1928)

predicted, within the city, both the familiar urban space that once belonged to the world of the *flâneur* and the space of monuments that had belonged to classical art would have to surrender to the modernist invasion.

Changing the urban identity: aspects of the emergence of a new urban reality

Like the millipedes of this modernist invasion, the iron construction of the elevated railway marched into the heart of the city, introducing a new rhythm to its peaceful setting and creating the unexpected encounter. In Berlin, the train would cut right through a museum complex and run next to a wall covered on the other side with Greek and Egyptian sculptures. The Berlin Elevated offers a rich example of the potent visual effect of the iron girders. Like knives they fragmented the classical architectural composition by isolating forms and disassembling the hierarchical canon with its progressive horizontal layers of *rustica*, *piano nobile*, etc. This interruption of the classical logic of load and support caused portions of the structure to appear suspended, hanging in the air, their girders blocked from view. Floating pediments, disconnected from their bases, underscored the fact that modern construction work was cutting architecture's legs off: in the urban realm, it not only spoiled frontal views but also ruptured the traditional concept, centrality. Furthermore, trains running on the level of the *bel-étage* violated the privacy of residential occupants. For a split second, passengers could peer into a stranger's apartment, suddenly exposing him to the surprise of having a train pass in front of the window. Not only could the train pass by close to one's window: it could even drive right through it, as one example of a train penetrating a Berlin apartment building and disappearing into the *bel-étage* shows.

Other, equally strange images resulting from new urban constellations that belonged to a modern 20th-century urban reality are to be found in painting and photography of this period. The eye of the artist seemed to be trained on the effect these new elements had on the imagery and identity of the traditional city. The urban realism of the Impressionists took early account of this change. In these paintings, modern bridges transformed into arcades or urban roofs that transformed streets and squares into steel-covered spaces, platforms of modern life, challenged the notion of inside and outside, adding excitement to the space of the *flâneur*. Some decades later, in the 20th-century city, the situation would look quite different: as Andre Kertész's photo *Meudon* (1928) seems to suggest, when trains fly through the sky, the familiar imagery can only belong to the past. It survives only as a picture for the living-room wall, to be wrapped up, carried under one's arm, and taken home.

Modern reality produced a city that could not be understood as a tableau.

Around 1900, crisscrossed by iron trajectories, the once-static body of the city began to move in a kind of mechanical ballet. Like Oskar Schlemmer's human figure with mechanical extensions, the modern metropolis, equipped with new iron extensions, all at once began to dance. In Berlin, the elevated railway ran straight into the walls of buildings or collided with a museum of ancient sculpture as if in a Dadaist collage, or trains would mysteriously disappear into the *bel-étage* of an apartment building through an opening in the facade. It would not be long before another moment of initiation would take place, when bridges would climb on top of one another like copulating animals, intermingling in their excitement to form clusters of steel webs, which, as multilevel viewing platforms, promised the pleasures of ever-greater visual experience of – and insight into – urban space. In the joints of this mechanical system, where underground train and tram, ships on the canal, interurban railway and long-distance trains intersected and met for a split second on their independent routes, the model for the city of the future was born. The image of a metropolis was laid bare in the multilayered movement and omnipresent bridges that were a response to the need for connections between the isolated objects of the cut-open city. Modern reality, already further advanced than traditional modes of perception, was only waiting to be kissed awake by a futurist imagination so that it could come to life in the icon of the modern city.

The modern city manifested itself as a new urban type: a city of fragmented space and isolated objects that assembled themselves to form an urbanized corridor, one that would be experienced from multiple *points de vue* rather than with traditional *Perspektivität*, or single point perspective. The space of this city would no longer be determined by the continuity of walls and facades, but would instead consist of a vast array of isolated objects gathered as a society of autonomous volumes. In opposition to the homogenizing and perspectival effects of the Serlian conception of the cityscape, the modern urban space would have no dominant centrality. It would instead engender a panoramic conception and perception as building came to be understood as object and fabric at once. This intrusion of modern technology into the city of monuments conjured up unfamiliar notions of space and urbanity. Railway trajectories, slicing through the homogeneous block system of the city, left behind the incoherence of fragments and voids. Modern construction work had deconstructed classical hierarchies and discounted monumental perspectivity, but furthermore, it confronted the eye with the previously unseen view of the 'backyard' of the city.

Writing on the subject of urbanism in 1890, Josef Stübben throws light on this peculiar late 19th-century urban condition from the point of view of an academic architect:

In most cases, in older parts of the city, the urban railway cannot assume a place in the middle of the street, but must instead cut right across the perimeter block system, and therefore has to bridge streets and intersections. Unfortunately, this type of construction has the disadvantage of causing great unpleasantness both for the pedestrian walking in the street, to whom the unadorned sidewalls due to the opened thoroughfare become visible in their bare crudity, and for the passenger on the train, who, on his journey through the city, already has tasted a sequence of disgusting images composed of backyards and rear views of buildings, and has thus gained obnoxious insights into the miseries of metropolitan life before ever having set foot on the magnificent boulevards. In these terms, the Berlin urban railway offers us an exemplary deterrent.

('Der Städtebau', in the *Handbuch der Architektur*, Darmstadt 1890, p. 217)

Cutting through the 19th-century city, the train paved the way for yet another urban phenomenon: the modern 'drive-through city'. As Stübben's observations make clear, with the train cutting through the urban block system, the disorderly character of the periphery is brought into the centre, whose interior is all the while becoming exteriorized. Once the eye was directed away from articulated spaces and facades, this 'other' city exposed the unpleasant, dark side of the well-built urban world, of the 'ugliness' of its interior, of things once shielded from view. Instead of a world governed by classical order, one would encounter a hitherto invisible urban desert of backyards and voids and fire-walls. This other, or 'second' city, crowded with absence, became apparent only as a collection of leftovers and fragments, of unadorned, impoverished buildings, masses of brick and windowless walls.

Lined up in unfamiliar spatial and rhythmical sequences, the urban corridors of the post-architectural landscape, with its zero-degree-architecture zone stretching out alongside traffic lanes, no longer had anything in common with the classical notion of the 'city as house' handed down to us from Plato and Alberti. Modern reality at work had left behind a violated urban context that no longer corresponded to the terms of classical urban topology. Perception of this city no longer depended upon the distinction between front and back; nor was it anchored by monuments or places for art. The modern urban reality of the drive-through city, with its cut-open and fragmented space and continuous boulevards, demanded a new urban optimism and new aesthetic terms to replace the classical ones.

With the cut-open space of this second-city-within-the-city, the margins invaded the urban centre, and the very structure and character of the buildings there caused its peripheralization. For this second city, the urban metaphor of the 'theatre' – the perspectival box of classical Serlian space – was no longer adequate. Neither was the traditional metaphor of the 'city as house', of the city as a sequence of *indoor* spaces, able to express this type of urban structure. Instead, it demanded an *outdoor* model as its new metaphor, one that would help us to understand the laws of a transformed visual world, because the clear distinction between actor and spectator, between inside and outside, was effaced as these spheres overlapped in the unpredictable movements of the city's mechanical ballet.

Like an embryo, this second city existed first as a drive-through city-within-the-city of the 19th century. Only in our century did this second-hand city begin to assume its autonomous urban life. Its fabric is characterized by the metropolitan fever of circulation, which causes the fragmentation of space and the isolation of objects and transforms the city into a composite of heterogeneous elements. Cross-programmed, juxtaposed and in permanent flux, this vibrant metropolitan plankton demands a dynamic perception instead of a static point of view in order to connect its piecemeal of parts into a sequence. The eye, moving through this modern landscape, is asked to construe an essentially new visual order, based on time, matter, space, and light in flux – driven by the perpetual activity of the modern city that forces us to reconsider our assumptions about what is urban.

Together with the necessity for another type of perception, that of the moving eye, goes a new notion of the urban object and its relation to architecture, even of its very identity as 'architecture' and as something 'urban'. The modern building does not belong to a precisely defined wall system anymore – for example, Hausmann Boulevard in Berlin – but has asserted its autonomy as one element in a rhythmic succession of space and matter, voids and solids. As 'lone' objects in the urban landscape, these solids 'without architecture' are not governed by the principle of frontality nor by the terms of the classical facade. The primacy of the facade is cancelled as one drives by, around or through these objects. Caught in an involuntary rotation, they now play a role in a larger kinetic composition that is the urban landscape.

The organization of space also depends upon a different sense of perspective. In the traditional city, the *point de vue* has been the perspectival organizer, but in the city-without-

Railway cutting through cityscape, Berlin (1900)

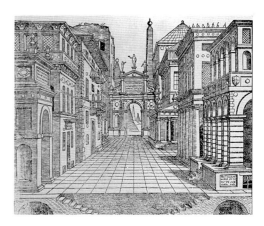

Sebastiano Serlio, 'Scena Tragedia' from *Tutte l'opere d'architettura e perspettiva* (Venice, 1584)

Drive-through city: Wim Wenders, Houston

Paul Citroen, *Metropolis* (photocollage, 1923)

centre, there is no fixed point of view. The absence of a focus in perspectival space allows – even demands – panoramic vision because no vanishing point arrests the movement of the eye. In the modern city, a new mode of establishing relations and connections is required to connect the kaleidoscopic impressions of independent objects and surfaces. There is a shift in the visual order that displaces the *object* from a now centreless space, and situates the *subject* at the centre of spatial as well as social experience. The fixed object, which demands to be looked at and visually determined from a single point of view, surrenders to the moving eye zooming through the urban plankton. The connecting view becomes the organizer of perception, replacing a built homogeneity imposed from above.

It seems to me that the train and the moving eye, or better a cinematic perception, obviously share a common tradition. Describing the train as a 'steam-camera on train tracks', the Japanese film director Ozu suggested this very relationship. There is also evidence of the mutual relationship between the train and the modern city, on the one hand, and the technology of film on the other hand which underlines the symbiotic nature of both faculties. In the process of shooting movies, the camera is mounted on a track of rails. The perception of the fragmented space of the modern city requires a mental construction that differs from traditional ones. The city caused by motion can virtually only be understood in motion, in terms of a sequence of singular images that, when connected in the mind of the viewer, reveals its sense and meaning.

Herman Sörgel, an early 20th-century German architectural theorist, sensed the fundamental change in perception that the modern city required by its very nature. In a short but notable text concerning New York written in 1926, Sörgel, contradicting fellow critics and architects who sharply attacked the appearance of neo-Gothic or other historical forms in Manhattan skyscrapers, developed a generosity of argument that indicated a deeper understanding. In the face of the grand rhythm of the metropolis, Sörgel argued, the question of the vocabulary of styles and forms has become totally irrelevant and obsolete. The grand rhythm of the metropolis is altogether indifferent to whether a building is Gothic or Renaissance or any other style.

The individual form disappears in the large scale; building-mass, continuity of change, life are what count. *In terms of architecture, New York can no longer be perceived in terms of isolated individual images, but only in terms of a continuously running film.*

When we consider the impact that modern technology had on the changing identity – and visual perception – of the city, the consequences (implications) for modern urban architecture immediately beg discussion. The demise of the Serlian section view in favour of directionless, continuous space, of panoramic vision devoid of aim and hierarchy, has liberated the architectural object and its surfaces from traditional restrictions to a substantial degree, allowing the body and its planes to be independent of one another. It is only when forms are distinguished from their parts that the skin of the building can be partially peeled away. This is not only true with respect to ornament stripped from the traditional facade, but also, in a more general way, for the dissolution of the wall itself. It transmutes – or deconstructs – into a system of rhetorical layers wrapped around the architectural object that tend to live their individual lives – a fashion of treating the wall highly favoured in today's architecture!

Historically, we may sense the beginning of this process at that moment when the clash between functional and symbolic eroded the consistency of architectural form; when modern technology first appeared in the public and aesthetic sphere of the city. This process results in architecture coming under attack by the sign, and losing its predominance as a constituent visual component of the cityscape. The fragmentation into systems of layers permits the billboard – not unlike the severed pediment of a classical building whose facade has been sliced through by elevated railway tracks – to gain an existence independent of the rest of the building. In this sense, the billboard indeed becomes a new type of urban architecture. It is this process that turns the cityscape into the 'ocean of signs' that make up the 'post-architectural urban landscape of the modern metropolis' (Roland Barthes). Its chaotic quality, demanding a different sense of urbanity and a sensitivity for difference rather than order, had already been captured by Bauhaus student Paul Citroen in his famous photocollage entitled *Metropolis* of 1923, an image that elevates the urban 'piecemeal' into the icon of the city of fragmentation.

Islands of urban order

Challenging the modern condition of urban fragmentation, the architect was confronted with the question of how to structure and make visible in built form the order of the modern urban world. At the turn of the century, Otto Wagner and Karl Scheffler – to mention only two important protagonists for a modern urban architecture, or *Groszstadt Architektur* – demanded a 'New Objectivity', a *Nutzstil*, taking account of both modern aesthetics and functional purposes at once. With the particular urban language of a 'functional prose' (Scheffler), the structuring of the architectural organism would be consciously connected to modern technology and the modern metropolis, both of which as totalities demanded form and character. The 19th-century Berlin architect Karl Friedrich Schinkel appears as a prominent precurser of this peculiar notion of modern urban architecture. His 'urbanism of the individual architectural object' emphasized isolation as well as departure from Baroque concatenation with its spatial uniformity and monotony of endless walls. And, with a building like his Bauakademie, Schinkel produced a prototype that assimilated modern technology at the same time as transforming it into urban architecture.

The Bauakademie appears as a massive cube of red bricks virtually plunged into the midst of the old city. In both its materials and construction techniques, the cube embodies Schinkel's encounter with the advanced industrial reality of the anonymous functional building he had the opportunity to see on his travels through England in 1826. Schinkel had remarked with surprise on the industrial landscape of Manchester, with its 'thousand smoking obelisks' and its 'enormous masses of red brick . . . erected without any thought of architecture.' This dark side of the industrial urban reality announced a future architecture not based on the laws of art, but rather intended to serve as a point of departure in the face of the challenge to arrive at new aesthetic virtues. Schinkel's functional classicism, embodied in the Bauakademie, assimilated this modern reality by utilizing the fireproof building construction of industrial mills and the soberness of purely functional building, and further, by bringing together art and commerce, as it provided shops for rent on the ground floor. It is not difficult to imagine the complaints of Schinkel's contemporaries about this building. It was criticized for its cubical shape, for the flatness of its facades, which lacked any plastic value, and for the uniformity of its appearance, with neither centre of gravity nor central axis. In a contemporary slogan, the Bauakademie was ridiculed as *Kasten dieser Stadt, Ringsum glatt und platt* ('Box of the town, flat and smooth all around'). Few were able – or willing — to appreciate Schinkel's building as a 'cornerstone of the urban space' (Friedrich Adler, 1869). A painting by Friedrich Klose from 1836 captures the essentially confrontational nature of this installation of a free-standing cube of red bricks in a district crowded with traditional stucco buildings. Like a horizontal divider, the 'mast of the ship' bisects both Klose's picture and the city. Two different types of cities are juxtaposed on the banks of the River Spree. On the left is the traditional city with its space enclosed by the 'old wall' whose failure would be ridiculed almost a century later; on the right bank of the river, we look into the modern cubical city composed as an association of free-standing cubes – typified by the Bauakademie as the modern solid 'without architecture' – in the opened-up, panoramic urban space.

It is not surprising that we find Schinkel's architecture of urban intervention and his vision of a cubical city echoed almost a century later in the urban projects of Mies van der Rohe and Ludwig Hilberseimer. Hilberseimer's sketch for the Alexander Platz competition of 1928 seems to propose the completion of Schinkel's view from the Schloßbrücke. Standing on this bridge, the viewer would be surrounded by regular cubical buildings in a full panoramic scope of more than 180 degrees. It was not a traditional concatenation of buildings, but instead a disposition of rather peculiarly dislocated structures that would become the guiding principle of modern architects who followed Schinkel. The view into the depth of urban space was no longer directed by the guiding lines of the wall, but – as Schinkel illustrates – by the corners of public buildings stepping forth in cubic relief. Hilberseimer's remark, 'better from Schinkel to Schinkel', found in an unpublished manuscript on the Architektur der Großstadt' of 1914, is illuminated from this point of view. If we recollect the unpleasant facts of the modernist invasion of the city – as exemplified in phenomena like windowless, unadorned walls, isolated objects without architecture, an almost aggressive presence of modern building materials and technology, the exteriorization of the interior space, cut-open block structures, and their patterns of dislocation allowing panoramic vision – there is, in particular, one project in the history of modern urban architecture that like a parasite absorbs all these 'negative' aspects in order to transform them into a completely new architectural language, one that would survive the 20th century. Of course, I am thinking of the Miesian design for a glass skyscraper on the Friedrichstrasse in Berlin of 1922, one of the most radical projects for urban architecture the modern movement offered, and one which left its imprint on the architectural mind of this century.

This prismatic design exposing modern technology – represented in the modern building material of glass as well as in the image of the steel skeleton – in an almost exhibitionistic manner towered over the city on a piece of land that, as the site plan shows, had been bisected by the railway some decades before and had been left a useless empty lot. Mies's tower summed up the windowless solid object without architecture, as it abolished all architectural decoration of the facade in order to transform the window into a wall. The window onto the city became the essential element of the wall, and the equilibrium of its former material and rhetorical qualities were now expressed in sheer transparency. The layers of

Karl Friedrich Schinkel, sketch of Manchester (1826)

Friedrich Wilhelm Klose, *Schinkel's Bauakademie* (1836)

Ludwig Hilberseimer, sketch for the Alexander Platz competition (1928)

Mies van der Rohe, glass skyscraper at Friedrichstrasse Station (1921–22)

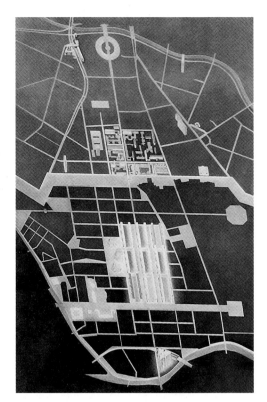

Rem Koolhaas, spaces in Berlin

Glass curtain wall of the Friedrichstrasse Station (1889)

architectural argumentation with which the old wall was composed were stripped away and replaced with new perceptual effects – including the reflection of light – to establish a new quality for the dialogue between the building and its surroundings. Elevated on a floating plane, one was lifted above ground and invited to enjoy a broader vista. Like twenty-two viewing platforms stacked one on top of another to provide the spectator with new panoramic sensations, the building became a viewing machine that stretched its corners out into three directions to embrace the urban spectacle. The transparency of the curtain wall allowed the passerby, struck by the visual punch of this dramatic object, to catch a glimpse of what existed behind the surface. In the same way that Schinkel's painting *View onto the Flowering of Greece* elevated the observer onto the level of the scaffolding in order to let him celebrate the sensation of being suspended above ground and participate *as viewer* in the making of civilization, the view out into the landscape of the modern city was made real. As the light reflected in the glass surface and the viewing angle suddenly made the building's skin transparent, private and public realms touched one another. Even if only for a moment, the division between inside and outside, surface and depth, was overcome: the auditorium and the stage of the urban theatre became one, and viewer and actor met on the same set.

Mies's vision of a skyscraper gave an edge to Schinkel's architecture of urban intervention. Schinkel's self-conscious urban architecture was raised to the level of dramatic key object, indeed acting as urban cornerstone, distancing modern civilization from the past. Towering over the cityscape, commanding the power to transform both space and context, the glass prism cut like a razorblade into the old Wilhelminian city, which was only waiting to be violated. But even if Mies let the urban surroundings sink into obscurity to become a kind of anonymous podium for his free-standing object, which appeared as a mere fragment of the future, it nevertheless complemented the composition of the city by echoing its fragmented urban condition.

Rem Koolhaas of OMA has taught us to relate the triangular shape of the urban site to a sequencing of spaces, which, like a string of pearls, adorned the city of Berlin: the roundel of the Baroque Friedrichstadt to the south, followed by the octagon of Leipziger Platz and the square of the Pariser Platz in front of the Brandenburg Gate. Other contextual references in the Miesian glass skyscraper – a project that has become notorious for its reputed disregard for its urban surroundings – can be found even in the choice of materials. The glass curtain wall of the tower picked up a theme introduced by its next-door neighbour,

the Friedrichstrasse Station, built in the late 19th century. Mies's curtain wall takes up a certain part of the station building, which, in Schinkel's terms, could also qualify as building 'without any thought of architecture', since it was the product of the engineer. It was the backside of the station that inspired those glass dreams of an architecture consisting of nothing more than the freely suspended glass curtain. Mies certainly had good reasons for not including the glass wall of the station building in any of his drawings or photomontages for the Friedrichstrasse project. Had he done so, the aura of originality of the avant-garde artist might have been compromised.

Mies's tower was the manifesto for a modern urban architecture that took into account both technological progress in building methods and the impact modern technology had already had on the identity of the city. The glass tower in a sense tested the traditional city as a backdrop for the insertions of modern presence, in the way that the gasometer and other functional and technological installations had already established themselves as new points of view within the fragmented urban tissue. In the 1920s, the cubical city took over the voids and remnants left behind by the urban desert of the 19th century. The voided corners of the grid structure, when cut open, provided ideal backdrops for striking implants. Like parasites on this context, modern urban architecture conquered these strategic urban positions by employing a 'cornerstone' strategy of its own: either dramatic new structures would be added, or already existing corner buildings would be remodelled in such a way that as individual objects they would express their disagreement and disgust at the notion of integration or harmony with the given context.

The modernist decontextualization, dehistoricization and intentional fragmentation made the process of urban transformation begun with the intrusion of modern technology into the cityscape a conscious one. Like Brunelleschi's autonomous and absolute architectural objects, modern urban architecture was bound to penetrate the structure of the traditional city, upsetting and altering its significance. The symbolic and constructive self-sufficiency of the new three-dimensional spatiality of the modern architectural object radiated into the urban space a rational order as the absolute emblem of a strict ethical will of transformation. Just as Brunelleschi's humanism suggested a new conception of the pre-existing town as a dying entity for transformation – ready to change its significance as soon as the introduction of compact architectural objects altered the balance of the Romanesque-Gothic 'continuous narrative' – modern urban architecture claimed to display visually the reverberation between rationality and the stratified urban texture.

Erich Mendelsohn's extension of the Mosse Building of 1922, stepping forth in bold relief, gave effective expression to the 'heroic caesura' of historical time by transmitting to architecture the velocity of modern machinery. Mendelsohn's staff jokingly declared that the addition represented 'the docking of the *Mauretania* in Berlin'. Their reference to one of the most famous oceanliners of the day captured both the building's intrusiveness and the flavour of machine-age speed it imparted. Indeed, Mendelsohn's almost Dadaist insertion of new fabric made the old building look as if it had been run over by an oceanliner steaming downtown, crashing into the block from behind, its prow raised up, and parts of its decks floating atop the facade of the street. The transformation of space and context, captured thirty years earlier in images like the train speeding down the middle of the street or the elevated railway system crashing into the *bel-étage* of an apartment building, found its proper architectural counterpart. In this kind of modern design, the violent intrusion of modernity was aesthetically balanced and smoothed into elegantly emphatic curves that would become the trademark for much continental modern architecture of the 1920s and 1930s. The cubical city, without distinguishable front and back, was shaped by machine-age aesthetics into a dynamics of movement, described by the architect as the effect he had sought:

An attempt had been made here to express the fact that the house is not an indifferent spectator of the careening motorcars and the tides of traffic in the streets, but that . . . it strives to be a living, cooperating factor of the movement. Just as it visibly expresses the swift tempo of the street, and takes up the accelerated tendency toward speed at the corners, so at the same time it subdues the nervousness of the street and of the passerby by the balance of its power.
(*Berliner Tageblatt*, 1924)

The engineered beauty found in modern machinery and objects like locomotives, bicycles, cars, aeroplanes and steamships became typical for the modern age, as van de Velde, Scheffler, J.A. Lux and others had observed at the turn of the century. The 'engineered' construction had been raised to the status of art. The modern architect, attempting to transform the urban space and the architectural object into a 'cooperating factor' of the modern movement, finally turned the city into a gigantic machine. Modern machinery became the symbol for both the aesthetic and functional concepts of the architecture of the metropolis in the era of Fordism. The dreams of a new architectural and urban

order were inspired by the much admired form and efficiency of modern machinery.

Hilberseimer's project for a Highrise City provided a frightening stereotypical vision of the metropolis of Fordism in the way it was inserted into the historic centre of the city, a crude urban brain transplant which transformed Berlin into a metropolitan Frankenstein. With this implantation of a scheme for 'operational units', each about the size of a small town, the exhausted metropolis could be given a new, economically and socially effective centre in order to resuscitate the old city with light, air and commerce.

As a second city, a city-within-a-city, the modernist downtown could be equated with a giant oceanliner anchored at Friedrichstrasse, adjacent to Schinkel's Theatre. This superimposition of an island of modernity brought the contemporary *Zeilenbau* to the heart of the city, and, to a large extent, utilized artistic techniques typical of the polemic collages of Dadaist artists. Deprived of all individuality, Hilberseimer's elementary design, with its stripped-naked walls, strongly resembled the urban architecture in George Grosz's paintings from the same period.

The essentially sober rhythm, emphasizing the definition of regularly articulated space, underscored the factory-like organization of these operational units that were lined up in a uniform scheme derived from industrial organization. With this grim and rather horrifying vision of the modern urban scenario – which, in the words of the late Hilberseimer, constituted 'a Necropolis rather than a Metropolis' – the threatening nocturnal machine that had been introduced by Fritz Lang's movie *Metropolis* in 1926 found its urban realization in the same year.

Avant-garde projects, like Hilberseimer's Highrise City, proposing an alternative order to the chaotic metropolitan condition as experienced in the American metropolis, were reductive instruments of utopian propaganda. With a crudity similar to the invasion by modern technology of the city's centre, these polemic islands of modernism emphasized the radical will to transform the urban environment with contemporary structures, thereby implying that 'modern life' would finally take place. The strategy of the polemic island – conceived of as a city-within-the-city – has its own history and tradition, reaching back in time to the Aérodômes of Henri-Jules Borie from 1867, and anticipating the projects of Rem Koolhaas, with his Office for Metropolitan Architecture and the Exodus project, dating from 1972, which transferred the Berlin Wall to the City of London in order to transform it into an island of maximum urban desirability.

Among the islands of order offered by the history of modern urban architecture, only a few projects embody both the 'metallic culture

Erich Mendelsohn, Mosse Building (1922)

Ludwig Hilberseimer, Highrise City (1925)

Henri-Jules Borie, Aérodômes, Paris (1867)

OMA, Exodus project (1972)

Mies van der Rohe, model of the Federal Center, Chicago (1959)

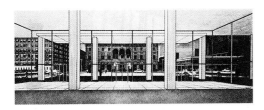

Mies van der Rohe, view from the lobby of the Seagram Building to the New York Racquet Club opposite

Piero della Francesca, *Prospect of an Ideal City* (c. 1490)

of the modern metropolis' (Malewitch) with its split-open space and also the sense for a clearly defined space endowed with a classical dignity. In this regard, Mies van der Rohe's late urban projects, like those for New York and Chicago, Toronto and Montreal, represent not *polemic*, but rather *Platonic islands of modernity*, where modern technology is adapted and balanced with a critical mind as a unique urban composition. Contrary to the modernist attempt to turn urban architecture into a 'living, cooperating factor of the movement' (Mendelsohn), the modern classical city of Mies establishes itself as an autonomous island of order and calmness, as a stable point of reference within the turbulent ocean of signs. Here, technology and art are married to allow a moment for stepping aside and for reflection *within* the frantic dynamics of metropolitan life.

As in the Federal Center in Chicago, Mies's silent black cubes mediated the facts of modern construction into the laconic splendour of the metal frame, and the disposition of these elegantly proportioned slabs that were well-attuned to one another formed a careful composition of dislocation, which referred at once to the modern opened-up and the classical closed form. From a certain vantage point, the silent dark slabs fuse and become a massive block that stands in the cityscape as an almost monumental urban cornerstone; but, when one begins to move around it, the composition gradually opens up and the mass separates into two solids of unequal sizes. The process of cutting open the urban space has lost all its violence and become an artful act of gradual unfolding – almost cinematic – motion. But the moving and the resting eye are given what they desire. As rotating objects, the buildings can be enjoyed on the level of modern cinematic perception; as stable objects in space, they can be appreciated on the level of the classical perspectival view governed by the laws of proportion.

The deliberate rhythm of voids and masses, volumes of bodies and atmospheric volumes, the empty spaces and full spaces, this almost Schinkelesque notion of a cubical city gave Mies's urban islands of reflection their distinctive character. His metropolitan architecture launched a dialogue between modernity and memory which made the stepping back of the Seagram Building from the front of Park Avenue a gesture symbolic of the necessity of distance and space within a highly congested urban world. At their cores, Mies's Platonic islands were at once modern and traditional. The lofty urban foyers on the plaza level of his highrises were reminiscent of the well-articulated, well-balanced space of the classical city as imagined in the famous prospects of the ideal city painted by Piero della Francesca in the 15th century.

With the return to classical typology and its traditionally constructed space in today's postmodernist urbanism, these 'prospects of the ideal city' have become the popular icons for a neat, nonviolent and polite urban architecture that supposedly refers to human scale and pedestrian needs. However, it seems to me that today, after the loss of utopia as a horizon for action, and with the disillusionment of postmodernist nostalgia, the necessity for an architecture of programmatic richness, of functional and formal complexity – with solutions not trapped by the oversimplifications of propaganda and narrow ideology – would be a more promising contribution to the architecture of the city. The city as a densely populated artificial landscape of modern civilization has become our second nature.

As an artifact, the city is a technological garden that promises neither redemption in paradise nor condemnation to darkness and despair. As long as the processes of making architecture and building civilization are related to one another, there will be a reason for some modest urban optimism, even for those of us who are architects.

New Directions in French Architecture and the Showcase of the Paris City Edge (1965–90)

Jean-Louis Cohen

French architectural thinking and practice have gone through radical changes in the past two decades, so much so that it is now difficult, considering the results of the *grands travaux*, or large-scale works, initiated in 1981 and a number of contemporaneous projects, particularly in Paris, to recognize the ruined landscape that existed at the end of the 1960s.

May 1968 and its consequences

Then, at the end of a period that was extraordinarily productive quantitatively in terms of dwellings and public buildings, French architecture as a whole was in a state of collapse due to various factors. The first of these was undoubtedly the craven consensus of the profession in the face of generous commissions for post-Second-World-War reconstruction and public works. This was the attitude that governed the encounter between the functional and constructive ideals of the functionalists and the compositional techniques of the École des Beaux-Arts when they met on the terrain of the new suburbs. The second factor relates precisely to the state of crisis existing at that time in the École, which had remained closed to any conceptual modernization notwithstanding individual efforts made on a practical level by Marcel Lods, Georges-Henri Pingusson and later Georges Candilis. The third and final factor concerns the lack of informed criticism and theory, notably the incapacity to call into question a naive modernist creed, deaf above all to the pleas that Ernesto N. Rogers in Italy had put forward for a 'critical revision' of the experiences of the modernist movement. No doubt it was also necessary to wait for Le Corbusier to disappear from the scene in 1965 before certain taboos could be broken.

The 1968 crisis, foreseeable in the light of the troubled attempts at reforms in the universities from 1965 onwards, brought about a fundamental shake-up of the former certainties of professional architects and brought new political and ethical possibilities to the forefront of their preoccupations. No immediate effect was apparent in projects or in the buildings actually constructed, and the products of the early 1970s can be assigned either to new brutalism on the one hand or to megastructures on the other. What architects proposed in the area of domestic building were 'proliferating' forms, pyramids or ziggurats which were looked on as an alternative both to the high-rise towers and low-rise blocks of big estates and also to individual houses. This tendency reached its height with Jean Renaudie's blocks of flats at Ivry (1970) and with the competition for the first district of Evry new town (1971), won by Michel Andrault and Pierre Parat, and notable also for the joint project for a megastructure by Paul Chemetov, Henri Ciriani and Ricardo Bofill.

New institutions, new discussions

In the middle of the '70s new orientations appeared as a result of greater openness to European and American experiences, and also because of the encouragement derived from public policies favouring architectural innovation. In 1973 a decree from the Minister of Public Works, Olivier Guichard, limited the length of low-rise blocks in big estates to 60 metres. Then the election of Valéry Giscard d'Estaing as President of the Republic in 1974 brought about a swing from the building of collective dwellings – which reached its height in 1975 with 550,000 units – towards individual houses. But on the edge of these political changes, the influence of contacts with Italy and America on the work of Bernard Huet, seen also in the new schools that came out of the transformation of the École des Beaux-Arts, and given expression in *L'Architecture d'Aujourd'hui* (1973–77), paved the way for new ideas. In Italy, Carlo Aymonino, Aldo Rossi and Manfredo Tafuri were concerned respectively with the urban dimension and the importance of history, while advances made in America by Louis Kahn and Robert Venturi needed to be assimilated. The parallel emergence of a specifically architectural branch of research leading to the appearance of theoretical and critical literature also had a certain impact on some young architects.

During the same period the operation of the *Plan Construction* and the *Programme Architecture Nouvelle* (PAN), both started at the beginning of the decade, encouraged mayors and prime contractors to place greater confidence in young architects who were at last prepared to think in terms of urban design. The Paris housing scheme of the Rue des Hautes-

Atelier de Montrouge, offices of Électricité de France, Porte de Sèvres, Paris (1970)

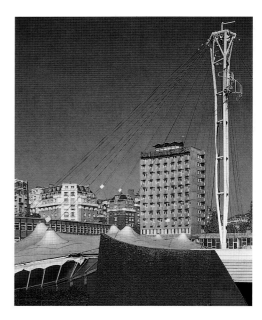

Roger Taillibert, René Le Gall swimming pool, Porte de Saint-Mandé, Paris (1973)

Formes, built in 1976–79 by Christian de Portzamparc, marked an essential change of course in the quality of its communal spaces and its plastic strength.

The initiation in 1981 of the debate on architectural 'post-modernism' with the Paris presentation of the 'Strada novissima' from the 1980 Venice Biennale came at a moment when Ricardo Bofill had long been paying court to the Paris authorities; but the debate was to some extent at cross-purposes, since it was in the end associated with a re-evaluation of certain categories of thought of the modern movement. Its impact was therefore relatively limited to the better-informed section of the profession, though its ravages in the field of large-scale production are better known. Always centred on the Paris region, and strongly influenced by public commissions for dwellings and communal buildings, French architecture set out on a course of conceptual and formal diversification.

The tendencies involved

Several important currents can thus be identified whose evolution is not likely to be complete by the end of the century. In the first place, the partisans of a renewed functionalism have not disappeared. Far from it. Those who favour Corbusian orthodoxy – admittedly relative, since it has shed some early or late ideas that could prove embarrassing – led by Henri Ciriani and Édith Girard, believe that such concepts as 'open plan' or the 'architectural promenade' are still valid. In this they are joined by some younger architects such as Michel Kagan, Maxime Kétoff and Marie Petit. Paul Chemetov, Roland Simounet and Pierre Riboulet have had to tackle a different task of adapting Corbusian theories in which strictly typological principles linked to calculated programmes tend to take first place alongside urban considerations. Parallel with the efforts of Jean-Pierre Buffi and Georges Maurios to link the forms of Corbusian modernism with theories of urban architecture, the work of Yves Lion shows a formal and intellectual rigour which at times achieves an explicit monumentality. A quite different philosophy directs the work of Henri Gaudin, whose poetic strategy rests on his fascination for the ambiguous densities of the medieval town, reflected in skilful preparatory sketches.

While these architects generally belong in the mainstream of the French obsession with reinforced concrete that characterized postwar architecture, another tendency is also visible. This carries on from Jean Prouvé's experiments in the field of architecture employing metal. Apparently inspired by new construction systems borrowed from aviation, Jean Nouvel proposes not only new outer skins, but also different and strongly individualized basic concepts in his buildings. Furthermore,

stimulated by the process of reintellectualization of French architecture begun in the 1970s, certain young architects like Antoine Grumbach or Patrick Berger have approached their work from the viewpoint of the urban structure of Paris or its vernacular architecture, creating from it projects both contextual and personal. The direction taken by Christian de Portzamparc, based on similar premises, has manifested itself in ever vaster projects, in the play of broad and mysterious forms.

Shaped by the debates that followed 1968 and stimulated by the policy of public competitions such as the *Programme Architecture Nouvelle*, a generation of architects barely out of school have had the opportunity of access to commissions early in their careers, notably in the field of dwellings and public buildings. Among this generation there coexist some very different figures, who are gradually freeing themselves of their allegiance to their seniors. Coming from the studio of Christian de Portzamparc, Frédéric Borel offers a personal interpretation of the Parisian vernacular, while Fabrice Dusapin and François Leclerc have elaborated a more graphic architecture shot through with the images of '50s late modernism. The policy of innovation carried into the domain of home-building has given this generation of explorers the opportunity to investigate new relationships between lifestyle and domestic space, breaking away from the simplifying hypotheses of 'large-scale complexes', and also from the over-emphasis of urban considerations to the detriment of interior arrangements within dwellings. The projects which received awards at the 14th session of the *Programme Architecture Nouvelle* (1988) or the first two EuroPAN competitions (1989 and 1991) have opened new horizons in this area.

The Paris city edge, a panorama of contemporary buildings

Certain places possess an almost magical capacity to register conceptual changes and conspicuous improvements in architectural achievement. Such a place is the city edge of Paris, built up since the 1920s on the site of the city's last ring of fortified ramparts. Establishing a continous belt that insulates the city within the former walls from the suburbs, the edge brings together low-cost housing and public buildings of the period between the wars with the functionalist 'large-scale complexes' of the '50s in a sort of linear townscape unique in Europe in that it brings the logic of the motorway into immediate proximity with a historic centre.

Built between 1957 and 1973, the Boulevard Périphérique has become one of the fundamental structures of an urban landscape whose pace of transformation is accelerating ever more rapidly. It is changing so swiftly

Paul Chemetov, Jean Perrottet, Christian Devillers, block of flats, Porte de Pantin, Paris (1978)

Paul Chemetov, block of flats, Saint-Ouen (1980)

because the strip formed by the old unbuilt-on zone now constitutes, together with the large expropriations made by the railways and industry, one of the city's main reserves of building land. However, side by side with this major urban function, the Périphérique has served as a showcase for all the main tendencies in French architecture mentioned above. The theoretical attitudes of architects manifested all along the 35 kilometres of the roadway can be read, to start with, in the general arrangement of the buildings along the artery, which ranges from totally ignoring its ground-plan to using it as a setting in which the boulevard is relegated to the background of the architect's formal strategy. But these attitudes differ as much in architectural rhetoric as in urban strategy.

The continuous circuit of Paris, free from traffic lights, at last became a reality in 1973. Since its opening it has been punctuated by Roger Taillibert's mast at the René Le Gall swimming pool, Raymond Lopez's tower blocks to the north of Paris, and the metallic signal of the Iran Pavilion by Claude Parent, André Bloc, Mohsen Foroughi and Hedar Ghiai. The work of multidisciplinary practices, which were among the new styles of working sought by younger architects at the beginning of the '60s, is also visible along the Périphérique in the offices of Électricité de France built by the Atelier de Montrouge and in the obstinately grey-toned tower blocks of the Atelier d'urbanisme et d'architecture at the Porte de Montreuil (1969).

Projects contemporary with the first stages of the Périphérique thus form a contrast to the background of housing operations initiated in the 1950s both in their verticality and in a somewhat exhibitionistic use of structure. Close to the new brutalist concrete of the Brazil Pavilion built by Le Corbusier at the Cité Universitaire, the Iran Pavilion with its cantilevers heroically celebrates the resources of folded sheet-metal, while Taillibert's swimming pool represents the first use in France of Frei Otto's retractable screens.

Now neighbouring the Parc de la Villette commissioned from Bernard Tschumi in 1983, the block of flats built by Paul Chemetov, Jean Perrottet and Christian Devillers on the suburban side at Pantin (1978) is the first recognition, with its red brick casing, of the visual unification of the two sides of the new boulevard, holding up a magnifying mirror to the low-cost housing of the 19th arrondissement built in the 1930s. Elsewhere, Chemetov is content with a sidelong glance at the world of the motor-car travelling along the Périphérique; the shape of the outer wall of his flats at Saint-Ouen echoes the silhouette of a line of cars. In the same register of autonomy relative to the route of the carriageway one can include Dominique Perrault's Berlier industrial build-

Henri Gaudin, Archives de Paris, Boulevard Sérurier, Paris (1989)

Pierre Riboulet, Robert Debré Hospital, Boulevard Sérurier, Paris (1988)

ing, a capacious glass oblong, tucked into the Ivry interchange but bearing no geometric relationship to it (1990), or the mute silos of Henri Gaudin's Archives de Paris at the Porte des Lilas (1989). Here there is a radical contrast between the transparency of the industrial building, with its interior spaces devoted to production open to the gaze of passersby, and the closed towers dedicated to conserving the documents of the Archives, which turn their backs squarely on the Périphérique, affording it at most a laconic symbol of permanence which is entirely missing from the much friendlier facade of the building on its public side.

Following on the same stretch of the Périphérique, the screen wall protecting Pierre Riboulet's Robert Debré Hospital (1988) from noise nuisance, and within whose shelter the building develops its galleries and patios, offers a well-thought-out alternative to the style of baffle walls that have come to enclose the Périphérique for a good part of its length. Acoustic stress is no longer absorbed by a paltry structure that canalizes the motorist's vision, but has become instead the primary determining factor in a style of architecture which exploits the general shape of the site with huge functionalist low-rise blocks planned by Robert Auzelle and started in 1954.

The relationship between the alignment of the building and that of the carriageway is based here on reasons of practicality and the acoustic factor. The latter is also present in the block of flats which Gérard Thurnauer has wrapped around the Porte de Bagnolet complex, built in 1956 by Édouard Crevel. However, acoustic considerations are undoubtedly secondary, and the symbolic dimension introduced by the architectural rewriting of a

Gérard Thurnauer, flats built around an earlier complex, Porte de Bagnolet, Paris (1990)

Michel W. Kagan, workshops and offices for the Ville de Paris, Rue Bruneseau (1991)

mediocre building will escape no one: it is evidently a kind of vengeance wreaked by the younger architects of the '50s on the Establishment of the time, finally achieved 35 years later.

In the metallic bubble of the Bercy II shopping centre built by the Renzo Piano group (see pp. 248–51), the relationship with the boulevard is systematically developed from an accidental affinity between the spatial envelope of the building – a curve whose orientation derives from the slip-roads of the Bercy interchange – and its structural basis, by way of an arch of glued and laminated wood of fixed profile clothed with a brilliant outer surface. On the other side of the Seine, the workshops and offices built by Michel Kagan on a rectangular site adjacent to the Périphérique make use of the carriageway as a landscape background which is ever present in a progress through an architectural promenade in the Corbusian idiom and which connects the disparate components of a very prosaic programme: workshops and sheds for the motorway maintenance vehicles.

Clearly the most powerful moments in recent building on the Paris city edge are linked to the formulation of individual relationships between each separate building and the Périphérique. However, we must not on that account overlook the buildings whose groundplan was determined by the Boulevard des Maréchaux, the earlier circular route concentric with the Périphérique, such as the Charléty Stadium undertaken by Henri Gaudin (1991), nor those based on sites laid out between the wars, like the Institut Français du Judo by the Architecture Studio at the Porte Brancion

(1992). In both these cases, the concern with the visibility of buildings from the Périphérique is associated with the exploitation of an earlier urban development, but the plasticity of Gaudin's stadium and blocks of flats exploits an extrovert dynamic register, whereas the metallic dome of the Institut du Judo encloses a sports area flattened into the ground.

An excessively Parisian picture

Side by side with the rediscovered quality and diversity displayed along the length of the Périphérique, there exist certain weaknesses in French architecture which must not be allowed to pass unnoticed. On the conceptual level, the fascination with the theme of transparency which has led all the major public commissions to be clothed in glass, mainly to 'integrate' them with their towns, sometimes produces architecture of a simplicity so naive as to end up in uniformity. On a more general level, the creation of new schools of architecture in the great provincial towns and the appearance of the decentralized commission, reinforced by the laws on administrative decentralization passed in 1983, have yet to deal with the fundamental problem of the imbalance between the architectural centre – which is still Paris – sucking in the elite, and the regional metropolises. Apart from the public buildings by Françoise-Hélène Jourda and Gilles Perraudin in Lyon, the Architecture School at Vaulx-en-Vélin (1989), or Laurent Beaudoin's blocks of flats at Nancy, the new identity of French cities is slow to reveal itself and remains culturally over-dependent on a centre that still overshadows the periphery.

The Dilemma of Technology

Peter Rice

Any essay on technology is about a very modern dilemma. In building and architecture, this has come to be typified by the argument between the modern and post-modern styles, between the Grande Arche de la Défense in Paris (pp. 224–25) on the one hand and the National Gallery extension in London (pp. 272–75) on the other. Both use the same modern building technology and have the same aims, in performance and comfort, and in efficiency, and yet they represent very different views of today's technological world.

Technology and its power define the essence of our life today. Not only is it everywhere, it is in and about everything, a continuous, massive, growing influence which controls and dominates every aspect of Western life. To talk of technology as something separate is to misunderstand the issue. Anything you touch or do is inextricably embedded in its own technology. It demands know-how and skill, and the utilization of an ever-growing amount of new information, mostly not fully comprehended. Technology is out of control, that is certain, and cannot now be stopped. But whether it will lead to our destruction or will continue to benefit us, as it has largely done up to now, is not so clear. There are ominous clouds overhead.

As a simple test, to understand technology and what it means, look at a non-technological activity like gardening. As I write, I am looking out on an English country garden, a haven, you would think, from all the aggressions of our technological age. But is it? The plants have all been bred and cross-bred to produce special strains to give extra colour, extra quality in the fruit, extra shelf-life. The mix of plants is carefully chosen to suit the soil. The lawn, filled with weeds though it is, demands to be treated and fed with special lawn compounds. Really there should not be a lawn there at all, as it is not the right soil, but that can be solved. The toolshed, with its lawnmower and other machines, its special organic feeds using 'traditional methods', is filled with the products of our industrial society. The farm opposite, which has 150 overweight cows, now confined because it is winter in an ugly industrial shed to improve the milk yield, pollutes this environment too and must keep up with the latest developments, otherwise it

cannot survive. And beyond are the Downs, with a prehistoric burial mound; cleared in Roman times, they have been preserved from change as a memory of our past.

Building, providing shelter and water and roads, was the first wholly man-made technology. It has a long history, containing as it does many of the leaps in understanding made by man as he sought to control and dominate his environment. The architecture and that understanding often went hand in hand. The Romans, the Gothic masons, the early-19th-century entrepreneurs and many, many others developed an architecture which reflected their understanding of the materials available to them and how these could be used. Architecture and technology were one. An architecture could be understood by looking at its technology – not always, of course, but there were generally clues of form, shape and texture which derived from the materials being used. Technology was simpler in those days. One man, an individual, could know all the rules of building and a talented individual could advance that understanding and invent new forms.

The structure of the architectural and construction professions reflects this long history. In most Western societies, especially in Europe, architecture remains with medicine and the law one of the liberal professions. This comes from those simpler times when one man could expect to understand how to build, and instruct others in what to do. Those days have long disappeared. First there were specialists. Structural engineers, like myself, calculated how a building would resist gravity and other environmental forces. Then came services engineers, deciding on plumbing, heating, cooling. In the beginning this was welcomed; it offered architects and designers a wonderful new freedom. But slowly all the functional aspects of construction were controlled by their specialists. The architect consulted and worked with them and, by teamwork, together they designed the building. This is where we are today. But this implies that the architect and his design team control the process of building. Sadly the reality is not quite so simple, because this model ignores the role of industry. It ignores above all the role of the industrial product called modern building.

Renzo Piano, The Menil Collection Museum, Houston, Texas

You could describe the process differently. Like the gardener, the architect, with his team of specialists, goes to the catalogue, selects the industrial products he will use and assembles them. He or the team may not even understand how these products work. And it is only those in the catalogue which he may use. In varying degrees, and depending on the development of the industrial nature of the society, the choice of what he builds, of what he may use, is becoming more and more limited. The industrial-financial framework in which building takes place is the overriding factor in deciding what we build and how it will be built. Today's building has moved a long way from the direct relationship between materials and form. What a building will look like is a completely separate discussion from the way it is built. Often, as I see a new building go up, I play a game of trying to guess the materials, the architectural lineage of its final appearance. Usually I am wrong, because there is no need for any relationship between the way a building is built and how it will look, and in the infinite variety of modern built form it is impossible to guess what the final image will be.

This, then, is the first and most important reality of technology today: substance and image are separate. And in the years since 1970, this has become more evident. We, the designers, are losing ground all the time. We can no longer decide what a building should be, but only how it should look. There are illusions of control. We may feel that we instruct the contractor, but in reality we select and suggest.

If America and Japan are the harbingers of the Europe of tomorrow, then the situation is disturbing. In the US, the choice for many building elements is very limited. Recently, in a project in Houston, Texas (The Menil Collection Museum), the European design team proposed roof elements in ferrocement, chosen because of its lightness and visual fragility. Houston is close to the Gulf of Mexico, where boat manufacture and the use of ferrocement would normally be found. After much research an American patent method of manufacture was chosen, but we were unable to find a US contractor to make the elements. Their manufacture did not fit in with management systems. They were too unusual. The contractors offered to make the closest precast parallel, by a standard production method. 'They would look the same,' they said, which was not true. Surface texture and certain critical dimensions would have been different and they would not have had the same durability or resistance to deterioration in the Houston weather. Eventually, a number of European companies willing to manufacture them to the specifications were found and they were shipped to site.

In Japan, this same monolithic approach permeates the industry. Then there is the added problem that most architects and engineers work for contractors. Most design is done in-house. This means that the company's latest technology dominates the decision making. And what is built, even when designed by one of the few independent designers, is translated into acceptable contractor designs before building actually takes place.

So the message is clear. Technology, with all its power and the investment made in it, is slowly but surely eliminating choice. And the trend is continuing that way. Part of the reason for this is the financial framework within which building is carried out. Time is money. Every building erected today is under enormous pressure to complete as quickly as possible. Perhaps it was always so. Even in 19th-century London, buildings such as the Savoy Hotel were finished in twelve months. The more efficient and quicker a building system is, the more financially viable the development becomes. American building techniques are typically 30 per cent faster than the best that can be achieved in Europe, and the typical Japanese construction is 10 per cent faster still. All this systemization, all the reduction in choice, gives buildings which are quicker to build, relatively cheaper, and more efficient than ever before.

This essay is not intended as a diatribe against modern technology. It is, however, important to understand it and its context. It is the reality of our life today, and tomorrow, and until or if there is some cataclysm which forces us to re-examine everything. Such a dramatic change could be brought about by the Green Movement. Slowly, all technology is becoming subject to scrutiny. The explosion at Chernobyl, the greenhouse effect and a general awareness of the fragility of our Earth are forcing us to reconsider the assumptions underlying our way of life. We are being asked to think about the long-terms effects of our decisions and to examine how the Earth's resources can best be used. The motor car, symbol of our modern way of life, is the first to be put to the test. Building cannot be far behind. No real analysis of the cost in environmental pollution, energy consumption and recycling exists for buildings. It will surely come, and when it does many of today's assumptions will be turned on their heads. This may become the catalyst which puts technology back in the hands of the designers.

What are the principal ingredients of this modern technological world which have changed most since 1970? I would choose three: manufacturing and assembly methods; old, new and redeveloped old materials; and information systems, which is by far the most important in the period since 1970. It is here that the real changes are taking place, and it is here also that we find the real hope, and fear, for the future. As the effect of the information revolution dominates everything else, we shall examine it first.

'Design by Computer' has become one of the icons of modern mythology. The term contains the essence of our dilemma, because it illustrates very clearly the way this exponential growth in our power to analyse has been used. It is perhaps inevitable that any new tool, like new materials, will be seen as a replacement for something that already exists. Computers can carry out much more complex and much more detailed calculations and analysis than were possible before. This has led to demands for more detailed proof that structures work, for example. No longer is it possible to hand-calculate a structure or environmental system and rely on engineering instinct to ensure that a structural solution is correct. Instead we must produce detailed computer justification for every effect and every detail. Complex detailed analysis, which the computer then sorts and explains, must be carried out even for the most banal structure.

The same is the case with computer drawing for architects. The computer can do it, therefore it must be done. The computer and its software has become an interface between designers and their product. Through this interface, designers are losing their physical feel for material and detail that was the hallmark of good designers in previous times. Computer programmes by their very nature are limited by the imagination and perception of those who write them. Good as they are, they are essentially replacing systems which already existed. Their principal use is to improve the flow of information between client, designers and site and to facilitate rapid change at a late stage. To date, very few people are using computers to explore areas where investigation is impossible without the machine's powers of analysis.

It is likely that this trend will grow; the principal use of computers and computer technology will continue to be as a communication and analysis tool. Clients, architects, engineers and contractors will seek an integrated computer system which enables each to understand and monitor the others' work. This trend has already happened in the case of larger, powerful clients, who often require their design team to equip themselves with computers and software which can be linked to their own in-house system. This enables them to record and monitor the flow of information between professionals and to store and archive information for the future when they are occupying the building. All this sophistication means that the process of design and project management has become more complex but more responsive. The client, the design team and the contractors become a single entity able to communicate quickly and simply, provided each has the ability to understand and manipulate the communication technology.

It is, of course, right that the building industry should become more efficient. Many outsiders, and indeed many insiders also, wonder how the industry can be so archaic in the age of the space shuttle and the intelligent bomb. The management changes and pressures just described have improved efficiency as their goal, and slowly this is happening. Many leading manufacturers and retailers have developed their products to the point that they can give a very precise specification and work method to their design and construction team, which enables them to have quickly and cheaply buildings which are suited to their needs. I see this becoming the industry norm, with effective and comprehensive packages available to the most unskilled client which will enable them to monitor the whole process of design and construction.

One further element needs to be noted in this general advance in the technology of management – the arrival in Europe of construction managers. These are 'management consultants' who carry out on the client's behalf all aspects of running the job, and many indeed run the site on the client's behalf as well. These construction management firms, which started in the US, have followed their US masters to Europe. Many major international projects in Europe, such as Euro-Disneyland, function in this way. It is likely that this too will become more common. It offers many advantages to clients, who can subcontract all those perplexing and unpleasant management tasks and can concentrate on just thinking of what they want.

All this offers the designer a confused picture of the impact of the computer revolution. Is this great change in the way we work and think really only going to lead to the designer becoming a small element in the whole process of design and construction of the modern building, or can it be used to reclaim the role of leader and progenitor of new ideas? The architect and designers must realize the possibilities that this new technology offers and use it positively to their advantage.

There is another aspect to the use of computers in design and analysis which is rarely explored, but which could in time lead to change as important and profound as the change in management structure. I am thinking of the use of computers to explore forms and shapes of construction not previously possible. The modern building is a complex machine. Not just in structure, but mechanically, electrically and electronically, and in environmental building management, modern buildings require a great deal of information to

Foster Associates, Stansted Air Terminal

Renzo Piano, isothermal simulation for Kansai Airport Terminal, Osaka

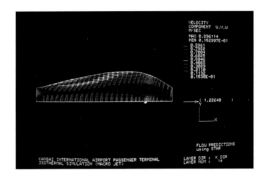

Future Systems, Green Building project

Michael Hopkins, the Mound Stand at Lords Cricket Ground, London

Jean Nouvel, Tour Sans Fin, proposed for La Défense, Paris

Paul Andreu/RFR, Peter Rice, Nuages du Parvis, Paris

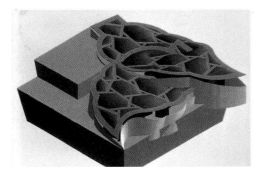

Frank Stella, computer simulation for the Groninger Museum, Holland

design and control them. This complexity is growing, but paradoxically it is also becoming simpler at the same time. Take fire and air. Firefighting methods and the prediction of how a building will perform in a fire are now much better understood, so old-fashioned blanket rules can be abandoned or relaxed and real-time simulations of disasters carried out. Large atriums and great voluminous conference centres and sports facilities can be safely built, thanks to advances in computer simulation and software. The new Stansted Air Terminal (pp. 258–59) is a case in point. This building far exceeds the guidelines for maximum volume in fire. But modern computer simulation techniques enabled a series of likely fire scenarios to be tested to demonstrate how the building would perform. Air flow inside and around buildings has become a positive factor in promoting form, as at Renzo Piano's Kansai International Airport Terminal Building in Osaka, Japan. These computer simulations have been used positively as a design tool to generate the building's form and are further justified because they improve comfort within the building and reduce energy consumption. Elsewhere, environmental wind engineering which can be done in the wind tunnel or by computer is used to study the impact of buildings on towns and to avoid unpleasant wind currents in the vicinity of new structures.

The Lloyd's Building in London (pp. 156–59) had air flow and smoke tests carried out on the atrium and had an environmental wind impact test to help design the entrance area. There are many other examples of the use of computers to promote change through improved environmental performance and perhaps one day we shall see a future, so far only a science-fiction invention, which has been stimulated by real technological issues, as in Future Systems' Green Building recently exhibited in London.

Structure and architecture are also candidates for change. Most structural solutions are adaptations of previous systems. Some, however, are now being developed using the new possibilities of analysing things differently now that powerful computers are commonplace. Tents and fabric structures are a good example. These require complex and sophisticated non-linear analysis and have grown in performance and form over time. The fabric roof of Lords Cricket Ground in London (Michael Hopkins) and the Nuages at Tête Défense in Paris (Paul Andreu/Peter Rice) are recent examples, and many more will follow, either as canopies or as full roofs to buildings. An earlier and two more recent examples are the Schlumberger Research Laboratories in Cambridge (pp. 124–25, Michael Hopkins), the Thompson Factory at Conflans Ste Honorine near Paris (Valode & Pistre) and the

R. Herron, the Imagination Building, London

Imagination Building in London (R. Herron), three buildings which use the diffused daylight created by fabric to enhance the ambience of internal spaces.

Structural forms too are advancing, as the structure for the Pyramid in Paris shows (pp. 226–29). Consisting of a highly prestressed frame with overlapping cable systems holding taut an outer glass layer, this is an example of a structure wholly rooted in the computer age. Towers and tall structures, such as Jean Nouvel's Tour Sans Fin, proposed for La Défense, Paris, require a great deal of analysis to ensure that they are comfortable and buildable, and that they will resist earthquake, wind and other environmental forces safely. The shape and form of these buildings are often computer led, and we shall no doubt see taller and thinner examples as engineers and architects explore the limits of the style and demonstrate to others their prowess.

The final area I would like to stimulate and hopefully help to explore is the rise of computer draughting programmes to generate change. One recent example was the Nuages du Parvis at La Défense. The structure is a canopy leading to and complementing the Nuages structure at Tête Défense. The intention of the design was to achieve complexity and variety using a standard element. The standard element chosen was a fabric panel with a warped geometry and non-parallel edges. This could be combined in a number of ways to create an undulating surface which overlapped and turned in a sensuous pattern. Another example is the Groninger Museum in Holland, designed by the American artist Frank Stella. Here the artist's original model was transferred to a computer, which was used to explore geometric and construction rules. The original artistic intention was the key to how the rules were developed, and the artist participated in the process. It was the computer which made possible the original model's transformation into a description recognizable to constructors and something they could price. Not only did the computer enable this exploration to take place, it also enabled it to be communicated to artist, contractors and client. The final project contains all the artist's intentions, but is quite different from the model and is made of simple contemporary building options. The artist becomes architect with the computer as palette.

Building materials and the way we use them have changed beyond recognition these last two decades. Many of them look the same. Indeed, most of them *are* the same, but the way we use them is quite different. Most building materials are now manufactured to be assembled in large elements on site. The crane and crane planning dictate the way buildings are built. Hand in hand with the need to deliver buildings in large sub-elements, industry has invented and developed methods of manufacture to enable this to happen. We are all familiar with steel and glass buildings, where this is obvious. Panels and sub-assemblies are used, totally manufactured off site, then clipped into position. Such methods often create an architectural feature which is used as a 'language' – Rogers' Lloyd's of London or Foster's Hong Kong and Shanghai Bank show this well. Whole sections of these buildings, manufactured and assembled off site, are a clear indication of one view of the future.

Traditional materials have also succumbed to this trend, and that is a surprise. We may not like it, and some of the more vociferous critics of modern architecture, such as Prince Charles in the UK, deeply regret the advent of modern methodology in the most conservative of professions. Take brick, that most traditional or artisanal of building materials. Gone are the bricklayer and mason, assembling bricks by hand to create an intricate facade (except, of course, in the repair of older buildings). Instead, bricks are now assembled into panels at the yard, backed with insulation and sent to site to be treated like precast concrete or steel. Stone too is cut into thin sheets, accurately formed and assembled on site to make designs similar in form and preparation to their antecedents. Nothing is as it seems. And yet at the heart of this there lies a challenge. How can we use these techniques to create new forms?

The extension to IRCAM in Paris (Renzo Piano), next to Centre Pompidou, is an example of the way things might go. There, the panels are sub-assembled like any other, but the jointing and the panel form are changed to return to a more vibrant past. Glass too can be used differently to express its innate character. The glass at La Villette in Paris (Adrien Fainsilber, pp. 172–73) or at the Willis, Faber & Dumas building in Ipswich (pp. 74–77) are two examples of the aesthetic results of exploring glass technology. Many others exist. These results are produced by an active involvement by designers, architects and engineers in the way materials work and are used, so that new uses and forms may emerge. In a way, no building is ever the same as any other. As in music or literature, variety is the objective as well as the norm. But variety within a restricted vocabulary. The vocabulary of building will expand, and that expansion must be stimulated by the designers as much as by constructors and be in some part controlled by them.

What of the new materials we hear so much about and eagerly await? The benefits from the space programme and other high-technology areas, where are they? The reason these new materials have not had an impact is largely because they are too expensive and because the performance conditions for construction are so demanding and difficult to test. Fire resistance is the most difficult obstacle, but long-term performance in sunlight is also a difficult criterion for many new materials to meet.

I think it is unlikely that wholly new materials will ever take over the role of the traditional ones, except as interior surfacing or other replaceable items. Some development of replacement materials, such as fibre-reinforced concrete, are currently being researched and developed, especially in Japan. These will offer options but will not, it seems, lead to large-scale change in construction methods, as glass-reinforced concrete did for a time in the 1970s. There is also talk of ceramics becoming an important material, especially in external cladding, but none of this is likely to alter the basic direction of industrial rationalization taking place, promoted by the information revolution.

Where then do we find ourselves? Technology out of control is the great challenge for the nineties and beyond, not just in the construction industry but generally. Not only do we have to make the impact of technology more acceptable, we designers and users of technology must take more responsibility for directing its growth. We can, if we make the effort. Ove Arup, an important thinker in the field of construction from the 1960s and '70s, became concerned at the end of his life about all the power and technology we direct without being aware of our responsibility. I would like to finish with a quotation from a speech he gave in London in 1983 when he was 88.

It is my conviction that whilst we have become very clever at doing almost anything

Foster Associates, Hong Kong and Shanghai Bank

Renzo Piano, extension to IRCAM, Paris

we like, we are very backward in choosing the right things to do. This is, of course, taking a global view of the behaviour of mankind and that, I submit, we are simply forced to do in view of the tremendous power for good and evil conferred on us by our sophisticated technology. It has brought us tremendous blessings, and it has also done tremendous damage to our planet and its inhabitants . . . And as mentioned, the decision about how to use it is not generally made by the engineers. But engineers are world citizens as we all are, and as they are largely represented on the design teams preparing the designs which determine what is made, they are in a good position to judge the consequences for mankind of proceeding with doing what we are about to do. Would it not be a good thing if they had a say in what we should do, and have they not a duty as citizens of the world to warn us of any dangerous consequences which would result from our actions?

My only hope is that this well-educated minority will swell to include the less well-educated majority so that even governments can start to think about how to alter course without creating world-wide chaos. It will be extremely difficult. It must be a slow and controlled process and its success depends on whether we can convince a majority of our leaders and their followers that we need to alter course. Doing a 'U-turn' in the mid-stream of traffic is dangerous: we can hardly avoid severe trouble and hardship. We are not helped by fanatic peacemongers, feeding on simplistic slogans, who think they can achieve universal peace by hate and destruction. Pulling down is easy, building up is difficult. We have to employ slogans which the great mass of people can understand and support, but they should appeal to their good instincts, not their bad ones. This is a source which is not so often tapped by our politicians, but I believe its power could be overwhelming if our leaders had the courage to build on it. Ideals must be tempered by realism but should not be poisoned by cynicism or hate. In the end all depends on our own integrity.

On Ecological Architecture: a Memo

From Lucius Burckhardt
To: The reader of *Architecture in Europe*

I have been asked to write an essay on the ecological aspect of architecture in Europe during the last twenty years. I found it impossible. Ecological architecture, or more precisely, the ecological house, was an issue of the 1970s. It turned out to be a trap!

The ecological house was a North American idea which others followed. You had to be rich and a drop-out, to have some technical skill and to be able to afford to live all alone in a remote, abandoned region – with, however, all the technological resources just around the corner. In addition you had to be abreast of the most advanced scientific breakthroughs of the day, and artistic enough to give your house a shape that reporters from magazines could immediately recognize as ecological.

The sport of ecological house building was adapted to local conditions in West Germany, as elsewhere, where there were no deserts or prairies; but there were farmers who could no longer compete in the modern market and would sell off their traditional houses. So ecologically minded people bought smallholdings and built on them. Or did they? I can't be sure any more. All I remember are plans and slides of sumptuous bathrooms with tree trunks inside, then other slides of apple tree branches framing lumicolour sketches of houses that were smaller than the bathrooms.

The ancestral clay houses, however, are hard to forget. They really did exist. Clay houses have a long history in Germany. They were built in the 18th century when wood was scarce. And they were built again in 1946. In the 1970s, some people did not realize that they were living in clay houses; when they did, the authorities pulled them down because it was considered backward and shameful to have such a thing in your parish.

While the authorities were demolishing old clay houses, the progressive, modern architects were building new ones. So much for ecological balance! But there was an additional problem to solve, one of appearance. If you did not want to use wooden cladding to protect the walls of your house in the rainy climate of Germany, because you were a modern, progressive architect, then you built a large, overhanging roof. As a result, the most recent of the German clay houses look like Swiss chalets. There is, by the way, an abundance of wood these days. This is because the dying forests of Eastern Europe that have been poisoned by lignite fumes (produced in part by the baking of clay for houses) are being sold off very cheaply.

By the end of the 1970s, the ecologists realized that the houses under the apple trees did not solve the energy problem. So the 1980s became the insulation decade.

Two-thirds of new housing in Germany, at least in larger towns and cities, are those bland structures dating from the reconstruction period of the 1950s. In the early 1980s, when you walked along a street with such buildings, which had not been very charming to begin with, you realized that the houses seemed suddenly to have put on weight. The windows, which had once been flush with the plaster, were now sunk deep inside the bulging walls. And inside these new apertures you could see new insulation glass lodged in large, shapeless frames. This is how owners obtained subsidies for insulation from the government. As a result, the occupants now had lower fuel bills – and mildew stains on their wallpaper. Other owners, with superior aesthetic sensibilities, preferred to add loggia-like glass corridors to the outside of their houses to create zones with intermediate temperatures between the open air and the living area. This was a kind of 'post-modern' version of ecological architecture.

It is true to say that by now the ecological house has 'improved', like everything else. Today, it looks like any quite ordinary one-family house erected by a speculator. But what may look like swimming pools inside and outside are not what they seem – facilities for the fitness and recreation of wealthy clients who might be tempted to buy such houses. As my experienced readers already know, the pools are used to collect rain water from the roof. This water is heated by the sun whose rays enter the house through openings that are regulated electronically. Electronic regulators decide what water will go where: to the swimming pool for family use; or to the tanks for the cultivation of perches; or to the kitchen for the dishwasher and washing machine. The one place the water will not go to is the toilet; there are now peat toilets which do not waste water. But the water with the excrement of the perches will be redirected to the garden, complete with ready-made fertilizer.

Every one of these houses has received an award from some ecological society and has attracted a circle of admirers. These houses also have severe critics, however, who say that the water or the air should have been circulating the other way round, first to the perches and then to the heating. Such people are no longer invited to the annual perch-eating party.

And there are other critics. They have thoughts that are even more threatening to the ecological house. The man with the self-heated swimming pool, they argue, would save even more energy if he lived in town, in an ordinary flat, and went to the office on foot or by bicycle. And sceptical criticism soon became even more sophisticated: where do all these materials, all these electronic gadgets and electronic pumps with which we try to economize energy and not pollute the environment come from? How much energy is consumed in producing and transporting them? Where do the obsolete and non-functioning pieces of equipment end up? And what can we do with this refuse of unknown materials? Shall we store it or burn it? Because the recycling of unknown materials is an impossibility. These are the sort of questions one may ask not only of ecological houses, but also of ordinary ones. A house is a complicated assembly of materials which are produced by methods involving a loss of energy and which produce pollution either when they are being made or after they have been used. Perhaps through cost benefit calculations of this kind we could develop an approach to shelters that would really be ecological.

Ecology's most important problem is that it is invisible. You cannot produce the visual sensation of harmony simply by being ecological any more than the reverse. This is obvious in gardening. Because we are all 'ecologists' now, no one has a lawn without weeds, everyone has a meadow in bloom. In agriculture, the meadow has its stability, but without cows it is an intermediate stage in a sequence of changing vegetable associations. To stop this sequence and to conserve the meadow is as expensive in terms of energy consumption and fertilizers as growing a weedless lawn used to be.

The same is the problem with architecture: you cannot see an ecological building. Of course you can build the image of an ecological house. The house under the apple tree, for instance. Or you can calculate how to save energy and how to clean up the environment. The problem with the second is that nobody will take pictures of it and publish it.

Atelier d'urbanisme, d'architecture et d'informatique Lucien Kroll
THE MEDICAL FACULTY AT WOLUWE-SAINT LAMBERT, 'LA MÉMÉ'
(Louvain, Belgium)
1968–72

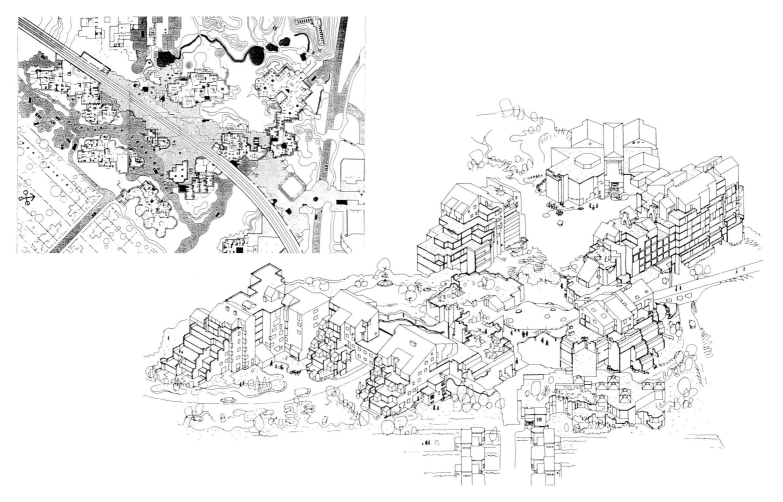

No other building can better claim the title of monument to the May 1968 utopian populist movement than Kroll's Medical Faculty of the University of Louvain. To conceive of it as a 'monument' is, of course, a contradiction in terms since it stands against the very notion of monumentality. But the need to preserve the memory of important events is a deep cognitive one that goes beyond transient ideologies, even if such events are paradoxically concerned with trying to abolish memory as something that inhibits liberation and invention. Therefore, as long as May 1968 continues to be seen as a significant moment in the history of the mentality of this century, the significance of Kroll's building as a 'monument' is undeniable.

'Two approaches to housing are possible', Kroll wrote when he began the design of this building in 1968. One is 'authoritarian', with 'specialists' producing 'objects to live in' which rationally, comfortably and hygienically 'reinforce the industrial division and boredom of students'; the other is 'participatory and pluralistic', involving each individual 'as a person and not as a function' in an 'exchange of responsibilities and a sharing of roles'. Considering the impasse that the first had lead to, the obvious choice was the second.

As opposed to the 'hard' 1960s high rises next to it, Kroll's building was intended to be soft, 'a big sponge', pierced 'with internal, exterior, horizontal, vertical, oblique, underground and rising pathways'. Kroll's premise was that it was 'irrational' to impose identical elements on different dwellings, because 'forms are not static, they change in ways that are always unexpected, and when walking through them they continuously change their configuration.' Hence the diversity in the materials of the windows, in their colours, their curtains, their balconies, their plants, in the surfaces of the facades, in the shapes of the apartments, all contributing to the impression of a coherent crowd of anarchic individuals taking part in a festive demonstration.

Kroll received the commission when, as a result of the students' protests over, among other things, housing conditions, the Catholic University of Louvain decided to change traditional procedures and consult its students in the choice of the architect for a new facility near Woluwe-Saint Lambert. The project was to accommodate a university hospital, medical facilities and residences for the personnel. The medical students bypassed professional organizations and asked the advice of their fellow students of the Ecole Nationale Supérieure of La Cambre of Brussels, with whom they shared a mistrust for established institutional professionalism and a common desire for a new, antielitist way of distributing specialized services in society. As a result of this consultation,

(Opposite, left) Site plan

(Opposite, right) The original scheme, as drawn by Lucien Kroll

(Above) A segment of the larger complex of La Mémé

Lucien Kroll – a graduate of La Cambre himself – was selected by the students as the architect of the project and, astonishingly, the University of Louvain approved the student decision and hired him.

Kroll had worked during the 1960s for the community of the Belgian Benedictines in Ruanda, an irrelevant experience at first glance. It made him, however, start looking at architecture through the eyes of an 'ethnologist', viewing the traditional life of Central Africa from within rather than as a professional, from the outside. Reasonable as it may appear today, after a significant shift of sensibility has occurred, this was a very compelling stance at the time. On his return to Europe, Kroll's viewpoint was similar to that of the dissenting students. He refused to accept the established division of labour between a paternalistic, oligarchic profession and submissive laymen. Furthermore, he refused to

adopt preconceived formulas to impose on the building. On the contrary, the solution was to emerge from within and out of a dialogue between users and architect.

The first step he took was to convince the university authorities to abandon their preliminary programmatic assumptions which meticulously divided the project into clear zones according to the function and status of the users. In this manner, one of the most fascinating, but also most questionable, experiments in architecture of this century started, challenging preconceptions not only about the form of buildings but also the very process through which this form was produced.

The principle of user participation in the design process was implemented architecturally through a design system which conceived the building as made from a dual structure: a fixed skeleton, accommodating structural and service elements, and the infilling or envelop-

ing building elements. This two-part system was at least a decade old as an idea; the Dutch architect Nicolaas John Habraken should be credited with formalizing it. But here the concept was put to the test and on a significant scale.

In addition, Kroll modified earlier proposals for the fixed skeleton. Instead of a repetitive, neutral, 'engineering grid' of the same form, Kroll moved around the bearing elements to accommodate the variety of the activities located between them, reflecting the plurality and individuality of needs as they were expressed by the users. Columns, to use Kroll's expression, 'ambled' rather than marched. To achieve this spatial flexibility technically, a 'mushroom' structure was applied, expensive in terms of materials, but cutting construction costs.

Once the structure skeleton was fixed, facade and partition components were to be inserted. This was done jointly by architects and users. Occasionally, the users fabricated and built in these infill pieces, participating not only conceptually, but also physically and even economically in the construction by investing their own time and effort.

Justified on functional and economic terms, the system was ultimately symbolic and its target educational-political. Kroll believed that the form of a building had an impact on its users' way of thinking. 'Regular columns', Kroll stated, 'make conformists. Irregular ones challenge the imagination.' The same attitude prevailed in the multi-colour, -size, -material and -proportion elements of the facade. The combination of the dictates of individual, functional reasons and their inscription within

(Top) General view of 'bricolaged' La Mémé, set against a background of post-war, modernist housing

(Above) Side view of La Mémé

(Opposite, below) Ground plan of a storey, chosen arbitrarily

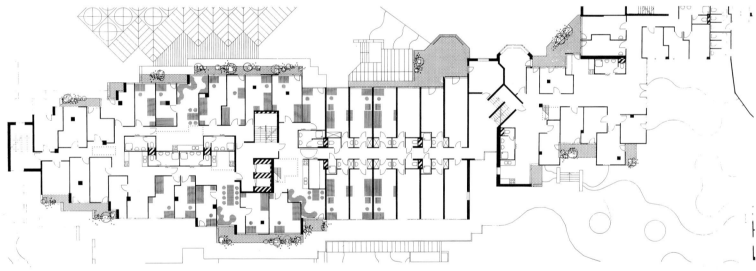

a modular coordination array led to unprecedented, irregular patterns that represented freedom from deadening everyday routines and induced creativity. A similar political message was carried out by the interior partitions. Mass-produced through highly industrialized processes, or 'bricolaged', and even sometimes handcrafted, the partitions were placed into the modular infrastructure without a predetermined plan, as individual needs arose. Thus they constituted a lived-in demonstration of the 'right to speak' of the users as citizens.

The origins of the ideas embodied in the architecture of the Medical Faculty of Louvain can be traced back to the Enlightenment theoreticians of the French Revolution, to Karl Friedrich Schiller's dictum 'that the most perfect work of art is the building of political freedom'. They come close to Kroll's belief in

using architecture as a means of developing a new cultural/political consciousness of openness. Rousseau, Condorcet and Kropotkin also come immediately to mind as providing many of the political organizational principles of the project. Closer to practice, during the post-war period André Lurçat had successfully introduced user participation into the design process in his pioneering work for Maubeuge in France in the late 1940s.

In addition, the appearance of the building, the 'organic' elements of the interior, the 'disordered' elements of the facade (occasionally generated by drawing cards from a pack at random), the earth and the vegetation-like textures, the 'non-finito' configurations, are reminiscent of another architect with strong political commitment of the 1900s: Victor Horta. As Horta's famous Maison du Peuple

(1896–99) served at a given moment actual functional needs in an innovative political framework, so did Kroll's project. And as Horta's building transcended this actuality to emerge as a monument, an abstract invention embodying concrete events – alas Horta's exists only on paper today – so did Kroll's university complex. But unlike Horta who, soon after the general mood of society changed, lost his enthusiasm and the supporters for his avant-garde architecture, Kroll, twenty years after the completion of the Medical Library, has continued to evolve in the same direction and has succeeded in finding a great number of clients for his architecture. (See also pp. 92–95.)

Architectenburo Herman Hertzberger b.v.
CENTRAAL BEHEER OFFICE BUILDING
(Apeldoorn, Holland)
1968–72

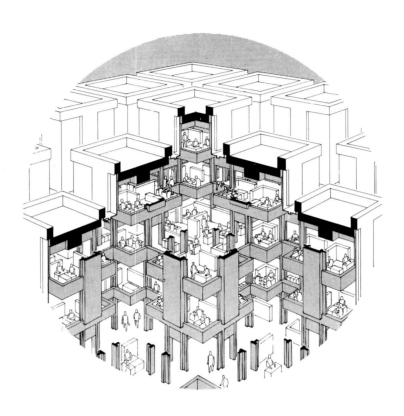

Despite their professed universality, Kroll's ideas about participatory architecture were mostly suited to residential facilities (pp. 44–47, 92–95). In his offices for the Centraal Beheer, an experienced and sophisticated insurance company, Herman Hertzberger focused on the problem of designing a workplace for white-collar workers of the post-Spring '68 era. He attempted to satisfy populist aspirations in an architecture that would serve the needs and aspirations of a younger generation, creating a new relationship between professionals and their clients, authorities and their subjects, managers and employees.

What Kroll did in de-institutionalizing a university facility (pp. 44–47), Hertzberger did with regard to the workplace; like Kroll, he was in search not only of a new building type, but also of a new design method. Like Kroll, he had to answer new questions about the hierarchization of public/private realms for contemporary users of architecture. Hertzberger and Kroll also shared several precedents: the idea of a dual spatial system dividing the plan of a building into two standard types of units, 'servant' and 'served', which goes back to Louis Kahn.

The infrastructure of Centraal Beheer differs in many respects from that of the Medical Faculty of the University of Louvain. The servicing units are more multi-functional, coordinating support, duct and circulation functions. The Centraal Beheer is also more structured and more structuring of the functions and people it contains. The 'plastic' manipulation of the service elements in Louvain and their accommodation is absent here. Its U-shaped bearing elements are standard in shape, size and in their spacing, which is specified by a standard grid; their only freedom is in their orientation, the direction their open side faces. Yet a remarkably rich variety of patterns emerges out of the combinations of facing, each resulting in a flexible system of servicing. A similar 'combinatorics' of standard furniture arrangement within the working cells provides a very rich repertory for organizing equipment and individuals and associating them in space around common productive tasks.

(Top) Isometric section of the Centraal Beheer building

(Above) View of the exterior

(Above) Internal light well and (right) staircase

(Far right) The roof garden

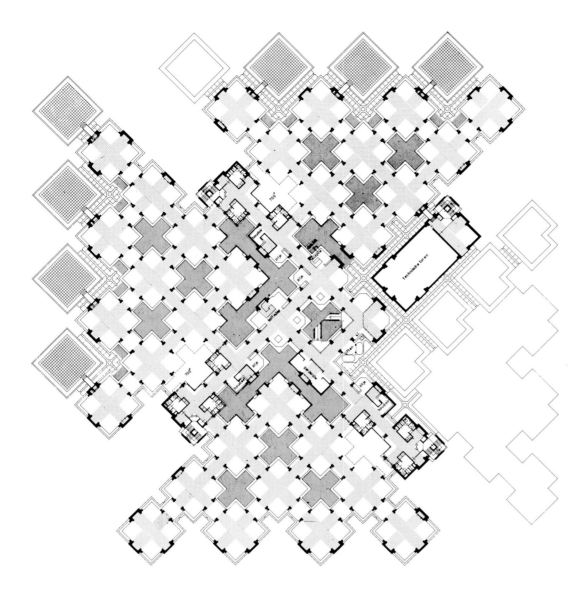

The system is 'open' in the sense that there are no other dividing partitions besides the vertical servicing elements to interrupt the continuity of the plan, or to prevent the project from growing. The vertical elements are allocated accumulating cells of work space forming, by implication, a public 'street', like a spine, or like the spaces defined spontaneously by individual blocks of buildings in a Mediterranean vernacular landscape, as if without a strict geometrical ordering plan.

The idea of such a central space operating not only for circulation and lighting purposes, but also as a collective representation of identity and of community, has precedents. Best known is Frank Lloyd Wright's Larkin Building (1904–05). But the 'de-institutional', improvised appearance of this space and the programmatic vision inspiring it is certainly a unique invention of Hertzberger's.

Although the internal organization of the building has been thought out in great detail, its external appearance seems to have been left to emerge spontaneously out of internal concerns. The building does not acknowledge its surroundings which, one has to admit, are characterless. As a result, the skyline of its

volume and the profile of its facade are imageless. While every effort has been made to identify a hierarchy of intimacy inside the facility, there is no indication of a transition between public and private territory as one enters the building. There is no representation of an 'urban' face on the outside of the building, the result perhaps of a polemical attitude against institutional, traditional architecture that insists on a separation of domains, private versus public, rather than negligence. If Centraal Beheer, however, presents no notable icon of the emerging fabric, it does offer an evocative climax of the interior spaces, which, without using any of the characteristics of institutional corporation lobbies, succeeds in giving not only legitimacy but also joy to the abstract idea of 'street contact' as put into action in the workplace of 1972.

Centraal Beheer's open workplace arrangement was a short-lived prototype, characteristic of the May '68 social experiments. Yet it has had a lasting impact. Not only has it enriched the thesaurus of similar architectural precedents of workplace and collective space in general, it represents uniquely the desires and aspirations of a generation.

(Top) Plan of the third floor

(Above) Aerial view of the roof terraces

(Opposite) Looking down into the building's interior

Ricardo Bofill Taller de Arquitectura
LA MURALLA ROJA
(Alicante, Spain)
1969–72

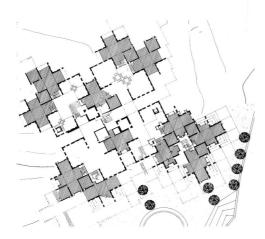

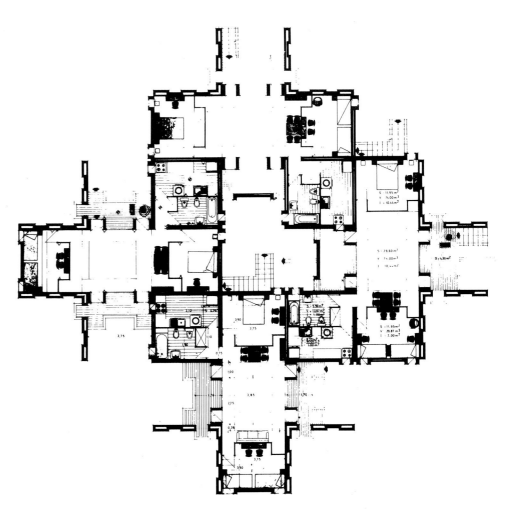

The Muralla Roja, or Red Wall, forms part of the large tourist complex on the Costa Blanca near Alicante, in Catalonia. Other buildings in the complex include Plexus, Xanadu and El Amphitheatro, all designed by Ricardo Bofill. In the latter cases, Bofill tried to incorporate regional elements, but in La Muralla Roja, he claimed to be 'breaking with the post-Renaissance tradition of the separation of the private and public' divisions in living quarters and to be reviving the 'Mediterranean tradition of the Casbah'. There is, however, more to this project than such declared programmatic intentions, and this is what sets it apart from the rest of the complex and gives it special distinction.

This building expresses a strangeness that is perhaps subliminal, but nevertheless great and even perhaps ultimately subversive. Its effect is to increase one's awareness of the artificiality and, indeed, absurdity of architecture and, by extension, of the functions that

take place within it. In the Muralla Roja, colour plays the most important role in creating this effect. Here, in contrast to those buildings which are inspired by 'popular, native' forms integrated into their context, Bofill applied bright shades of red to the exterior, thus accentuating its contrast with the landscape. He then used different mixtures of blue for the interior, such as indigo, violet and pink, because of the illusory fusion that they form with the sky. The route through the building was designed specifically to heighten the sense of unreality. As one walks through its patios, one has the additional 'sensation of crossing a labyrinth' – which is simply 'an assemblage of concave and convex volumes generated by a predetermined geometrical spatial structure'.

At the end of the 1960s, there was a tendency to de-institutionalize public space by de-aestheticizing it; Herman Hertzberger's

Centraal Beheer (1968–72, pp. 48–51) is an obvious example of this strategy applied to the workplace. At the Muralla Roja, Bofill aimed at the same objective but chose the extreme opposite design strategy – over-aestheticizing. Ornament, colour and spatial articulation are greatly emphasized, indeed exaggerated. In the same way that the film *La Grande Bouffe* (Marco Ferreri, 1973) offered a critique of consumer culture by presenting scenes of over-consumption, so in the Muralla Roja consumerist values are subverted by awakening in people a consciousness of their conformism. Bofill comments on the seductive power of design objects by making them over-voluptuous.

Whatever its political message, the Muralla Roja is one of the rare, and certainly most successful, examples of the application of paint to architecture in Europe since the Second World War.

(Opposite, above left and right) General plan and a typical floor plan

(Opposite, below left) Rooftop swimming pool

(Below) Exterior view

(Bottom left and right) Interior court; detail of the composition of the facade

Studio Arquitectos PER (Clotet & Tusquets)
BELVEDERE GEORGINA
(Gerona, Spain)
1972

This small residence replicates a Renaissance belvedere, a look-out tower over a landscape. Disconcertingly, on its roof under a pergola stands a parked car. Unexpected combinations of different elements, each with its own references and evocative power, give it a dream-like, 'magical real' quality.

'It was hard for us to imagine a very small isolated house in this landscape,' these young architects wrote at the time. 'Those little houses, with elements of great villas at a reduced scale, are usually a mess. We thought it would be more fruitful to use a different object whose proper scale could be maintained and to adapt it to the function of a house.

'We admired the agreeable way in which some historical architectures had fitted buildings with their own personality into the landscape without having to resort to a masquerade. The simple geometrical and round forms of pavilions, rotundas and belvederes were the best ones we could think of.

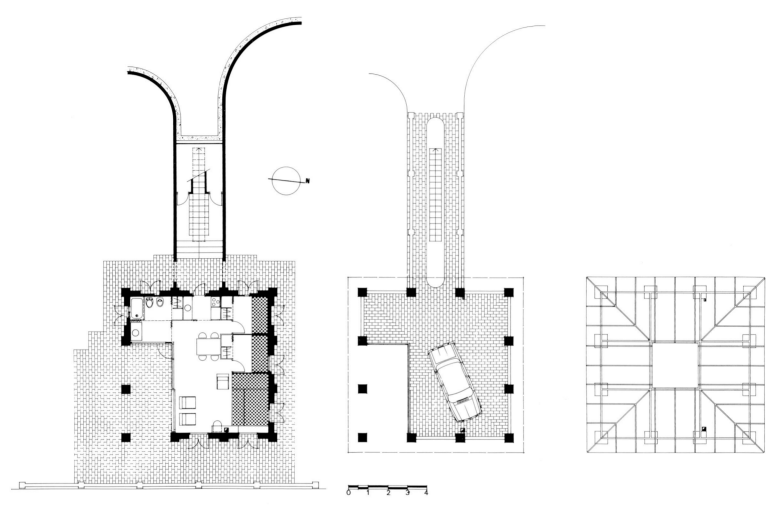

'We decided to exploit as much as we could this intuitive image, not only in relation to the overall volumetric appearance, but also to the anecdotal details that would reinforce it and that were already present in many classical-inspired popular Catalan buildings.

'To insert a functional house into a Palladian belvedere seemed to us like something that would generate a still stranger superimposition. Looking at these photographs we are reminded of the much more beautiful Neo-classical pergolas, and of the no less ridiculous 40-square-metre houses.'

The elements are unquestionably regional, the aura of the work overtly Catalonian and Mediterranean. Nevertheless, the composition transcends the merely folkloristic, regional aspect of the elements by using them in arresting, novel ways. But there is another value in the work, its function as a kind of analogy. It seems that the building says that belvederes are car parks, or rather, in a more cynical mode, parking lots are the belvederes of our time. This forces us to reconsider our stereotypes of both and consequently to reconsider stereotypes in general. By its inventiveness, Belvedere Georgina fired an appetite for inventive thinking at a moment when too many clichés appeared to have been accumulating in Spain, but also in Europe. In the words of the Spanish architectural critic Anton Capitel, Belvedere Georgina became 'one of the most powerful and significant – it may even be said one of the earliest – images, and one which seemed most clearly to trigger a new way of thinking and acting'. Its great appeal, to quote the psychologist and philosopher Jerome Bruner on the cognitive function of literature as art, was to open 'us to dilemmas, to the hypothetical, to the range of the possible', protecting us from 'the boredom induced by empty ideas pretentiously paraded'.

(Opposite, top) The rooftop terrace with its parked car

(Opposite, left) The colonnade seen from the ground floor

(Opposite, right) The house within its landscape

(Above) Plans for (left to right) the ground floor; the terrace with the parked car; the roof

The utopian radical idea of a world whose political, economic, cultural and aesthetic order was to be overthrown, 'the pyramid turned upside down', as the architect Giancarlo De Carlo called the anti-institutional, anti-authoritarian vision of May '68, affected not only the appearance of architectural artifacts, but also the very processes of their conception and production. This challenge to established values was deeply felt in most professions throughout the Western world.

But in Italy, where experiences of pluralistic collective bargaining were scarce and subject to exhaustive socio-historical analysis (Gramscian in their sophistication), the populist, 'reformist', 'anarcho-architecture' proposed by Lucien Kroll (see pp. 44–47) or Herman Hertzberger (see pp. 48–51) was looked on as naive. With very few exceptions such as the work of Giancarlo De Carlo (see pp. 198–201), the May '68 campaign for cultural renewal was very quickly succeeded by either extremist activist movements which demanded the total and fundamental dismantling of the established power structure, or by a profound pessimism about the possibility of any change at all. In the midst of this crisis – allegorically portrayed by Federico Fellini at the end of the '70s in his film, *Prova d'Orchestra* (1979) – a third position emerged.

This called for a return to traditional, professional values, the norms of the 'craft' and the 'workshop', as the architect Giorgio Grassi called them. They were 'small things certainly', Aldo Rossi wrote in his *Scientific Autobiography* (1981), yet, 'having seen that the possibility of the great ones was historically precluded', architects realized that these were the only objects they 'could have aspired to'. Under most circumstances, this *retour à l'ordre* advice would have been perceived as conservatism, despite the fact that it came from the least conservative of architects. Given the excessive, self-destructive situation of the architectural profession at the end of the 1960s, it was simply a sensible suggestion.

Central to the craft of architecture was 'typology'. Rossi's idea of typology (see pp. 60–63) was more complex than the standard one – the identification and choice of building types according to agreed architectural characteristics, a division of architectural

(Above) The ossuary

(Right) General plan

theory with a long and strong Italian tradition, notably in the theories of Saverio Muratori. Rossi's idea of typology was grounded, on the one hand, on abstract and metaphysical concepts, Platonic principles claiming the universality and eternity of certain architectural forms; and, on the other, on concrete ideas related to the programme and context of specific buildings with a deeper cultural and political past. Occasionally, in the somewhat obscure writings of Rossi, there is a third meaning attached to typology, which echoes Gyorgy Lukács's.

A new project was related to typological precedents 'by analogy'. Rossi's meaning of analogy was close to the way in which associations between objects were perceived by depth psychology. Memory, to Rossi, was a mechanism used to produce a design, as much as design was a means through which to pay homage to a memory, or to the idea of memory, abstractly, as a value on which culture and society are founded. The Cemetery of San Cataldo in Modena, the most characteristic, if not the most significant product of Rossi's career, emerged out of such a theory of typology.

The programme required the enlargement of the old Neo-classical cemetery of del Costa. Rossi's was the winning project in the 1971 national competition. The basic elements of the design were the porticoed, rectilinear pathway, the columbarium, the sanctuary, the common grave and the ossuary. The flat surfaces of the ossuary and columbarium were meant to enhance the abstraction of the architecture. The red cube of the ossuary dominates the site, its punched openings artfully framing vistas of other cemetery buildings. The roofless interior contains a grid-work of niches where ashes are placed. Metal-grate stairs and galleries, supported on slender steel columns, surround the paved inner court. In line with the columbarium, a tiered bridge structure links two linear ossuaries that form the long cemetery wall bordering the town.

Following Rossi's principles of 'typology', the form of the sanctuary, a large cubic structure, was derived from that of a house – an abstract, prismatic, 'universal' idea of a house which surprisingly bore a striking resemblance to traditional houses of northern Italy. Lacking floors, windows or roof, it was an 'incomplete', abandoned house 'analogical' to death. The common grave was a conic structure 'analogical' to a large chimney. The columbarium was arranged in a succession of parallelepipeds, a series of corridors inscribed in an isosceles triangle made up of 'osteological' figures 'analogical' to the arrangement of bones within the torso. Grave and sanctuary were arranged at the two ends of an axis, the columbarium lying between them in a classical tripartite manner, a composition with a beginning, middle and conclusion. The overall composition was of an anthropomorphic concrete object evoking the body devoid of life and flesh – the skeleton.

The striking schematic pattern of the project was derived by an application of regular shapes and volumes from the top down, as well as a reduction of concrete objects to pure masses from the bottom up, forcing them into canonical 'Platonic' volumes. Hence, the turn-of-the-century, toy-like appearance of scale-less, game-like building type.

The theme of the cemetery gave Rossi an excellent opportunity to demonstrate his ideas about architecture without major difficulties. His credo, using elementary volumes undisturbed by functional requirements, could easily be put into practice in the world of the dead whose everyday needs were non-existent. Furthermore, the oppositional theme of death as the negation of life provided a helpful cognitive mechanism for putting forward a critique of the present human state of affairs, a mode of what Adorno called 'negative critical thinking'.

Thus memory, history, orderliness, the values cherished by Rossi, expressions of collective will which had been expelled from the contemporary city, could find a home again in the *luogo architettonico*, the 'architectonic place' of the cemetery. Following the bankruptcy of any other means, according to Rossi, this negative city built by negative architecture could act as the base for a different kind of assault against the anti-values of the functionalist and populist 'Babylon'.

(Right) Perspective view of the cemetery

(Below right) The cemetery wall

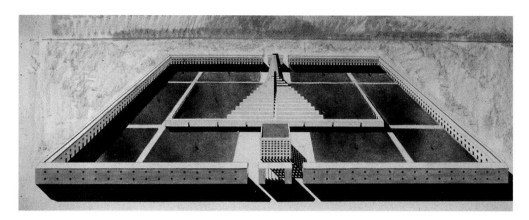

Aldo Rossi
GALLARATESE HOUSING PROJECT
(Milan, Italy)
1969–73

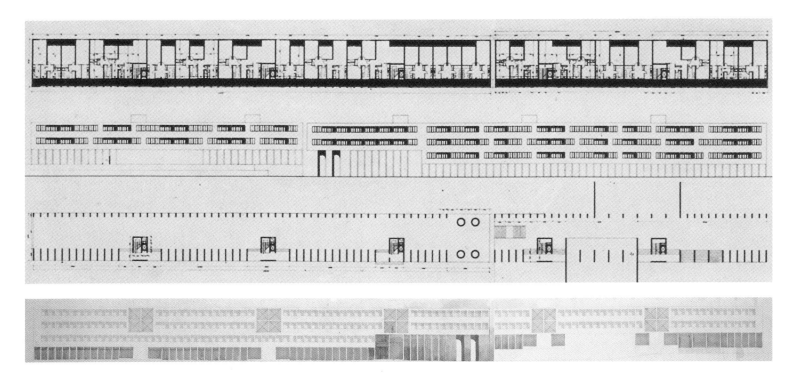

The Gallaratese housing project was as paradigmatic of Aldo Rossi's ideas as its contemporary, the San Cataldo Cemetery in Modena (pp. 56–59). It was as if he had been engaged in a comparative study to demonstrate that his principles of architecture were sufficiently universal to be applied both to the houses of the living and of the dead. Indeed, the projects share the same elementary units (triangles, cubes, cylinders, cones). Similar composition rules (absence of termination, lack of hierarchization of parts – i.e. a reduced but also rigidified classical canon – bilateral axial symmetry, serial repetition, orthogonality) govern both.

Seen from the point of view of modern architecture, which demanded functionalist 'authenticity', the similarities between the housing project and the cemetery amounted to a scandal. They did not correspond to shared programmatic, operational features nor did they arise from a shared technology of construction, as was the case when Mies aroused controversy by dressing housing and offices in the same curtain wall clothes and placing one next to the other. When populist criteria were applied, such as those which dictated Kroll's (pp. 44–47, 92–95) or Hertzberger's (pp. 48–51) architecture, the common features of

cemetery and housing invited characterization of authoritarianism, cultural imperialism – even necrophilia.

However, in the context of Rossi's own beliefs about culture and society – his 'typological' theory of architecture – the use of the same attributes in apartments for the living and in a cemetery that represents collective silence and memory was entirely justifiable.

Kroll's so-called ethnological approach maintained an open, complete confidence in the non-professional users of architecture and in their spontaneous demands. By contrast, Rossi was suspicious of such populism. He believed instead that architectural norms had to be derived from patient professional research. While Kroll's methodology focused strictly on the present demands of a specific group of users of a building, Rossi's typological methodology dug into the past (with vague references to antiquity), into a 'universal', Western European past, in an attempt to identify the pre-existing invariant architectural elements. 'The cemetery, as a building,' Rossi argued, 'is the house of the dead. The typology of the house and of the tomb are in origin indistinguishable.'

The Gallaratese housing, therefore, employs what Rossi identified as the 'elements of

(Opposite)

(Top) Plans and elevations

(Centre) Facade

(Below) Conceptual drawing

(This page, above) Exterior view

architecture, and not only of residential architecture.' For him, similarities with funereal architecture arose not from confusion of function or content, but from the priority given to form, a practice common in classical architecture. Gallaratese's facade, which to the functionalists was 'false', was likened by Rossi to the built stage of the Roman theatre and to the facade of the Palladian basilica, which were employed irrespective of functional specifics. Contrary to the views of modernists, functionalists, rigorists and populists alike, preservation of order for Rossi was more important than functional fit, accommodation of individual aspirations, flexibility, openness to an unknown and unknowable future, or promoting a pluralistic, agnostic society.

Following these almost Poundian presumptions about the inherent superiority of certain cultural forms (minus Ezra Pound's admiration for oriental culture), it is not surprising that the formal aspects of the Gallaratese housing not only resemble those of a cemetery but are also diametrically opposed to those of the Medical Faculty of Louvain, designed by Kroll for its rowdy, light-hearted, forgetful students.

Yet there was also a realistic dimension to Rossi's general, transcendental and quasi-metaphysical theory of typology. When the moment for its specific application arrived, he did take account of existing conditions. This was the case in the cemetery of Modena. In the Gallaratese housing also, *a priori* abstract, spatial components – the cube, the cylinder, the equilateral triangle – were joined with pre-existing physical features. For Rossi, typological investigations did not only search for universal forms; they also sought the 'union of geometry with use' and the 'history of use', as he states in his *L'architettura della città* (1966). Investigating the terrain where a building is going to be constructed, identifying the location's inherited built structures, the reality of their predominant and unique features and the reality of their past workings – all these factors were seen as necessary components of the design.

Gallaratese derives its long rectilinear form from the traditional Milanese tenement house which Rossi identified as a type. The building itself is 182 metres in length and 12 metres deep. The ground floor is an implacably rhythmical portico made up of pilaster elements, while the mostly 2-room housing units are located above, along a corridor.

Besides the neo-Platonic volumetric presuppositions or the historical typologies of the region, precedents for Rossi's approach in the Gallaratese housing project can be found in the work of Giovanni Muzio, one of the leading Milanese architects of the pre-Second World War era, and in that of Le Corbusier. Of particular significance is the latter's La Tourette; Rossi had written with admiration about its abstract compositional values before he chose his own formal path.

Despite the highly abstract language of Rossi's texts, the Gallaratese housing had many practical implications, hence its paradigmatic character. Rossi's was an architecture of *Gestalt*, not of detail. Construction aspects were not important, a justifiable approach since the formal paradigms adopted demanded minimal construction technique. Its starkness and simplicity demonstrated how over-complicated the forms used in housing projects had been during the late 1960s, which had been feebly justified by pseudo-sociological and pseudo-organizational jargon. It also showed that the study of previously accumulated knowledge, implicit in the pervasive and persistent spatial arrangements of buildings of the past (the 'types'), could render effective help in the first steps of design.

What is beyond doubt is the uniqueness of the Gallaratese project. It stood as a symbol representing a reaction to the 1968 spirit of disintegration that threatened institutional destruction and social decomposition – a threat in many ways over-exaggerated at the time. In the cemetery of Modena, the formal integrity of the *luogo architettonico* of the city of the dead was intended as an alternative to the 'ugly growth' of the contemporary city. So, in the same way, the Gallaratese houses seemed to defy the false deductions of vulgar materialism which proclaimed that 'form follows function', or those of early modernist architecture, as well as the utopian naivety of post-war architecture, that 'function will follow form'. Similarly, Gallaratese asserted that, contrary to the fashionable slogans, the result of the populist sentiments of 1968 resulted only in building 'internal barricades' of neo-tribalism. Despite Gallaratese's overwhelming formalism, Rossi conceived it as social architecture; but a social architecture distinct from that of functionalists and populists, and not only in terms of architectural means, but also social ends. It was meant as a 'collective representation'. Nevertheless, one has to ask whether the socio-cultural values proclaimed by the strict geometrical formulas of the Gallaratese housing as symbolic collective representations were important enough to justify their constraining impact on the everyday life of its individual occupants. Was the regimenting effect on the ordinary activities of individuals a legitimate cost in representing their alleged 'collectivity'?

Whatever the effect of Rossi's architecture on the comfort of the users of Gallaratese, he became a hero to grateful architects who embraced him for having almost singlehandedly restored their confidence in the profession. The simplicity of his toy-like forms and his domino-like rule system was seductively, even exhilaratingly easy to follow. His slogan-recipes were memorable, hypnotic, charismatic, like Le Corbusier's. And, as in the case of Le Corbusier, their adoption was the result of an act of faith rather than a rational decision.

In the misty Milan dusk, the Gallaratese housing with its neo-Platonist, arcane composition rises as if to exorcise the evil spirit of contemporary Babylon rather than as a cry of protest, or a constructive vision.

(Above) Typological study

(Right) Drawing of the facade

Mario Botta Architetto
HOUSE AT RIVA SAN VITALE
(Ticino, Switzerland)
1971–73

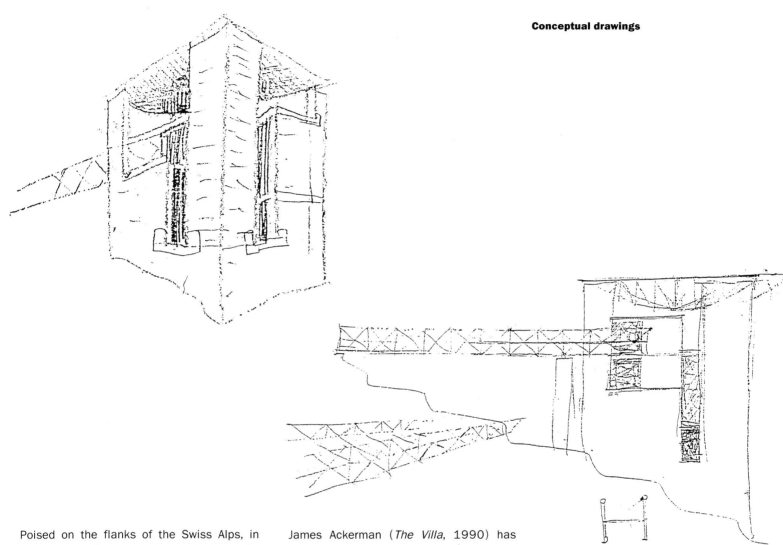

Poised on the flanks of the Swiss Alps, in Monte San Giorgio which encircles Lake Lugano, this modest building by the young Mario Botta – like that of his friend and colleague Luigi Snozzi in Locarno (pp. 80–81) – had an exhilarating impact when it appeared. Like Rossi's San Cataldo cemetery (pp. 56–59), it seemed to mark a return to order and traditional values after the crisis of 1968: nature, the family, geometry, craftsmanship in construction. However, the Riva San Vitale House differed from Rossi's architecture, which was not concerned with projecting positive models. It appeared to be offering to restore a moral way of life, spatially represented not only in the composition but also in the small, embedded details, using precedents derived from the tradition of the villa – a 'utopian topos', a world within a world, a refuge in natural wilderness from urban 'totalism'.

James Ackerman (*The Villa*, 1990) has enumerated the elements of the 'mythology' the villa expresses. The Riva San Vitale House can be considered as a successful example of the type: its tall, prismatic volume is firmly 'engaged' in the land, while at the same time, in its exaggerated erectedness, it maintains a distance from it. The idea of distance is underlined by the very means through which the building is linked to its surroundings by the long, light bridge made of steel which, in its suspension, length and lightness, keeps on distinguishing the artifice and its ground. The house really does appear, as the architect himself wrote, to 'emerge from the terrain in a dialectical game with the environment, emphasized by the minimal occupation of the terrain and by the subtle bridge of steel that, standing on the limits of the road, stabilizes the physical relation to the mountain.'

The entrance bridge

Platonic geometry, with its rigorously square shape, and the artificial materials of the project, both products of culture, set the building apart from the natural landscape, while their artificiality exalts the landscape's physical character by contrast. Although contained in the landscape, the building conceptually 'frames' the landscape. As in all villas, the dialectic of view is also expressed in Riva San Vitale House. Much as the building is designed as a distinguished, well-formed object to look at, at the same time it is a place to look out from, a belvedere. In fact, in its tower form, the San Vitale villa resembles an expressly made artifice for enjoying a prospect.

According to Ackerman, the villa mythology expresses 'the prerogatives of privilege' and 'regional pride'. Indeed, the Botta villa, in its aloof and pristine physiognomy, has a super-

ior, an aristocratic air which the heaviness and roughness of the material – echoing the tradition of Renaissance rustication – in fact exaggerate. One could be critical of this manifestation of 'power and class aspiration'. One could be equally critical of the exaltation of the regional Ticinese architectural qualities which the building evokes in the rigour of its geometry, the robustness of its material and the elegance of construction details. However, the Riva San Vitale House can in fact be seen as an expression of a critical manifesto. As Kenneth Frampton has pointed out in his perceptive writings on Botta and the school of Ticino in *Modern Architecture* (1985), the building derives from the *roccolo*, a bird catching tower, a rustic building type to be found in this Italian part of Switzerland. In choosing this unusual prototype, and promoting it to the status of a symbol embodying the true values

of the region, Botta appears to be using it as a means of criticizing the debased, kitsch version of Ticino commercial regionalism, and of the commercialism of culture in general.

The villa has been linked through history with two traditions, in its formal spatial expression: on the one hand, the master-servant dialectic confirming the legitimacy of the master; and on the other, the perennial *otium-negotium* antithesis supporting the 'sweet and honorable otium' of the 'contemplative life', as opposed to 'active', commercial engagement. The villa, without loosing its strong formal identity in history, has oscillated between a conservative and a liberating approach. In the context of the post-1968 world, it has surely taken in Botta's work the latter position.

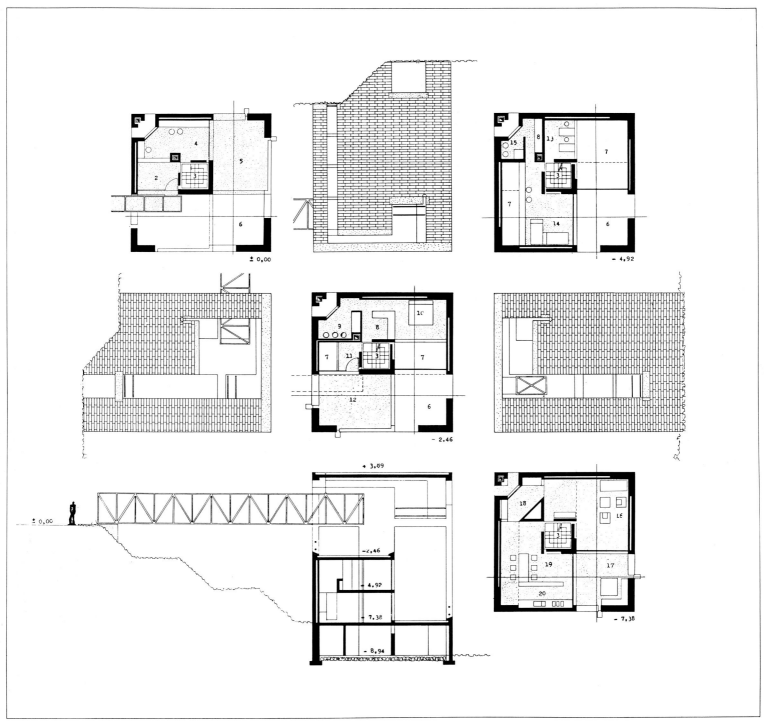

(Above) A selection of plans and elevations

(Left) Detail of the house's construction

(Opposite) The entrance bridge connecting the house to the mountainous surrounding landscape

Ralph Erskine
BYKER WALL
(Newcastle upon Tyne, England)
1968–74

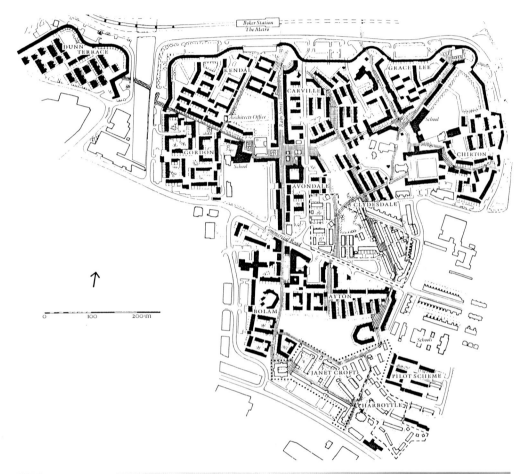

Ralph Erskine's Byker housing project is one of the most celebrated episodes in the brief history of the populist movement in architecture following the cultural-social explosion of May 1968. Although the project is unique, the story it tells is characteristic.

Byker began as a settlement built in haste for shipyard craftsmen. A ten-thousand-strong village of skilled workers who lived in red-brick flats and enjoyed a strong sense of community, it was declared overcrowded by the officials of the city of Newcastle upon Tyne. The conflict between an obsolete built tissue and a still vital social fabric demanding to be accommo-

(Opposite, above) **Urban plan**

(Opposite, below) **Byker Wall from the outside**

(Above) **From the inside**

dated within it is a common problem worldwide. The old solutions of massive demolition and redevelopment conceived and imposed from above, as practised at least since the end of the Second World War in Europe, Great Britain and in Newcastle itself, were rejected in the case of Byker. It is to the credit of the local authorities that they reached this conclusion early on, and equally to the credit of the private developer, whose understanding of the nature of the problem was enhanced by the populist movement of the end of the 1960s.

Ralph Erskine was invited to design the project because of his previous successful involvement over a period of fifteen years with social housing in Sweden. His success was partly due to his commitment to making no design decisions unless close consultation with the users of the project had first taken place. At that time, such procedures were still unorthodox in most parts of the world, although very much in tune with the polyarchic spirit of Scandinavian Welfare State policies.

When he was invited to work on the Byker Wall project, Erskine was professionally located in Sweden and had therefore to arrange for an office annex on site. Consequently, it was not as easy for him to embark on a participatory process of design as it had been for Lucien Kroll in his Louvain Medical Faculty housing (pp. 44–47). Luckily, an old collaborator of Erskine, Vernon Gracie, turned down a more lucrative job in the Middle East in order to move to Byker. Together with Gracie, Erskine set up a local practice similar to American examples of 'storefront architecture' of the late 1960s in Harlem (New York), Mantua (Philadelphia), and in Boston's South End.

Byker became a way of life. By contrast to the atmosphere prevailing on most such projects, Erskine's attitude was not one of agitation and antagonism towards the authorities. His ties with his client, the Newcastle District Council Housing Committee, were close and his contribution as a professional positive rather than critical. He in fact assumed an enviable, and certainly rare, dual role: on the one hand, he acted as an architect for the Council, and on the other as a planning consultant. This meant that he was able to rewrite his own architectural programmes before actually accepting the commission as architect, and to maintain an overview of the future development of Byker by other agencies and firms. Because of his highly responsible ethos of self-control – in his dual capacity as supervisor and supervised – this privileged position led to creative innovations rather than either bland compromises or unchecked extravagances.

The intentions of client and architect were from the start to assist the economic development and modernization of the area. To do this, they improved Byker's accessibility by bringing in a road running along the north/east sides of the site and linking it to public transport. They supplied new housing, but at the same time preserved family and social links – the essential component of the programme.

The basic concept of space organization emerged out of the seemingly conflicting programmatic forces: the invention of the architect and scrutiny of the users, who were informed in detail about every decision. An early pilot project of 46 houses was built for testing by the development's future residents. Their post-occupancy criticisms were incorporated in the final project.

The fundamental design scheme was that of a large wall created by the high-rise perimeter block of flats. This turned its back to the planned highway and enclosed low-rise housing terraces, interwoven tightly with paths, open areas and gardens in a territory almost free of cars. The duality of the scheme reflected the bipolarity of the programme, the mass of the wall block acting as a barrier against the negative environmental impact of the road, the low, traditional, village-like frame sustaining the social fabric.

The curved volume of the project dominates the hilltop landscape impressively and has a dream-like effect. It rises, a weird huge mass, partly in silhouette, evoking memories of medieval fortifications from illustrations in children's books. The design of the wall, with its scenographic ornamental patterns, is indebted to Erskine's schooling in Northern European Expressionist architecture, which had been tried in social housing projects of the past – for instance Michel de Klerk's housing projects of Amsterdam South of the 1910s. Passing from the open landscape into the walled-in, intimately articulated area is a stunning dramatic experience similar to that one has in historical fortified cities that grew up over long stretches of time. Byker's exterior irregular gigantism, coupled with the informal humility of its interior, is exceedingly appropriate to the open site where it is situated, beyond urban constraints. Despite its fabulistic image, however, Byker is not merely a scenographic setting. And yet it is true that such a scheme probably could not serve as a prototype for an urban situation, where a less walled-in spatial concept and a more explicit public face are required.

The strongest impression of community cohesion emerges less from Byker's visual effects than from its spatial-functional organization and its functional details. Even though many of these physical details and their technical craftsmanship – for instance its rapidly aging external balconies – have not lasted well, its larger vision of the will of a community to survive as a community and of professional diligence and accountability remain intact.

Ten years after the project was completed, 90 per cent of the users expressed satisfaction, a remarkably high rate for low-budget rented housing. Byker won the Award of Britain in the Bloom competition, in the summer of 1980, as the 'best-kept village'. In 1989, it received the Prince of Wales Prize at Harvard University's Graduate School of Design, along with Alvaro Siza's Evora-Malaguera housing project (1988).

It is ironic that just when such new, creative ideas about the architecture of social housing had started to emerge and to overcome the failures of the past, reasons beyond the architects' control – political and financial – made this kind of architecture largely impossible to pursue.

Close up of Byker Wall from the inside

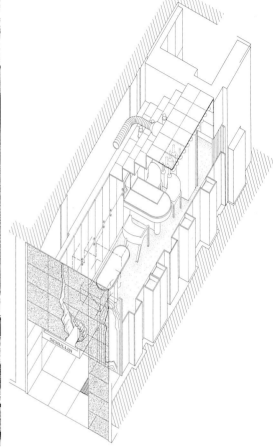

In the 1960s Hollein had completed a number of 'paper' and actual projects before undertaking the design of the Schullin Jewelry shop. Most of these had been small-scale art galleries or commercial shops, their design always a balancing act between consumption and imagination, and very Viennese, reminiscent of the turn of the century. In connection with his architectural practice, Hollein also emerged as one of the major forces behind new, high-quality industrial design. In the context of a practice reflecting the innovations of pre-war, avant-garde architecture, Hollein's early 'fantasies' are both stimulating inventions, but also powerful critical statements.

The Schullin shop is a modest project, but the ambitious ideas it incorporates, and certainly its influence, are disproportionately large. In an era of piecemeal functional accommodation of facilities, Hollein produced

a genuine *Gesamtkunstwerk* with a remarkable unity of materials, where even the most minute, 'uninteresting' detail is treated with great and loving attention. Granite slabs, ducts, a niche, a portal, plates, frames are all carefully layered in contrast to anything that surrounds the shop, or that pre-existed on its site.

Against the bland, conventional and depersonalized post-war mainstream buildings, the Schullin shop appeared as a shocking, gilded eccentricity when it was opened in 1974. Although it fulfilled all its functional requirements, the architect did not choose to be content with that. Its facade cried out and was a most conspicuous image. In the context of the functionalist tradition, Hollein had created something that defiantly turned its back on it.

Yet, very much as in the case of Robert Venturi's so-called 'witty', or even 'perverse'

design statements, the Schullin shop delivered a disconcerting, and uncompromising lesson. Instead of replaying the 'form follows function' routine, this 'modest' undertaking took upon itself to pose questions about the relationship between truth and poetry, language and reality: the sort of questions that grand works of art belonging to the Viennese, if not the entire Western tradition, had always posed in the past.

The project was one of the most important works to bring back to post-war architecture the idea of narration through iconic architectural means. At a time when facades were according to current practice means of 'communicating' the operation of the building programme (which, anyhow, was trivial for the Schullin shop), Hollein decided to use it to tell an exotic story, the story of the gold mine and the cracked stone. A cracked object? How

strange that this object appeared when architecture could tolerate at most an organic object's informality within a highly controlled universe of mechanical products! What an anomaly, this geometry of disorder and chaos in the midst of so much rational perfection, well-formedness, *bien fini*!

The fabulism of the Schullin shop, like that of the other shops Hollein designed during the previous decade, can be criticized and condemned for delinquency or indifference to the prevailing urban and social problems; its mythographic luxury can be seen as decadent and irresponsible, as erecting temples to fetishism and fanning the flames of the bourgeois thirst for consumption. But the sheer anarchic fantasy and creative invention which went into the project's design were, paradoxically, not dissimilar, in terms of fantasy and imagination, to the previous decade's cultural revolt.

Foster Associates Ltd
WILLIS, FABER & DUMAS HEAD OFFICE
(Ipswich, England)
1970–75

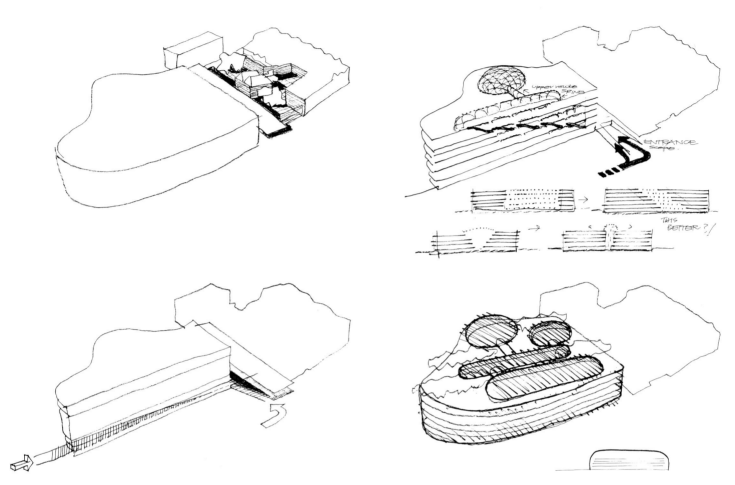

The architecture of the workplace enjoyed predominance in the first two decades after the Second World War and many innovative ideas about the form, structure and function of buildings were associated with it. Most major architects of the time engaged in this field with great inventiveness. This has not, however, been the case in the last twenty years. With few exceptions, such as Herman Hertzberger's Centraal Beheer (1968–72, pp. 48–51) and Richard Rogers' Lloyd's of London (1978–86, pp. 156–59), little creative attention has been given to offices and factories architecturally. Norman Foster is among these rare exceptions and one of the most singular and significant ones. His Willis, Faber & Dumas offices are one of his most inventive and influential contributions to this design problem, at once so urgent and so neglected.

Starting from the need to develop an architecture of the workplace that would be appropriate to a new generation of employees with a new attitude to work and discipline, Foster arrived at a very different solution from Hertzberger's Centraal Beheer. Foster, like his old friend, classmate and associate Richard Rogers, believed in using 'appropriate technologies to social goals', in achieving emancipation through innovation. Influenced by the vision of Buckminster Fuller's Dymaxion House and by the notion of the 'well-serviced shed', as described by the influential British architectural historian and critic Reyner Banham, Foster placed great emphasis on problem-solving techniques and searched for an integration of structure, services and external skin, in words paraphrasing Mies, 'to do more with less'.

A programme responding to new ideas about labour, human relations, management and flow of information required a spatial layout 'based on short lines of communication' and an 'open-door' management policy. It also required the integration of social and sports activities into the production facility. These programmatic demands led to an open-plan architectural scheme with 'offices without doors', without enclaves or hierarchization of spaces and a careful clustering of activities. Natural and socializing amenities and visual contact with the outside were provided for all. A swimming pool at ground level, a restaurant pavilion and a large roof garden also became essential components of the building. As in the case of Centraal Beheer, arriving at this solution was not the result of one-way decisions by the architect. The design followed detailed analysis and investigation of the organization of the office and public presentations and discussions, with both staff and management.

The building has been likened to a 'sandwich'. Two 'served' floors of open-plan office space (to use Louis Kahn's notions of 'served' and 'servant', which were influential in the development of Foster's approach) are situated between two 'servant' floors within which special amenities – swimming pool, restaurant, roof garden – are interspersed. The

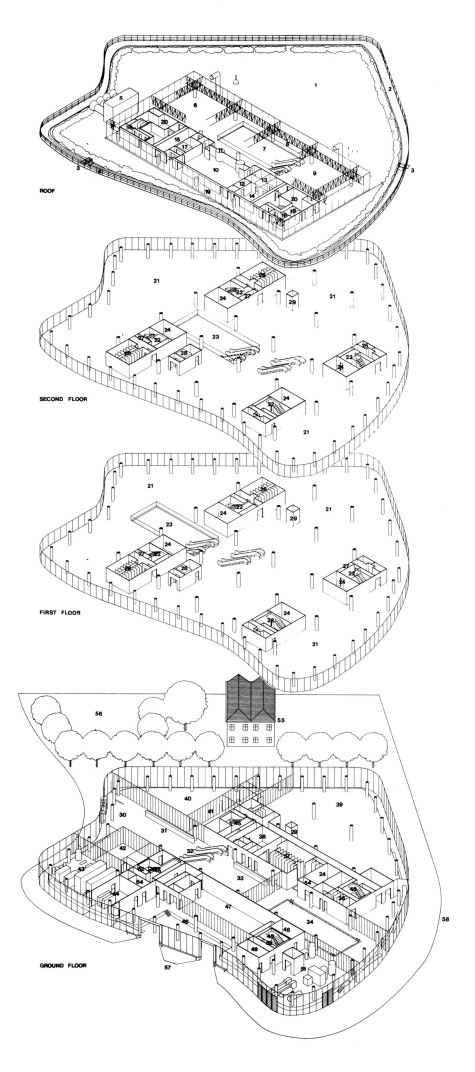

ROOF

SECOND FLOOR

FIRST FLOOR

GROUND FLOOR

(Opposite) Series of conceptual drawings
(Upper left) Walls, paving, trees and landscaping create a network of related spaces; the glass lobby acts as a wind break

(Lower left) Flooding hazard indicators show need to raise areas in use; entrance is restricted to high elevation

(Upper right) Reintroduction in a different, more appropriate form of escalator routes

(Lower right) Sketch for a 'predominantly' glazed roof for the building

(This page) Floor plans

sandwich is held together by a vertical core consisting of a circulation lobby topped by the all-glass pavilion located on the roof garden.

The technological means for implementing this architecture were also carefully studied. Essential to establishing the desirable transparency was the absence of any bulky, space-occupying structural elements. The basic concept of structural organization adopted was that of a dual system: a major one for the main body of the building and a minor one for its periphery. The major columnar support system was constructed as a regular, square grid, the minor an irregular one, using smaller columns. A series of regularly spaced columns was lined up around the periphery of the site's amoeboid configuration, leaving an irregular zone surrounding the grid. This is a classic approach, avoiding a single-grid pattern that contains multiple distortions, a kind of 'organic' deformation schema such as Alvar Aalto or several other contemporary architects might have employed. Going further back in history, such a

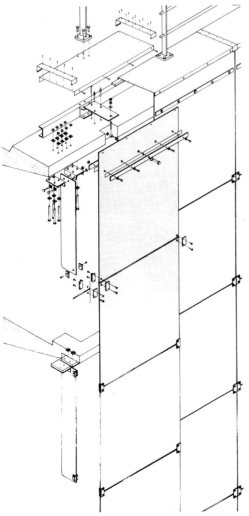

solution was first invented by the Renaissance architect Serlio in his efforts to reconcile classical *taxis* with the typically disordered shapes of the medieval urban sites.

Also essential for establishing visual contact with the outside, so desirable for the employees, was the detailing of the glass. The ingenious system of its suspension and the absence of mullions in the floor-to-ceiling glazing were all designed and calculated by the architect's office. The glass manufacturer offered guarantees for the design in return for the rights to it. Important also towards achieving a feeling of openness and accessibility was the 'dematerialization' of lighting features, diffusers, pipes, ducts. A sandwich structure absorbed them between ceiling and slab.

In a reversal of the usual institutional hierarchization of quality materials and design, whereby the most precious and well-crafted environment is created for the public lobby and the most restrained for the actual working areas, Foster designed a simple entrance/reception for Willis, Faber & Dumas. As one penetrates the building, walking and rising by escalators, one encounters increasingly more luxurious and comfortable areas.

The building was carefully designed from the point of view of energy control and efficiency, which are achieved through a low periphery plan, low proportion of glass-to-floor area, high-efficiency lighting and very effective insulation provided by roof landscaping, a Le Corbusier-type method.

But the most celebrated feature of the project is its external wall, its skin, which transforms this wonderfully pragmatic shelter into a poetic object. The solution marks the beginning of a major shift in sensitivity, away from the sculpted, plastic, spatially exhibitionistic architecture, as well as away from the structural, rhythmic and skeletal, both of which types had been predominant since the Second World War, and towards one that focused on the qualities of occlusions, covering, impermeability, folding – that is, on surface. The Willis, Faber & Dumas office is entirely clad in an almost seamless solar mirror glass curtain that extends to the edge of the site in a manner reminiscent in plan to Mies's Berlin 1923 glass skyscraper. The effect is a miraculous disappearing act by the building, and at the same time a doubling of the architectural features of the surroundings reflected on its surface skin. The irregularity of the mirroring glass adds to the magic, the unreality and the deep sense of play, our turn-of-the-20th-century, economical, people's answer to the challenge of Louis XIV's Galerie des Glaces at Versailles. Foster's invention was soon imitated around the world, and it still is at the moment of writing. But almost without exception, these attempts are poor reflections which fail to capture the unique experience offered by the mirrors of the Willis, Faber & Dumas building.

Foster was not interested in the discussions about the de-institutionalization and re-appropriation by the individual of the workplace, so predominant among populists after the events of Spring '68. As a trade-off for individualized, enwrapping workstations, Foster opted for commonsense environmental and social amenities such as light, spaciousness, long vistas and visual contact with the outside, together with excellence in the detailing of the inanimate objects that surround the worker. He was also from the outset determined to treat aspects of the external impact of the building as being of equal importance to determinants internal to the building. It appears retrospectively that almost all these decisions were taken with imagination and good judgment.

(Above left) Exterior view with entrance

(Left) Detail showing the attachment of the glass facade to the roof

(Below) Section

(Opposite, above) The building by night

(Opposite) Site plan

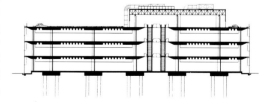

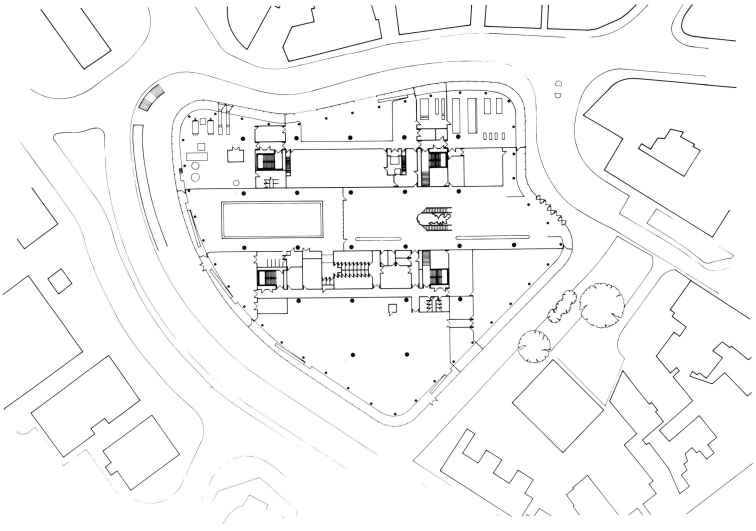

Estudio Rafael Moneo
BANKINTER
(Madrid, Spain)
1973–76

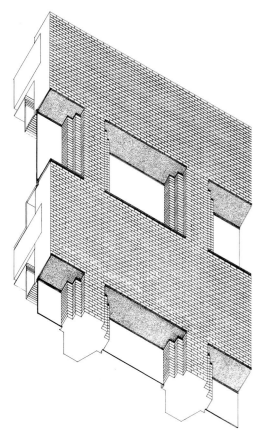

Bankinter stands in the grounds of the small, late-19th-century villa of the Marques de Mudela. The site is among the last vestiges of the urban tissue that once made up Madrid's Paseo de la Castellana; it is now occupied by the massive, mighty, high-rise business area carved out of the city centre during the later part of the Franco years. In the early 1970s, in an effort to preserve what little of the historic fabric survived there, new regulations were enacted that strictly limited the volume of new construction. This was an important step towards arresting the destruction of the historically defined, characteristic Madrilenian sense of place by the spread of mainstream commercial, bureaucratic buildings. Bankinter was the first building erected in accordance with these regulations, and it was also one of the key buildings that triggered a 'critical regionalist' movement in Spain. The desire to respect the original house and grounds and keep their integrity was among the principal reasons for the selection of Rafael Moneo, an architect already known for his devotion to the

problem of continuity in architectural evolution.

As Moneo has written, the 'authentic protagonist' in this building is brick construction, a regional attribute. If there is one image the visitor retains of Madrid's architecture, it is the prismatic volumes, the rigorist, jointless, red brickwork. Although the majority of Spanish architects of the previous generation – Alejandro de la Sota and Julio Cano Lasso, for instance – had used this architectural vocabulary, Moneo made a point of choosing as his model the architecture of Francisco Cabrero's Casa Sindical in Madrid, from the end of the 1940s.

The brick, 'cubic' project of Cabrero had succeeded in creating a building with a public face beyond the pompous Escorialism of many of his contemporaries. He amalgamated a more vernacular Madrid tradition with the neomonumentalism of the Milan architects of the 1930s. Moneo went one step further in this approach towards inclusiveness and syncretism by introducing rules of composition derived from a distant and unexpected source, the Finnish architect Alvar Aalto.

During the 1950s Aalto was virtually unknown in Spain. His sensitivity to site conditions, his openness to regional context and his concern for 'place' proved to have a special appeal to Spanish architects at a moment of crisis, when the alienating 'urban sprawl' was taking hold during the 1960s. Several projects by another Spanish architect of the period, Antonio Fernandez Alba, testify in their design to Aalto's influence and warm reception in

Spain. In Moneo's project, given the severely constrained site conditions, physical as well as cultural, Aalto provided the necessary balance to Cabrero's lack of response to site conditions. The pin-wheel composition, the shift of scales on each side of the building, the facade with many faces, the breaking of the monolithic volume into discrete units, their fit into the urban setting of the Paseo de la Castellana, resulted in a paradigmatic contextual urban design.

Bankinter displays the same planarity, the same play of recesses and appearance of solidity as Cabrero's Casa Sindical. However, with its sharp wedge to one side and a rounded wall to the other, the building is also obviously taking liberties with this meticulous geometric rigorism, breaking the familiar regionalist pattern.

In its syncretism, the creative combination of architectural precedents, the project can be seen as a representation of the inclusiveness, reconciliation and opening up of the new, post-Franco dynamic Spain. In the same spirit of conciliation, no doubt, are the cast bronze floral reliefs on the upper part of the facade; by the Spanish artist Francisco Lopez Hernandez, they are directly inspired by Louis Sullivan's buildings in Chicago.

The impact of the project was immediate and was felt as strongly outside Spain as within its borders. This doubtless contributed, along with Moneo's Museum in Merida (1980–86, pp. 148–51), to his appointment as chairman of the Graduate School of Design at Harvard in 1984.

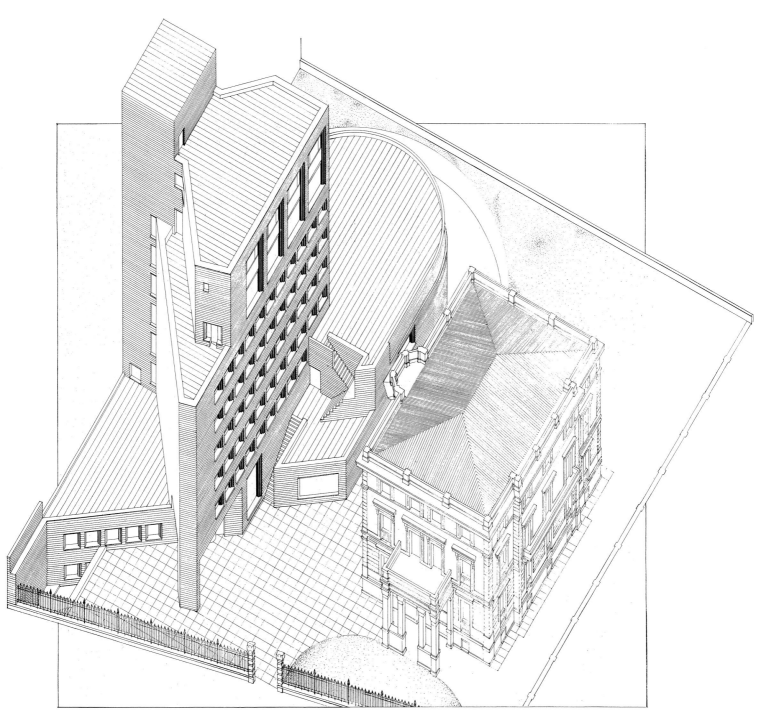

(Opposite, left) Axonometric section showing
detail of the wall

(Opposite) The facade on the entrance side
(centre) and in relation to the villa (right)

(Above) Axonometric drawing of Bankinter
and the villa

(Right) General plan of the two buildings

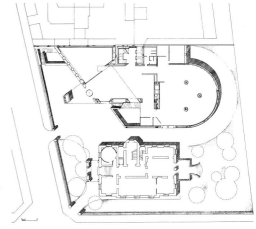

Luigi Snozzi
CASA KALMAN
(Locarno, Switzerland)
1974–76

This small house in Locarno, overlooking Lake Maggiore, is an intentional act of provocation in relation to the gaudy, vulgar, nouveau-riche vacation houses that surround it. It marks a return, like his collaborator and friend Mario Botta's critical regionalist Riva San Vitale House on Lake Lugano (pp. 64–67), to the moral values associated with the original Hellenistic Roman villa: the espousal of a moral, healthy, natural way of life and the exaltation of the land. However, unlike Mario Botta's project – in fact unlike most of the critical regionalist projects of the 1980s internationally – it makes no reference to an existing vernacular building type. With its roughcast concrete walls that seem to fuse with the craggy terrain, and its minimalist, self-effacing, austere volume, the building is an attempt to be true to the topographic rather than the architectural *genius loci*. As such, it can also be seen as a return to the aesthetics of wilderness and natural roughness associated with another Swiss, the 18th-century figure Jean Jacques Rousseau, author of the celebrated *Promenades*. Snozzi's building expresses the idea of yet another Swiss, Le Corbusier, and his notion of the *promenade architecturale*.

The design of the Casa Kalman is dominated by circulation. It is entered by a walkway bridging a small stream in front of the house. One can follow the building's curved retaining

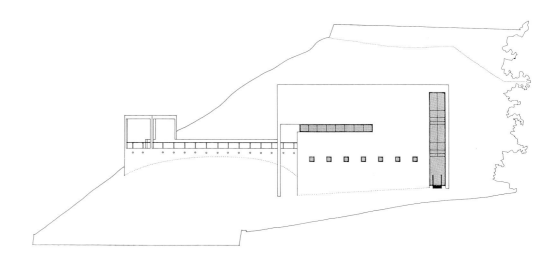

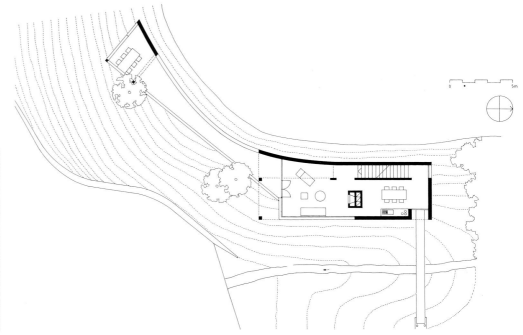

(Opposite) Exterior view of the Casa Kalman within its landscape

(Above) The terrace, leading down to the pergola

(Top right) Elevation of the house

(Above right) Plan of the site and house (drawing-room floor level)

wall along the line of the steep hill, pass to an outside terrace and, continuing that line, arrive at a miniature pergola. Throughout this itinerary consistent with the Picturesque and Rousseauist traditions, a memorable hierarchy of views is encountered by the *promeneur*. As Snozzi writes, 'The visitor's first impression is one of bold outlines and a progressive disclosure of spaces: the initial architectural encounter at the entry, then across the stream, up the steps through the living room and along the terrace to the pergola.'

There is something heroic about Casa Kalman's refutation of bourgeois domestic comfort, its austerity, its exaltation of the landscape, its back-to-nature viewpoint of

foregrounding the landscape, of 'defamiliarizing' the sense of place and, therefore, of making the viewer aware of its real values. But in addition, the purpose of this latter-day Rousseauiste appears therapeutic, 'sentimental' in the original 18th-century sense, a 'sweet and deep revery' to restore health to the psyche through the eye's contact with the outside objects. The contemplation of the surroundings is meant to occur, in Snozzi's words, 'in a number of ways, ranging from the immediate impression of nearby meadows, vineyards and trees and ending in a view of the Bay of Locarno'.

Antonio Cruz Villalon   Antonio Ortiz Garcia

HOUSING BLOCK ON DOÑA MARIA CORONEL STREET

(Seville, Spain)
1974–76

Neither the geometry of its curved internal court nor any of the decorative elements of the facade is borrowed from the regional architectural tradition of Seville. Yet this building by these two young architects at the beginning of their career does exude a strong sense of the city. At a time when the spread of unchecked urban development was threatening what was left of the long-neglected, declining structure of the historical centre of Seville as a place of encounter and identity, this project was one of the first carried out in what we have identified as the 'critical regionalist spirit' – a call for 'placeness' and community, much like Rafael Moneo's Bankinter building (1976, pp. 78–79) and, a little later, Alvaro Siza's Bouça Housing (1977, pp. 90–91). Such regionalism has nothing to do with tourist folklorism or chauvinistic sentimentalism. Selecting a few but key memories of local, artifacted space, divorced from nostalgia and escapism, regionalist architecture provides a critique against mounting, flattening technocracy and bureaucracy.

This housing block is in the historical centre of Seville, built on an irregularly shaped site, about 500 square metres in surface. Each apartment had to measure approximately 110 square metres. According to planning regulations, 25 per cent of the space of the site had to remain unoccupied as a means of controlling the high density of this area of the city. Given these constraints, the architects chose to concentrate all the free space into one collective patio, a reference to the traditional Sevillian house, but they were required to accommodate it to the irregular lot by making it kidney shaped. This unusual form became a feature which both referred to the traditional patio and preserved a critical distance from it, while at the same time maintaining the deeper social, communal values inherent in the patio space. This was rightly seen as an act of faith in traditional forms of urban life and as a critical statement about the choking of the old city centre by wanton development, on one hand, and by a tawdry, inane, folkloristic regionalism, on the other.

(Opposite, far left) The housing block seen from the street

(Far left and left) Two views of the kidney-shaped internal courtyard

(Below) Plans of the roof (left) and ground floor (right)

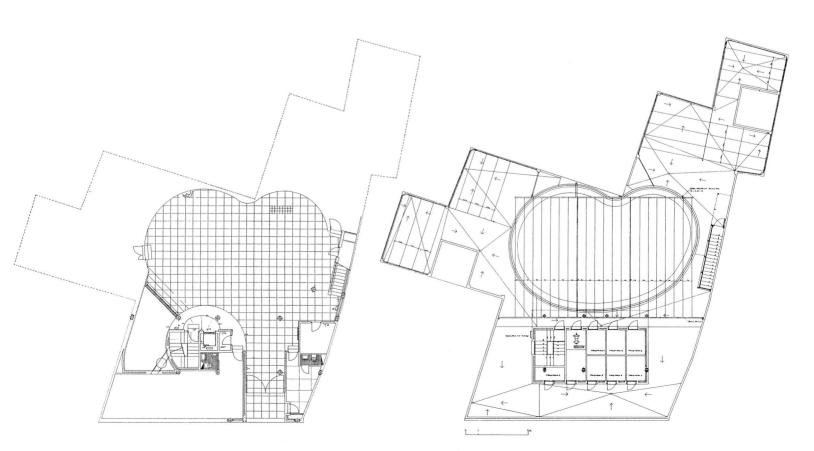

Renzo Piano & Richard Rogers
CENTRE CULTUREL D'ART GEORGES POMPIDOU
(Paris, France)
1971–77

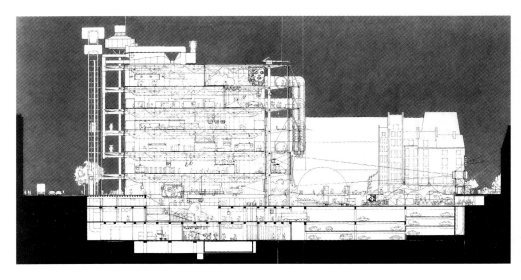

The Pompidou project is, in terms of its references, an amalgam of the architectural visions of the Russian Constructivists, Buckminster Fuller, Yona Friedman, Serge Chermayeff and, to a lesser degree, Louis and Albert Kahn, Marshall McLuhan and Archigram. It is the first implementation in a long tradition of significant, but previously not fully realized, conceptual inventions on the construction and operation of buildings. A feat of what is called 'architectural syncretism' – the deliberate and conscious bringing together of different elements and styles to create a new type of building – it is the *chef d'oeuvre* of two young but experienced architects. It can also be seen as a wholehearted act of faith in the Enlightenment ideals of development and progress, technique and emancipation. Its spatial organization can be traced to various planning ideas of Serge Chermayeff; the zoning, at least partly, to Louis Kahn; and the general space concept to Albert Kahn. Archigram's influence provides the inspiration for its gigantic, visceral exhibitionism, and Yona Friedman's the vision of total flexibility. To Fuller and to the Constructivists one can credit its technological spirit and to Marshall McLuhan the belief that information is ultimately the building block of any product, including buildings. Finally, the Enlightenment encyclopaedists could be said to have provided inspiration for its commitment to knowledge, democratic values, unity between the arts and techniques, and exhilarating optimism. The exceptional invention of this work lies in the

way such ideas have been brought together into a synthesis.

The programme for the Centre was extremely ambitious, requiring a building which, within its 93,000 square metres, would accommodate a museum of modern art, a reference library, a centre for industrial design and a centre for acoustic research and music, as well as bookshops, cinemas, restaurants, a children's centre, administrative offices and parking. Behind this programme lay a multitude of other ambitions: to try to recapture for Paris its status, lost since the Second World War, as the centre of the international avantgarde art community; to try to use such regained territory as a springboard in a bid to achieve superiority in other fields, such as fashion, publishing, mass-media and culture in general, areas in which France had fallen behind. Paris had to compete, at the beginning of the 1970s, with other European capitals as the predominant cultural, commercial and banking centre of the European Community. This was the moment to assert its predominance after a long period of economic growth had produced significant capital. Furthermore, the French establishment, after the shock of Spring '68, had to prove that it was not as culturally sclerotic as the young students claimed and that it was the leader of the field in creativity and innovation.

There was also a need to revitalize prime areas of real estate in decline, such as Le Marais, where the Centre was finally located. Implanting such a major magnet project into

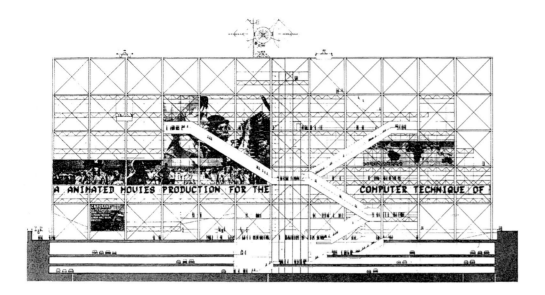

this area was seen as a good way of activating it. The Centre, with the Concorde and the new business centre of La Défense, was meant to proclaim the new French self-confidence. No wonder it was Robert Bordaz, the man who had negotiated the French withdrawal from Vietnam and ex-director of the French radio and television systems, who was appointed administrator of the project, directly accountable to President Pompidou and in charge of a staff of about 150.

Bordaz's style of administration was that of an enlightened head of a multi-national corporation. The programme for the international competition for the Centre was visionary, the staging and organization clear, the committee excellent, headed by Jean Prouvé, Oscar Niemeyer and Philip Johnson, among others. A total of 681 entries were received from all over the world and the final choice, announced on 15 July 1971, was a stunning 'anti-monument', a 'spaceship', an object that captured both in its radical populist content and its science-fiction form the wildest dreams of the May '68 generation.

Interpreting the programme and the mood of the times, Piano and Rogers submitted an entry in which they saw the opportunity to create not just a major cultural facility, in the traditional sense, but, in the spirit of Spring '68, a 'dynamic communications machine', a 'people's centre, a university of the street reflecting the constantly changing needs of users', mobilizing the most up-to-date technology for putting together and running the building, open to constant change and development.

Once the winners of the competition had been chosen, many complex negotiations between client, technical specialists and architects followed. These resulted in several serious modifications to the original plan. For instance, the proposed virtually complete flexibility of the interior and an amazing, architecturally de-materialized screen-facade – an idea prefigured in the J.W.E Buijs and J.B. Lursen building for 'De Volharding' in The Hague – did not survive. Yet, much to the amazement of the international public, this ultra-radical first prize was completed and

delivered as scheduled, on time and under budget, in January 1977, with most of its original ideas triumphant. It has since functioned with great success, at a running cost of one hundred million dollars, with an average attendance of approximately seven million people a year.

More than a decade after its opening, despite some serious difficulties in its operation and several changes in the programme and in the interior (carried out by Gae Aulenti), the complex is still enormously popular – too popular, many might say – and still maintains its aura of youthfulness, still continues to amaze, despite major shifts in sensibility and world outlook, and still retains its identity.

This extraordinary success was a result of the programme's vision and inventiveness, and was also due to the rigour with which technology was applied to realize that vision. The building occupied only half the site provided; the rest was turned into a public square in order to enhance the project's civic character and to encourage the urban piazza activities meant to take place in it. This space

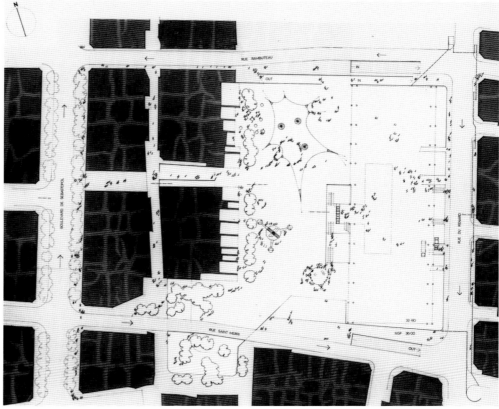

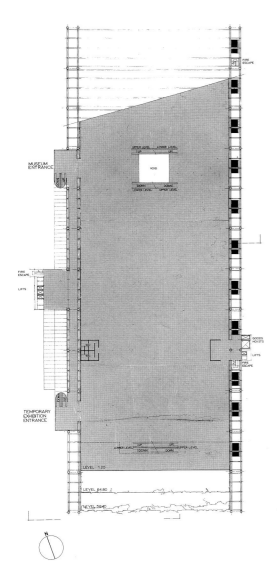

was paved and sloped, like an amphitheatre, and the three roads bordering it closed to traffic. The piazza became one of the most captivating open spaces in Paris.

The simplicity of the building's spatial scheme is brilliantly conceived. It is divided into several discrete zones. The entrance-level zone accommodates information services, shops and a large internal piazza which complements the one outside. The core zone consists of the floors conceived as open platforms to contain exhibitions, temporary shows and administrative services, with minimum permanent subdivision structure, to be constantly adapted to new needs. (This extreme concept and the initial allocation of functions on each level were later modified.) The top floor is devoted to evening activities, including a restaurant offering a panorama of the city. Two parallel, vertical zones at the front and back of the building, 7 metres wide and 50 metres apart, contain the vertical structure, a series of spun-steel hollow columns 800 mm in diameter, each holding six 10-ton gerberettes. These flanking zones also contain circu-

lation and services. The west, facing the square, accommodates vertical and horizontal circulation systems, lifts, walkways, escape stairs and, hanging on the outside of the zone, a 150-metre-long escalator system moving 3000 people an hour and feeding all levels. The system overlooks the activities in the square and the surrounding facades, and provides a splendid view of Paris.

Seen from the piazza's amphitheatre, the structure and movement, equipment and service paraphernalia – pipes, cables, decks, stairs, towers, moving stairs and landings, something like a cross between an ocean liner and a space ship – provide a genuine late-20th-century alternative to the late-16th-century Italian architect Serlio's urban piazza backdrop. Interestingly, these elements rise in great accord with the classical facades of the surrounding buildings from previous centuries, a harmony achieved thanks to the colour of the building, its horizontality, its unexpected respect for the height of its neighbouring structures and, most importantly, thanks to an aura of an underlying common spirit of rigour

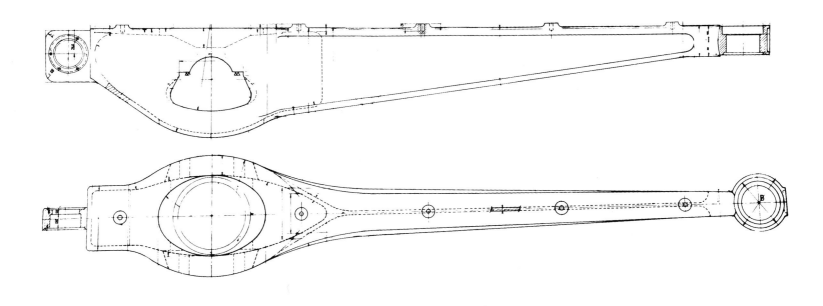

and robustness which exists between the Centre and the historical structures of Le Marais. The east zone holds all the mechanical services. As one approaches the building by car along the rue de Renard, the multi-coloured contraptions give the motorist a fascinating surprise – but this is not the case if one walks down the less-than-delightful street abutting its front. Finally, the roof zone contains air handling plant rooms (for air processing and ventilation), cooling towers and other such mechanical services.

Movement, change and flexibility were the top priorities of the Centre's programme, according to the architects. This dictated the displaying of all the building's movement systems, whether of people or works of art, all along the two facades. Even potential move-ment is allowed for in that most divisions, whether vertical or horizontal, can be taken apart and reassembled with ease; even the facades of the building can be disconnected from the columns. And the partitions of the structural movement are themselves movable, of dry construction. 'All [components] are movable and express their movability', was the credo of the architects, a cry reminiscent of the Futurists and the Constructivists.

Perhaps even more significant than the appearance of the building is its programme, projecting a new way of life. And from this point of view, it can be considered as the last building that reflects the optimism of the Enlightenment. Few can dispute the Centre's architectural consistency in the execution of its programme. What is beyond argument is that its uniqueness does not lie in disembo-died ideas about design and construction, but in the way that these ideas serve with great consistency, imagination and vigour a given programme. And in this, the Centre achieves what a grand monument is supposed to do.

(Above) Construction details

(Opposite) The rear facade

Alvaro Siza
BOUÇA SOCIAL HOUSING
(Porto, Portugal)
1973–77

In a country where social housing standards had always been inadequate, the Bouça housing development, when it was completed in 1977, offered, despite its modest standards of quality, an image of lightness, colour and one might say *alegria*, something which had been suppressed in Portugal for a long time.

This urban infill project was commissioned by the residential housing associations set up by the state in the wake of the Portuguese revolution of April 1974. It was intended to accommodate the slum dwellers of Porto who had been victims, in Siza's words, of 'rent racketeering, illegal housing, overcrowding and lack of sanitary facilities'.

Like Bruno Taut's 'Uncle Tom's Cabin' housing project for workers (1926–31) and Alvar Aalto's at Paimio (1929–33) and Sunila (1936–39), which Siza explicitly cites as his prototypes, the original design of the Bouça scheme is extremely simple and direct. A spine wall screened the scheme from the adjoining railway embankment. Perpendicular to this, four linear terraces of double maisonettes formed long courtyards. At the end of each row, facing the existing urban context, there were public facilities such as a laundry, a library and shops. Each unit was provided with every possible comfort, within the restricted budget, without catering to any exceptional demands. While alluding to the local tradition of vernacular architecture, Bouça Housing is stripped of any nationalist or scenographic elements. The rows of houses with the spine wall are intended to 'celebrate the communal values which the revolution had brought to the surface.'

The project was meant as more than a mere facility or a shelter; it was to be perceived as a cultural statement. It carried within its fabric a commentary on contemporary architecture, life and society. It was a protest against the destruction of community, the splitting of human associations, the dissolution of human contact. It was thus one of the most powerful expressions of the critical regionalist movement in Europe of the 1970s. Despite its lean, almost poverty-stricken character, its message had a tremendous appeal. Many of its formal aspects were echoed in Europe and around the world for more than a decade, especially in Spain. But it was mainly the implied aura of the scheme that inspired other

(Opposite) Conceptual sketch

(Left) Model of the original design, showing the screen wall with four housing blocks projecting from it

(Below) Plans and section

(Bottom) Front facade (left) and rear facade (right)

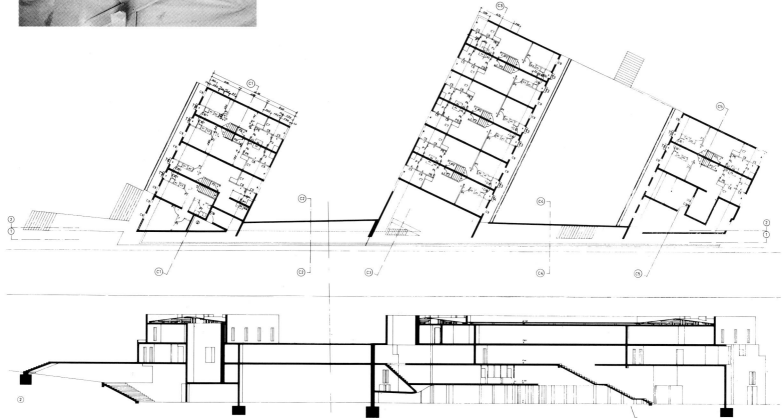

architects and that elevated Siza and his colleagues of Porto to the status of a school.

Offering an optimistic message, directness and honesty of expression, this project's regionalist populism brings to mind an equivalent tendency that lasted briefly during the late 1950s in Europe. One of its most eloquent and enthusiastic representatives was James Stirling; his Preston Infill Housing (1957–59) adhered to the 1920s and '30s image of modern architecture as an upholder of social democracy without succumbing to its formalist intellectualism.

Bouça brought back the air of social change in which architecture was a significant partner – but with an innocence which failed to foresee the upheavals of the subsequent stormy years. To the outsider, Siza made it seem for a moment as if the technocratic and bureaucratic developments which had occurred between the 1920s and the 1970s had never existed, and that the purity of the dream of avant-garde architecture remained untarnished. Unfortunately, and ironically, only two short sections of the planned four rows of houses were actually completed because of the lack of sustained political support.

Atelier d'urbanisme, d'architecture et d'informatique Lucien Kroll
ZUP PERSEIGNE
(Alençon, France)
1978

ZUP (*zone à urbaniser en priorité*) is a typical, state-subsidized, moderate-income, mega-residential project constructed using industrialized techniques between 1958 and 1969, at the end of the post-war wave of massive prefabricated construction in France. This particular one provided 2300 units for 6500 inhabitants. Within the first year of completion, 15 per cent of the constructed units showed signs of malfunction. As early as 1971, the ZUP Perseigne had become the object of specialized behavioural research which diagnosed that social life was suppressed by the empty, monotonous and alien spaces spawned by the architecture. As a result of the sociologists' recommendation, a therapeutic reconstruction of the ZUP was proposed and Lucien Kroll, on the basis of his design for *'La Mémé'* in Louvain (1968–72, pp. 44–47), was called to carry it out.

Consistent with his principles, Kroll refused to operate on the old 'pathological' plan as an outsider and to rebuild the project according to a preconceived normative plan. He chose instead to try and 'rehabilitate', or restore it to health, in accordance with what the users of the project felt was wrong with it. The first phase of the design consisted therefore in listening, like a doctor and an ethnographer: 'listening to the history of the neighbourhood, listening to the inhabitants, individually and collectively.' Once the period of diagnostic consulting was over, Kroll and his collaborators continued to pursue a participatory approach in implementing the new programmatic directives architecturally.

They inserted new units, planted trees, grew vines, paved paths, added outdoor furniture and lighting fixtures. A haphazard series of two-storey units appeared, creating the impression of a village street. New accesses, balconies, roofs, exterior surfaces, started to grow all over the old ZUP. Finally, and more importantly, changes were also carried out inside a limited number of units – not without a struggle with the local housing authorities – by knocking down walls, thus expanding the unit sizes.

Superficially, Kroll's 'interventions' looked like drawing a moustache on the Mona Lisa. This is how a bird's-eye view of his generated 'chaos', insertions of units, services and vege-

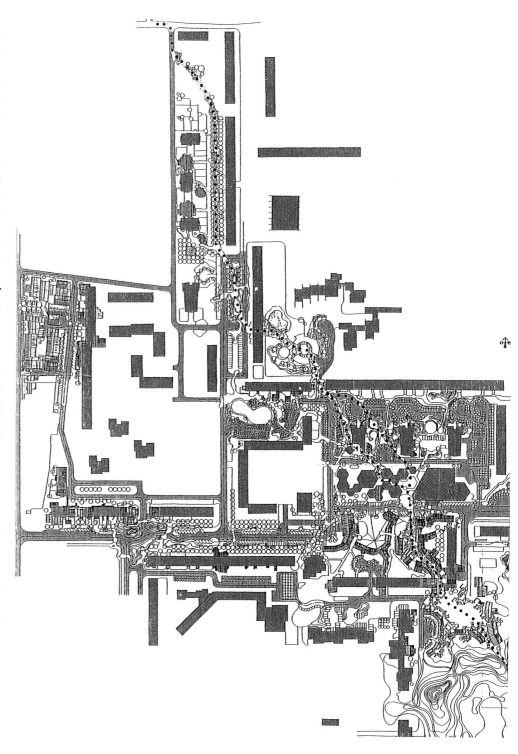

(Opposite) Urban plan

(Right) Kroll's new buildings seen against a background of the earlier development

In addition to inserting completely new houses, Kroll also made changes to existing buildings

(Below right and far right) A modification to an earlier construction; a rehabilitated facade

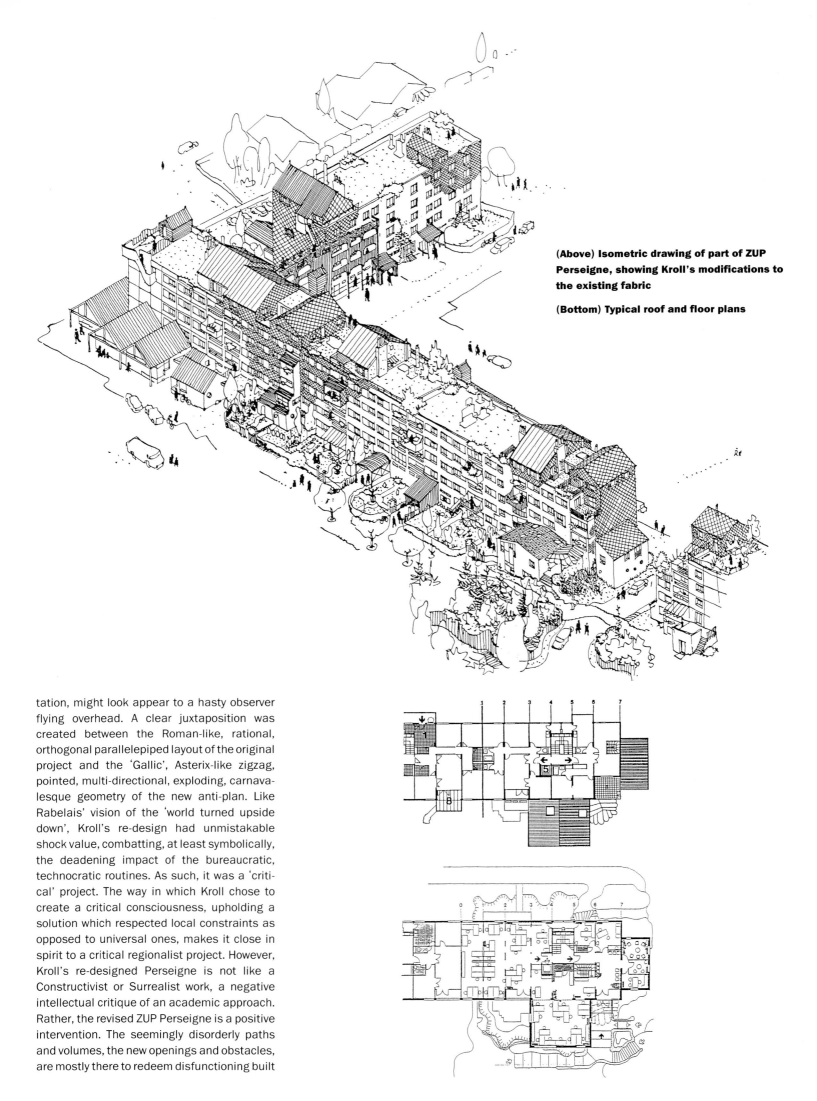

(Above) Isometric drawing of part of ZUP Perseigne, showing Kroll's modifications to the existing fabric

(Bottom) Typical roof and floor plans

tation, might look appear to a hasty observer flying overhead. A clear juxtaposition was created between the Roman-like, rational, orthogonal parallelepiped layout of the original project and the 'Gallic', Asterix-like zigzag, pointed, multi-directional, exploding, carnavalesque geometry of the new anti-plan. Like Rabelais' vision of the 'world turned upside down', Kroll's re-design had unmistakable shock value, combatting, at least symbolically, the deadening impact of the bureaucratic, technocratic routines. As such, it was a 'critical' project. The way in which Kroll chose to create a critical consciousness, upholding a solution which respected local constraints as opposed to universal ones, makes it close in spirit to a critical regionalist project. However, Kroll's re-designed Perseigne is not like a Constructivist or Surrealist work, a negative intellectual critique of an academic approach. Rather, the revised ZUP Perseigne is a positive intervention. The seemingly disorderly paths and volumes, the new openings and obstacles, are mostly there to redeem disfunctioning built

patterns, especially as they affected social operations and generated a pathology of human relations. The result is a restoration of social life, invented and inserted in the midst of severe constraints and scarce resources, accommodating residential, recreational and communal needs previously impoverished by conformist, reductive, arbitrary ideas. The intricacy of the new project, its organic picturesqueness, are not only meant to represent untamable nature: it results from building intelligently within it. If forms appear traditional, the thinking behind them is forward looking. And it is not only the political philosophy, the design methodology, that are forward looking; the very instruments of implementing them are at the cutting edge of invention. Kroll and his collaborators believe that it is through computer technology that we can achieve ultimately the best results to satisfy the emancipatory programme of what he calls 'ethnological' architecture.

Three stages in the transformation of a typical facade
(Top) The original version

(Middle) An early design stage of Kroll's intervention

(Bottom) The facade after his modifications

Neave Brown
ALEXANDRA ROAD HOUSING
(London, England)
1968–78

This is a project which created considerable animosity among critics because of its surprising initial success. To start with, it was public housing, which always arouses controversy. Next, it was unfashionable, constructed in reinforced concrete, and looked naked, brute, in the tradition of Le Corbusier. Neither in its materials, type nor overall geometrical figure did the building acknowledge its context by citation, and it was not built incrementally. Furthermore, it was planned as a high-density development, with high intensity circulation patterns and collective services.

In the ideology-loaded debates of the last fifteen years, many of the accomplishments of Alexandra Road have been overlooked. This is much to the detriment of current architectural practice, which needs to learn from experiences, both positive and negative, but especially positive, since so much bad design surrounds us with the failures that not surprisingly result from it.

Alexandra Road does not conform to the clichés of many current trends which overlook those commonsense facts that count so much in housing: that relatively generous dimen-

sions, buildings that do not obstruct one another, good lighting conditions, contact with the outside and good solid detailing are essential to public success, irrespective of stylistic, mood or institutional matters.

In many respects the uniqueness of the project is in its scale and its serenity, as if in response to the anxieties of the post-1968 shock. It relies heavily on neo-brutalist precedents which it filters and combines purely on criteria based on quality, something which undeniably gives an air of pragmatic conservatism to the project. The architects themselves refer to 18th- and early 19th-century housing which, they believe, 'established place and parity for every dwelling in which the whole exceeded the part . . . an architecture composed of elements belonging to a common culture, rendering irrelevant the sad distinction between public and private housing.'

The scheme covers an area of 6.47 ha. To the north, there runs a main railway line; to the south, there lies an area of Victorian houses extending down to St John's Wood; to the east, the shopping centre at Swiss Cottage; and to the west, a new mixed development of low and

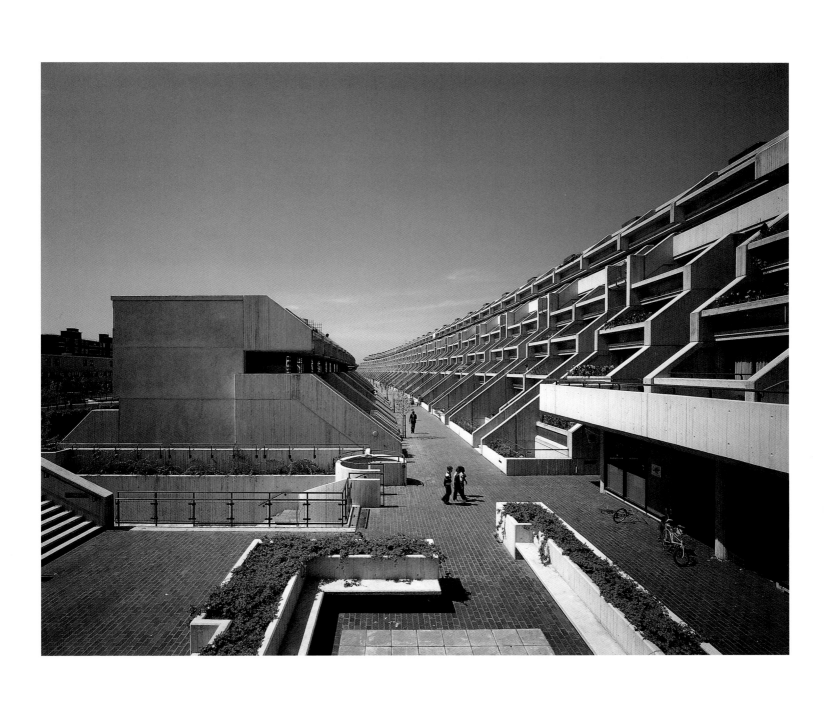

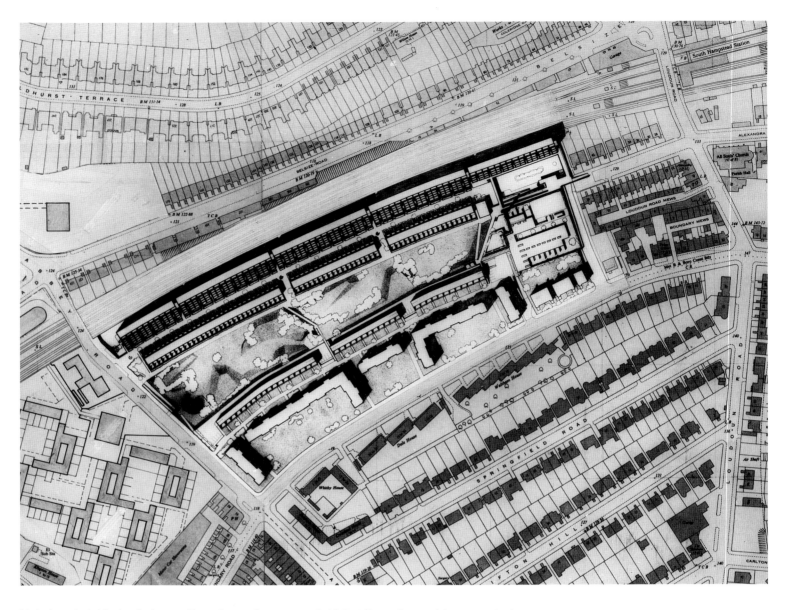

high housing blocks between the site and Kilburn.

The layout comprises two almost parallel pedestrian streets of terraced six- and four-storey housing, between which is a central park. The arrangement is similar to that of Regency or Victorian London and the scale approximates that of nearby Belsize Park.

Noise is blocked from the site by the northernmost terrace, which presents a solid wall of building against the railway track. This block is sound-insulated by anti-vibration pads in the foundations and by double glazing. A set-back section gives each dwelling a balcony open to the sky, catching sun from the east, west and south; it also provides more light and space for the pedestrian streets by reducing over-shadowing. From these streets, access is to paired dwellings around external staircases which, in the tall northern block, lead to an upper-level gallery. In addition, at intervals along this terrace, lifts link the gallery to the pedestrian streets and the ground-level garages. The lifts have large glazed panels and are set in glazed shafts. Parallel to the two main streets are paths alongside the park, which join at the vehicle centre, and continue as one, bridging the entry road to connect at ground level with the main pedestrian entrance to the scheme at Loudoun Road.

The project felicitously combines street pattern, which one would have expected to be accompanied with upright row housing, with housing organized along a terrace, which one would associate more with sites overlooking vistas. As a result, both the privacy of the houses is safeguarded and there is a resort-life air of leisure about it.

In addition to the careful proportioning of the units, what gives Alexandra Road a definite civic character and urbaneness is the curving of the street. Without resorting to collective enclosed spaces which most of the time have negative social repercussions, this offers a representation of common ground and common identity to the inhabitants.

Despite these qualities, Alexandra Road fails to overcome those difficulties of maintenance and cost of servicing that are typical of such projects of social housing. Nevertheless, if this remarkable housing has been insufficiently appreciated in the 1980s, it is to be hoped that closer attention will be given to it in the future.

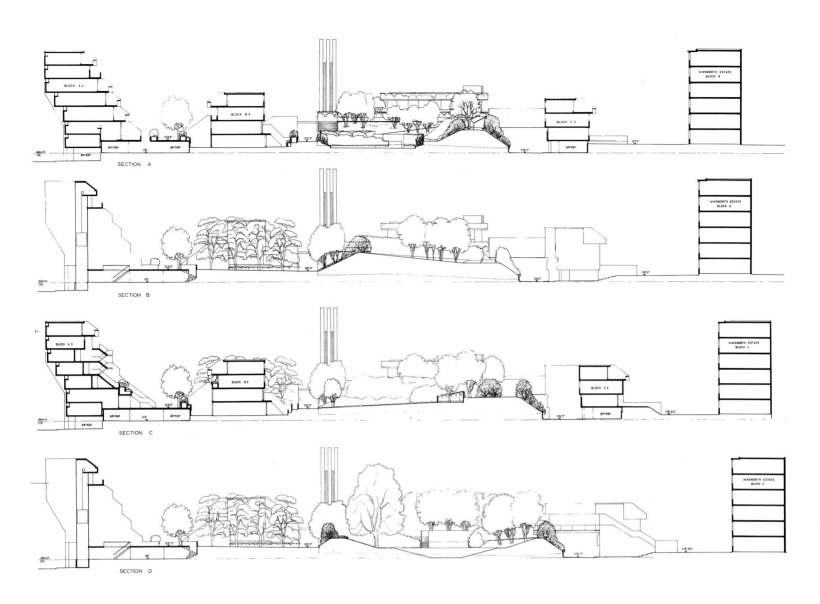

SECTION A

SECTION B

SECTION C

SECTION D

(Opposite) Diagram of the urban plan of the Alexandra Road development

(Above) Site sections

(Right) Plan of a typical unit

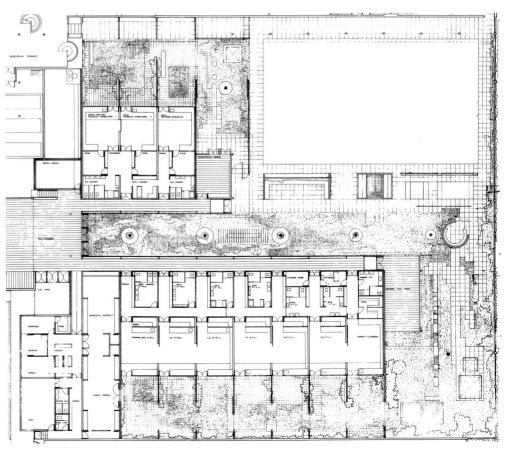

Francisco Javier Saenz de Oiza
BANCO DE BILBAO
(Madrid, Spain)
1971–78

The Banco de Bilbao in Madrid is one of the most elegant towers built in Europe since the Second World War and probably the most distinguished tall office building of the period in this book. Surprisingly, it was not primarily formal visual considerations that were the architect's main concerns in conceiving and carrying out the design; these were, instead, functional organization, the flow of information and energy conservation.

The building stands on the Paseo de la Castellana, the high-rise business section in the centre of Madrid created during the period of economic boom, in the twilight of the Franco era. It has 29 floors and an underground service area. The building is divided into two horizontal servicing duct zones. The mechanical servicing is located on the eleventh, twentieth and top floors. The top floor, under the servicing, is used for meetings and public relation functions. The auditorium and other meeting rooms are on the fifteenth floor. Most work areas are on the periphery of the building with good views and natural light.

A basic concern of the architect was the reduction of glare and overheating because of the intense sunlight. An extended peripheral awning of metal that projects at almost every storey has solved this problem and gives the building its characteristic silhouette. Together with another unusual feature, its warm hues of maroon and copper, it demonstrates the architect's sensitivity to regional contextual factors, as well as conferring on the building a sense of place, scale and craftsmanship sadly absent from the exteriors of most contemporary

(Opposite, right) The entrance

(Opposite, left) Interior

(Above) Lift

(Right) One of the rounded corners

towers. The corners of the Banco de Bilbao are rounded, and, once more, there are functional benefits to be derived from such a design: the carved niches create a better place for work. Rounded corners also have a pleasant visual impact. The curved glass is modelled on a Frank Lloyd Wright masterpiece, the Johnson Wax Building (Racine, Wisconsin, 1936–39), a detail that makes the Banco de Bilbao stand apart from the overwhelming majority of post-war office towers which have tended to follow the tradition of Mies van der Rohe.

The columns of the structure of the building are set back from the external glass wall, leaving a zone for easy circulation around its periphery. By hiding the bearing structure and the vertical service elements in this way, by minimizing the detailing of the building, curving its corners and projecting the awning elements, Oiza has given to the Banco de Bilbao an overall feeling of smoothness and continuity rather than angularity and a markedly discontinuous articulation of elements. These qualities produce the impression of a sensuously crafted object rather than a mechanically reproduced artifact. Characterized more by skin than skeleton, the tower integrates well with the surrounding buildings, which explains the rather warm feelings of the inhabitants of Madrid towards this imposing structure.

The building also differs from the majority of office towers in that its main entrance is neither monumental nor forbidding. One descends to enter from ground level. The doors are set back from the plane of the facade, thus providing a recessed, covered area planted with greenery, which at once invites and protects the visitor. Once in the lobby, one is surrounded by an unexpectedly polychromatic, cheerful interior. It is a double-floor space which includes a reception area, the entrances to the lifts and a ramp.

The organization of the tower follows the prototypes of the 1930s and '40s: there is a central service core, while most offices are attached to the periphery of the building. From the point of view of livability and efficiency, this solution remains an unsurpassable prototype.

In defending his functionalist position, Saenz de Oiza echoes the pre-war champion of anti-formalism, Hannes Meyer, who, submitting his proposal for the Palace for the League of Nations in 1926–27, said that 'as an organic structure it expresses sincerely that it wishes to be a building for work and cooperation . . . As a deliberately conceived man-made product, it presents itself as in legitimate contrast with nature. This building is neither beautiful nor horrible. It asks to be evaluated as a structural invention.'

With a renewed interest, in the 1990s, in realism, Oiza's propensity for problem-solving rather than critical commentary, functionality rather than rhetoric, innovation rather than stereotyping, offers an important precedent.

(This page) Exterior view and section

(Opposite, above) Plan of the twenty-seventh floor

(Opposite, below) General plan of the ground floor

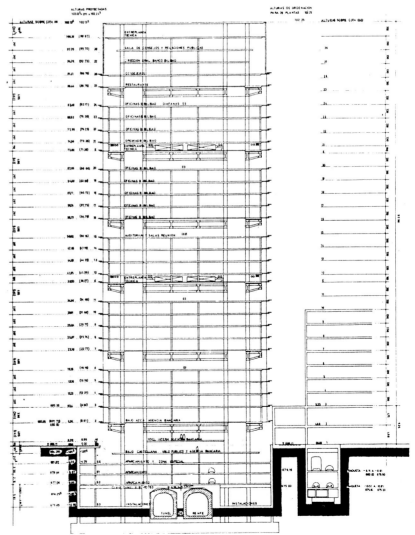

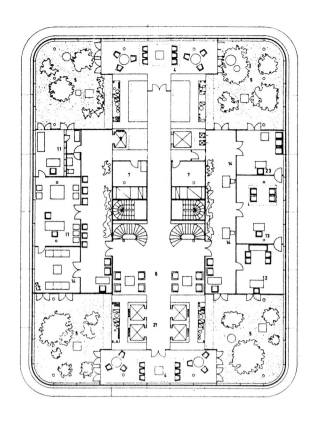

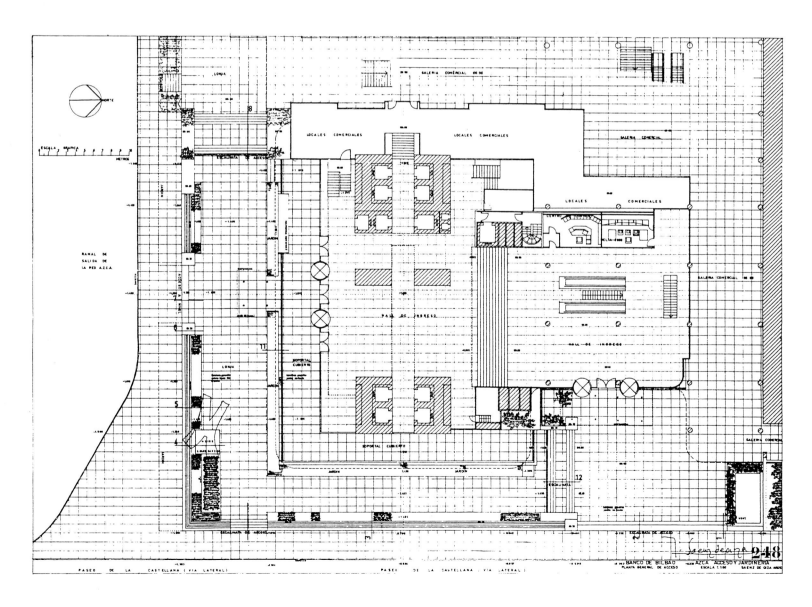

Nicholas Grimshaw and Partners Ltd
SPORTS HALL FOR IBM
(Hampshire, England)
1980–82

Very much in the tradition of 'high-tech' architecture, Nicholas Grimshaw, a one-time collaborator of Terry Farrell, believes in the virtues of technology and in exposing it on the surface of a building. In his Sports Hall for IBM, one of his first projects, the five space-frame portals that support the walls and roof of this 18-metre long, clear-span building are painted black to stand out, somewhat exhibitionistically, against the white exterior of the building. The pivot at their base and the diagonal bracing that connects them is bare and open to view. As a spatial concept, this is a 'universal space' as it was practised in the 1940s, using updated technology and a light structure. In borrowing techniques previously associated exclusively with industrial buildings, Grimshaw is very much in the tradition of Mies's Crown Hall in Chicago (1952–56), Charles and Ray Eames' house (1949) and Jean Prouvé's Palais des Expositions in Grenoble of 1967 (especially in the hall's curving corners).

The wall panels of the IBM Centre are highly glazed in a laminate of grey-tinted, dark

plastic. 5250 mm long by 500 mm high and 42 mm thick, they are simple industrial door panels, bolted at each corner to cleats on the frame. PVC sheeting and preformed upstands of rigid PVC were used for the roof, a solution that makes it watertight, unlike the glass and steel roof of Crown Hall, the great prototype of clear-span buildings, as John Winter has pointed out in his discussion on the building in the *Architectural Review*. The gaps that separate the four walls and the gaps between walls and ceiling are filled with fibreglass. This has the additional advantage of translucency and lets in natural light without glare. At night when the lights are on, the translucent rounded corners, viewed from the outside, are luminous.

The undemanding programme for a low-cost building equipped for badminton and other indoor sports allows for future expansion. The exposed external structure consists of five tubular steel trussed portal frames 5.25 metres high at the centre and spanning 18 metres. This results in flush walls inside. The

cladding sandwich panels are bolted to cleats welded to the main frame and to the gable mullions. The mullions have been detailed for easy modification of the structure. The entire gable wall can be unbolted and taken down.

This shed is appropriately easy to use and, more significantly, easy to understand. Its athletic image of lightness and physical agility is achieved without having to resort to unnecessary violations of space, a Venturi 'duck', or to Venturi's other roadside publicity decorations.

Moreover, it sits in the middle of the green park, where the intricate contraption of its space-frame supports, pivoted at the base, gives a strong impression of the 'machine in the garden'. But if one looks at the same elements as space-ordering devices, something of the English classical-picturesque tradition also comes to mind: the placing of simple, articulate, highly geometrical structures in nature to stress its wilderness.

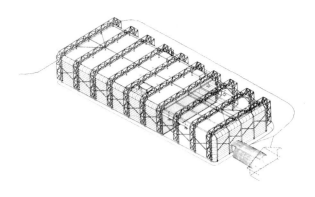

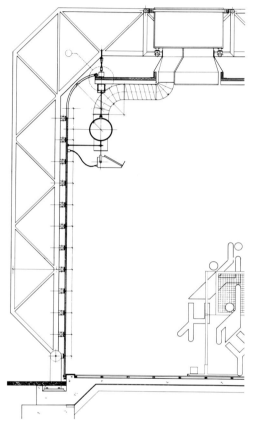

(Opposite) Exterior view

(Top) Isometric view, including possible future extension

(Above) Detailed section of the facade

(Right) Detail of the facade

Oscar Niemeyer Office
COMMUNIST PARTY HEADQUARTERS
(Paris, France)
1965–80

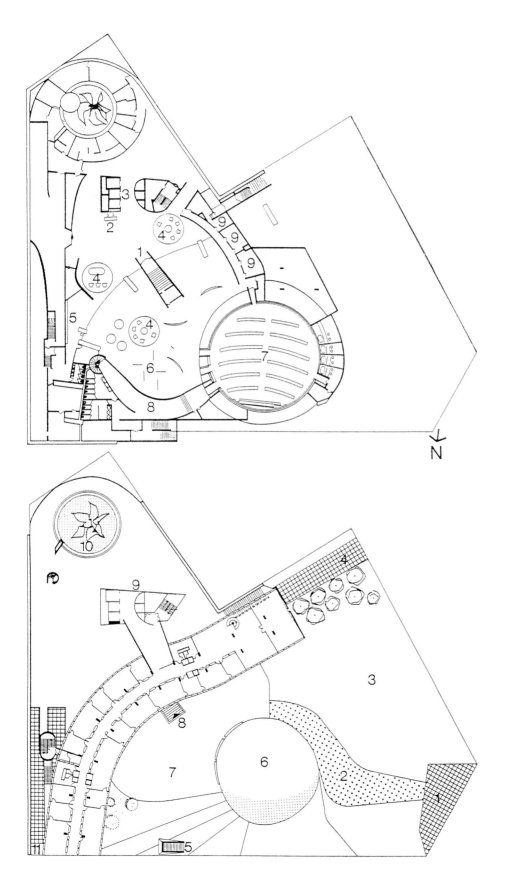

(Left) Ground floor plan of the Communist Party Headquarters
Key: 1 main entrance; 2 reception; 3 lifts; 4 waiting area; 5 library; 6 exhibition area; 7 Hall of the Central Committee; 8 access to meeting rooms in the basement; 9 offices

(Below left) Typical floor plan
Key: 1 entrance from the Place du Colonel Fabien; 2 pedestrian ramps; 3 green area; 4 service entrance from the Blvd de la Villette; 5 entrance from the Avenue Mathurin Moreau; 6 cupola; 7 esplanade; 8 main entrance; 9 service tower; 10 patio; 11 entrance to car park

(Opposite) The facade seen by night and by day – the cupola covers the Hall of the Central Committee

At the height of its political power, the French Communist Party decided to commission Oscar Niemeyer as the architect of its headquarters in Paris – with Jean Prouvé as the engineer of its building's curtain wall facade. By 1972, a year still reverberating from the May '68 revolt, to which the PCF had shown a neutral if not hostile attitude, the silhouette of the building had already risen over the site. Embodying the heroic antics of the old cultural, political, technological avant-garde, it made Niemeyer and Prouvé appear like two sacred cows distinctly out of tune, a monument to

irrevocably lost certainties. One has only to glance at the PCF headquarters and compare them to Kroll's (pp. 44–47, 92–95) and Rossi's (pp. 56–63) projects to see how deep was the chasm separating the two sides of the May '68 divide.

Yet, twenty years on, with 'negative' historicist design fading away, and the interest in the pleasure of formal invention and in the re-emergence of technological construction, the Niemeyer and Prouvé building suddenly appears both youthful and relevant, thanks not only to the unique personal talents of its

creators but also to many of the general architectural principles it employed. The affinities with Koolhaas's Dance Theatre (1987, pp. 182–85), de Portzamparc's Cité de la Musique (1990, pp. 190–93) and Hans Kollhoff's Luisenplatz Housing project (1988, pp. 210–13) are suggestive of how much the present generation of designers responds to Niemeyer and Prouvé, and for good reasons.

Functionalist principles demanded that each major function in a building be expressed by a particular volume and gave to this volume a form fit for the function it contained. The rule

system is conventional, but its flexibility has proved indisputable, allowing the form of each volume to change in accordance with changes in function and without disturbing the rest of the volumes. In this functionalist framework, Niemeyer considers the form of the building to be the result of a fusion between internal and external 'forces'. The internal ones are comprised of the requirements of the operations the building contains: a conference hall, an exhibition space and office spaces for the secretariat. By external ones he means the conditions of the site on which the project is

placed. These include the formation of the ground, the views from within and the orientation.

The curved form of the facade, for example, emerged, in Niemeyer's words, 'naturally from the necessity to hide the neighbouring building and to create between it and the new building the spaces necessary for vertical access that we wanted outside the building in order to guarantee the indispensable flexibility of its interior'. The most interesting aspect of the interior, he finds, is the main hall. In the same vein, he explains that 'we did not want it on pilotis with the glassed-in hall giving onto the street or gardens. This would have occupied the entire site and precluded that correct relation between volumes and empty space, all too often forgotten by architects. Therefore, we designed it half buried: a great hall that the small entrance makes even greater, with the foyer, the exhibition hall, the little bookstore and the auditorium, its cupola emerging onto the garden like major elements of the composition.'

Seen from the air, one might read into the composite configuration the hammer and sickle emblem of the PCF, but the sobriety and rigour of the project do not support this. The Baroque-like effect, as one moves around and through the streamlined contours of the building, the overpowering presence of the materials, the intricacy of the industrial details and the rich repertory of compositional arrangements – stairs to planes, columns to panels, panels to walls – may not be startlingly original. They are, however, authentically and 'grammatically' represented, condensed and displayed in a small, compact space and in an almost didactic, erudite manner, offering a textbook application of modernist architecture at its most purist and rigorist phase. And it is remarkable how inexhaustible such canonical modernism still is, decades after Niemeyer's collaboration with Le Corbusier in Brazil.

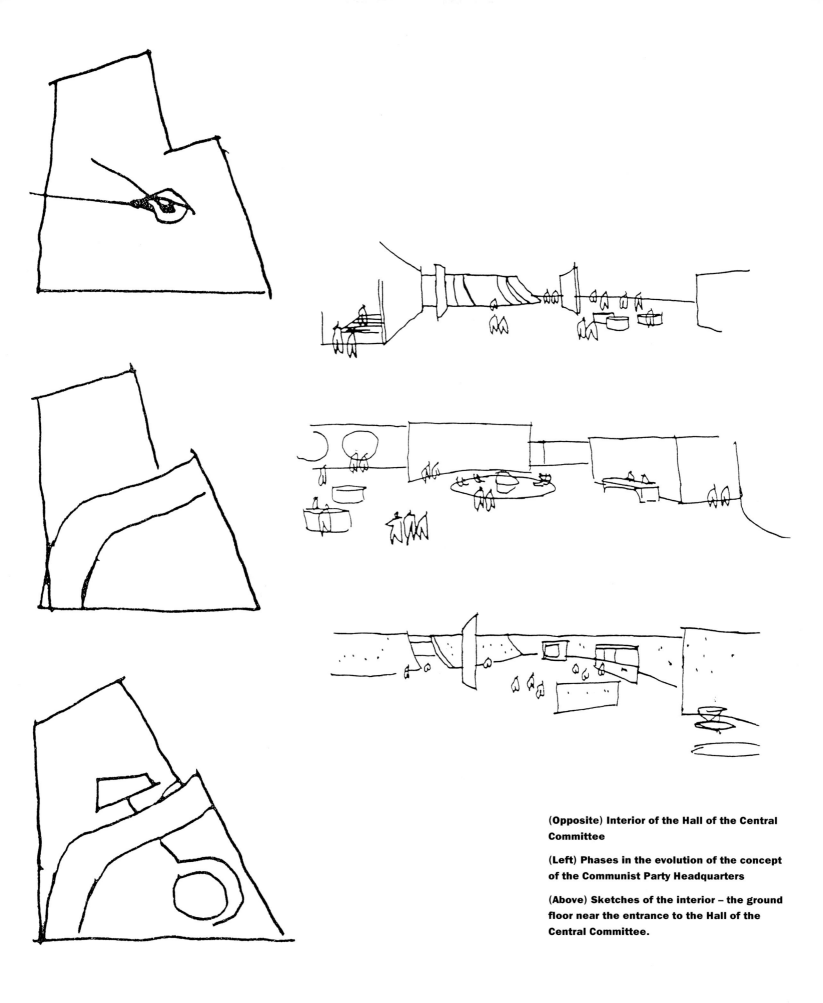

(Opposite) Interior of the Hall of the Central Committee

(Left) Phases in the evolution of the concept of the Communist Party Headquarters

(Above) Sketches of the interior – the ground floor near the entrance to the Hall of the Central Committee.

Atelier Gustav Peichl
ORF-STUDIO
(Graz, Austria)
1978–1981

Austria is a federation in which each state of the union has been encouraged to develop its own cultural identity. To reinforce this policy, each has its own broadcasting station, and six have been built since 1970, all designed by Gustav Peichl. Except for only slight variations, virtually all are identical.

It is no coincidence that Gustav Peichl is also a highly popular socio-political cartoonist working under the pen-name of 'Ironimus'. Taken as a whole, the broadcasting stations are obviously meant to enshrine the uniformity and conformism of his fellow countrymen. They are perhaps also allegorical comments on what happens when creative forces come into contact with bureaucratic control.

Like the one in Graz, each broadcasting station presents an image of contradiction and collision. On one side there is a swirling, dynamic, spiralling shape in which the studio work takes place. This is modelled on an eccentrically diverse variety of prototypes of spirals which Peichl identifies as a nautilus,

the Disc of Phaestos, Bruce Goff's snail house, the volute of an Ionic capital and Marcel Duchamp's Anaemic-Cinema. On the other, we have a matrix-like grid plan, symbolizing the regimented and rigid orthogonal matrix grid of classical architecture. This is where the offices are housed. The sharp corner of the latter cleaves the former, causing it to splinter and fan out in irregular, calibrated, discontinuous wedges.

The point of collision of the two building plans is the fulcrum of the entire complex. Onto its cylindrical well, which contains a staircase, are hinged the office block with its stepped articulation and precise, orthogonal composition, and the 'fan' of the studios. However strange and complex, the plan pattern is extremely economical. It allows most of the circulation to be concentrated at the centre, which makes a complicated building convenient to use.

But the significance of these forms goes beyond the search either for humorous effect

or for functionality, to the very heart of what we have referred to elsewhere as the 'classical poetics of order' and the poetics of pre-war modernism which was predicated on the negation of the classical poetics. This building is a playful, creative exercise based on a systematic, disciplined, rigorous knowledge of both classical and anti-classical modes. Peichl inherited this knowledge from the older generation of Viennese architects like Adolf Loos and has helped to transmit it to the younger generation of Austrian architects like Klaus Kada (pp. 208–209) and Coop Himmelblau (pp. 220–23), for whom he has been a great inspiration.

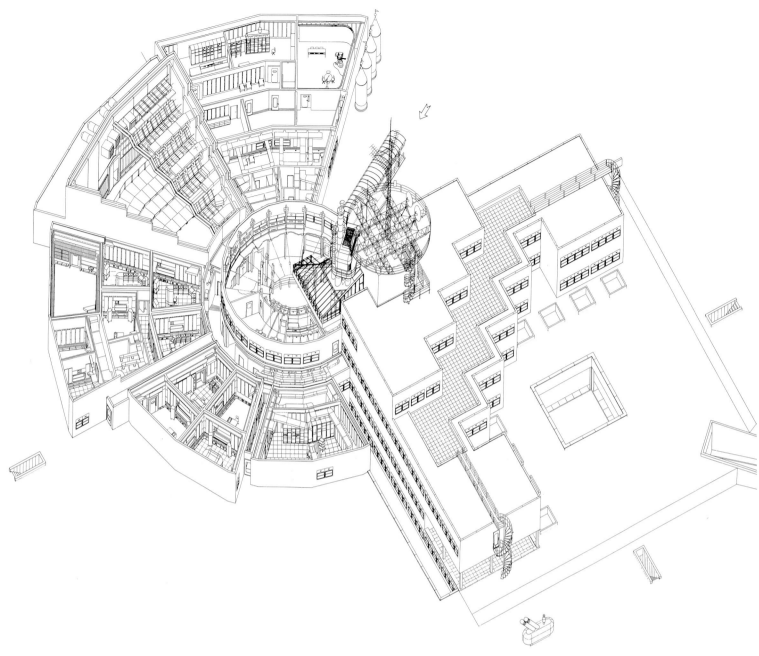

(Opposite) Entrance and general exterior view of Peichl's ORF-Studio

(Above) Axonometric drawing

(Right) Light shaft at the building's centre

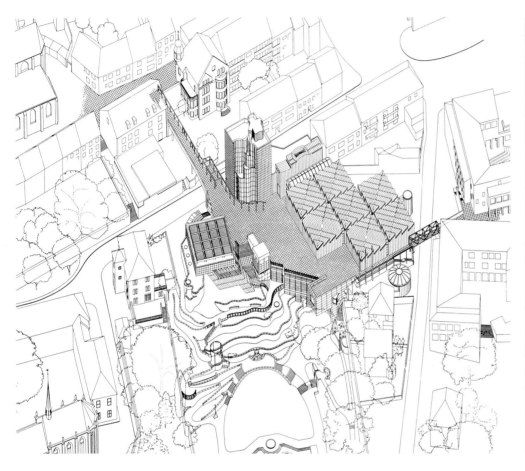

Throughout a long series of architectural projects, Hollein has declared his conviction that architecture is above all an 'art of space', of relationships between pure solids and voids, as this was defined by 19th-century aesthetics. His investigations, however, in the design of furniture, industrial products, shops and display rooms, which manifest a great agility and knowledge in ordering and manipulating spatial structures, are ultimately dominated by a 'narrative desire'. Almost every shop designed by Hollein tells a different story using iconic architectural means, and the ingredients of each fabula are objects rather than abstract relations of voids (pp. 72–73). In fact, in much of Hollein's work narrative displaces spatial composition.

The Mönchengladbach museum was Hollein's first major constructed work in which 'negative space' was the predominant building block of the architecture, an idea he first tried out in his design for Washington University's Experimental Theater (1963–64). The spatial composition of the museum is not a goal in itself, and as with many of his earlier smaller projects, such as galleries and stores, it perspicuously serves to preserve and present to the public a number of works of art.

By contrast to the idea of a museum as a universal, neutral container where objects float in seemingly unlimited space, arrested only temporarily by free panels, Hollein's approach has been to provide a variety of spaces – wide or small, open or closed, circular, square or winding – which serve the specific attributes of the objects displayed in a specific sequence. The feeling of individuality is further enhanced by the dissimilarity of entrances, ramps, stairways, bridges. Spatial contrast is underlined by the contrasting multiple viewpoints and contact with the outside. Natural light comes through skylights and large windows; artificial light, when needed, is neon. The sense of overlapping narratives survives in the routing and the ensuing variety of spatial types.

The commitment to the individuality, discreteness and multiformity of space complements the museum's programme, which demands a variety of settings in order to display a multitude of objects in different lighting and volumes of space and at different distances (not to mention shifting curatorial attitudes). Most museums that provide a universal space normally try to meet these requirements with ad-hoc panels and lighting installations.

Despite the overriding attention to the organization of the interior spaces, the integration of the complex within its urban context has not been overlooked. Rather than developing the external skin of the building as a quasi-autonomous system, a variable tissue that responds to the different surrounding conditions – a path followed to a great extent in the Sainsbury Wing of London's National Gallery (pp. 272–75) – Hollein uses here, as in the interior, purely spatial volumetric means, with great success. The spatial components of the

project are 'folded' to fit the spaces inbetween and around existing urban constraints. They are attached around a wide, sand-paved platform, which forms the roof of the museum's lower levels, while on ground level it serves as a plaza which provides access to the side street and gardens. A subdued classicist entrance contrasts with the expanse of the plaza and the soaring volumes of a gothicizing tower.

In Hollein's museum, there is no sense of tortured investigation about time and the interdependence of present and past, as in the Merida museum by Moneo (pp. 148–51). Despite the presence of architectural motifs, such as the classical-looking entrance, that have strong associations with the past, the Städtisches Museum lives in the context of the present, a context of pure spatial events. Equally absent is any conflict between private and civic ways of life. The building is neither hidden behind nor overwhelmed by the surrounding urban fabric. As in the case of Stirling's extension to the Staatsgalerie in Stuttgart (pp. 126–31), the fictional and poetic worlds evoked by the contents of the museum, different salient worlds, are implied by the way in which the building itself is an outsider amid its urban surroundings. But in contrast to Stirling's flamboyant civic architecture, which reaches out to invite people in, Hollein's museum is like a visitor from another world, a version of the end of this century's idea of a *temenos*, a temple, a world within a world. Its style is neither the idealist, eclectic historicism of the 19th-century museum, nor is it the Miesian, transcendental and neo-idealist temple. What it aims to convey is a belief in the idea of art as coherence and purity. Placed solemnly between hill and city centre, its sand-finished walls, its glass, steel, chrome and aluminium are like a mantle emphasizing its silky, silvery strangeness.

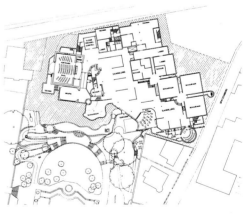

(Opposite) Axonometric projection of the museum and surrounding site

(Top) Looking towards the entrance

(Above) Ground floor plan

Antonio Barrionuevo Ferrer
HOUSING BLOCK IN PINO MONTANO
(Seville, Spain)
1981–83

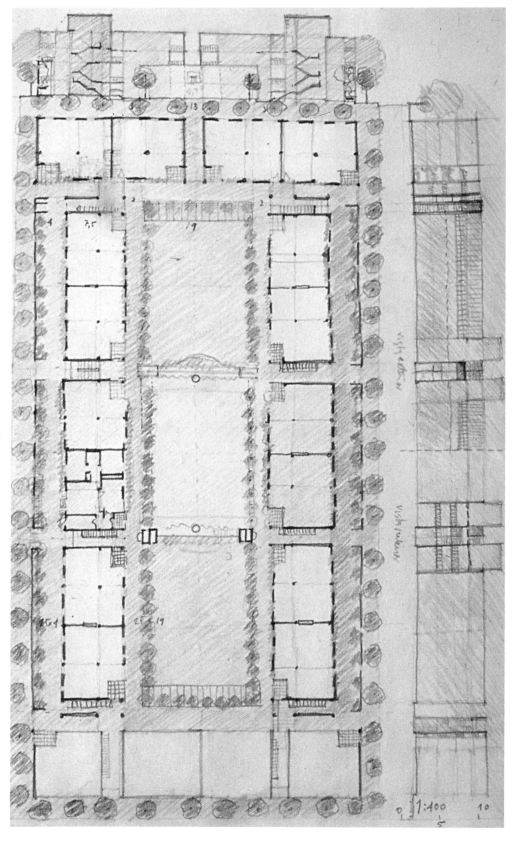

This housing project for eighty agrarian fami-
lies is situated in Pino Montano, where the
periphery of Seville gives way to the vast
expanses of the *huertas*, or fields of the
agricultural heartland, an area left outside the
general planning policies of 1960s and '70s.
Antonio Barrionuevo saw in this project the
chance to attempt 'a new type of communal
dwelling for its humble proprietors that would
contribute, as a new alternative, to giving a new
form to the working class housing other than
that which characterized the metropolitan
condition inside Seville.'

Antonio Barrionuevo, like Giancarlo De Carlo
(pp. 198–201) and Alvaro Siza (pp. 90–91),
placed major emphasis on collective space, its
hierarchical structure and its collective
memory. He tried to recapture 'the way in which
the population of Seville occupies the street,
the square or the internal courts (the renowned
corral) of traditional neighbourhoods, as well
as the different degrees of privacy that free
space possesses, from the street to the private
patio.' To do this, he has opted for a perimeter
block, a spatial schema which provides ventilation and orientation but also offers the possibility of creating a communal, open space which
is even more public than the traditional patio,
but which still preserves the patio's relative
privacy and collective intimacy.

Beyond iconographic considerations, in this working class, low-budget housing, through its colours, materials and scale, Barrionuevo has tried to instil a sense of joyfulness. Without succumbing to imitation and nostalgia, other regional devices have been applied, such as a temple-monument to mark the centre of the patio. Above the entrances, the structures are covered in the same traditional ceramic tiles which were used on the mudejar minarets that were transformed into church towers. These are intended, according to the architect, as 'signs of identity of the collectivity'. Pergolas for shade, benches for meetings, kiosks, orange and palm trees, running water, all suggest not only the local gardens and patios, but also the 19th-century squares in the historic centre of Seville.

The design of this housing block bears all the features typical of the regionalist trend. so dominant in Spain. Barrionuevo has remarked that in this work he was trying to bring back all those native elements which were 'lacking in the panorama of social housing of our country for so long'. If critical regionalism succeeds only in this, in bringing back this sense of *alegría* (traditional joyfulness), its task in preserving the sense of local community has been accomplished.

(Opposite, left) General plan and sections

(Opposite, right) Conceptual drawing

(Above) The interior court

(Right) Typical unit plan

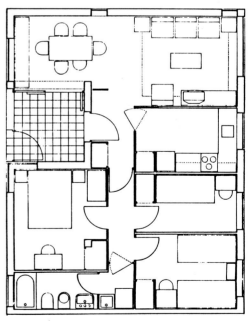

Foster Associates Ltd
RENAULT PARTS DISTRIBUTION CENTRE

(Swindon, England)
1980–83

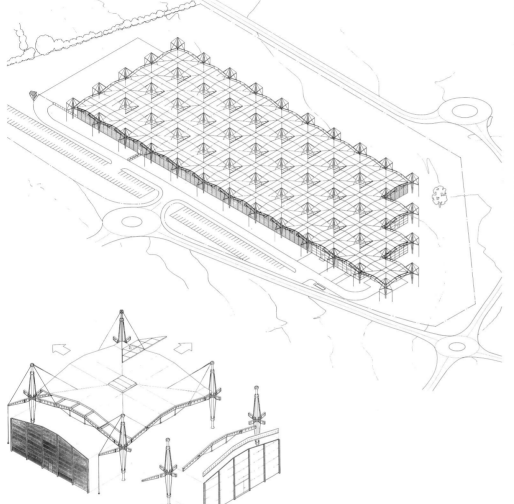

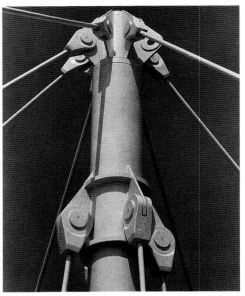

(Above, left) Isometric view of the Renault Centre

(Left) A structural bay

(Above) Detail of the top of a mast

(Opposite) General view

Norman Foster's ideas about design are often seen as highly iconoclastic applications of unprecedented technological inventions. In fact, this is merely an impression gained from his bold use of industrial components, his emphasis on strong outlines without shadow modulations, on muscled figures on the outside and loud colour, sometimes reminiscent of a Fernand Léger painting turned into architecture. And like Léger's pictorial universe, Foster's architectural world and predilection for newness has a long tradition: Charles and Ray Eames, Jean Prouvé, Buckminster Fuller, not to mention ship and aeroplane design, with which the building has not only an elective affinity, but of which it is a direct technological citation. In addition to antecedents, Foster's style also has contemporaries, such as

Richard Rogers' Fleetguard manufacturing and distribution centre in Quimper, France (1981), which, like Foster's Renault Centre, also uses masts and a suspension system for the roof.

The Renault Centre accommodates offices, a restaurant and an exhibition space, and is eventually intended to expand to a 30,000-square-metre warehouse with 10,000 square metres of office space. The emphasis is on flexibility. The building is constructed on an irregularly shaped sloping site of 6.5 hectares using a single, regular, square grid. In order to adapt to the site's configuration, a number of grid units have been removed from one side of the plan, a solution that keeps the mutilation of the overall order of space to a minimum. On the other hand, to satisfy the needs of eventual

development, the plan can grow by adding units over time in any direction, without disturbing the basic grid system.

Each unit of the grid is 7.5 metres high at its lowest point and 9.5 metres at the apex. The roof of each unit is suspended from cables attached to a central 16-metre-high, pre-stressed, circular mast of rolled, hollow steel, with 8 radiating steel beams, very much as in Buckminster Fuller's 4D structures of the 1920s. Unlike Fuller's free-standing units, however, Foster's 'suspended umbrellas' are assembled to form a system. As a result, the partly cantilevered, partly hung beams of the units come together to unite into arches, which in turn are strengthened by a system of cables. Construction follows the 'guy' principle: weak structural elements are reinforced at their

particularly weak points. In the case of the long span of the Renault arched roof, reinforcement is implemented through the use of an under-spanning cable and two studs in combination with external cable stayed strengthening. It is an elaborate, highly reliable structure where suspension and support are strategically combined to maximize its effectiveness and efficiency. But it is not only economy that is gained through this intricate space system. The structure is an essay on how forces travel in space and how materials behave, a cognitive mapping of how resolution and composition of forces work, how compression and tension stresses combine.

Natural lighting and transparency are key features of the building. Light comes from the sides as well as from the roof, a clear glass panel being placed at each column. In addition, a roof-light unit made out of double-skin, translucent PVC louvres is positioned in the centre of each module. These units, placed strategically at the apex of the roof system, can be opened to ventilate the space. The external walls of the space are made out of special panels of expanded polyurethane foam insulation encased between two sheets of steel. Roof lights and walls are glazed with an assembly of reinforced glass, the overall construction detail being that of the Pilkington 'Planar' system.

The office, showroom and restaurant furniture, the chairs and storage units, are a combination of special systems designed by the architects and items re-used from other Renault facilities.

The building offers a wonderful series of connections, of intricate joints, of details of compression and tension, which have an emblematic quality, almost as elegant and memorable as a classical Ionic capital. The masts too have an emblematic character, half resembling machine parts, half totemic, anthropomorphic figures that appear to hover in the open landscape.

(Left and opposite, top) Detail and sketch of external staircase against the facade

(Opposite, centre) Entrance hall and showroom

(Below) Distant view of the Centre from the floodplain

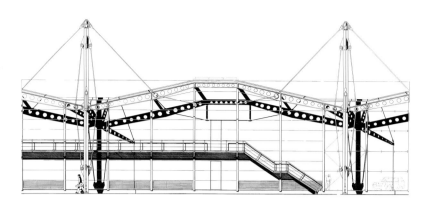

Building Workshop Renzo Piano
SCHLUMBERGER INDUSTRIAL SITE
(Paris, France)
1981–84

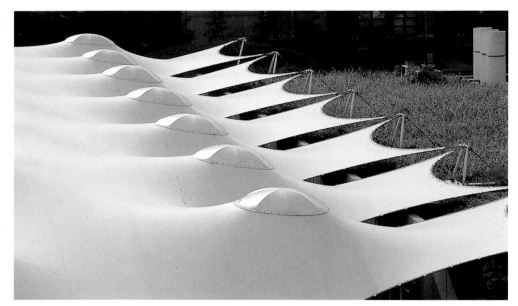

(Left) The translucent fibreglass membrane coated with teflon, seen from above and below

(Opposite) The support points of the membrane, viewed from below

This project followed soon after Piano's collaboration with Richard Rogers on the Centre Pompidou (pp. 84–89). Although it was located outside the city centre of Paris, the Schlumberger project had to submit to greater constaints, which defined its particular challenge.

It represented an early attempt, typical of the 1980s, to deal with the problem of an obsolescent industrial structure without demolishing it. Similar projects were the old Fiat plant in Turin, the Lingotto, and the old Pirelli plant in Milan, the La Biccocca factory complex. In both these cases, the creative contribution of the architects was thought to be important; the definition of the programme was very much part of the problem posed to them. By contrast, Schlumberger had a very clear idea of what re-use meant: to turn the old factories into a new research centre, or, to use Lewis Mumford's terms, to transform a 'palaeo-technic' workplace into a 'neo-technic' one.

As Piano stated in an interview, 'in practical terms we [had to] oversee the firm's transition from assembly line to the computer: a very stimulating experience. The president of the company asked me, at the beginning, to modernize the old site without erasing the industrial memory of the factory's original activities. What happened was this: while working on the headquarters, we ended up also working on the reorganization of the firm. Having started from the container, we arrived at the contained.'

Piano tried to implement architecturally a programme that had already been well defined by the organization. His approach was to respect the roughness of the old structures

and the memory of the hardness of the old work style, on the one hand; and, on the other, to emphasize through the greatest contrast the character of the new conditions of work. Two strategies were followed. First, the restoration of nature amid brutal industrial blight and, second, the installation of a new artifact expressing the qualities of the neo-technic age – intelligence, openness, friendliness.

The main factory, located in the middle of the site, was torn down and replaced by a garden designed by Piano in collaboration with Alexandre Chemetoff. This came to surround, smother and even break into the older buildings in the form of greenhouses, so reversing the previous process that had characterized the spread of industrialization. 'Often', explained Piano, 'construction has suffocated, overloaded, killed nature. This is why when I have to deal with a re-use project, I tend, on the contrary, to favour nature over the city.'

Complementary to the garden was a tent whose structure did not serve any specific operation. It was simply a protected 'forum' where many activities could occur. It did, however, serve an important iconographic function; like the garden, it contrasted the new ways with the old ways of production and, implicitly, the old style of management with the new, enlightened one. It also reflected on the nature of the product itself – the old industrial one being hardware, the result of processed matter, the new electronic one being software, the result of processed information. Finally, the tent served to demonstrate the current state of knowledge of structural laws. As in the case of Norman Foster's Renault Parts Distribution Centre (1980–83, pp. 116–19), the Schlumberger tent offered a chance to show how structural forces operate in space and the optimal allocation of matter whereby maximal spans are achieved with minimum resources. Certainly, the vocabulary of the tent and its highly expressive contrasting components – masts, strings, tissue – are excellent means towards this goal, probably the best, as yacht

design has demonstrated in the past. The tissue used was fibreglass membrane spun in France and woven in Germany, a self-cleaning material of excellent luminosity which took two months to put together. Arup Associates contributed towards finalizing the form of the structure.

The tent is asymmetrical, the north side supported by 'palm trees', the south by rods abutted to the walls of the forum. The result is a weightless image of flying, although not like Coop Himmelblau's Rooftop Remodelling (pp. 220–23) or the expressionistic dynamism of Santiago Calatrava's railway stations (pp. 254–57, 284–85). This is an explicitly light surface whose form results from the play and balance of forces. On a different plane, one does not contemplate for too long the abstractly representational qualities of the structure without being struck as was the photographer Deidi Von Schaewen by the subliminal metaphor at play in its sinuous curves and inflections.

(Opposite, above) An existing industrial building, converted to a new use, is colonized by the garden

(Opposite, centre page) Site sections

(Right and above) Plan and aerial view of the site

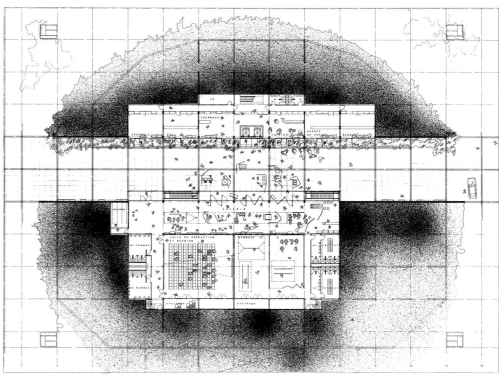

Michael Hopkins & Partners
RESEARCH LABORATORIES FOR SCHLUMBERGER
(Cambridge, England)
1984

The Schlumberger oil company required a scientific facility for testing machinery for oil exploration, drilling and fluid mechanics, rock and wellbore physics, and related computer-based research. Accordingly, Hopkins' building contains scientists' offices, laboratories, a kitchen, computer stations, a service yard and a drilling test station, as well as administrative offices, a restaurant and a terrace.

The concept of the plan is indebted to a spatial schema developed by Serge Chermayeff in his work on the prototypical organization of buildings. Hopkins' building is a skilful application of this most functional model, first reflected in projects by the members of the Team X group at the end of the 1960s, then exemplified with ingenuity by Piano and Rogers' Pompidou Centre (pp. 84–89), and in part by the Medical Faculty of Aachen of Weber, Brandt & Partners (pp. 168–71). Following Chermayeff's model, the Schlumberger Laboratories are divided into parallel zones, the outer ones reserved for activities which are the most service orientated and private in nature, while the central spine is taken up by communal and general purpose functions. The space in between these two topological extremes of the spectrum is allocated to activities which are functionally intermediary. The merits of such a layout are evident in Hopkins' plan. The scientific researchers are offered the maximum of privacy, tranquillity and view, the laboratories the best accessibility. Researchers and personnel are provided with opportunities for contact in conveniently central areas. Without any major disruption in the organization of function and services, the building can be expanded at the two ends of the spine, reproducing the same principles of the basic plan.

Demountable, PVC-laced, ship-board panels make up the internal partitions and also form a storage wall system. 50 per cent of the corridor walls are glazed while doors are plate glass. The ceilings are covered in acoustic metal tiles. Servicing is carried out from the floor. This is also the case for the complex machinery for the drilling test station and underground high-pressure pump chamber, as well as the ventilation system which draws fresh air from the outside and serves all areas, including the

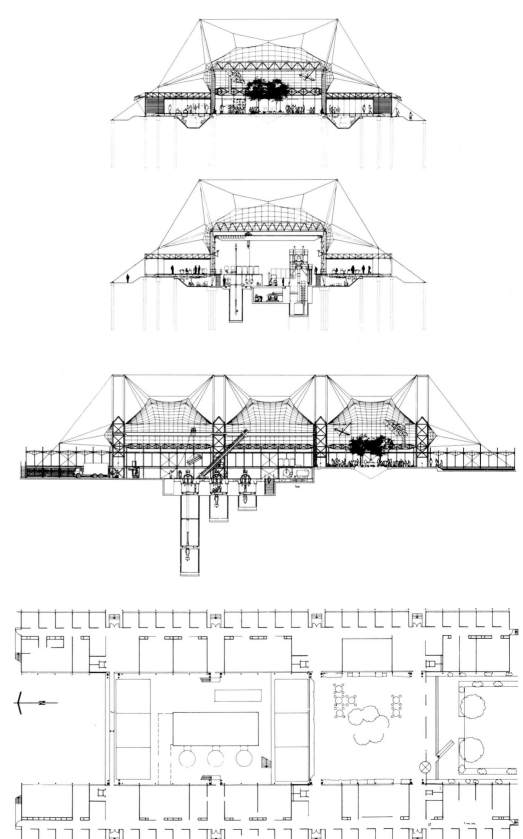

(Opposite, top to bottom) Cross sections through the winter garden and test station; longitudinal section; plan

(Top) Detail of the construction

(Above) Two views of the structure from a distance

sealed, air-conditioned, internal laboratories. Most of the heating of the spine areas of the building comes from the surrounding zones of the laboratories, an additional benefit of the layout. Functionally, as Peter Rice has pointed out, the suspended roof system enhances the ambience of internal areas of the spine. The translucent teflon membrane hoisted above the flat roof of the building, or above the winter garden and restaurant, which have no intermediary roof, admits high-quality natural light.

As in the case of the buildings of Norman Foster and Richard Rogers, the structure is deliberately exposed to view from the outside. Three zones of construction coincide with the tripartite functional division of the plan. The two zones formed by the research wings are spanned by trusses from which a flat roof, covered with a single-layer polymeric membrane on a profiled steel deck, is hung.

But if this kind of suspended roof is strongly reminiscent of many of Mies van der Rohe's buildings, the main, central zone with the larger span, containing the winter garden, restaurant and test station, owes more to Buckminster Fuller's vision of roof structures suspended by cables from a mast. What is suspended in this case, however, is an altogether different kind of roof from, for instance,

the metallic hood of Fuller's Dymaxion House. It is a tensile material, a translucent teflon-coated glass-fibre membrane. It rises in great contrast to the rigid geometry of the steel truss structure of the two outer zones. Although structural elements, again, remain on the outside of the building and the roof is suspended, the main medium here is not the truss and the flat roof but the cable and the tensile material. The latter is suspended through a system of cables from twinned masts forming a tent-like envelope. The masts in turn are stabilized through another system of cables and interconnecting three-dimensional trusses anchored to the ground.

There is a romantic aura to this tensile structure that is rare in buildings characterized by so-called 'high-tech' architecture, founded upon the faithful exhibition of all technological elements and the promotion, as a solution, of the most advanced technological means. Indeed, the main core of the present building recalls the tents which explorers used to set up in uncharted parts of the world in bygone days, an image which seems apt for an institution which, like the Research Laboratories for Schlumberger, is devoted to advanced research into natural science and technology.

James Stirling, Michael Wilford and Associates
NEW STATE GALLERY
(Stuttgart, Germany)
1977–84

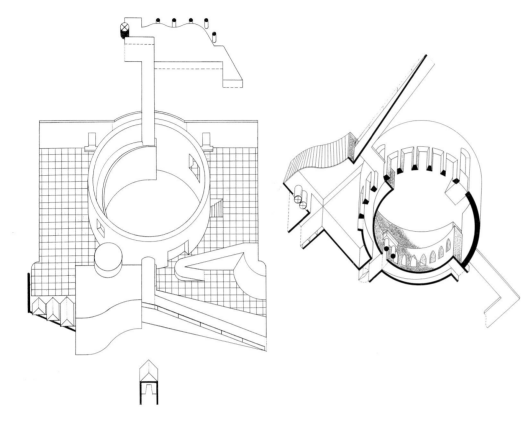

In September 1977 James Stirling and his partners were informed that they had won the competition to design an extension for the Stuttgart Staatsgalerie. The client was the local government of Baden-Württemburg. The project included, in addition to an art gallery, a theatre, a museum school and a library. The site, 90 metres by 140 metres of abandoned space, was separated by a dual carriageway from the Staatstheater south of the existing Staatsgalerie. The anonymity of this character-less area was not unlike what one often finds in most technologically developed cities in Europe and around the world. As a result of rapid and ruthless economic growth, built structures are often abandoned as soon as they appear unable to keep up with mounting demands for efficiency, without much consideration for social and cultural costs. In this case, the site contained in its fragmentary, existing structures a latent but strong urban potential. Stirling and his partners decided to make this potential manifest; they succeeded with great inventiveness and wit.

The Staatsgalerie extension is one of the best examples of a shift in attitudes in the mid-1970s away from both the self-destructive excesses of the populist tendencies of around 1968 and the alienating, bureaucratic and technocratic mainstream of so-called moder-nist design. Here we have an architecture whose urban character was expected to res-tore a public face to the buildings and a civic consciousness to the users – or, as the American sociologist Richard Sennett has put it, to restore the 'fallen public man'.

Such considerations played an important role in Stirling's decision to move away from the post-war stereotypical attitudes about museums that were predominant among cura-tors, designers and critics, who saw them as simply well-controlled environments whose fundamental task was to preserve and present information about art objects with a minimum of interference. As a consequence of such attitudes, the museum was still regarded as cut off from its surroundings, even when site conditions and factors of context were taken into consideration. By contrast, the leading consideration for Stirling's design of the Staatsgalerie extension was the building's *urban* identity.

A promenade, like the ones in a traditional city, was designed to bring pedestrian visitors through the building itself. The route cuts diagonally across the site, providing 'mean-ingful contact with the new building'. The public can descend into the sculpture yard – and gaze at the sculpture without actually visiting the gallery, an act of urban voyeurism – and down to the entrance terrace, then through the theatre arch to the Eugenstrasse corner. The entrance to the gallery and theatre also makes visible an uninterrupted pedestrian walkway network latent in the present site. This makes the gate to the building part of a system of public 'squares', thus serving as an inter-face between roads and built complex. This inventive urban-architectural device functions as a spatial rhetorical prologue to the museum's activities. It also suggests a kind of theatrical setting; the visitors become actors, the building a public stage. In addition, this walkway relates the basic layout of the exten-sion, a U-shaped plan, to the H-shape of the original building.

Participation in cultural activities is per-ceived here as a public, 'urban' event, a

secular ritual for citizens – what Harold Rosenberg called the contemplative experience of the post-war museum, rather than a private, intimate, confessional experience. This spirit of civic design led to the principles of frontality, seriality and hierarchy determining the spatial, formal composition of both the outside spaces and the internal areas of the new gallery. This gives the building an objective and ceremonial, rather than an individual, confessional character. The museum's programme, a straightforward, 'chronological journey through the history of painting and sculpture', dictated the topology of the exhibition rooms. The orthogonal-prismatic configuration of the rooms seems equally objective.

The restaurant, an important feature socially and commercially in most contemporary cultural facilities today, is placed apart from cultural events, but not, as in many museums, in a secluded, private internal yard. In the tradition of the piazza, it is attached to the terrace where performances and temporary shows take place.

Equally 'public' and 'objective' is the lighting of the exhibition areas inside the gallery –

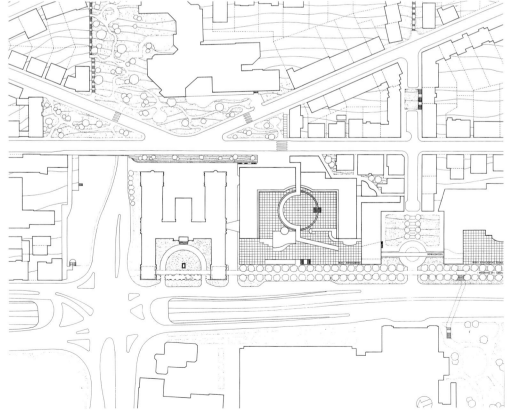

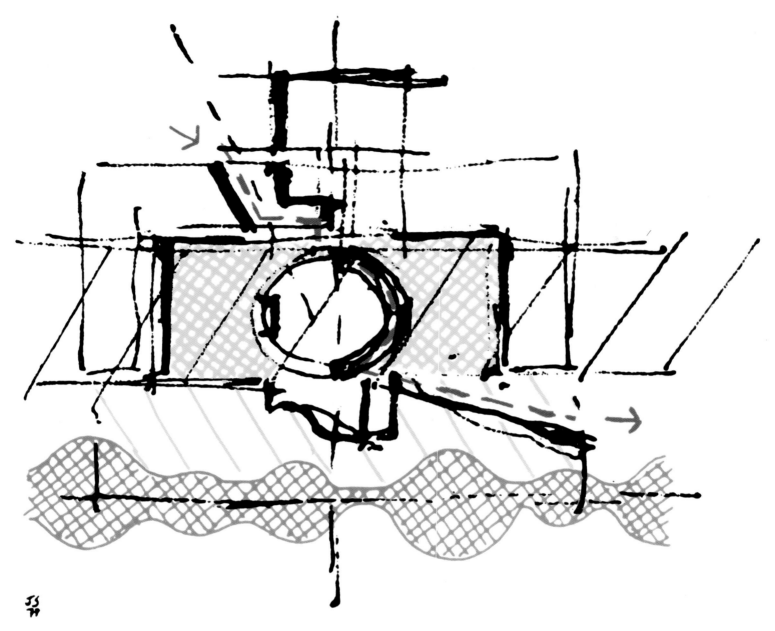

natural light controlled by adjustable, motor-
ized louvres mounted in the ceiling, together
with high-efficiency, fluorescent lamps in the
fibrous plaster ceilings. This combination
avoids an atmosphere of interior cosiness. The
external exhibition areas are endowed with
their civic character by virtue of their geometry
and texture; 'dressing' them appropriately in
colourful local marble and sandstone creates
a festive, joyful atmosphere which emphasizes
the impression of everyday action having
become, once again, acting.

A further contribution to the civic-theatrical
character of the project was made by deliberately recycling architectural antecedents from
known, strong civic successes of the past.
Stirling, who had led a succession of contradictory architectural trends, is, in the Stuttgart
museum, once more attuned to the emerging
historicist mood of architecture of the 1970s.
This project is without doubt the most extreme,
and also his most successful example of the
intensive exploitation of cannibalized fragments of antecedents from the past twenty
years.

There have been many kinds of retrospective
uses of past architecture: 'a variation on a
theme' is what Robert Venturi and Denise Scott
Brown have done at the Sainsbury Wing of
London's National Gallery, employing as a
motif the Corinthian column from the original
Wilkins Gallery next door (pp. 272–75). There
is an abundance of antecedents in recent
buildings – citations, references, allusions or
even collages. In some cases, as a result of
cross references and semantic cross fertiliza-
tion, meaning is blurred and the idea of
meaningfulness in architecture is trivialized
and debased. In other cases, however, different contexts are joined together to enhance
the horizon of interpretation, thus enriching the
meaning of a work: for example, the Banco de
España headquarters by Clotet and Paricio
(pp. 132–33). Stirling, in the Stuttgart gallery,
has done precisely that. He has invented a new
urban setting, rediscovering motifs and spatial
structures in British, German and Italian buildings. It is noteworthy that he has done so with
erudition and an implicit spirit of comic irony,
not tragic heaviness.

(Above) Conceptual sketch

**(Opposite) Detailed view of the exterior – the
sculpture yard**

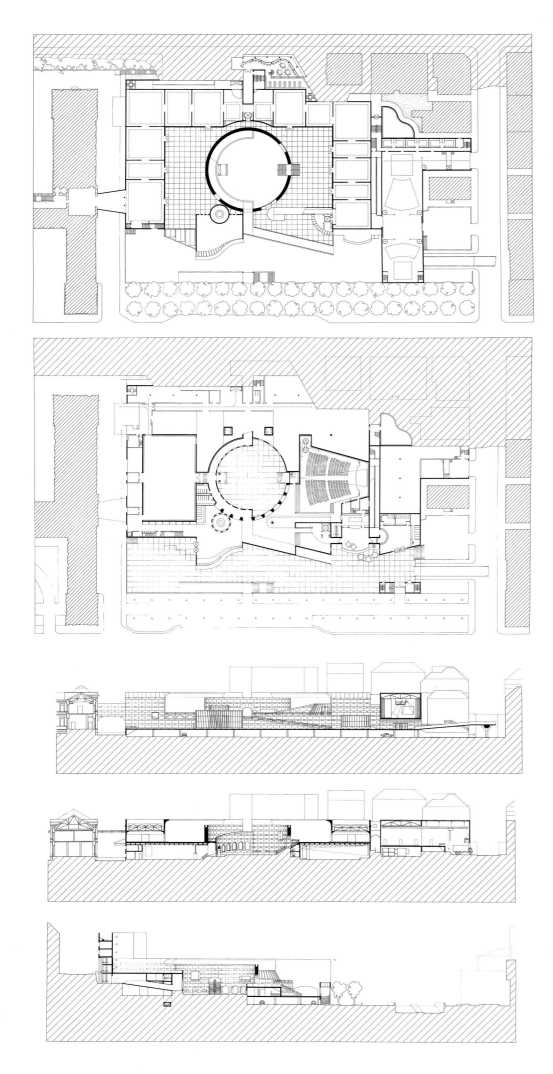

(Opposite, top to bottom) Gallery level plan; entrance level plan; sections

(Right) Exhibition space inside the gallery

But why this irony? To imply that every act repeats itself in history, once as tragedy and once as joke? Is he saying that the dream of restoring civic architecture and an urban society by reinventing 'the relation between stage and street' is chimerical? Or is it self-mockery, hinting at the silliness of the eclectic, nostalgic retro-fashion which emerged in architecture at the beginning of the 1970s – as it had in the post-May '68 adversary culture (a fashion which, to some extent, some of Stirling's ex-collaborators had helped to launch)? Claude Parent, the French modernist architect and critic, has taken this view, commenting that 'in Stuttgart, Stirling has built the tomb of post-modernism, no longer by criticisms without effect, but by giving a second look at the exemplary modern architecture liberated from the arid codifications of the 1950s–1960s, ready for adventures that will permit him to measure up to the past.'

There is, however, another possible, parallel critical interpretation of the building's 'historicist' character – and from a certain point of view more convincing – which explains the undisputed sense of joy the gallery evokes.

This interpretation has to do more with the basic level of spatial cognition, and of design as an act of invention, which the gallery embodies. Accordingly, the project is seen as born from the fusion of two fundamental, formal spatial canons, the classical and the anti-classical. Like the 1838 Staatsgalerie, the extension is organized along the constraints of a classical tripartite division schema and a half-atrium spatial formula. Over this classically composed arrangement, and at the open side of the half-atrium, lie a crowd of architectural elements whose configuration is alien to the classical rules, a Niemeyer-type streamlined, double wall of curved glass in the foyer, an oblique Constructivist steel lattice canopy, curved zig-zag ramps, each element breaking, in its own way, the classical canon and collectively making up a counter-canon. The two systems, classical/anti-classical, may be contradictory, but the historical confrontation creates a third canon, a meta-canon, that makes thinking in and about space more encompassing, and makes the world, according to Stirling's optimistic message, appear richer and more familiar.

Clotet, Paricio & Assoc., S.A.
BANCO DE ESPAÑA HEADQUARTERS
(Gerona, Spain)
1982–85

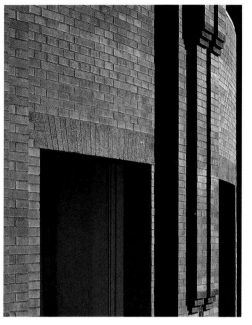

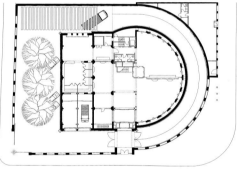

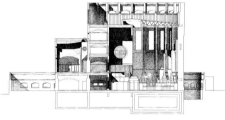

The Banco de España headquarters is an exercise in urbanity. The entrance faces onto a small park, in a small street. As one moves clockwise towards the corner on the left, one soon realizes that this corner, and not the front, is the most important exposure of the building. At this awkward point, the site opens onto the Gran Via Jaime I, a major 19th-century avenue of the *ensanche*, or extension, of Gerona, with a vista stretching for several hundred metres. Clotet and Paricio's problem was how to be faithful to the real facade while avoiding the

impression that the building was turning its back to the rest of the city. The remarkably simple cylindrical form was an agile solution to the dilemma. It allows the bank to present an all-round, continuous, genial facade to its surroundings and at the same time allows the avenue to preserve its character.

The building's elemental, rounded arcaded forms reveal clearly the influence of the architecture of Louis Kahn, who was himself inspired by Roman models. Kahn's style is perfectly attuned to the strong element of

critical regionalism which is characteristic of Clotet and Paricio's work. Its indebtedness to the Roman tradition of large-scale brick constructions, which still loom large in Iberian landscapes and cityscapes, is great. The Roman heritage is apparent in the ancient aqueducts, in the amphitheatres and in the craftsmanship demonstrated in their use of brick. Spanish buildings of the 19th and 20th centuries, most particularly the bull-rings, so beloved by the Spaniards, also draw on these Roman precedents.

(Opposite, left and top right) Exterior view and detail of the facade

(Opposite, right centre and below) Ground floor plan and section

(This page) Views of the bank's interior

What is most distinctive about the Banco de España building is the extraordinary and incongruous metaphor which gives it its visual identity: a bank in bull-ring's clothing. It is the same kind of unexpected association, a Luis Buñuel kind of metaphor, revealing discrete elective affinities, as one finds in the Belvedere Georgina of 1972, of which Clotet was one of the architects (pp. 54–55).

Superficially, the form of the building and its mode of detailing have very little to do with its functional programme as one of the many branches around the world of the Banco de España, all of which have more or less similar organizational requirements. Within the framework of the critical regionalist movement, however, this seemingly arbitrary choice of form in terms of the building's function serves to create a necessary and desirable identification of place and community. In Clotet's words, this idiosyncratic-looking, anti-monumental 'monument', whimsically at odds with its institutional role as a bank, is far from being 'the product of nostalgia for a lost paradise that never existed'. On the contrary, the semantic dissonance it has set up is intended as a playfully subliminal means of reminding the viewer about 'our own origins and roots'.

Oswald Matthias Ungers Architekt
ARCHITECTURAL MUSEUM
(Frankfurt-am-Main, Germany)
1981–84

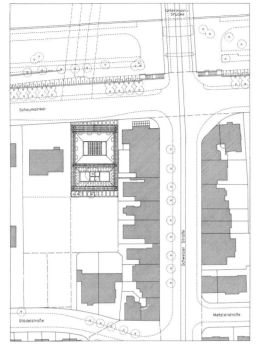

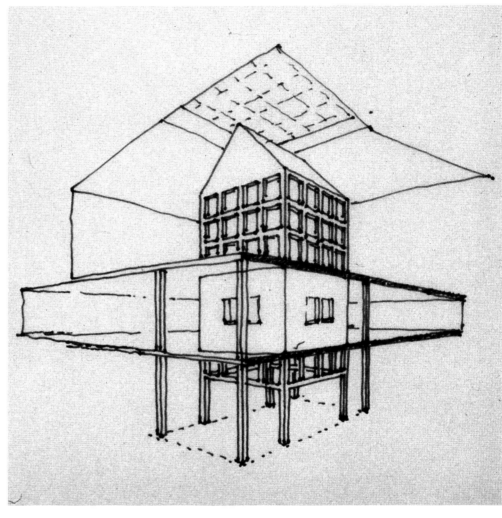

In this building within a building, Ungers succeeded in capturing the obsessive self-reflective preoccupations of post-modernism probably more than in any other project of its kind. The fact that this is a museum of architecture helps significantly in giving the impression that such preoccupations have found a natural home.

The Architectural Museum is located on the left bank of the River Main, a mainly 19th-century residential area occupied by villas which the city of Frankfurt planned to turn into an area of museums, the so-called Museum-ufer. Located inside a nondescript villa of the turn of the century whose interior has been gutted, the building consists of a simple four-storey structure painted white and constructed like a schema, a spatial, cognitive abstraction of a building.

The building within a building is one of the oldest themes in the history of architecture and is associated with archaic cosmological structures of macro-microcosm analogies. In the tradition of Christian architecture, it is often seen in the design of baldaquins. It is also encountered in the tradition of domestic architecture, especially in sleeping areas which are defined as a kind of building within a building with obvious erotic connotations. A recent current example is a project by Charles Moore who has imbedded inside his house (1960–62) at Orinda, California, two *aedicu-lae* (small dwellings) which resembled not only each other but the house as a whole. Here the intention was to comment on the idea of place and architecture rather than make a statement about cosmology, or simply an associative, mood-inducing design. It is with this

tendency of architecture reflecting on itself that Ungers' *aedicula* belongs.

Ungers had been concerned over a long period with the idea of the origins of architectural rules and architectural typology. Like Aldo Rossi (pp. 56–63), he had searched to identify generic structures to which architecture owes its development, what came to be known as 'morphological design method'. This led him to formulate the notion of what he called New Abstraction in architecture. He hoped that this would 'revive basic concepts of space' . . . which as 'universal orders of abstraction represent a quality of permanence'.

Despite its abstraction and the careful avoidance of scenographic effects to give a dimension of time to the building and introduce the historical dimension – an effect on which Moneo's museum (pp. 148–51) relies

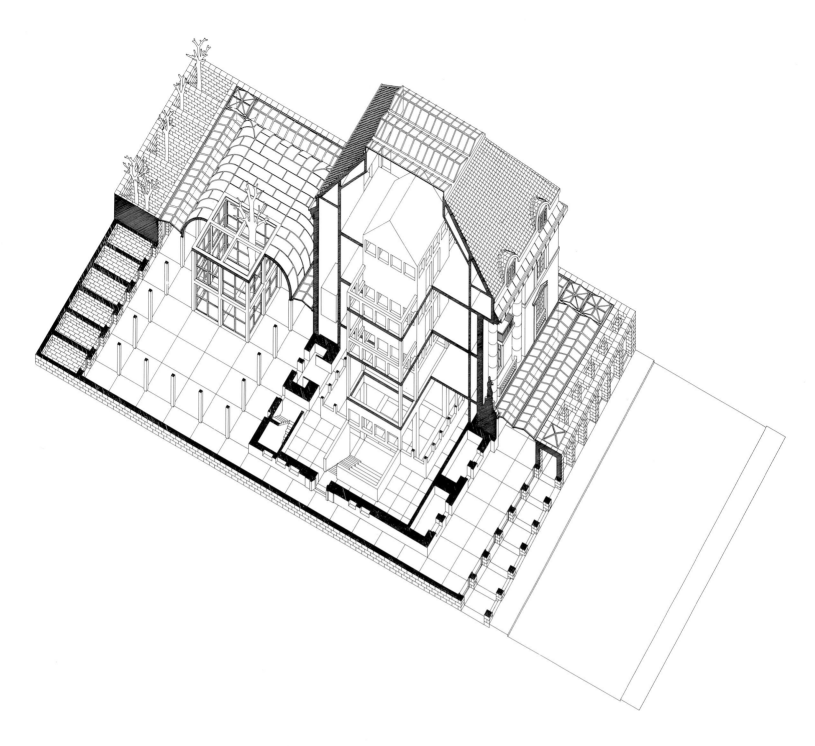

to a great extent – this building within a building represents more a nostalgia for such a type than a type itself, probably the result, ironically, of a lack of abstraction and analysis despite Ungers' intentions. In the context of a museum of architecture, it is as if the enclosed building became the museum's first item to be collected, the ancestral, original prototype of architecture. Topologically, as it is placed in the centre, it is positioned like the seed out of which all architecture grows, as well as the villa which encloses it. Any building other than an architectural museum that played such mirroring games might be criticized as self-indulgent. But for an architectural museum, and especially one under the directorship of the post-modern theoretician Heinrich Klotz, the idea was most felicitous.

(Opposite) Site plan and conceptual drawing for Ungers' Architectural Museum

(Above) Axonometric section through the building

(Left) The top of the *aedicula*

Richard Meier & Partners
MUSEUM FOR THE DECORATIVE ARTS
(Frankfurt-am-Main, Germany)
1979–85

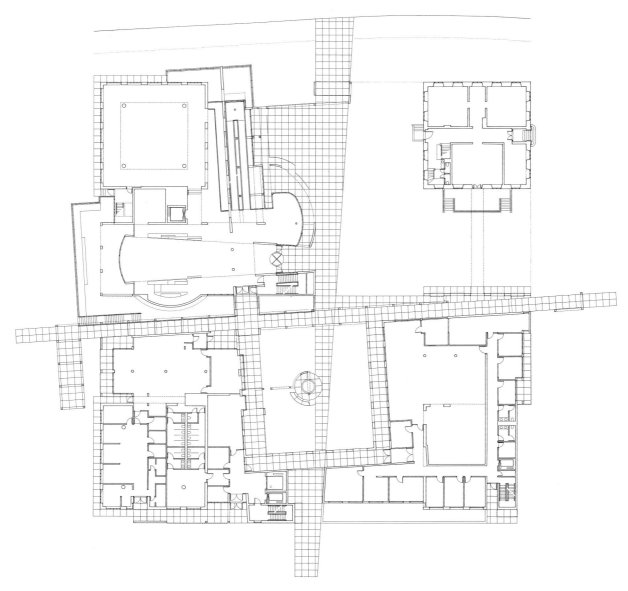

Designed as part of a new cultural district on the banks of the River Main – the so-called Museumufer – the Museum for the Decorative Arts is an elegant exercise in the interplay of the old and the new in white reflected light modulation, integrating different modular and grid systems.

As in other work by Meier, choices about the organization of circulation were decisive in determining the spatial scheme. Given the didactic character of the museum, the anti-clockwise circulation path leads the visitor through a sequence of displays which reflect developments in the history of European art. The linearity of this way of ordering the space is

varied by intercepting it with openings. Still more important in the shaping of the new museum is the concern with its relation to the adjacent Villa Metzler – built in 1816 in the Biedermeier style.

This highly successful inscription of a new structure into an environment constrained by its natural and cultural character is achieved not through easy scenographic effects, but by using subtle design strategies: number, proportion, spatial coordinates. The building is subdivided into interconnected units which respond to the proportions of the adjoining Biedermeier structure, creating an indispensable bond with it, not only by responding to it,

but also by reinterpreting it. Proportions and dimensions of the project are thus determined as if radiating from the villa. The 1.10-metre module of metal panels is used in the greater part of the new building. This module is derived from the basic dimensions – 17.6 metres width and height – of the villa. The shape of the fenestration of the new building is extracted also out of the proportions of the villa windows. The concentrated form of the building allows part of the site to be a park open to the surrounding community, the Sachenhausen, in the south, and the city across the river, in the north. The site is further opened up by introducing pathways and vistas through the barrier

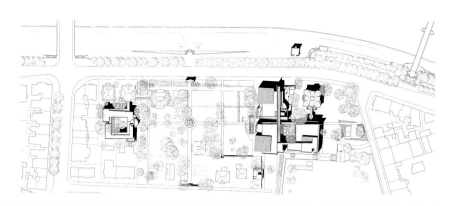

(Opposite) Ground floor plan

(Top) Site plan

(Above) Exterior view

formed by the villas lining the Main. An orthogonal grid, abstracted from the Villa Metzler, and a discrepant second grid oriented towards the river are overlaid, generating the skewed spatial structure of the plan. The formal order of the building is thus generated by superimposition.

Characteristic of Meier's work, there are echoes here of pre-war 'purism', an aura of floating and refined, modulated light reminiscent of German Rococo. As one proceeds from room to room, one's impression is of calculated elegance and studied calmness, appropriate qualities for a museum building and felicitous to the character of its location. There is, too, an

atmosphere of opulence, clarity, polite conservatism, even predictability, removed from any surprises. This helps to underline the 'minor' character of the objects displayed in the museum, but perhaps it overlooks the innovative quality that at least some of them share with 'high' art. But then, surprise and adventure are not the qualities of Meier's impeccably, implacably purist oeuvre.

Alejandro de la Sota
POST OFFICE AND TELECOMMUNICATIONS BUILDING

(León, Spain)
1985

This building crowns a prolific career of poetical research and technical invention by Alejandro de la Sota. It also demonstrates the long creative evolution of modern architecture in Europe. Two of his earlier buildings, the Government Building of Tarragona, in the late 1950s, and the Colegio Maravillas in Madrid, of 1961, are among the most outstanding examples of the kind of post-war architecture we call 'realist'. The León building shows that the trend is not exhausted. It is a public building but de la Sota in his realist, anti-rhetorical way has excluded all rhetorical devices from it. In his characteristically anti-monumental approach, his concerns are pragmatic.

For the walls, he used panels usually employed in Spanish supermarkets, remarking, 'Here they were used for a quite singular, very important building, and the result is perfectly acceptable.' *Couleur local* was respected by painting them in 'León colour'. Equally pragmatic was the spatial organization of the building which, in accordance with implicit realist principles, had to take account of the constraints of the programme interpreted in the framework of spatial structure.

This organization is of paradigmatic simplicity: a rectangular prism divides space into $4 \times 8 \times 11$ 3-dimensional grid units. Within this subdivision a $4 \times 8 \times 4$ sub-system is embedded for bearing elements. Finally, interwoven in a parallelepiped pattern, partitions are positioned to create a paratactic arrangement of functional zones. Such an overlay of three systems could have belonged to any ordinary, mainstream building, but in this case the effortless exactness with which each system nestles inside the other results in a faultless, original synthesis. As the prominent Spanish architect Julio Cano Lasso has observed, de la Sota 'has transformed reality into poetic material' and, indeed, the building gives the kind of satisfaction works of poetry offer.

Envisaging as a coherent whole every component of a building, structural, spatial or functional, requires skills acquired from a long-accumulated knowledge of the tradition of classical and modern international architecture. This tradition involves the practice of physically embedding heterogeneous spatial components – structural, functional, ornamental, iconographic – one inside the other without imposing on each other's integrity and without creating new contradictions. This was successfully accomplished in Spain at least as far back as the work of the Renaissance architect Juan Herrera. But it can be regarded as going even further back, to the classical principle of *taxis*, the rule system for partitioning space, and its prime paradigm, the classical temple.

De la Sota dutifully acknowledges this debt, and in an essay, 'Experiences', he placed a photograph of himself posing in front of the Parthenon and referred to Schinkel as the 'passport' that saw him through his studies. He also credited Juan and Emilio Moya, Modesto Lopez Otero and Pascual Bravo, all adherents of the classical tradition.

Nevertheless, de la Sota refers to another tradition, that of going beyond tradition. In the entirely original structural, divisional and functional zoning frames of the Post Office building, the freshness of his approach to such coordination problems is inspired by the work of two other great Spanish innovators, Antonio Flores and Antonio Palacios.

'We suffer from the ceiling', de la Sota says, referring to the low level of accumulated knowledge and 'collective memory'. This leads to 'an architecture that was – and threatened always to be – the same'. His solution is to recommend the 'union of different elements in order to obtain a third . . . [which] contains something new'. And this is precisely the case with the León building. As much as one can identify in its conception the classical canon (the formidable Herreran 'cube', with all its historical connotations of repressive order), one is equally reminded, in the scheme's poetics of newness, of early Gropius, Breuer and Neutra, and even Hannes Meyer, Max Bill or the Eameses. Characteristically, de la Sota's unpretentious description of his building was that 'the idea was to make a cube that works, and that would be adaptable to future changes'.

Memory and invention, de la Sota tells us, can be turned into conflicting tyrants: 'Legacies from the past tend to be overvalued, so that fear and nostalgia are mixed together to create a way of thinking in which restoration is deemed more worthy than re-creation. But it is

(Above) The east side

(Opposite) Conceptual drawing and first floor plan

not so.' Newness might also win, he reminds us. For a realist, much as memory is not an overriding norm, newness is not autonomous. According to de la Sota, newness is endowed with precedent experience. As in a game of chess, one of de la Sota's favourite metaphors for design, 'Moving a simple pawn can be enough for the whole game to take on a new light . . . a change in the placing of a pillar, a change in the quality of one of the materials . . . in the . . . conception of the job will completely alter the resulting architecture.' The way in which different components are combined in the León Post Office does indeed bring to mind the intelligence required in a game of chess.

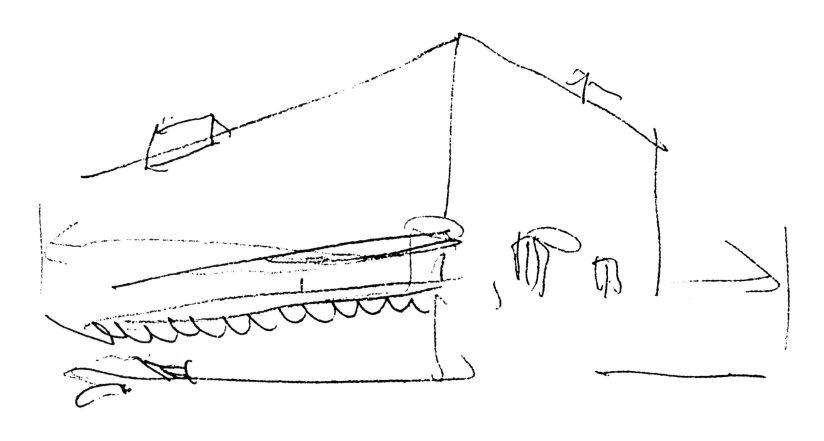

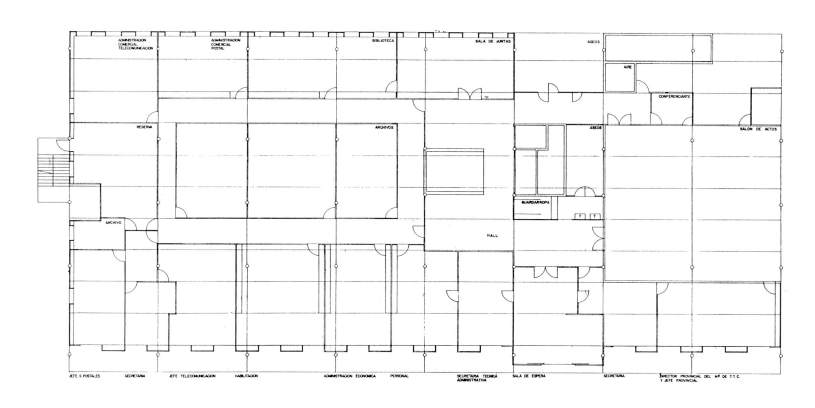

(Opposite) The south facade

(Left) Corner balcony

(Below left) Staircase

Studio d'Architettura Aurelio Galfetti
PUBLIC TENNIS CLUB
(Bellinzona, Switzerland)
1982–85

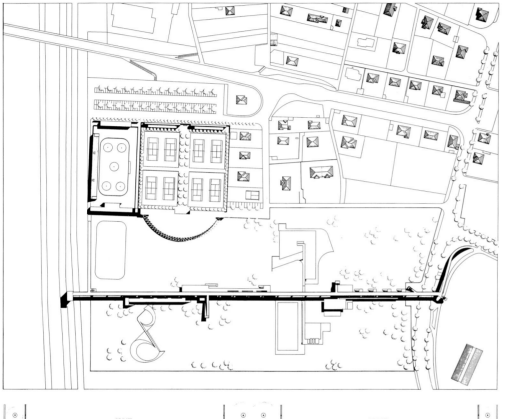

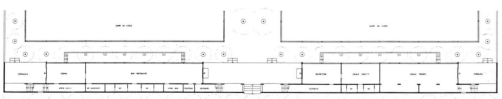

(Left) Site plan of the tennis club

(Below left) Detail of ground floor plan

(Opposite) Exterior view of the long, wall-like structure

(Above and opposite, above) Two views of the entrance

Galfetti is one of the major figures of the group of Ticinese architects made up of Mario Botta (pp. 64–67), Flora Ruchat and Luigi Snozzi (pp. 80–81) among others, who were identified by the architectural historian Kenneth Frampton with the broader international trend of critical regionalism and assigned the function of cultural critics.

Galfetti and his associates designed a community swimming facility in 1967–70. It is now the nucleus of a new recreational complex that includes this tennis club. The brief envisaged, in addition to 8 courts, a small restaurant and clubhouse, 4 changing rooms, 32 showers, 12 toilets and various storehouses and technical installations. The special feature of the new building is that, like a wall, it supports but also encloses; it both houses the services of the club and forms a barrier

separating the facilities from the rest of the town.

There are precedents for such wall-like buildings. Galfetti acknowledges the influence of Le Corbusier's plans for Rio and Tangiers. But he also refers to the more regional prototype that is particular to its location. A hill town in the Italian Swiss Alps, Bellinzona is situated at the point where the valley of the Ticino river widens to form Lake Maggiore. With its complex of three castles and their connecting fortified walls, the town was the barrier that controlled access to the three high mountain passes of San Gottardo, San Bernardino and Lucomagno, as Gerardo Brown-Manrique notes in his architectural guide to the Ticino area (1989). Castelgrande, dating from the late 4th century, is the oldest of the three castles and is a small acropolis fifty metres

above the valley floor. The magnificent walls still dominate the morphology and life of the city and its passageways remain important public spaces and pedestrian circulation paths. Once their restoration, which Galfetti is directing, is complete, they will house banquet rooms, a restaurant, exhibition halls and meeting rooms.

Besides its identity as a building type, the wall of the Public Tennis Club embodies a feature of Galfetti's work which has been consistent since the early 1960s and which inspired the Ticinese critical regionalist movement as a whole: construction craftsmanship. It implied a resistance, or rather one should say a representation of resistance, to the advancement of technocratic commercialism. In this connection, Galfetti's work can be seen as a continuation of a long and celebrated tradition

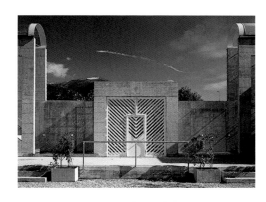

which goes back to great figures like Fontana, Maderno, Borromini, but also to generations of humble, anonymous builders whose excellence and skill have been renowned since the Renaissance in Italy and Switzerland and whose dignified and dedicated way of life the market and industry have ended.

Indeed, the exposed reinforced concrete wall has a highly photogenic sculptural surface texture as a result of the intricacy of the construction technique. It allows for deep horizontal stripes of shadow alternating with thin, flat, lighted surfaces immaculately executed through the use of form-work. The plastic quality of the technique is made to emerge by exposing the materials of the object and the means of its production. Concrete is left uncovered and the fact that it has been cast is foregrounded by giving to the wood forms an

expressive profile and by letting the joints between form-work be visible. Certainly, neo-brutalism did precisely that, and 'brutally', but the Bellinzona Club does it with extreme refinement.

From the purely formal point of view, this technique of casting has a wonderful optical effect of horizontality which helps to underline the distinct profile of the mountainscape in the background. By contrast to it the same technique is also used in the early Botta and Snozzi work (pp. 64–67, 80–81), in which the use of pure prismatic volumes serves to foreground the specific irregular forms of the natural landscape as well as their irregularity.

It is remarkable how the cult of what the late Renaissance called *agutezza* (purposeful neglect) has managed to survive in the heart of one of the most prosperous and technology-

dominated societies in the world, where exposed concrete is treated as if it were made out of precious material. One would search in vain here for a nostalgic return to the past. In fact, Galfetti is polemically opposed to such easy formulas. His architecture may come from a strong attachment to memory, but it is also the product of a search for inventive ways of renewing it and adapting to the new realities of an increasingly international world. This is what makes it not just regionalist, but critical regionalist. It is intriguing also how in a reversal of roles, the refined and precious, as well as the regional and crafted, have increasingly become, in the midst of the devaluation of culture and community, the aesthetics of radicalism and an expression of what the American critic Lionel Trilling called 'adversary culture'.

Ricardo Bofill Taller de Arquitectura
LES COLONNES DE SAINT CHRISTOPHE
(Cergy-Pontoise, Paris, France)
1981–86

Classical and industrial, proletarian and aristocratic, reminiscent of Louis XIV facades, but inspired by the garden city ideal; serving equally well absolutist and socialist politicians, claiming monumentality and fulfilling to the last detail the pedestrian requirements of planning authorities, this housing project is one of the most coherent examples in the constellation of neo-monumental complexes by Ricardo Bofill. The architect of 'subsidized Doric', he has been likened in the same breath to Michelangelo, Gaudí, Cecil B. de Mille and Albert Speer. While such characterizations of Bofill express the polymorphous nature of his oeuvre, they are also a measure of the slackness of the media of our time.

Les Colonnes dominates the valley of the River Oise in the new town of Cergy-Pontoise, on the plateau of Le Puiseau. It occupies the highest point, where the principal axis of the new neighbourhood intersects a linear layout of parks, hanging gardens and terraces over the river. It is composed of two distinctly morphological parts: a six-storeyed crescent to the south, oriented towards the valley; and two symmetrical, square plazas with four storeys to the north, connected by a cross-shaped plaza and cross-axis.

The composition, which is structured by a complex geometric system based on the square, draws upon the precedents of the classical English architecture of squares and gardens, such as the Circus and Royal Crescent by the John Woods in Bath. It departs, however, from a classical scheme in the way in which it relates and articulates buildings and regulates controlled interior spaces.

The complex, which is both eclectic and picturesque in its planning, is not closed to the surrounding landscape. At the edge of the plateau, above the valley, the facade of the crescent is, according to Bofill, 'treated like a grand city hall, punctuated by solid towers between which are placed apartment blocks, their French windows overlooking the natural theatre, like so many historic walls that have been progressively domesticated and transformed (for example Urbino, or the cities so characteristic of the Yemen).' The facade is intended to serve as the termination of the perspective created by the axis of the gardens and terraces rising from the river.

(Below, centre and bottom) Site plan and perspective view

(Below) Plan of a typical floor

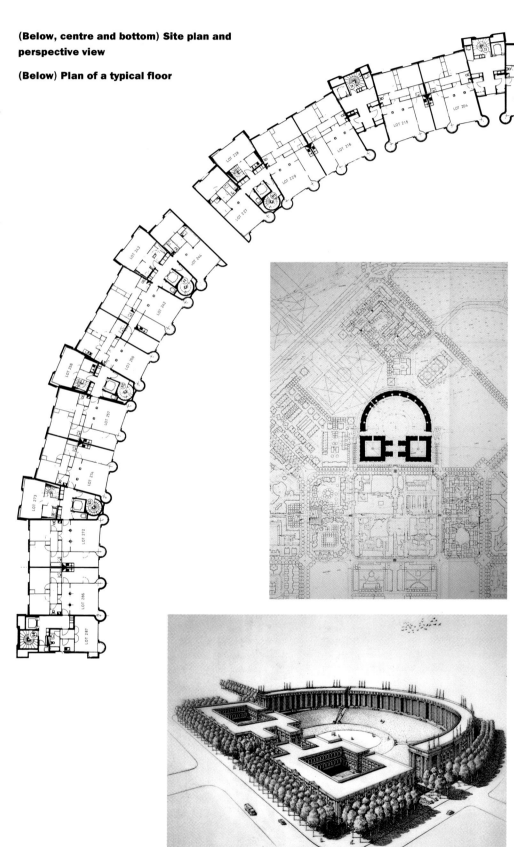

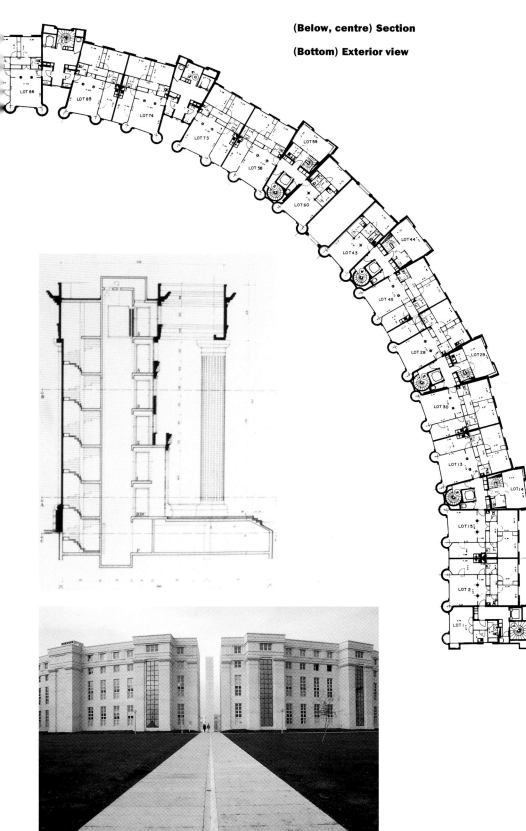

(Below, centre) Section

(Bottom) Exterior view

The architecture of the details is also characterized by a reliance on the architectural 'language' of the classical tradition. But it is, to extend the metaphor, a peculiar use of the language. Isolated 'words', or motifs, are applied in an exaggerated, overblown manner, almost to the point of caricature. On the other hand, it is debatable to what extent the classical rules of composition, its 'grammar' and 'syntax', are used. The effect is partly expressionistic, occasionally oneiric – as in a dream, certain details loom larger than life and are obsessively repeated. But the result is at the same time comically corrupted and solecistic.

Leaving aside the use of details in order to consider the large-scale arrangement of the masses in the landscape, the residential character of the property is emphasized by extending the clean green lawns of the grand, continuous park into the interior spaces. This green amphitheatre is surrounded by a wide colonnade of exposed concrete, covered with climbing vines, which reinforces the calm horizontality of the project and stresses its unity. On a more intimate scale, the two interior squares are similarly treated like small green courtyards.

For Bofill, apparently, the functionalist claim that a building's objectives must be consistent with its technology and the lifestyle of its users is merely a superstitious dogma. And Saint Christophe tests this theory.

Bofill makes us think again about our ideas of what sort of architecture is appropriate for today, as well as the very meaning of 'appropriateness' in architecture, now that the 20th century is drawing to a close. He also makes us reflect on the stagnation in their programmes that housing projects demonstrate.

Les Colonnes de Saint Christophe has a purportedly therapeutic aim: to salvage its inhabitants from the boredom of post-industrial technology and bureaucracy; to restore the sense of security that comes from belonging to a community; and to induce a collective consciousness in their behaviour. Bofill remarked in a 1983 interview to Jane Holtz Kay of the *Christian Science Monitor* that 'from the social point, the problem I'm interested in is not the lone block or single-family home, because that produces an individualistic

society and confines the range of alternatives to the amassing of housing units which exclude the more fundamental constituents of programmatic innovation.' But this kind of innovation is achieved neither in this project nor in most housing of the last twenty years. What Saint Christophe does achieve is a higher density combined with a collective configuration implanted in a landscape, where the collective units are not modernist blocks but palatial prototypes heavily loaded with historical citations. Whether this new hybrid of architectural composition fulfils its therapeutic objective, only time will tell. Ironically, the project appears to be still burdened with the deterministic presuppositions of modernist architecture, that a building can have a salutary effect on our way of thinking.

Saint Christophe is neither the best known nor the most publicized of Bofill's 'as-if' classical projects, but it is probably the most relaxed and well-balanced example of a rare architectural talent operating in a period of affluence, an affluence given expression in terms of its architectural means, but which remains paradoxically poor in its vision of architectural programmes.

(Top) Detail of the facade

(Right) View across the semicircular court

Estudio Rafael Moneo
MUSEO NACIONAL DE ARTE ROMANO
(Merida, Spain)
1980–86

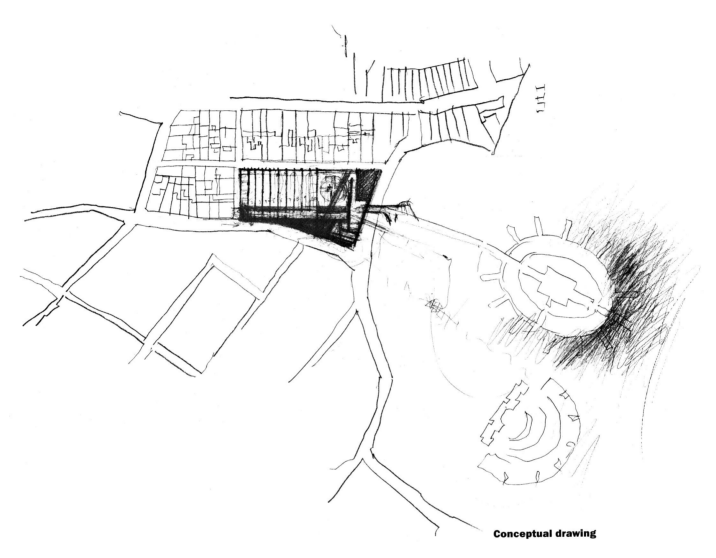

Conceptual drawing

The Merida museum is one of a handful of buildings that best represents, from many points of view, the prevailing mood of the 1980s for a return to tradition and classical coherence. The main programmatic goal of this project, to preserve and show artifacts from the past, is appropriately realized in Rafael Moneo's building. The objects for exhibition and the location of the museum are both intended to present the Roman world, upholder of the traditional and the classical, and to demonstrate the values of continuity and consistency. The architectural implementation, the relation of the building to the site, the space composition, construction and the materials used implicitly represent conservation and tenaciousness. The happy coincidence of these three elements – mood, subject

and implementation – contribute to the sense of synthesis in stone with which the project is identified – to its being, in Moneo's words, a living 'Archive-Museum'.

The museum houses more than 20,000 Roman finds that make Merida's collection the richest in Spain. It rises next to the ruins of the Roman theatre, which attracts about 400,000 visitors a year. The historical and geographical significance of the city, one of the most remote Mediterranean outposts of the Roman Empire, was not lost on the Spanish authorities. When the building was completed, the opportunity for demonstrating Spain's *romanidad*, its ancient ties with Europe and its strong association with Italy was seized; it was opened jointly by the President of Italy, Francesco Cossiga, and King Juan Carlos of Spain.

The museum is built directly on top of the archaeological site of the Roman city. The organization of the plan appears straightforward: the space is divided by ten arched walls. A great nave running down the centre divides the arched walls in two parts. The visitor can wander freely down the nave, through its arcades and along the arched walls, and can 'zig-zag . . . with absolute continuity', grasping 'the entire collection almost in one glance', according to Moneo's stated intention. Light comes down through windows placed between each arched wall.

The intricate grid-pattern formed by arched walls and naves provides more than a structure for a protective shell above the archaeological finds and functional paths for viewing them. It suggests a meaning which interacts with the

(Right) Plan of the Roman ruins

(Bottom left) View of the site with the museum under construction

(Centre, left) Isometric projection of the arched wall system

(Centre, right) Isometric section showing arched walls

(Upper left) Section – partial view of the facade with entrance

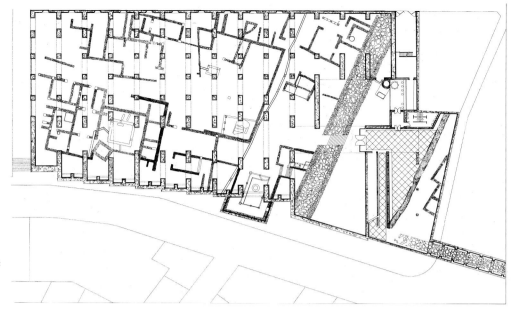

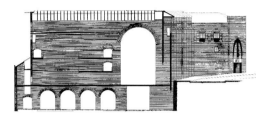

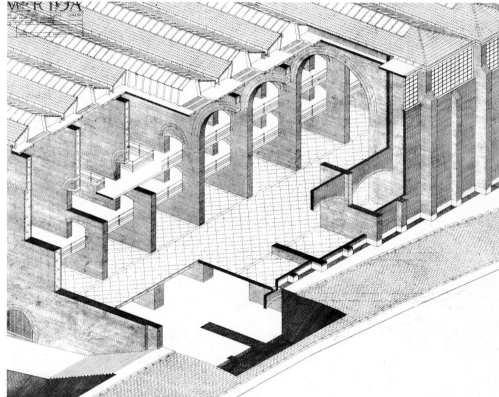

meaning of the exhibited objects, creating a higher level of understanding, a quasi-metaphysical interpretation of the Roman remains and of architecture. The museum thus emerges as if mediating between 'time present and time past', and the visitor moving through it becomes an unceasing explorer. To achieve this, Moneo skilfully uses basic architectural devices: geometry, orientation, materials. First, the grid structure which organizes the elements of the building, arched walls and naves, the spatial schema, is orientated in conformity with the schema of the structures in the present city. This orientation contrasts with that of the Roman ruins. The arched walls of the museum, however, conform with the ruins in terms of their geometry and materials — made of handcrafted brick in Seville, of similar

dimensions to the Roman ones. The structure of the museum therefore has a double identity. In terms of its orientation, it is part of the present; in terms of its materials and geometry, part of the past. In other words, the architectural space elements are simultaneously tagged with reference to two distinct points in time. Thus, the building testifies to the conflict between memory and actuality and represents a creative synthesis of the two. However, Moneo's architecture is not only concerned with the metaphysics of time and the idea of historical continuum, but also with the ideal of conservation of human institutions.

There is an interesting contrast between Moneo's over-interpretation of the contents of the museum through the architecture which

Interior views of the museum

contains them and Richard Meier's neutral lightness in the Museum for the Decorative Arts in Frankfurt (pp. 136–37). The overpowering presence of the grid in the Merida museum, the 'brickness' of the building blocks, the geometry of the arched walls, the solemnity of the composition which characterizes it, have their roots in 20th-century Spanish architectural tradition and, more specifically, in the buildings of the 'Madrid School', which have become one with the region in the memory of the people. The emphatic restatement of such regional design devices in a cultural building – at a moment of proliferation in Spain, as well as in the rest of the world, of technocratic, bureaucratic and anomic projects – may imply a topical and critical message, a critical regionalist commentary similar to that of other architects in Spain and other European countries. This critical, humanistic message could

be one of the many possible 'ontological landscapes', to quote Thomas Pavel, which the building fosters, in addition to that of *romanidad*, and the metaphysical yearning for the conservation of time.

The museum offers extraordinarily evocative, concatenated views of Roman sculpture which appears to be rising out of the Roman ruins, inscribed within the arches of the new structure and dramatically lit from above by natural light. The drama presented is a pictorial and theatrical experience of still objects in space, the results of the obstinate and unequivocal way in which the architectural elements of the building are organized. The frontality of the naves does not allow alternative ways of relating objects to viewers. Similarly, the absence of directionality and the Mies-like purity and singlemindedness of the configuration of the arches is a hindrance to joining

the horizontal floor subdivisions; the arches are their roof. Thus, the vertical elements remain unintegrated with the horizontal.

Compared, for instance, to Venturi's extension to the National Gallery in London (pp. 272–75), with its equivocal, inclusive architecture, which addresses the chaos of the multiplicity of contemporary functional requirements, world outlooks and ways of living found in abundance in the contemporary metropolis, the Merida museum is a sombre, silent building whose enviable serenity is achieved often by exclusion. Yet the impression of unity the building gives to the visitor is salutory and memorable, even if it is so abstractly put forward in pursuit of a sense of the eternal rather than the speculative.

The explicit reference represented in this building is a Metso, a large wood-grouse or blackcock, making a mating call or cooing. According to Reima Pietilä, the wood-grouse, which lives in the 'deep primeval woodlands' of Finland, has become 'the *genius loci* of virgin nature' for the Finnish people.

The emblematic bird shape is frequently encountered in the work of northern European architects. Two famous examples come immediately to mind – although built outside northern Europe: the Finnish architect Eero Saarinen's TWA Terminal in New York's Kennedy airport and the Danish architect Jørn Utzon's Sydney Opera House in Australia. Seeking truth in primeval forms and the espousal of regionalism in northern Europe in order to find a *genius loci* characterizes late Romantic and Symbolist aesthetics of the turn of the century in reaction to dominant classical poetics. Such regionalist attitudes were certainly influential in Alvar Aalto's anti-classical formal poetics and have in turn been influential in the Pietiläs' Tampere Library. The regionalism of this project is, however, more folkloristic and less abstract than Aalto's, closer to such contemporary Hungarian architects as Beno Taba and Imre Mackovecz.

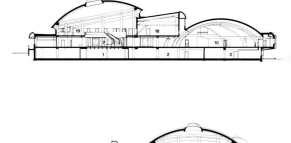

(Opposite, left) Site plan

(Opposite, right, top to bottom) First floor plan; ground floor plan; two sections

(Above) Exterior view of the library's entrance

The frames and mullions of the wooden windows of the Tampere building have 'tree-trunk', circular sections and the columns are circular or semicircular, 'bending down as trees do' and 'thereby giving the impression that the external space continues into the large main hall'. Situated at the crossroads of two parks, the book halls open towards both directions allowing the green spaces to continue into the interior, uniting the parks visually and symbolically creating 'a cosmic interior, with configurations [which] are as mysterious as the signs of the Zodiac'. Pietilä continues, 'As the trees grow, the park-like atmosphere will intensify as the building isolates itself from the rectilinearity of its neighbouring houses, thus allowing for a close relationship with nature.' And he concludes, 'All the building materials are of Finnish origin. The basement cladding and steps are of granite, the facades and curving eaves are of copper, the windows of greenish impregnated pine.'

Neither the symbolist aesthetics nor the regionalist elements, however, are a replay of pre-First World War themes. Rather, Pietilä's concerns echo the 1960s views of Team X, held by theoreticians such as Aldo van Eyck

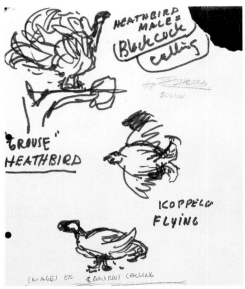

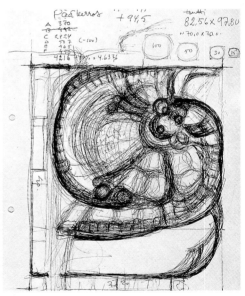

who, through buildings highly charged with poetry and myth, criticized the reductive, utilitarian, over-regimented post-war modernism. In a similar vein, Pietilä stresses that the grouse-shaped building 'is no functionalist form. Form follows the hints of expression and composition.' The Pietiläs' melancholic dissent, however, is expressed in lyrical rather than rhetorical terms. As architect-poets the Pietiläs are interested less in the art of convincing and more in the act of contemplating. Rather than trying to press on the viewer a striking, persuasive image, they have composed a memorable icon which, like the black-bird in Wallace Steven's famous poem, is open to many interpretations. The images projected by this building are changeable and relative, and each reading is a response to the changing context in which the building is seen at different seasons of the year. The architects themselves, in the process of conceiving the building, were actually undecided about its image and envisaged at different times a building in the shape of a bending branch, a lamb's head and, finally, the Finnish woodgrouse, believing that architectural form is a projection of the designer's and viewer's world-image.

(Opposite) Three conceptual drawings, including a volumetric sketch (left) and a sketch of the plan (below right)

(Above) Interior view

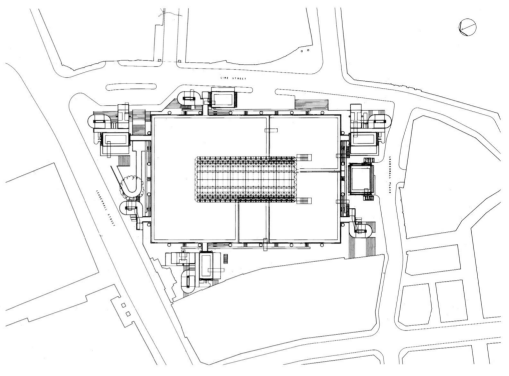

Just as Richard Rogers' and Renzo Piano's Pompidou Centre seemed to bring the space age to the middle of Renaissance Paris, next to its medieval and Roman quarters (pp. 84–89), so did Rogers' Lloyd's of London in the equally historic part of the British capital almost ten years later. The circumstances could not have been more different. The Paris building was a high-tech Parnassus, a 'people's centre', as the architects interpreted it. Lloyd's, by contrast, was a temple to Hermes and Tyche, the centre of a global market place.

President Pompidou and his advisors saw the Cultural Centre as an opportunity to revolutionize the stagnant waters of French culture and revitalize the declining area of Les Halles and Le Marais. In London, Lloyd's, a private 'society of underwriters formed into syndicates', asked for an 'owner-occupied' building which would help to take the established, dynamic and essentially commercial institution into the 21st century; it should also help Lloyd's maintain its leading world position and allow for its continuing expansion. At the same time, Lloyd's wanted a building 'contributing to the environment of the City of London'. Openness, flexibility, innovation were priorities in the programmes of both facilities.

Architecturally, the two projects may appear similar, and not only because they are both designed by Rogers. Other, more specific common programmatic considerations contribute to their physical similarities. The need for large, open exhibition areas, in the case of the Pompidou Centre, and the requirement for a single underwriting room (reinstating the old Lloyd's Adam Room, but many times larger), together with large, open floor areas for offices in the case of Lloyd's, led to schemes with a characteristic topology. Both locate most structure, movement and service elements in special 'servant' zones in the outer edges of the 'served' core. Equally important in this decision to establish distinct service zones in the outside of the building was the belief in technological 'legibility', the credo that all components of the building should be 'movable and express their movability'.

Behind this design concept – defining a new building type, polarizing its zoning between 'servant' and 'served', as well as turning inside out traditional locations of services within the building volume – lies an important precedent in the architecture of Louis Kahn. But whereas Kahn gave these duct-filled, outside towers the romantic, historicist look of medieval castles,

Rogers, reflecting Reyner Banham's ideas for an architecture of 'the second Machine Age' and Buckminster Fuller's 'liberated attitude to those mechanical services', made such 'packed together' equipment not only visible but also symbolic.

In the case of Lloyd's, the topological concept of 'servant' and 'served' satisfied the need for a major central space, a 'pantheon', for the workplace. In cases such as Petrus Berlage's Main Hall of the Amsterdam Stock Exchange (1903), Frank Lloyd Wright's Larkin Building in Buffalo (1904–05) and, more recently, Herman Hertzberger's Centraal Beheer (pp. 48–51) the central space acts as a mechanism for sustaining a corporate identity, but also as a de-alienating device. It provides an icon of community over a divisive world of private enterprise and division of labour. Hence, in Lloyd's, the memorable, inward-facing great atrium overlooking the new Adam Room and surrounded by an outward zone of six service towers.

For this 'package of services', Rogers uses highly expressive construction details, a lyrical universe of 'nuts and bolts', as well as a very high standard of finish and cladding in stainless steel. All this contrasts favourably with the

(Opposite, left) Exterior view

(Opposite, right) Roof plan and surroundings

(Right) Section

(Below right) Plan of galleries

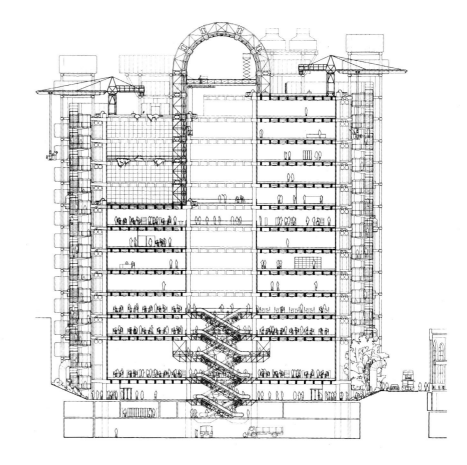

surrounding new but traditional-looking, pseudo-modernist, stony 'monolithic blocks'. But, as the British architectural critic Colin Amery remarked in an article in the London *Financial Times*, commenting on the newspaper's presenting to Lloyd's the Architecture at Work Award, 'a whole city of Lloyd's buildings would not be an entirely agreeable place'. From the urbanistic point of view, what seems questionable is the idea of dressing a building in an envelope, which, whatever its sculptural, symbolic or functional character, leaves no significant openings from which to look out at the neighbouring buildings or open areas, as traditional architecture does. While this is acceptable, if not actually commendable, for a cultural complex like the Pompidou, it is infelicitous for a workplace. Thus while Lloyd's in its well-formed structure offers a highly civic image, in its highly introspective topology it lacks an urbane character.

One of the most carefully studied, designed and manufactured components of the building – a true feat of innovation in building history – involved a 'transfer of technology from other industries'. For instance, a contractor had to be found with qualifications beyond those of the building industry for the 33 prefabricated

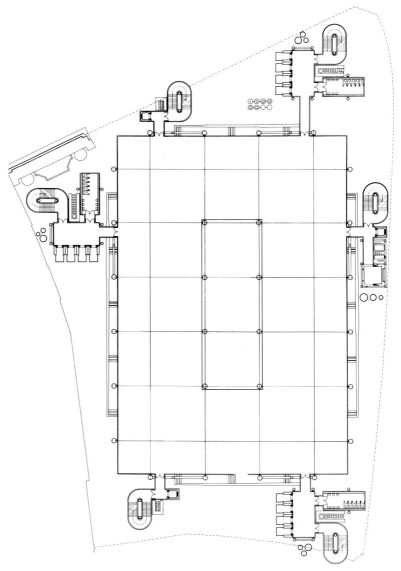

toilet modules that 'clipped on' to the core of the complex. The one selected specialized in the fabrication of vessels for the nuclear industry. Discovery and invention often follow strange paths. Seemingly specialized novelties, such as those involving the prefabricated toilets, used by the architect and the Arup Industrial Engineering Group, are likely to have implications in building beyond the limited problems at hand. Even so, when a building represents so few of its other functions in its overall appearance, to assign to these units such an important position seems quite deliberately to invite controversy.

The project has been criticized for the claustrophobic quality of the work spaces, their lack of contact with the outside, their minimal dimensions. Such complaints led Lloyd's in 1990, less than two years after the occupation of the building, to reorganize these spaces. Of coure, complaints such as these are often resistance to the new; it takes time for the users of a building, who have set habits, to enter the new lifestyle that a new building creates. However, other problems also emerged which could not be easily solved, such as the use of new technology by the brokers and underwriters and, most importantly, the unforeseen massive growth of the organization. These complaints were magnified by the loud, mostly negative, publicity the project received in connection with its commitment to technology and its corollaries, flexibility and change. On a deeper level, criticisms may also lie in the limitations of the scheme's topology which places the zone of structure and services at the periphery of the served volume – limitations which, in the case of Lloyd's, are even more restrictive and circumscribing than in the Pompidou Centre. Perhaps the problems of Lloyd's lie, ultimately, not so much in its newness or radicalism, but in its conservatism. In the last analysis, the scheme's rationale is iconological, and therefore restrictive, a preservation of the spatial ideal of the temple, albeit a Futurist-Constructivist one, whose peripheral columnar orders are, in addition to support elements, lifts, risers, toilets, pipes, ducts.

Located between memory and invention, raising as many questions as the ingenious answers it offers, a building of superb craftsmanship and sublime effect, Lloyd's is a major stepping stone in the history of the workplace and its adventures of discovery.

(Opposite) The upper levels of the atrium

(Left) Escalators link the dealing room to the lower tiers of the atrium

Atelier Peter Zumthor
PROTECTION SHED OVER ROMAN RUINS

(Chur, Switzerland)

1985–86

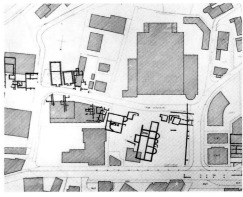

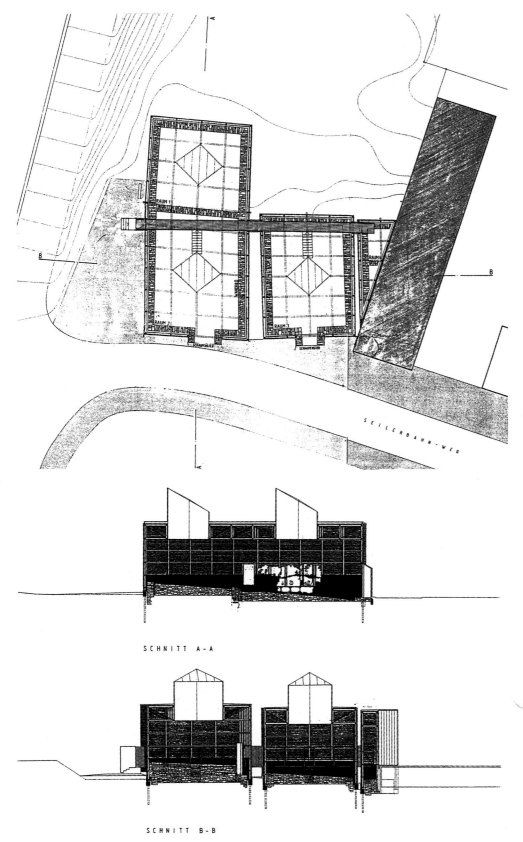

SCHNITT A-A

SCHNITT B-B

In many respects, this building is a simple, straightforward, functional structure, a shed for sheltering an archaeological excavation of Roman ruins in the town of Chur in the Swiss Alps. Made of thin, parallel, interspaced horizontal slats of wood that tilt downwards towards the outside, it protects against the elements, enhances natural light and ventilation and is economical to maintain.

But, in its radically rigorous way, this drastically stripped-down structure does in the end carry meaning. It symbolizes its strong statement of opposition to the crassly commercial or even 'cultural' buildings Robert Venturi calls 'decorated sheds'. The Chur building is a representation of a humble but at the same time severe and precise idea of architecture. It does not show off but concentrates only on what is necessary and sufficient, continuing the tradition that goes back to the ancient wooden constructions of the region. The Chur structure stands in contrast to the world of conspicuous consumption, real as well as fictional, a world conducive to exaggeration, exhibitionism and occasional falsity. It is, therefore, a moral statement about honesty and integrity. Like the revolt of Abbé Laugier, the celebrated early functionalist of the mid-18th century, against the overcrowding of architecture by court ornament, which led him to propose stripping down buildings to their essential hut prototype, Peter Zumthor's rebellion against mainstream architecture and its domination by images for mass-consumption demands the return to the same stripped-down prototype, even though his method differs from Laugier's. Rather than concentrating on the structural essentials, Zumthor focuses on the

(Opposite, left) Ground plan and sections

(Opposite, right) Site plan

(Above) Exterior of the protection shed

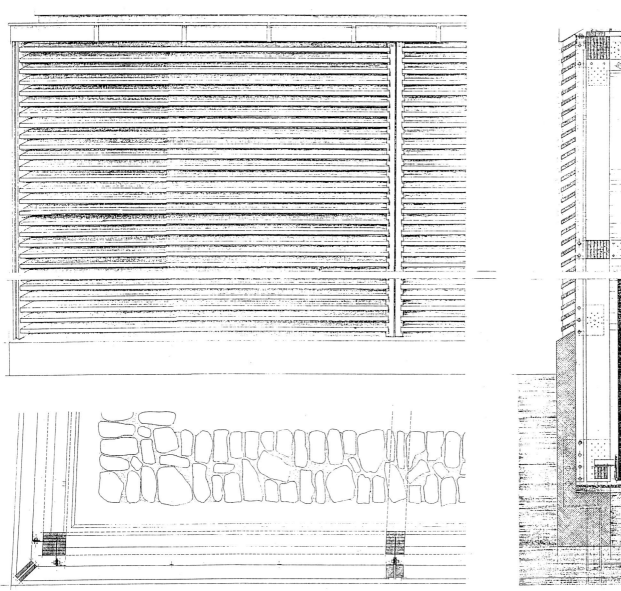
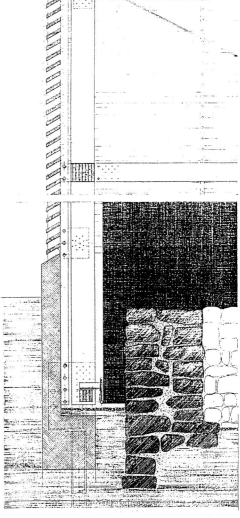

exterior covering, the skin of the building, expressing the love for traditional wood construction which he revealed in articles and interviews, in the late 1970s and 1980s, in the Swiss periodical *Archithèse*.

Without falling back on the facile, shallow formulas of the 'Swiss-style chalet' type of architecture, Zumthor exploits traditional elements both in the volume configuration of his shelters and in their outward appearance. He makes the onlooker aware of the particular qualities of wood which are often taken for granted, the fact that it can be hewed, hacked, cleaved, trimmed, bevelled, skived, whittled.

Zumthor's architecture can very easily be interpreted as Purist and Minimalist. It can be likened to Donald Judd's sculpture and to his recent experiments in architecture in Marfa, Texas. Zumthor might even be mistaken for a Platonist because of the impression that he is using primary volumes. A closer look, however, reveals that he is more concerned with the uniqueness of the concrete object and its particular details than with the perfection of an ideal prototype. He is, therefore, more like a Minimalist rooted in realism. For instance, the prismatic volume of the shed is skewed imperceptibly. This is done not only to meet the unique requirements of the site, but also in order to represent singularity in the way northern naturalist artists did, depicting with great devotion the exceptional and the characteris-

tic. Similarly, the details of joinery play a role in the overall composition that is as significant as the configuration of the whole.

In its rigorous attention to the skin of the building, the shelter upholds the values of humility, honesty and truth, of nominalist *Naturwarheit*, as Max Dvorak, the great art historian of northern naturalist art, would have said.

(Opposite) Construction details

(Above) The shed's interior

Philippe Chaix   Jean Paul Morel Architectes
ZENITH OF MONTPELLIER
(Montpellier, France)
1985–86

(Left) Detail of roof

(Above) Main facade by night

(Opposite) Section and view of entrance

Zenith is more of a system than a building – a frame for a shelter to be instantiated where and when needed according to specific requirements, to satisfy the growing demand for large-scale popular spectacles. The Montpellier project shown here followed a previous application of the concept, that of La Villette at the crossroads of Bagnolet, on the outskirts of Paris. It is a kind of temporary architecture conceived for performances by rock stars or jazz musicians. The Zeniths were commissioned by Jack Lang, the French Minister of Culture, within the framework of the *Grands Projets* programme and as part of the policy to support youth culture announced in 1982 by President François Mitterand. More are bound to be constructed as pop-related spectacles continue to blossom in France and elsewhere.

The Zeniths' creators cite as inspiration the ideas of the Egyptian populist architect Hassan Fathy and his concept of 'implicitness'. Consequently, it is very much an anti-rhetorical, anti-monumental, unpretentious architecture that professes to be simply a sign of the times.

In the Zeniths, the structure is designed to carry the sheathing of the building, along with support for the equipment and cat-walk, without the help of masts, as these would interfere with visibility. For reasons of economy and

rapidity of construction, the whole of the building's covering is totally assembled and equipped on the ground, then hoisted onto the summit of the peripheral posts.

The Zenith of La Villette, designed in 1983, was a project carried out under strict constraints of budget and time. It had a capacity of 6,500 places – more than almost any other performance space in France. Two years later, the Montpellier version, which adapted the general principles to a new context and site, provided an opportunity to modify, enlarge and improve the first trial.

The basic scheme is that of a square hall covered by a lightweight structure. The 80-metre clear span trusses contain all services necessary for the shows – lighting, acoustics, fittings, stage design, projectors – besides supporting the modular, double-curved covering envelope which is made of PVC polyester. The acoustic performance of the structure is high, thanks to advanced studies both in insulation and acoustic correction. The interior envelope is made up of an overlay of plaster tiles for insulation and an absorbing panel made of PVC and glass wool. On the outside, acoustic insulation is ensured by alternating heavy PVC material and dense glass wool, which, incidentally, also provides excellent thermal insulation.

The air inside the capsule is renewed by 16 vents located in the upper part of the envelope. Safety precautions include the use of fire-resistant materials and 16 emergency exits.

The square shape of the plan aims for maximum visibility and flexibility, minimizing the distance of the back row from the stage. It offers relative compactness, a satisfactory rapport between stage and audience, and permits a good utilization of the angles of the structure for storage spaces and loggias on either side of the stage.

Outside, on the parvis that opens onto the park, a large wire-mesh structure carries announcements and information. This mesh constitutes the building's 'facade'; as in a circus big top, one does not enter the sheath of the building directly, but via the intermediary of a built and, as the designers put it, 'architecturalized' facade.

Zenith's metallic structure with its stainless steel facade is shiny but quiet during the day; at night it awakens, a radiant, magical box on the outskirts of the city. True to the centuries-old European tradition of ephemeral architecture of spectacle, it signals an invitation for a brief escape from the drudgery of everyday life into a world of alternative counter-factualities.

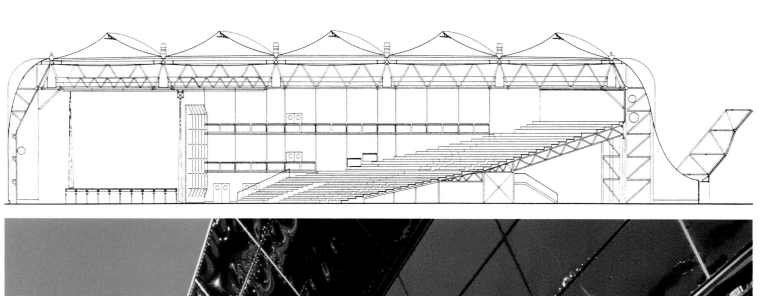

Alain Sarfati-AREA
88 HOUSING UNITS IN SAVIGNY-LE-TEMPLE
(Ville Nouvelle de Melun-Sénart, France)
1982–86

(Left) View of the facade

(Below) Site plan

(Opposite)
(Above) Exterior view of the corner of the block

(Below left) An entrance staircase

(Below right) Plans and elevations of one of the blocks

In 1967 Alain Sarfati, together with fellow students Philippe Boudon and Bernard Hamburger, founded in Paris the architectural review *Mouvement-Architecture-Continuité*. This became one of the most important cultural forums for architecture in Europe, and still remains so, long after the founding team has disbanded. From the start, the review's main interest was the relation between architecture and the city. The first issue contained a translation of Christopher Alexander's article 'A City is not a Tree'; subsequent issues centred around Robert Venturi's *Complexity and Contradiction in Architecture* and Kevin Lynch's *The Image of the City*. Ironically, then, much of the search for a truly urban, urbane architecture in France at this time was strongly influenced by American writers.

Almost twenty years later, not only the viewpoint but also the influence of American theorists of city planning is still evident in this housing project by Sarfati for a new district surrounding the city hall in the *ville nouvelle* of Melun-Sénart, in the countryside on the edge of Paris. The concepts behind it are unmistakably, on the one hand, Venturi's 'complexity and contradiction' and, on the other, Lynch's 'street' and 'imaginability'.

'Emerging out of the station,' Sarfati writes of the finished project, 'one gets the extraordinary impression of having set foot in the country, while at the same time an invisible line, an immaterial boundary, gives the distinct feeling that one is in a city.'

As opposed to those typically regimented, subsidized public-housing projects which are characterized by their simplified built form and reductive lifestyle, the Savigny-le-Temple housing is like an adventure playground in the individualization of the units, their entrances, their small-scale elements, the disrupted rhythms and contrasts usually associated with a historical street: smooth and rough, see-through and opaque, old and new, private and public, 'dirty real' and fabulistic, regionalist and international.

The aim was, as Sarfati remarked in his article 'The Exploded City', at a moment when 'the world has become a world of the interior', to provide 'an exterior, a public space which projects our ambitions'. The design of the street is his answer to this demand. The first building of the complex, with its strong gable element of concrete, is conceived as the beginning of a succession of widely divergent visual experiences, laid out along a route which ends in a corner made of white metal. The intention of the architect is to make the buildings look like the gleaming sides of the prow of a ship, 'marching in the street' like objects of 'envies, passions, dreams', Roland Barthes would say, as if 'the dream of a city [were] temporarily grounded but waiting to go forward.'

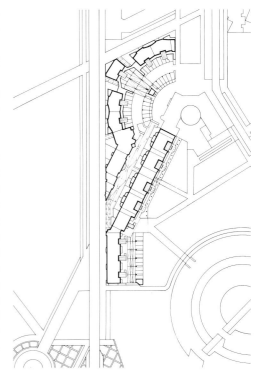

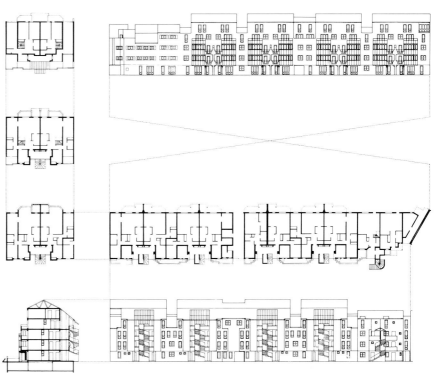

Weber, Brandt and Partners
NEW MEDICAL FACULTY, TECHNICAL UNIVERSITY OF AACHEN
(Aachen, Germany)
1968–86

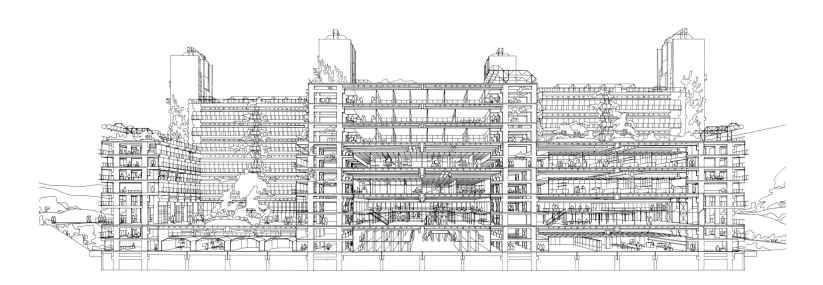

The hospital of the medical faculty of the University of Aachen, the largest in Europe, accommodates 1500 patients and 3000 students. It is conceived as 'nothing but organization: social, technical, economic, mental', in the words of Hannes Meyer (1928) whom the architect cites. The basic material infrastructure is a system of routes for the circulation of people, goods and messages, as well as air, light and water, all aimed at restoring health.

The scheme draws heavily on ideas developed during the early 1960s by Team X, particularly those of Shadrach Woods in the Free University of Berlin, and Giancarlo De Carlo's proposal for the University of Dublin, Serge Chermayeff and his collaborators in the USA, and Kenzo Tange in Japan. All those studies looked at buildings as general-purpose networks for information processing, mechanisms for sustaining human communication through a minimal structure of circulation and services within which individuals and groups would interact not only purposely but also playfully and randomly, as in the case of traditional city neighbourhoods.

The gridiron street-avenue circulation system of Manhattan has been repeatedly cited as a paradigm for the general plan layout of many types of building complexes, especially universities. Manhattan's layout as a guiding precedent is apparent in the medical faculty's east-west street pattern which intersects the avenue-like mega-corridors of the hospital. In the words of the architects, the hospital was with its service towers and, at different levels, green courtyards, 'nothing less than a mini-town . . . being blueprinted, even if it was a somewhat specialized one.' Within this overwhelming structure, a gigantic global organization was to be housed, 'everything in any way relevant to the process of regaining health under a single roof'. Assembling under the same roof a large number of apparatuses and services had obvious benefits of accessibility and what managers call economies of scale. But the architect also had other reasons in mind. Fitting such a diversity of specialists and technicians under a common shelter was intended, for reasons beyond efficiency and effectiveness, to create a sense of common purpose and solidarity

through the use of a complete transparency of means for total awareness of the 'interconnected factors involved in restoring health'.

Its Manhattan-like organization allowed the project to be flexible and open to growth in stages. Thus, consistent with the ideas of the British Archigram group, and in many respects resembling the Piano and Rogers Pompidou Centre (pp. 84–89 – the Aachen hospital was in fact conceived shortly before), the project exposes its mechanical and structural systems 'deliberately and shamelessly'. Colour is also used to foreground their identity and there is no overwhelming framework inside which all these diverse contraptions are inscribed, other than the grid. As a result, its individual components are free of any formalistic presuppositions. Given, however, the explosion of new technological, electronic means of information processing, of simulation and uses of artificial intelligence, one wonders if the very technology which created this efficient and sublime cathedral of health will not soon make it obsolete in its gigantism by relocating much of it onto the family doctor's desk.

(Opposite) Perspective section showing construction and services of the New Medical Faculty of the Technical University of Aachen

(Below) Isometric drawing of the building and its interior

(Right) The facade at the rear of the building

(Above) Interior

(Left) One of the internal courts

(Opposite) Detail of the tower-like structures

Adrien Fainsilber
CITÉ DES SCIENCES ET DE L'INDUSTRIE, PARC DE LA VILLETTE
(Paris, France)
1980–86

Like the New Medical Faculty of the Technical University of Aachen by Weber, Brandt and Partners (1968–86, pp. 168–71), the Cité des Sciences et de l'Industrie manifests the megaphiliac and technophiliac as well as universalist spirit of the 1960s, bent on assembling everything under one roof. And as in the case of Piano and Rogers' Centre Pompidou (1971–77, pp. 84–89), the global nature of its programme, the size of the structure and the lack of formalist pre-conceptions create a festive, circus-like mood. Yet neither overcrowding nor the roar that accompanies its holiday atmosphere prevent this building from fulfilling its aim: the communication of the joy to be derived from science, technology and invention.

The largest science museum in the world, it occupies an area of 165,000 square metres. A permanent exhibition area covers 40,000 square metres. To accommodate the many activities it hosts, it has a convention centre with a main auditorium for 1000, a multimedia library, temporary exhibition spaces, a 'discovery' area for children's science clubs, restaurants, and so on.

The museum building reused a large auction hall (270 metres long by 110 metres wide) which had been begun on the site in the 1960s and never completed. This was accomplished by removing existing construction elements from the original building structure, which consisted of 20 hollow, concrete towers, each 40 metres high, until their foundations 13 metres below ground level were exposed. As a result, the entire facade now receives daylight. Similarly, the 16 steel trusses, with a 65-metre span, have been exposed and painted deep cobalt blue, to contrast with the granite-clad concrete towers.

The museum's objective of celebrating technology within its walls is furthered by the building itself. Three aspects contribute significantly to this: the natural lighting devices; the bio-climatic greenhouses; and the mirroring surface of the Géode globe.

The provision of natural light was a key concern of the architect. The original multi-layered volume was gutted and a huge, open, central light well was carved out of the roof. Two domes 26 metres in diameter and equipped with robot-operated mirrors bring light deep into the building. The rotating cupolas were coated with stretched teflon.

The north and south facades of the building are among the most important features of the project, not so much as conscious spatial compositions, but rather as artifacts that perform significant processes. The singular feature of the south facade is its three green-houses of a monumental scale, 32 metres by 32 metres in surface and 8 metres deep. They act as bio-climatic fronts, buffer areas to collect daylight and store solar energy which they redistribute according to the needs of the facility. The glasshouse details were designed in collaboration with Peter Rice of the engineering firm Ove Arup. What makes it special is the original way in which the panes are mounted and suspended. The design for this enormous glass surface, so sensitive to pressure and depression, was tested carefully in a wind tunnel before construction. Meticulous investigations were also carried out to ensure that the envelope was weatherproof, as well as being rigid.

The creation of this structure, with its qualities of extreme lightness combined with especial stability (most notably to withstand wind), constitutes a true technological feat. But in addition, it demonstrates that the amazing technology developed in our time – much of it employed in Fainsilber's building – can be used in an architecture that celebrates the very idea of technology.

The north facade is divided by a horizontal safety walkway linking the terraces on the east and west sides. Its upper part is made of stainless steel, while the lower is glazed. The effect of transparency and reflection which

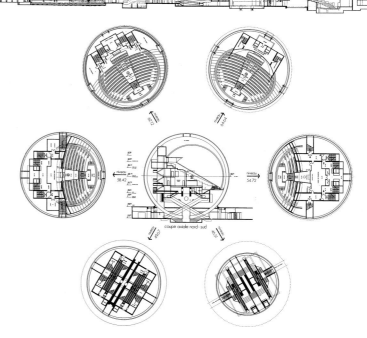

dominates the composition is enhanced by the reflecting pool around the building.

In front of the south facade, born from a pool of water and centred on the main entrance hall, rises the Géode, a geodesic dome in stainless steel with a brilliant mirror finish, which houses a cinema. The architect saw in it a symbolic representation of knowledge, expressed both through its mirroring of the sky, water and earth in its spherical form, and in its placement as a 'beacon' in the overall plan. Inside, people are transported between the surrounding sunken sitting area and the auditorium by four escalators. They enter a world within a world of sound and image. The Géode contains a highly sophisticated audio-visual system, the Omni-max, with a 180-degree projection capability onto a hemispherical screen of over 1000 square metres, suspended under the dome. If the visitor standing outside has the feeling that the universe is contracting onto the sphere, once inside, the 370 spectators have the opposite feeling, that their perception of the universe reaches out to its infinity.

(Opposite, left) The facade with greenhouses

(Opposite, right) Natural light floods the interior

(This page, centre) Site section

(Top and bottom) The Géode, with plans and section

Jean Nouvel, Gilbert Lezènes, Pierre Soria, Architecture Studio
INSTITUT DU MONDE ARABE
(Paris, France)
1983–87

The site of the Institut du Monde Arabe was notorious for its bad location. Used for a long time as a car park, it is immediately adjacent to the university campus of Paris Jussieu, which is a typical, unfriendly project of the 1960s. The site is also on the fringe of Paris's periphery, near the Gare d'Austerlitz and the Salpêtrière Hospital, an area strewn with the languishing carcasses of great architectural monuments of the past, such as the Menagerie of the Jardin des Plantes. Moreover, it stands at the very point where the street along the Left Bank now turns into a super-highway; this has destroyed the possibility of the site coming into contact with the river, a luxury that still survives in the older parts of Paris. Although so close to the centre of Paris, such developments as the Institut have created a Manhattan-like condition of isolation which characterized this site of the urban periphery.

The Institut du Monde Arabe responded to this 'dirty real' environment in a lyrical way, foregrounding its harshness rather than trying to cover it up or prettify it. The cinematic coolness of its glass and metal surfaces are highly charged with the kind of poetic references and beauty found in French *films noirs*. Ultimately, however, its aesthetics are more inclined to the cool and minimal. The metallic textures of the interiors are reminiscent, for

(Below) Site plan

(Right) Plans of the ground floor and basement

(Opposite) Sunscreen panels operate by means of automatic photosensitive diaphragms

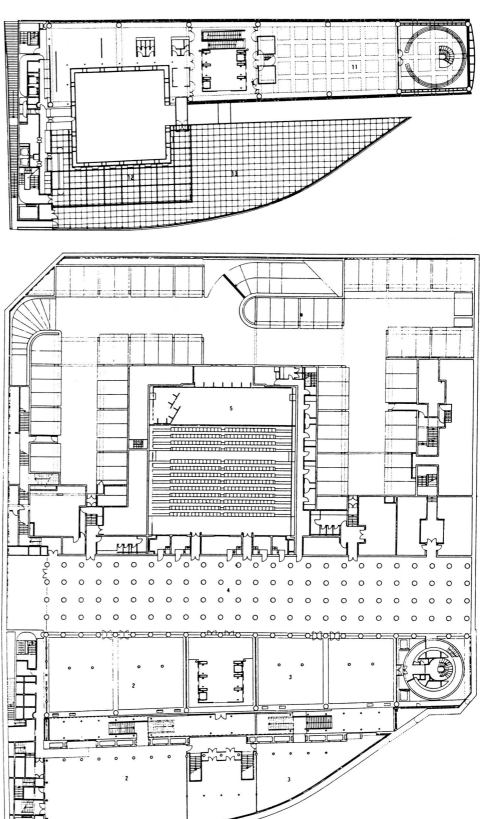

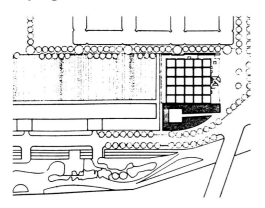

example, of Michel Andrault and Pierre Parat's Agence Havas, in Neuilly-sur-Seine (1971–73). They can be traced back to the prototypes of Jean Prouvé, in particular to his design for the Maison du Peuple of 1939 in Clichy, with its industrial skin of metal, lightweight and thin, pierced with railway-carriage-type windows, and certainly to Pierre Chareau's Maison de Verre (1928–32). As in these antecedents, Nouvel has succeeded in infusing into the industrial products he has used a sense of intention and intelligence, through, for instance, the 'humanization' of the mass-produced details, and he has succeeded in incorporating into them a fictionalized, narrative quality which renders the industrial fabric pleasurable. The building thus has the surface harshness of a factory, but not its aggressiveness, while making the best of its disadvantaged context.

French architectural critics and others have praised Nouvel for adopting a height that fits in with the surrounding buildings, thus allowing the overall configuration of the complex to be consistent with the city's skyline. As in the case of the Pompidou Centre (pp. 84–89), the Institut's respect for its surroundings has made the project felicitous. The way in which the building encloses the maximum number of activities in extraordinarily compact forms concentrated along the riverside – thus leaving space for the creation of a generous public square on the south side of the building where it is protected from the flow of traffic, a fragment of urbanity in the midst of an anomic and atopic part of the city – has also been highly praised. The open-air café on the top floor, overlooking the Seine – another precedent set by the Pompidou Centre, which should be imitated more often – also establishes

contact with the river, with the Ile St-Louis, the Quai Henri IV, in fact, with the entire Paris skyline, while maintaining a comfortable distance from the noise and pollution of the traffic below.

The institute, which is devoted to Arab studies, contains a library of 35,000 books, an auditorium with 352 seats, reading rooms, a museum and audio-visual facilities. The generally hard, 'northern', industrial aesthetic employed makes a contrasting and ingenious use of appropriate references to Arabic culture. In the library, a gently sloping spiral staircase, based on the minaret of Samara in Iraq, rises a full 32 metres in the air. Lined with reference books, it provides a view of the outside through a glass wall on the west side, oriented towards the Ile St-Louis. The building's main *arabisant* feature is the glass-and-aluminium panels, more than 240 in number, which include 27,000 light-sensitive apertures on the side facing the open square. These work like the shutters of a camera, adapting to the shifts in light conditions, so that its intensity remains constant. The apertures cast onto the interior geometrical shadows shaped like *masharabieh*, the traditional sculpted wooden screens. Each mobile shutter panel is sandwiched between double-glazed windows on the outside and single ones on the inside. The latter can be opened for easy access to the screen to facilitate repairs or cleaning. Of the building's cost, 60 per cent was borne by the French and 40 per cent by the Arab States – with the exception of Egypt. Expenditure was high; each shutter element, for example, cost 45,000 francs (in 1985) excluding the glass and the aluminium frame, as the *Wall Street Journal* noted at the time.

The building's friendly interior is no less felicitous than its exterior. It is broken down into two volumes, one square and one wedge-shaped. These are separated by a slit which allows vehicular access to the second floor and acts as the entrance to a patio whose facade is of white marble tiles from Thasos, held in aluminium frames. The white marble is so finely hewn that it is translucent, and acts as a filter through which light enters the building. The main exhibition hall is in the wedge-shaped part of the building and is primarily made of glass windows which are inscribed with a *trompe-l'oeil* silkscreen print by P.M. Jacquot. This reproduces a mirror image of the view of trees and houses on the Ile St-Louis across the Seine, directly opposite the building.

Jean Nouvel's interest in the cinema is reflected in the Institut's architecture, not so much in its capacity to serve as a backdrop for movies, but in its evocation of the intrigue of the silver screen. It is a building which, in the words of Roland Barthes, appears 'not as [an] illusion, but as fiction'.

**Jean Nouvel et Associés
NÉMAUSUS**
(Nîmes, France)
1985–87

In contrast to Jean Nouvel's Institut du Monde Arabe (pp. 174–77), which was one of the most expensive buildings per square metre in recent memory, his Némausus social housing project, directly commissioned by the socialist mayor of Nîmes, was cheap to build because of its use of inexpensive industrial materials. As a result, the tenants gained approximately 30 per cent more space. As an additional benefit, the 114 apartments, contained in the two almost identical buildings that make up the project, were provided with features rarely available even in the private housing sector: double orientation, cross ventilation, sunny balconies 2 metres wide, 15-metre-square bathrooms with large windows, and double-

height living rooms 5 metres high. Further-more, it provided an unusually rich selection of 17 different apartment types, either simplex, duplex or triplex.

As the French architectural critic Lionel Duroy notes, the materials used include corru-gated aluminium sheeting for the exterior and staircases, together with perforated and galva-nized aluminium for the footbridges that provide inner links of the type used in the engine rooms of freighters. Office-type glazed partitions are used to enclose rooms and bathrooms; wardrobes, cupboards and plate metal shelves are all fitted onto a perforated framework. The flooring is simple grey plastic, the rough concrete walls and ceilings bare

concrete. The sole concession to luxury is the prototype accordion garage doors made by the German firm Hormann that make up the entire facade of the apartments on the south side and permit maximum access to the balconies, to make the most of one of the finest climates France has to offer.

There are precedents for the overt imitation of industrial buildings in housing. Prouvé's housing in Meudon as well as his own house are two notable examples in France. The Eames' house in Pacific Palisades, California, with its steel decking, walls, joists and steel-framed windows bought from a catalogue, is another. A most influential precedent, of course, is Buckminster Fuller's Dymaxion

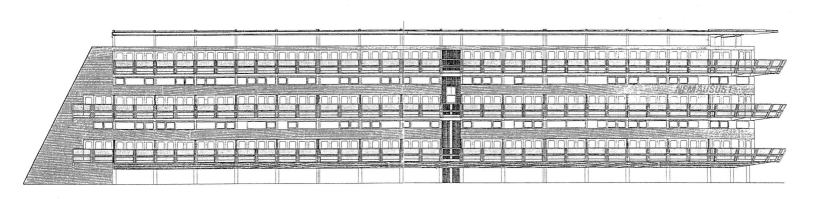

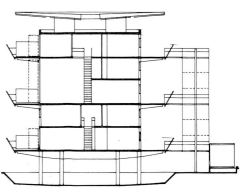

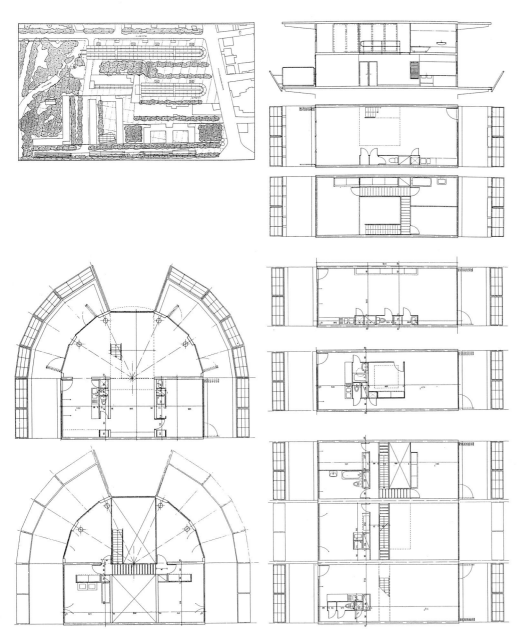

(Opposite) The balcony

(Top) Elevation

(Left column, top) General site plan

Different units within Némausus
(Left column, bottom two sketches) Plans for
5-room units in the 'prow' of the ship-like
building

(Centre column, top three sketches) Section
and plan of a 3-room duplex unit

(Centre column, middle two sketches) Types
of 2-room simplex apartments

(Centre column, bottom three sketches) A 4-
room triplex type

(Above) Cross-section showing duplex and
triplex apartments, external circulation,
parking area and pilotis

(Far and below left) The balcony and building by night

(Left) Detail of staircase

(Opposite) The exterior, looking towards the prow

House with its use of metallic cladding, 'clip-on' appendages and rounded forms shaded by *brises-soleil*. That precedent, meant for serial reproduction, was also doubtless the source of Némausus's remarkable configuration: almost identical parallel twin buildings separated by a thicket of sycamore trees.

But there is an additional, contextualist dimension to Nouvel's choice of industrial materials and forms. Némausus is built on a 'periphery' site: the buildings are located in an old industrial area close to the peripheral road around the city. The 'dirty real' landscape is populated by futuristic gas stations, rough garages, industrial plants and warehouses. The Némausus units respond in kind. With their rough concrete interiors, accordion doors, red and white bands and exclusive use of perforated and galvanized industrial aluminium staircases, the buildings are metaphorical garages or industrial warehouses. The painter François Seigneur was commissioned to work on the concrete walls of four apartments, but otherwise the inhabitants were forbidden to change their intentionally 'unfinished' appearance.

One of the key metaphors that shaped Le Corbusier's Unité d'Habitation in Marseille was the building as sea-going vessel. The same is true of the two Némausus units; equipped as they are with a poop, decks and prow, the buildings are also obviously intended as representations of ships. However, whereas Le Corbusier's prototype was the ocean liner, Nouvel's model seems to be a lightweight, economically conceived, jet hovercraft. The

irony of the Nouvel metaphor is apparent in the sunken parking lot below the apartments: only the curves of the car roofs are visible from the outside. The intention is to make the building look like a vessel sailing across metallic waves – a metaphor one would expect from someone such as Nouvel, a long-time collaborator of the neo-futurist theoretician Paul Virilio, for whom the representation of movement is the essence of modernity.

The buildings are more than a graceful formal statement. According to a recent study, they are popular among their inhabitants. They are machines for living in, to use Corbusier's famous expression (but less metaphorically and more pragmatically meant than by Le Corbusier). They achieve extremely high standards of livability in a public-sector housing development by overcoming infelicitous conditions and refusing to accept conventional constraints. In this respect, Jean Nouvel is what has been described, in the words of the French critic Jacques Lucan, as a 'critical' architect.

Rem Koolhaas (OMA)
THE NETHERLANDS DANCE THEATRE
(The Hague, Holland)
1984–87

A major problem in Europe, over the last twenty years or so, has been how to cope with the chaotic, derelict areas of cities on their peripheries and in their centres that the wanton urban development schemes of the post-war era have turned into no-man's-land. At a time when many architects were preoccupied with 'memory' or the 'sense of place' in historic urban areas, Rem Koolhaas was among the first to address the 'degree zero' urbanity of the fractured city edges and disembowelled inner cities. The Hague Dance Theatre was an ironically appropriate first commission.

A crueller case of urban blight, created by what Koolhaas has referred to as our contemporary 'culture of congestion', would be hard to imagine. Once the very heart of historic The Hague, the site for The Netherlands Dance Theatre is now squeezed between an elevated eight-lane highway, a major tram and bus interchange, the oppressive concrete slabs of the Ministries of Justice and Defence and a multitude of derelict two-storey buildings alternating with littered vacant lots (not to mention the claustrophobia induced by the zoning and planning scheme of the site chosen for the Dance Theatre). To make things still more difficult, the budget for the theatre was low.

Like the early-1970s followers of Robert Venturi's and Denise Scott Brown's *Learning from Las Vegas*, Koolhaas responded to the commission in a contextualist manner instead of approaching the problem with *a priori* architectural values, finding guidelines for design in the specifics of the site and its surroundings. In comparison to the so-called pop contextualists, the mood of his response was no longer so light-hearted; it had a hard edge because of the harsher urban realities. The result is the deliberately provocative and critical 'dirty real' quality of the building, the building's contextual reality in all its urban or industrial roughness. To the south-east, it lunges almost pugnaciously over the traffic lights at the intersection of the road and the tram and bus lines. Its consciously nondescript facade is that of a governmental building rather than a cultural institution, more suited to bureaucrats than art lovers. The corrugated metal walls at the back are garage-like. Finally, and most disconcertingly, the main entrance to the theatre looks distinctly like a side door.

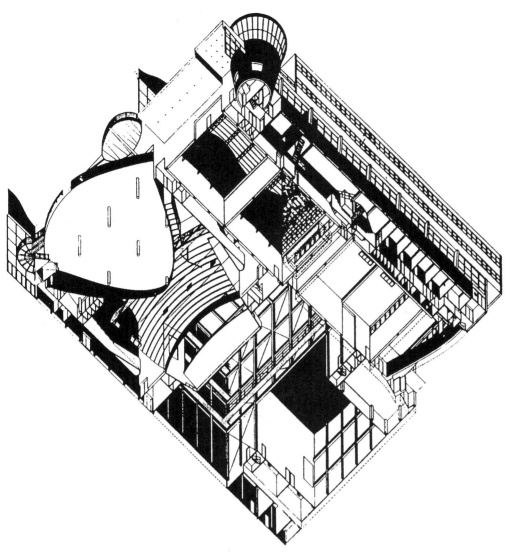

(Left) A worm's-eye view of The Netherlands Dance Theatre building

Two views of the interior
(Opposite) The sky bar, balanced on a single beam, seen from the foyer below

(Below) The theatre, looking towards the stage

(Below left) The side of the building projects over the road

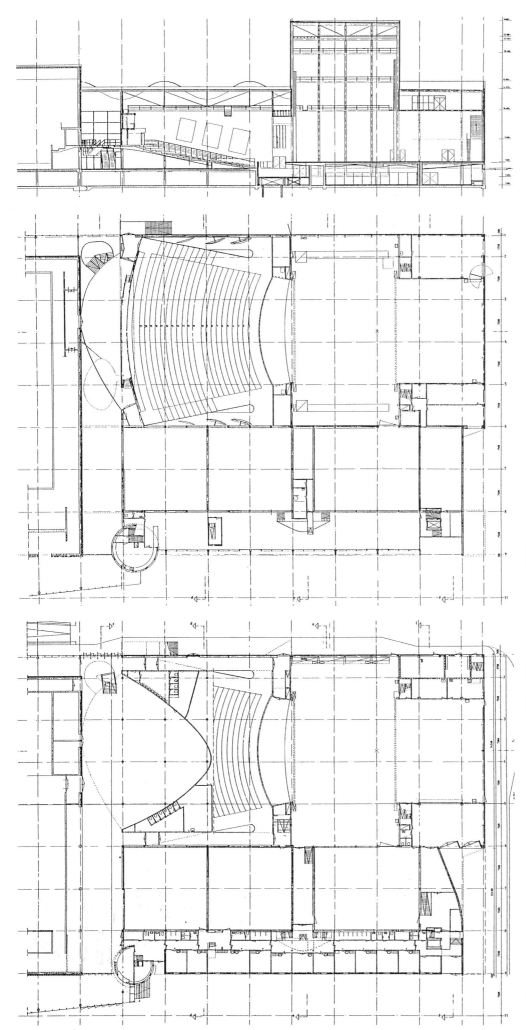

**Plans of the Dance Theatre
(Top to bottom) Section; floor plan at balcony
level; ground floor plan**

**(Opposite) The main facade, with Madelon
Vriesendorp's fresco, in its site context**

(Above) The rear facade

However, the response of the Dance Theatre to the surrounding urban harshness is not just to reflect it. The giant fresco of dancers by Madelon Vriesendorp that adorns the wall rising above the rest of the building is a vibrant affirmation of sensuality, as if to negate the abysmal surroundings. The same is the case with the dominating visual effects in the interior of the building, especially the polychromatic explosion in the foyer in canary yellow, cardinal red, copper and gold.

As in an Alexander Calder mobile, in this setting for the celebration of the body in motion nothing is a strict geometrical form and everything seems somehow slightly out of joint, as if poised on the brink of imbalance. The concave shape of the coffee bar and the curve of the balcony of the first floor are not paraboles, just

as the platform of the second-floor balcony, the sky bar, is not an ellipse but an ovoid. Seen from below, the two balconies above the foyer seem to float, or to rather dance. The sky bar literally does bob and dip in response to shifting movements of visitors, precariously balanced as it is on a single beam. In the theatre proper, painted black, the tension resulting from the buoyant, fluid effect is similar. The undulated ceiling, which is simply the underside of the roof, with insulation held between the two layers of corrugated steel, is swung up over a light truss spine, swaying rhythmically with the rippling corrugated metallic walls below.

The one indulgence of the extremely economical theatre is concealed: a suspended swimming pool, an element that became almost an

emblem in Koolhaas's early paper designs, which is reserved for the dancers. In the imaginative provision of this amenity, as well as in several other small functional details, OMA, Koolhaas's Office of Metropolitan Architecture, demonstrates that it is one of the very few architectural firms today which continue to dare to think seriously and inventively about programme and programmatic innovation rather than just compositional newness. It is troubling that outside the refuge of the Dance Theatre, the dirty realities go on, a fact intentionally brought to mind as one slips back out through the 'side door' entrance.

Rob Krier
SCHINKELPLATZ HOUSING PROJECT
(Berlin, Germany)
1983–87

In 1957, Interbau, the International Exposition of Architecture, took place in the Hansa Viertel neighbourhood of West Berlin. Its purpose was to present itself as a major example of urbanism demonstrating the sacred principles established by the Athens Charter in the Congrès Internationaux d'Architecture Moderne (CIAM) in 1933. Its post-war modernist buildings placed individually in a park were meant to stand as symbols of newness, health, liberty – at once a critique of and an alternative to the Stalin Allee of East Berlin, to its blind historicist obedience to models of the past in city planning and architecture.

By the early 1980s, however, a complete reversal was well under way. West Berlin, in the spirit typical of Western industrial democracies, had begun to re-evaluate in a positive manner Stalinist architecture (a revisionism which included the reinstatement of Albert Speer as a great architect), City Beautiful Planning and Academic Monumentalism. The decision was taken to organize a new international exhibition in Berlin, the IBA Stadt-Neubau, which opened in 1987. The purpose of the exhibition was to try to save Berlin from a danger, in the words of Jean-Louis Cohen, that had been 'more destructive than the bombardments' – that of modernist, Athens Charter type urbanism. As in the case of Interbau, architects were called in to participate from all over the world.

It is within this framework that Rob Krier's projects in Berlin try to rediscover and reconstruct the art of traditional city building and to reintroduce the idea of monumentalism in housing. Krier is concerned with maintaining the architectural memory of the city as a

(Above) Axonometric showing analysis of courtyard and public places

(Above left) Architect displaying plans

(Opposite, above) Drawing of the internal court concept

(Opposite, below) View of internal court

precious discovery whose value is still untarnished. The Schinkelplatz project possesses the unquestionable merits of livability inherent in the traditional building type that it reuses. Nevertheless, its cognitive power to make us understand time through space by affecting our perceptions – which is, after all, what a history-based architecture is all about – is limited to scenographic effects. To paraphrase Proust's observation in *Contre Sainte Beuve*, 'time never assumed a dimension of space' here. Moreover, one questions the relevance of these effects to the inhabitants of the project; as Krier himself points out, they are mainly of Turkish extraction. Despite the project's rhetorical urbanity, it is difficult to ignore the narcissistic qualities of what appears to be little more than a retreat to the past – coloured by what Heinrich Klotz has called a Luddite

reaction against the idea of progress. Despite its scale, the project fails to address any of the key issues of contemporary urbanism, such as transportation or the relationship between employment, residence and services. It cannot therefore be used as a model for similar developments.

Dominique Perrault Architecte
ÉSIÉÉ, ÉCOLE D'INGÉNIEURS EN ÉLECTRONIQUE ET ÉLECTROTECHNIQUE
(Cité Descartes, Marne-la-Vallée, France)
1985–1987

Perrault's building resembles a colossal, 40,000-square-metre computer keyboard rising on the edge of the superhighway in the heart of the Cité Descartes, the green-belt science park of Marne-la-Vallée, on the outskirts of Paris. The building houses the 1100 students and faculty of the prestigious College for Electrical and Electronic Engineers, which specializes in advanced micro and optical electronics, robotics and computer science.

Perrault has said that he was influenced by land art in the conception of this enormous plastic structure, which gracefully fits the contours of the site. Equally successful are the interior public circulation spaces. But the most significant feature of the project is the use of

innovative materials and techniques of construction and the rich visual effects of celebration it achieves through them.

This cathedral to computation manifests an almost mystical, obsessive fascination with photogenic, artificial materials and the light effects associated with them. It successfully transcends the tackiness which might so easily have been attributed to it because of the presence of so much plastic and the naive use of the computer icon to shape the scheme. In fact, it brings to mind Abbot Suger's comments about the materials used in St-Denis, which show an equally obsessive and mystical fascination with the light-reflecting qualities of precious stones – sardius, topaz, jasper,

chrysolite, onyx, sapphires, carbuncles and emeralds. Indeed, Perrault boasts, above all else, of the use of building materials and techniques: silicone-jointed structural glazing, for example, already standard in the USA and Britain, but first introduced in France in I.M. Pei's Pyramid of the Grand Louvre (pp. 226–29). This technique is employed in most of the building's exterior and interior, in the north, east and south facades of the library, the main entrance and the restaurant. Polyester in the form of tiles is also used in cladding the inclined plane of the building. Their composition is described with something approaching wonderment in the project description: 'These panels are 6 metres long and 1.20

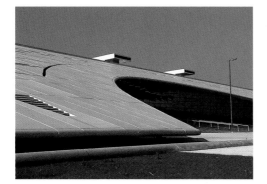

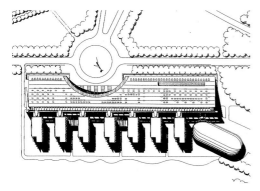

(Opposite) The glass wall

(Above) Volumetric plan

(Top centre) Detail of the exterior

(Top right) Aerial view of the building and its surroundings

(Right) The interior

metres wide; they have been fabricated thanks to a perfectly smooth metal mould in which the following layers were superimposed: a demoulding agent, a layer of gelcoat, a coat of resin, a coat of fibreglass, a coat of resin, a coat of foam, a coat of fibreglass, a coat of resin.' Acrylic and polycarbon are used for the gallery concourse toptighting which takes the form of double bowstring strutted 'lenses' to control solar gain. Finally, PVC fabric is stretched over laminated arches throughout the forebuilding where it provides an economical false ceiling, and is continued uninterrupted beneath skylights where it acts as a light diffuser, as well as in the canopy covering the entrance to the building.

Christian de Portzamparc
CITÉ DE LA MUSIQUE
(Paris, France)
1984–90

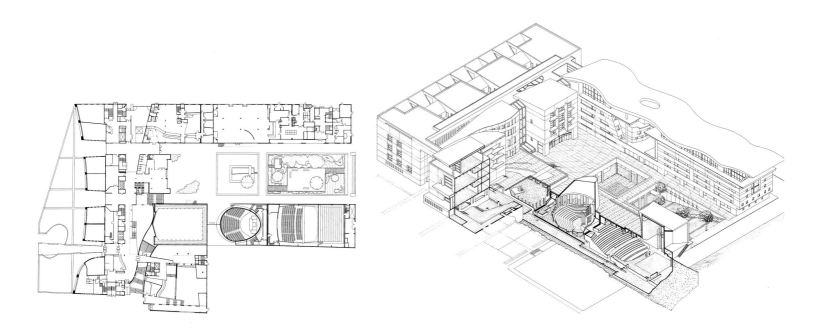

Conceived as a 'city within the city', a work composed of many compositions, a spatial structure expressing the 'art of movement' and 'made for sound', this project sits at the southern entrance of the Parc de la Villette, one of the last in the *Grands Projets* series of President Mitterand.

The highly heterogeneous character of the complex emerged out of its intricate, multi-functional programme, 'a unique collection of places devoted to music and dance'. The building is divided roughly into two zones. The western zone is devoted to teaching and study; it also contains large halls for group rehearsals. This zone is itself partitioned further into 'four north-south bands separated by hallways of light'.

In the centre of the complex there is an interior court, a patio and a cloistered garden seven metres below street level. The conical form belongs to the organ hall next to the theatre shell.

The activities housed in the eastern zone are more public. The zone contains an elliptical cylinder-shaped concert hall (capacity 1200 persons) for symphonic music and contemporary performances, a Museum of Music (for listening to and viewing one of the most beautiful collections of instruments in the world), a Centre for Organ Studies, an amphitheatre, the headquarters of the Ensemble Intercontemporain, the Institute of Music Instruction, student residences and shops specializing in music. As with the western zone, the eastern is further divided into explicitly articulated locations, each housing an individual activity. All the locations are joined by a circulation network stressing the integrity of each space and the transparency of the overall volume.

The plurality of elements which make up the spatial composition did not result only from the nature of the programme. It was also the outcome of the anti-monistic design principle of de Portzamparc: a building should not be an arbitrarily shaped, universal envelope, but a multiform assemblage of volumes and facades responding to the different conditions of the site, some requesting openness, some suggesting insularity, some a symmetrical treatment, some an asymmetrical, free, geometric design. 'What more natural', de Portzamparc writes, 'than that a building [should] propose all kinds of different faces . . . No one side should be more decisive than the others . . . they are all different, without expressing a hierarchy'.

In addition to the compositional motivation, there are several other benefits to be derived from a spatial arrangement of such highly particularized units which, de Portzamparc believes, the project achieves. First, the effect

(Above left) Underground plan

(Above) Isometric projection with section view of the concert hall

(Opposite) Views from the court

of scale: the building, despite its size, avoids inspiring those feelings of claustrophobia and vertigo so common to 'grand structure' projects. Secondly, there is a functional requirement: a facility so devoted to the contemplation of sound structures and the production of 'noise' needs powerful insulation devices. In housing each musical event in distinct volumes or sub-groups of spaces, de Portzamparc found an efficient and effective way of solving the problem of acoustical protection. A third benefit from this individualization of parts is the urban-friendly quality of the building: natural light and long views, and diverse outdoor 'in-between' locations provide public areas for socializing at the same size and frequency as in traditional, historical city centres.

This project makes use of Corbusier's 'bricolage' manner of composition and has a strong aura of his work: the shell covering the concert hall is a replica of the Chandigarh Assembly Hall and of the church of Firminy; the western facade emulates the curved and rhythmical portico of the Palace of the Assembly of Chandigarh; the rounded walls are a hallmark of any number of Corbusier's designs; and the undulating roof can be traced back to Corbusier's utopian and never-completed project at La Sainte-Baume. When all the sources of inspiration are identified and the 'intertextual' interpretation of the citations is carried out in this project's rich memory labyrinth, one may feel overpowered by a sense of wonder at the brilliance of the original *bricoleur*.

(Above) View from the court

(Opposite) East facade

Hans Hollein
NEUES HAAS HAUS
(Vienna, Austria)
1985–90

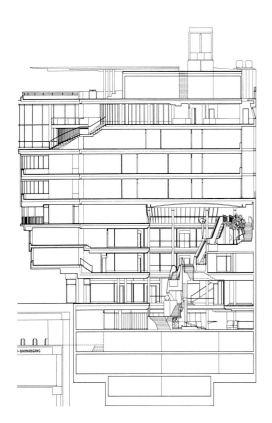

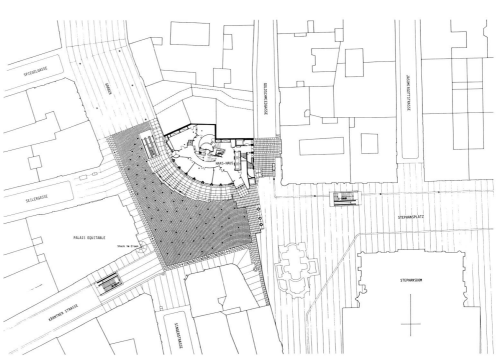

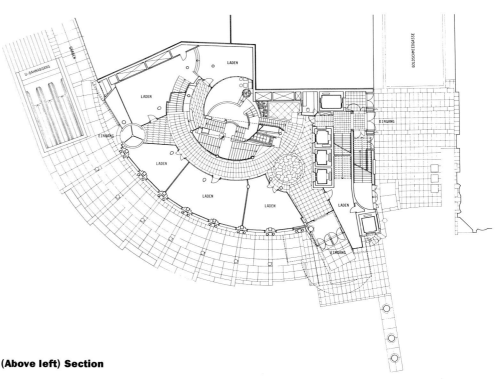

The Neues Haas Haus stands on the site of earlier Roman fortifications, in the heart of the historic First District of Vienna, opposite St Stephen's Cathedral. But it also lies inside a territory defined very much by Hollein's own mental world; three decades of stage design, exhibitions, industrial design, artifacts, furniture, the radiant Retti candle shop (1964), the florid Chista Metek boutique (1967), the precious Schullin Jewelry Shop (1972, pp. 72–73). The Neues Haas Haus is an ambitious commercial project of eight storeys: four sales floors facing onto a glassed-in courtyard, three office floors and a restaurant on top. As in most buildings by Hans Hollein, functionally the organization of the project is an ordinary response to the needs of the programme. The extraordinary aspects of the project relate mainly to the treatment of the facade and to the reading it invites.

There is an aura of Richard Strauss in the building: contrast, paradox, irony, a delicate balance between classical and anti-classical views of spatial composition. In short, it is characterized by what have been called 'oxymoric poetics', and it is these that make it one of the most intriguing works of Hollein's career.

At first glance, the eye is caught by an apparently strange sight. A graceful, classical,

(Above left) Section

(Above) General plan and ground floor plan

(Opposite, above) Exterior view

(Opposite, below) Interior view from the glassed-in courtyard

belvedere-like temple stands at the top of the massive volume of the building, where it dominates the structure. It is as if the building's only reason for existing were to serve as a foundation for this delicate pavilion.

Another strange aspect emerges when one looks at the facades of the building. It is encased in two stone walls which remain open at the corner, their place being taken by an imposing wall of curved glass. The Roman baroque-like stone walls, with their solidly mounted and sombre convex forms, rise up as if to refortify the city on this very site of its ancient walls; then they suddenly disappear, to expose a radiant, all-glass turret. There is a contextual explanation for this highly contrasted manner of treating a facade: according to Hollein himself, the periphery of the building varies in response to changing conditions of the site around it. Thus we find 'stone towards the Graben and the Goldschiedgasse' and glass 'where the view is more open', that is, overlooking the main square which faces the corner of the building. The idea of contextual interpretation is reinforced by the fact that the building's curved outline follows the contour of the Roman fortification.

But there is probably another way of reading the project, more complex and more in line with

Hollein's idea of architecture – his preoccupation with creating 'fiction' through buildings and giving birth to 'salient worlds of design', as in the case of the Schullin Jewelry Shop (pp. 72–73). The building in its design narrates, in an urban-theatrical and highly abstract manner, the act of stripping, the state of undress acted out architecturally by the exposure of the sparkling epidermis of the curtain wall. The 'plot' of the suggestive stripping away of the fabric of the perforated stone wall offers a 'commercial' image *par excellence*. This is a fitting image for a super-emporium trying to revive the lifestyle of a bygone, typically Viennese pre-war department store.

But ultimately there is a bitter-sweet moral allegory within this image of the built and unbuilt, the covered and revealed, which ties the project to the high and low art tradition of *fin-de-siècle* Vienna – also an obsessive theme present in most of Hollein's prolific works. The cracking of the stone wall can be interpreted simultaneously as covering as well as stripping, as revealing nudity as well as laceration, as the coupling of libido and abstinence, as eros and thanatos. More abstractly, this ambiguous architectural pattern can be seen as representing the cognitive acts of spatial composition and decomposition.

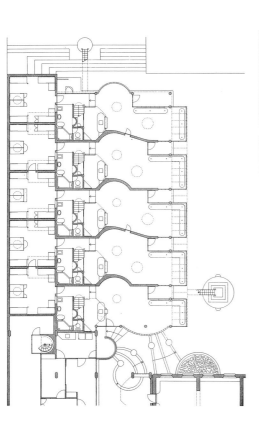

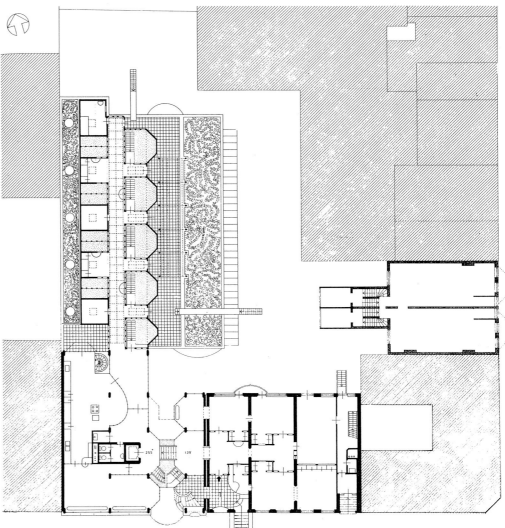

Aldo van Eyck's views first came into prominence in 1946 when, as an employee of the Office of Public Works in Amsterdam under the direction of Cornelis van Eesteren, he took a dissenting position against the massive projects of urban reconstruction typical of the post-war, militant 'progressive' approach that advocated the 'total' rebuilding of European cities. Van Eyck proposed, instead, small-scale 'infill' interventions, to be inserted in the voids of the bombed or abandoned urban fabric, which would spontaneously accommodate urgent needs in a focused, flexible and humane way. Three decades later, when most of such anti-planning, so-called 'incremental' ideas about urban intervention had become standard thinking in the architectural profession at large, and van Eyck himself had

gone in different directions, he returned to the idea of designing an infill project consistent with his life-long vision of a socially committed architecture. The result was Hubertus, a home for single mothers (now for single parents of either sex) and their children.

The commission came from the Hubertus Association, a Christian charity that had moved away from its original 19th-century paternalistic character. The building houses around 16 parents and a total of 73 children. Each family unit stays for about six months, during which time the single working parents are helped with their problems by 65 qualified professionals. The institutional principles are inspired by Carl Rogers' 'client centred' therapy and his ideals of a 'therapeutic', but also 'democratic' community.

This building stands in one of the most interesting parts of Amsterdam. It is inserted into a row of typical bourgeois, parallelepiped town houses in Plantage, an area associated with the Amsterdam Zoo, Berlage's Diamond Workers Union and theatres such as the Hollandse Schouwburg, which is just across the street from Hubertus. The site of the project itself was once occupied by the Talmud Thora Synagogue. Besides being an infill, Hubertus is partly a re-utilization of an existing adjacent building.

Van Eyck had to invent a new spatial organization for the new institution and he did this by introducing existing principles of the rule system of composition, colour and construction, all of which were put to work in the service of the building's programme; but they

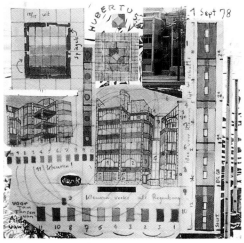

(Opposite, left) **Plan of five children's units**

(Opposite, right) **Mezzanine plan**

(Above) **Conceptual drawing**

(Right) **Views of the facade and the interior open area**

were also developed independently, rather like a quasi-autonomous essay on space and its cognition.

The front of the new building is a pushed-in and broken version of the well-ordered, reserved, frontal classicist Amsterdam facade typical of its street. The front door is set back, to create an open porch behind the building line and at the same time a kind of bay window, as well as a light well right on the street. An additional light well lies immediately behind the entrance, while the bay-window motif is taken up at the back of the building. This fragmentation has the effect of producing a sense of intimacy. Equally unconventional is the organization of the interior space, which does not, however, completely abandon the traditional orthogonal grid plan. There is also a wonderful transparency and spatial depth typical of the domestic architecture so often featured in Dutch 17th-century paintings. The new design uses a number of van Eyck's characteristic motifs: the unexpected syncopation which cheerfully subverts the composition's tripartite system of taxis, the chopped-off corners creating a 45-degree angle, the over-emphasized doorsteps and stair, the mixing of the square and the circle.

Many of these devices are drawn from the thesaurus of precedents of world architecture, ranging from African homesteads to Guarini churches and Santorini streets, to complexes by Johannes Duiker and, most definitely, projects by Le Corbusier. But none of them is employed for cognitive reasons alone, separate from meaning and use. In all their eccentricity and iconoclasm, they can be seen to be delivering, in sticks and stones, a critique of the conformist and routine obedience of order. But they also serve to celebrate a child's sense of place, in the manner of another van Eyck project, his famous Municipal Orphanage in Amsterdam (1960). Hubertus, by the use of colour, forms a total contrast to the sombre, generally uneventful facades around it. A polychromic 'rainbow bouquet', it is in van Eyck's words an icon of joy, affection and optimism. In the last analysis, his contribution is deeply human. It lies in creating what he calls a sense of 'homecoming' through a paradox: by making us feel momentarily like strangers in a new world.

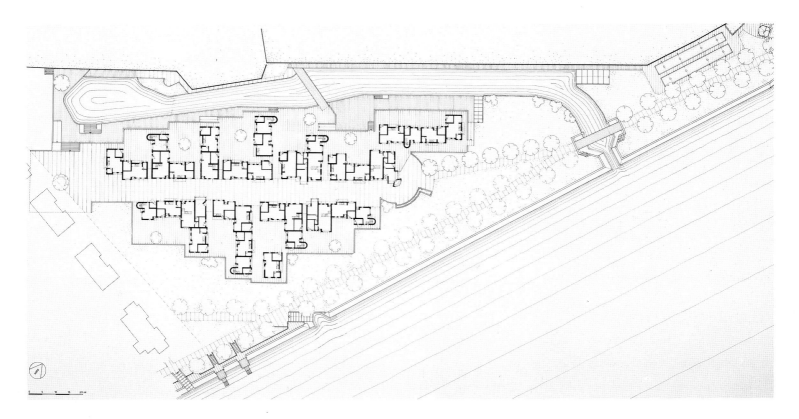

A housing project for just eighty dwellings would have normally passed unremarked in most cases, as Giancarlo De Carlo has observed. Eighty dwellings on the Venetian Lagoon, however, are a different matter and have a significant impact. De Carlo claims that his greatest concern has been the delicate, almost imperceptible structure of a 'myriad of minute signs' which, for him, has always had a 'clear meaning', indicating the movement of the various types of boats, the niches where fish gather, the topography of mooring. Observing the project, on the island of Mazzorbo, across from the islands of Burano and Torcello and only a few minutes from Venice itself, makes it immediately obvious that historical considerations, the 'gentle invasion' of new houses in a landscape charged with a cultural past, were of paramount importance.

In a passage quoted by Richard MacCormac in his inaugural address as the RIBA's new president, on 2 July 1991, he summarized De Carlo's life-long efforts to build within highly constrained cultural contexts: 'De Carlo says: "To design in a historic place, one should first of all read its layers of architectural strata and try to understand the significance of each layer before superimposing a new one. This does not mean indulging in imitation, as this would be a mean-spirited approach, saying nothing about the present and spreading confusion over the past. What is called for is the invention of new architectural images that are authentic and at the same time reciprocal with images already existing."'

De Carlo's most important inventions are not, however, limited to coping with problems of historical context. His architecture embraces history as part of the design process towards broader cultural and social objectives. Since the design of his early housing project in Matera of the mid-1950s, in the south of Italy, De Carlo has asserted that historical knowledge is a means through which architecture can bring about what he considers emancipation – a participatory rather than a hierarchical, regimented society. Historical knowledge can be achieved, according to De Carlo, very effectively through *participatory* methods aimed at stimulating and re-activating the memory of the inhabitants of a place. It is this sense of historical and hermeneutical dimension that makes De Carlo's design, through participation, so distinct from other, more

(Above) General plan of the Mazzorbo housing project

(Opposite) Two studies for individual units

(Opposite, above) The housing development seen from the lagoon

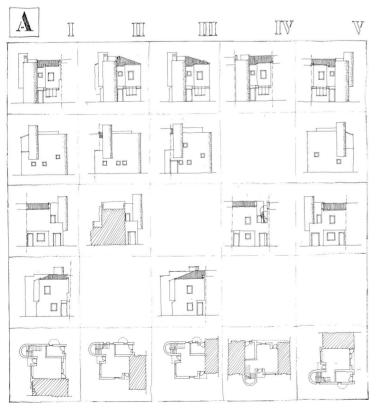

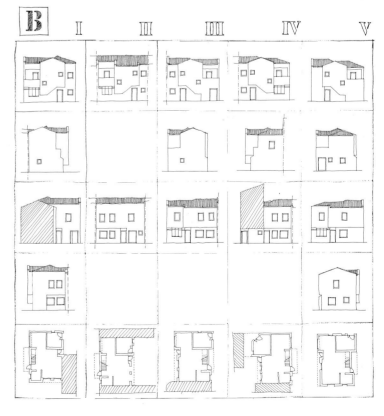

'positivistic', user-oriented approaches, from André Lurçat's first attempt, after World War II, to that of the more current practitioners, such as Lucien Kroll (pp. 44–47) and Herman Hertzberger (pp. 48–51).

In the case of the housing project presented here, there were hardly any existing structures on the site, and the only identifiable topographical element was the canal – or rather the memory of it, as the canal bed had been filled in. Given, however, the proximity of the Mazzorbo site to other small towns, not least Venice itself, 'the enemy, yet dreamed capital', and given also the strong architectural identity of these towns and the fact that most of the inhabitants of the new housing complex were to move there from them – physical images and also past ways of living deeply engraved on their minds – De Carlo acknowledged such contextual constraints.

Through systematic observation, structured interviews and informal meetings, De Carlo and his collaborators began to gather the information needed. The initial phase of research did not just involve people expressing their needs while the architects passively transcribed them. The reconstruction of history they were attempting was not only on the level of constructing a narrative 'truth'. It was, rather, a reciprocal, interactive process. Participation was an attempt at mutual *de-alienation*, engaging not only the users but the

architects themselves, who also suffered from exclusion and isolation. Moreover, even though the contribution of the future 'unskilled' users who lacked specialized knowledge was considered fundamental in tackling the problem at hand, the knowledge of the skilled architects was equally significant in attempting 'to invent and modify the space at hand'.

The initial observational and historical study followed procedures similar to previous studies by De Carlo, especially his acclaimed work on Urbino of the 1960s. In these studies he had developed a number of fundamental characteristic criteria used to analyse urban fabric and through which he could guide his interviews and observations of the users' lifestyle. It was these criteria which later helped to prescribe the results of his research into architecture. In their investigation, De Carlo and his collaborators dug deep into time, revealing layer upon layer of the underlying organization of space patterns, and the activities which took place within them, which finally determined the built forms.

Materials used for edges, steps and moorings are in white Istria stone, the same as in Venice. The layouts of the houses are based on carefully identified patterns of rooms and room relations, windows and window groupings, doors and thresholds, found in the area. In a similar manner, the colours of the facades are derived from the 'chromatic structures' (rather

than using isolated colours) that exist in Burano and Mazzorbo. The preservation of all such contextual architectural elements reveals an emphasis on maintaining contact and community, echoing De Carlo's affiliation with the 1960s Team X. The historicism of the resulting forms of the houses does not reflect a sense of nostalgia or regression, nor have such historical norms been imposed by the authority of the architect in this respect. There is no similarity in De Carlo's approach to the use of memory that, for instance, Aldo Rossi makes (pp. 56–63). What is unique in De Carlo's method is masterfully revealed in the Mazzorbo housing, a blend of historical 'socio-analysis', fundamental architectural structuralist conceptions and, most importantly, the belief that neither meaning nor quality in architecture are autonomous values. For De Carlo, meaning is the result of the transaction between human beings and the quality of the organization of physical space, which depends on the way space is peopled and forms are inhabited, on the manner which allows 'every human being' to be 'a potential protagonist'. This is an architecture of human dignity.

(Above) Houses along the canal

(Opposite, left) Disembarking from a boat on the canal

(Opposite, right) The central spine between housing rows

Erith & Terry
RICHMOND RIVERSIDE
(Richmond, England)
1985–88

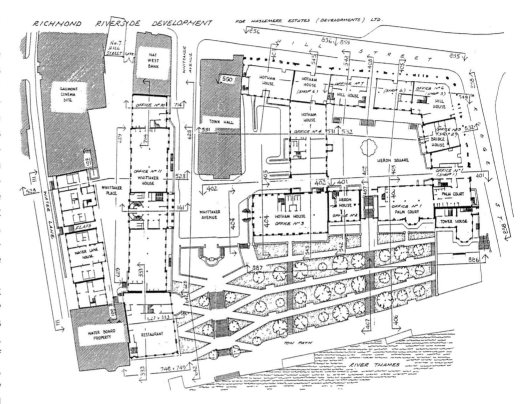

'Richmond Riverside is best approached from the river. This is the way the Queen arrived when she opened it in October 1988, on the same day that the Prince of Wales gave his remarkable attack on modern architecture.' This opening to the British architectural historian David Watkin's commentary on Quinlan Terry's project, written in a tone which echoes old guide books to important national monuments, encapsulates perfectly the union intended by the architect between architectural form, event and institution. It is the search for such a union that led to the explicit references, if not a direct revival of classicism, and an uncompromising continuity with historical setting that underlie this project of the classical revival movement of the 1980s.

Terry's gateway-building to the complex employs Burlingtonian details. The archway that leads to the townscape cites Palladio's Basilica at Vicenza. Once inside the complex, one encounters the 'Anglo-Dutch flavour of houses like Pratt's Coleshill of c. 1650', Watkin writes. Hotham House has eleven-bay piles and a balustraded belvedere; its external staircase 'recalls that of Poole Guildhall'. In the same vein, Watkin informs us, the Gothic of Venetian back-street houses is used in Bridge Street, along with 'further details recalling Ammanati's work at the Pitti Palace, and the Palazzo Venezia in Rome'.

Despite the excessive load of historical references, and the consequent amount of strict programme constraints, Terry incorporates facilities which make use of modern technology to serve the twenty-eight apartments, in what is predominantly a commercial development of about 9,850 square metres of offices and about 1,000 square metres of shops. There are throughways for lorries and fire-engines, air conditioning for all but Whittaker House, and parking for 135 cars. All basic provisions for users with physical disabilities are made in accordance with the humanistic principles of the architect, whose intention is to create a quality of humanity and care. The architectural organization of the buildings is contextually harmonious with the adjacent London riverside of Georgian Richmond, Kew and Twickenham and is related to their urban character. The scheme is adapted to the major landscape element, the river, through a skilful but simple use of terraces and lawns, ramps and stairs. The relation between river and project is so simple and successful one wonders, with David Watkin, why such obvious and intelligent solutions were not applied to projects of the recent past like the Hayward Gallery and the National Theatre complex. Richmond Riverside is one of the best projects of the last two decades in its fit to the site.

The project has been criticized for its inconsistency in using up-to-date technology at the same time as the spatial grammar of the past. One may argue, however, that this is in fact one of its most successful features: the independent pursuit of different systems that together make up an architectural whole, whether these systems are technological, functional or cultural, and the rational pursuit of each aspect independently and with the minimum of conflict. In this respect, the project appears particularly successful in terms of its contemporaneity – paradoxically because of, and not despite, its use of historical precedents coupled with avant-garde technology used for domestic comfort.

Perhaps it is not enough, however, simply to identify with intelligence and treat separately only in intellectual terms these distinct aspects, as Terry does. The architect, as producer of culture, has to provide deeper justification of the consequences of such discoveries on our life, and to comment critically upon them, to go beyond a mechanistic exposition of a system's complexity. More needs to be said on a higher level of abstraction as well as in architectural terms. Yet this project seems to turn its back to such questions, as non-existent.

Terry is undoubtedly a highly knowledgeable, conscientious and pragmatic architect. He is also opposed to what he considers to be 'progressive charlatanism and demagogy', current among many architects. Terry has most wittily expressed his views, for instance in a recent interview when he said, 'I wouldn't have a qualified architect in the office. They're just argumentative. They've got lots of political ideas which aren't of interest to me; they want a partnership, they're quarrelsome, they're lazy, they arrive late, they don't shave.' He clearly sees projects like Richmond Riverside, despite the business-like manner in which they are carried out, despite their 'lettability' and their popularity (the Richmond project won the

(Opposite) General plan

(Right) The development seen from the river

(Below) The South Gate

(Below right) Detail of the capital of a Corinthian pilaster

Johnnie Walker Award for 'being popular with the man in the street', and the Prince of Wales likes it too), as being on the same frontier where Kroll, Rossi or Rogers see themselves working. Terry perceives himself as part of an avant-garde, only one that is even more persecuted and excluded as a professional establishment than its 'radical' members. His campaign for a return to the traditional, classical values is carried out with as much intolerance and consistency as that of the radical avant-gardists he seems to deplore so much. In the same interview quoted above, he confesses how much he dislikes Grieg and Rachmaninov, how much he adores the classical music of Mozart and Purcell, and with what extreme devotion he traces and proportions the profiles of his classical orders. And yet his own work rarely succeeds in comparison to the genuine classical compositions. It is almost as if he could read correctly the individual notes and chords of Mozart without being able to produce the phrases, to perceive the thematic structures, or to understand that the classical edifice as culture has more to do with cognition and drama than simply with the parade of capitals and cornices.

Gregotti Associati International
UNIVERSITY OF PALERMO SCIENCE DEPARTMENTS
(Palermo, Italy)
1969–88

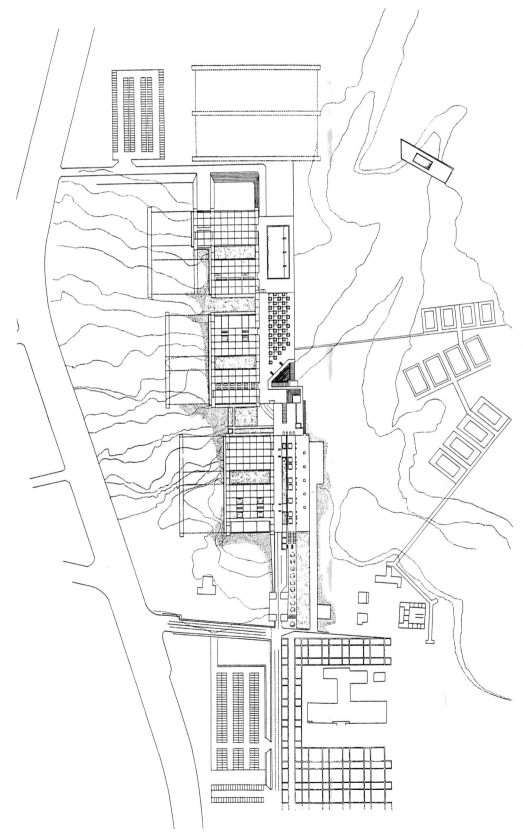

(Left) General plan of Gregotti's complex for the science departments of the University of Palermo

(Above) Aerial view of the buildings

Like many of the buildings of the critical regionalists in Spain, the complex of Gregotti's University of Palermo stands in a historical town. However, the difference in attitude to location could hardly be greater between them and him. Whereas the critical regionalists seek to reflect the memory of a place in their projects, Gregotti's buildings make not the slightest concession to it.

The new science departments of the University of Palermo (chemistry, physics, biology, mathematics and geology) is not only Gregotti's largest project, but one of the greatest in Italy in the last twenty years. For better or worse, the rejection of contextualism has yielded a functional megastructure that almost approaches in scale the Aachen Hospital Complex by Weber & Brandt (pp. 168–71), although entirely different in terms of its street allocation system and its treatment of structure and servicing.

The complex of Gregotti's science departments is arranged on the axis of the present Viale delle Scienze and laid out around a set of three elongated pedestrian precincts on different levels, with all the science departments

(Above) Site section and elevations

(Right) Detailed plan of a unit

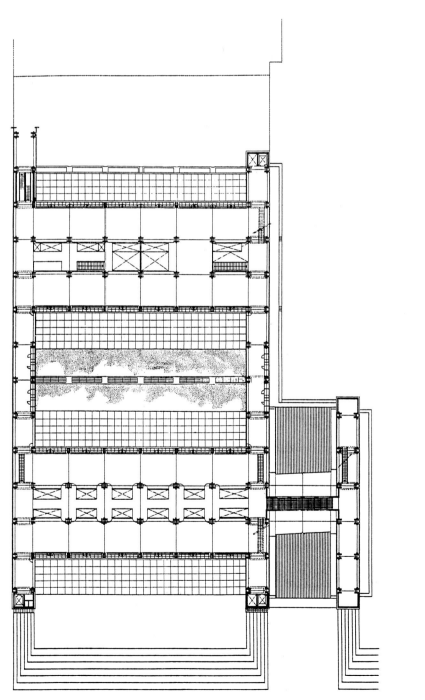

abutting onto them and the collective services for the student residences aligned along those. Each department consists of two connected blocks, one essentially intended for teaching preliminary courses and the other for advanced courses and research. Each of these blocks has two floors and a basement level for parking and services. The basic module for both construction and installations of each block is 7.20 metres square. In addition to its research block, the physics department has a workshop located along the axis of the research block. The vertical bearing elements are composed of a prefabricated double pillar (with an interaxis of 7.20 metres both ways) which will permit the vertical passage of the conduits and utilities – electric power lines, compressed air, gas, water pipes, distilled water supply, ventilation shafts, etc. These can then run horizontally, and open to inspection, under the prefabricated ceilings, which are so shaped as to permit the continuous horizontal arrangement of the conduits in both directions. This is the first earthquake-proof prefabricated and precompressed structure of any importance to be put up in Italy.

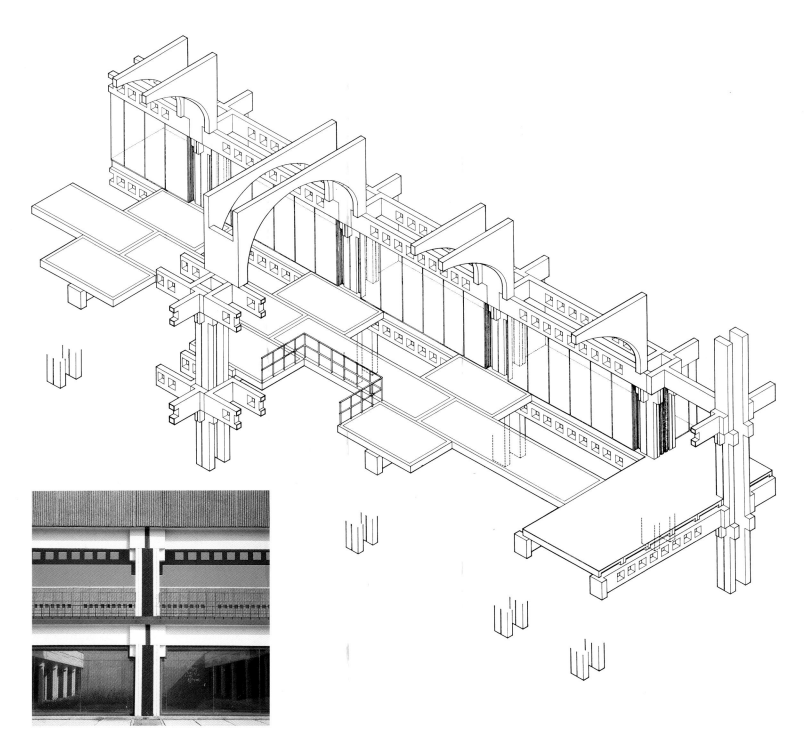

The Italian architectural historian and critic Manfredo Tafuri has pointed out that Gregotti's architecture is the outcome of the reaction of his generation to the 'neo-realists' of the 1950s and 1960s. They were, predominantly, Ernesto Rogers, Lodovico Quaroni and Mario Ridolfi. The most prominent was Ernesto Rogers, the architect of, among others, the Torre Velasca in Milan; he was also editor of the influential architectural review *Casabella Continuità*. Rogers was particularly concerned with the relation between modern architecture and the historical and regional fabric of its context. He supported an architecture which stood for the physiognomic and the specific and which avoided abstraction and adherence to general systems.

At the opposite end of the scale, Gregotti, a designer, and currently editor of *Casabella*, has taken sides in the European debate about such issues against the emphasis on architectural 'memory'. In his book, *Il territorio dell' architettura* (1965), he dismisses what he disparagingly refers to as 'neo-Proustean' attitudes. He argues, instead, for a highly abstract ideal of 'modernity' which is opposed to mimesis and memory. As is evident, on the other hand, in the University of Palermo, he is equally against an ad hoc, chaotic accumulation of spaces. In a manner, later followed by Paul Chemetov (see pp. 244–45), his project departs from a rigid minimalism or geometrical orthogonality – which slowly fills in with equally elementary, rigidly geometrical components. The result, in Gregotti's case, is measured and guarantees that it never falls short of a minimum quality of usage.

(Above) Isometric section showing the construction

(Above left) Detail of the facade

(Above) Interior view of corridors, connected to the floor below by staircases

(Right) Seating area in the open-air theatre

Architekt Dipl. Ing. Klaus Kada
GLASMUSEUM
(Bärnbach, Austria)
1988

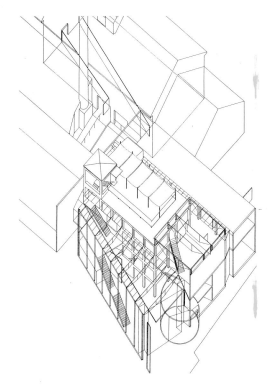

This design was the winning entry in a competition for an exhibition building on the theme of glass and coal on the site of the 1950s Bärnbach glass works. The building was then converted into a permanent glass museum and cultural centre. The use of glass as the most significant material for the building made the structure at once an 'exhibit and part of the display', Klaus Kada has stated.

What strikes the viewer is a sense of movement implicit in the design of the Glasmuseum. There is one's own movement as one is drawn into the structure, presented with 'prospects and retrospects', and offered multiple vistas of all aspects of the building and its surroundings in a 'conquest of flatness'. There is also the implicit movement of the parts which make up the structure, as if they had all been arrested in the process of being taken apart. Another sense of movement comes from the light: the way it is caught by the intersecting surfaces as it penetrates the loosely defined volumes of the building through their wide-open seams.

What holds the building together and makes possible all such implicit interpenetrations, while explicitly the volume is sealed, is glass. But the building is also held together as a composition. There is rigour in its formal spatial organization despite its apparent lack. The design is anchored onto a steel skeleton, a remnant and testimony of the old factory, which Kada views as a welcome accident, an architectural *objet trouvé*. The composition unfolds spirally, reaching out to the limits of the site and acknowledging the major axis of the town. The wall of hand-made glass tiles, carried by a filigree structure, runs parallel to the railway and the river.

In similar terms, Kada sees basic components of the composition as shaped by urban determinants. He writes, 'a glass stele . . . creates the pivot to the street frontage, along the second town-development line. On this line, the closure of the hall is formed by a pure, self-supporting glass construction, which at the same time dissolves the materiality of this boundary; urban space penetrates a house and can be experienced from outside. A solid wall follows, as the faceted outline of the grid-like front of the "shelving" in spatial distance – a stratum which has moved into the space by detaching itself from the steel-concrete framework.'

There is also a deeper logic which informs the building. It derives from the systematic breaking of one of the most fundamental structuring devices of classical architecture, what Vitruvius, following ancient Greek writings, referred to as *taxis*, the well-formed division of space into parts. Most often, this spatial rule system used an orthogonal grid as a basis for locating all architectural elements. It also prescribed that buildings and their parts must have clearly circumscribed limits and a perceptible beginning, middle and end. All that is carefully violated in Klaus Kada's Glasmuseum. In its place we have the jagged outline of the plan, dissolved boundaries, a faceted front of the building, an uneven succession of 'floating' roofs of galvanized tin.

In this elaborate exercise in anti-classicism, the role of glass, as a necessary condition for it, is central. But glass, ultimately, is only the means towards an end. Kada's architecture, like that of a large number of his Austrian colleagues, Günther Domenig, Michael Szyszkowitz and Karla Kowalski, Coop Himmelblau, Gustav Peichl, seems obsessed with the will to represent the unfolding of time through space.

(Left) Axonometric drawing of the Glasmuseum

(Opposite) Detail of the roof seen from inside the building

(Opposite, bottom row, left to right) The exterior; detail of the facade; the entrance

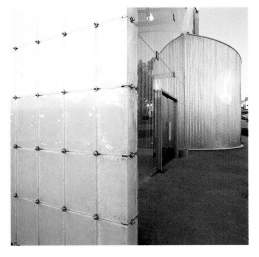

Hans Kollhoff
LUISENPLATZ HOUSING PROJECT
(Charlottenburg, Berlin, Germany)
1982–88

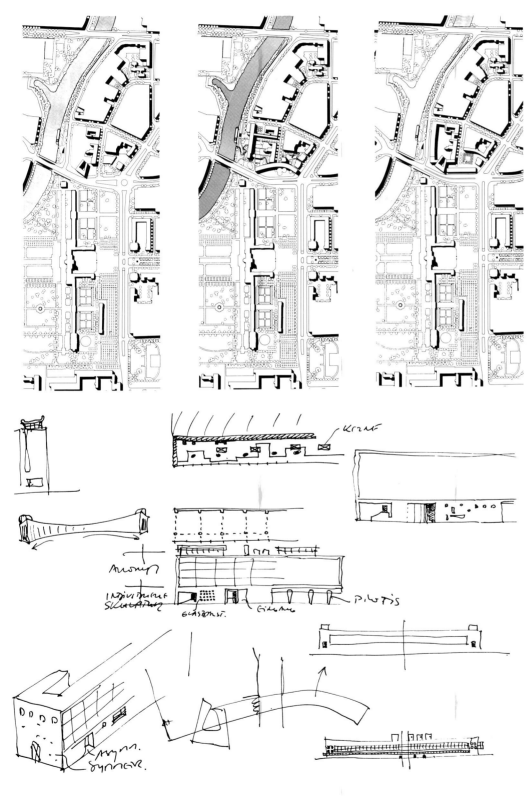

Two main principles characterized the housing projects presented at the IBA (the International Architecture Exhibition held in Berlin in 1987): a rejection of modernism in architecture and in the design of the urban fabric; and the perception of the city as a series of disconnected fragments, a view influenced by Colin Rowe's idea of a 'collage city' in the planning and organization of its fabric. If there is one feature which marks the Luisenplatz project by Hans Kollhoff, a representative of the younger generation of German architects, it is a polemical rejection of both those IBA principles.

This project is located in the heart of a district rich in historical styles – Jugendstil apartment houses, a Neo-classical Schinkel pavilion and the great Baroque Charlottenburg Palace. With its heavy blue brick inspired by Peter Behrens' industrial buildings and the wing-like form on the roof derived from Le Corbusier's design for Chandigarh, it is overtly attached to the ideals of modernist architecture. On the urbanistic level, it is an expression of the search for unity rather than fragmentation. Despite its eclectic assemblage of elements from modernist precedents, the building's tripartite composition of base, main structure and exaggerated celebratory crown is reminiscent of the compromise techniques of the 'New Monumentality' movement of the 1950s, formally reinforcing rather than destroying the spatial unity of the street. In Kollhoff's words, the building strives to create

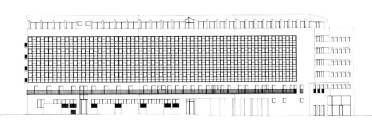

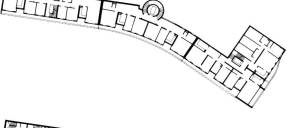

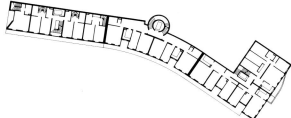

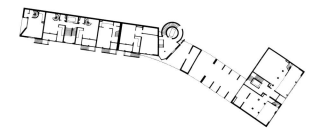

(Opposite)
(Above left, left to right) Plans of the site before the competition; the competition entry; the final plan

(Below left) Sketches and conceptual drawings

(Right) The facade

(This page) Plans and elevations

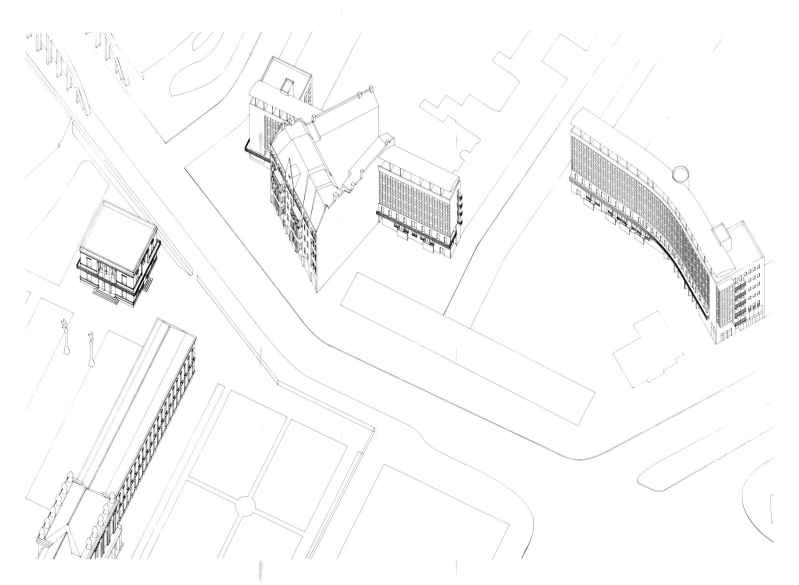

a 'wholeness' with the overall urban texture. Surprisingly, however, this coherence is derived from the classical canon rather than the anti-classical modernist rules from which the antecedent design elements of the project are derived. It is achieved, Kollhoff argues, 'through Schinkel's principle of relationship of axes, in spite of the repeated fragmentation'. In particular, Kollhoff sees the curved wall 'together with the Schloss, the Schinkel Pavilion and the bridge [forming] a signet-like constellation', in the spirit of the 19th century.

Kollhoff's general principles of urban design reflected in this project assume a highly contextual, quasi-critical regionalist character, more concerned with the local, *longue durée*, deep continuities and the site's quality of place than the IBA's appeals to tradition.

Kollhoff considers a building to be more than just an object; to him, it is a structure 'that implies a very different notion of living in a city'. This point of view is realized, in the Luisenplatz project, in 'the way the apartment opens to the sun and to the castle and its garden', in the possibility 'of private expression in the facade in spite of its elegant and reserved' character, in the allocation 'of a continuous, generous porch'. It is in these respects that this project offers specific alternatives beyond the essentially nostalgic approach of most of the IBA buildings.

(Opposite) Axonometric drawing of the buildings and site

(Above) View of the building and surroundings

Myrto Vitart (for Jean Nouvel Associés)
ONYX CULTURAL CENTRE
(Saint Herblain, France)
1987–88

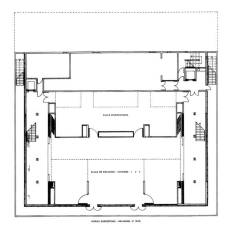

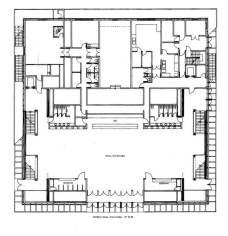

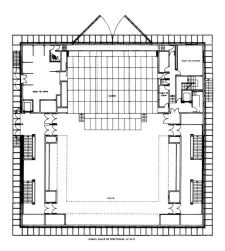

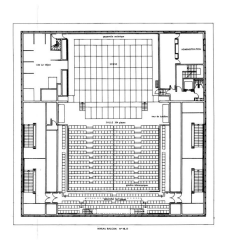

A parking lot in the midst of a vast void on the remote periphery of the town of Saint Herblain, near Nantes, is the unlikely site on which Myrto Vitart was commissioned to build a 4-storey cultural centre containing a theatre with 354 seats, as well as an exhibition area and three halls for conventions. Despite its relatively small scale and simple programme, the building is significant; what makes it so is the incongruous relation between the building's function and its context.

The centre is balanced on a borderline between two radically different environments. On the entrance side to the south, it overlooks what will eventually become a lush Edenic garden. At the back, to the north, just the opposite: an expanse of empty space, an asphalt desert. Beyond the huge, 10-hectare, V-shaped parking lot whose distant sharp point sinks beneath the surface of a mirage-like body of water, the only signs of life are a colossal hypermarket (by Richard Rogers) and gigantic factory warehouses that seem dwarfed in the distance. The topography of the site seems transposed from Wim Wenders' *Paris, Texas*.

Rather than try to dissimulate or camouflage the surroundings consecrated to the cult of the car and mass consumption, Vitart has chosen to confront them. This contextual response

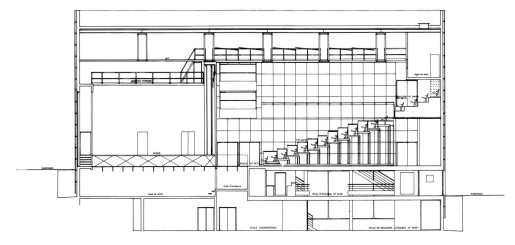

(Opposite) Plans and section of the ONYX Centre

(Above) Interior view with staircase

(Opposite, bottom right) Exterior seen from the north

(Below) Perspective view of the site from the lake

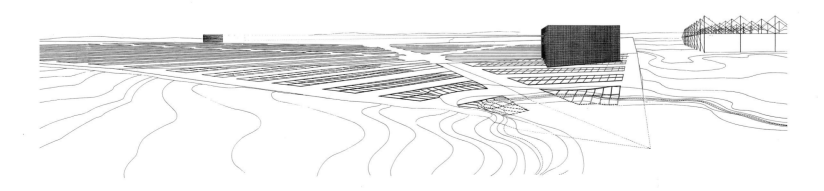

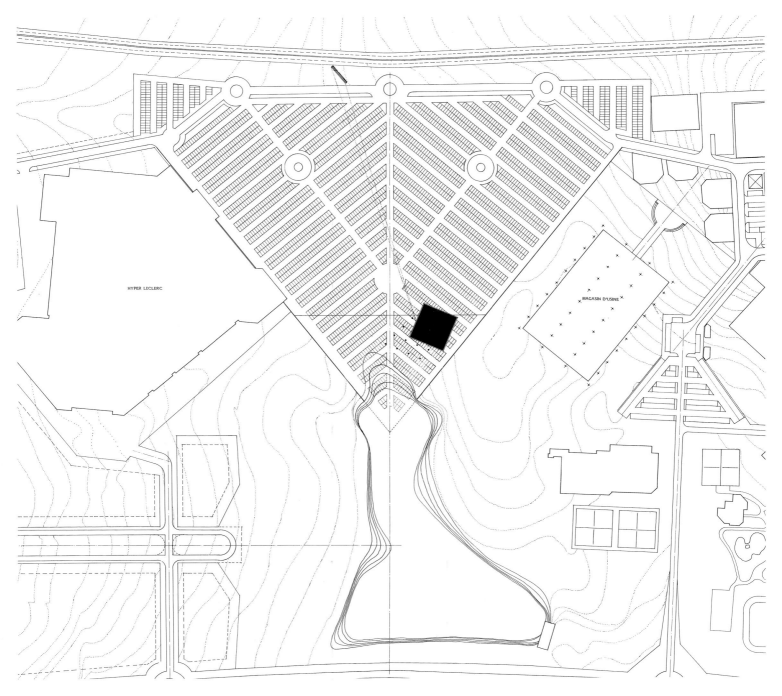

HYPER LECLERC

MAGASIN D'USINE

seems surprising. During the 1960s and '70s the idea of contextualism had to do with the preservation or continuation of something positive, a way of increasing something good that was already in the surrounding environment. This certainly presupposed that there *was* something good that was being threatened in the first place. Here, however, the context, a true commercial/industrial wilderness, is 'foregrounded' or 'de-familiarized'. By means of the great bay window which is carved out of the facade, the V-shaped parking lot is transformed into a stage setting for a Robert Wilson opera or a James Turrell installation. Light becomes a scenographic or sculptural element to be looked at, and one finds oneself actually looking at dusk or at the dark slashed by headlamps. In turn, looking at the bay window from the parking lot, it becomes the illuminated screen of a drive-in cinema. The building itself becomes part of the spectacle it

overlooks, a participant in the performance art it serves to frame.

ONYX keeps a low profile in its site. Its chief device is understatement. Amid its measureless, bearingless surroundings, it too loses any sense of scale. A gleaming black box, it reflects the void around it, sending the image of emptiness back where it came from. And like a black box, it remains enigmatic. It carries no signs. Its skin of metal grating allows only fragmentary messages to pass through from an interior where cold galvanized metallic surfaces shimmer under orange lights.

This building in a desert of urbanity and humanity makes no effort to improve the aesthetic conditions of its surroundings or to improve the human condition. Neither does it make any overt critical statement. Yet it is a work in which, as in a piece of fiction of the school of young 'dirty realist' writers, 'you hope some readers hear the whispers, catch the

feints and shadows, gather the traces, sense the pressures, and that the prose tricks them into the drama, and the drama breaks their hearts' (Frederick Barthelme, *New York Times Book Review*, 3 April, 1988).

(Opposite) Site plan

(This page) Day and night view from the lake

Mario Bellini
INDUSTRIAL AND OFFICE COMPLEX ON THE VIA KULISCIOFF
(Milan, Italy)
1982–88

Conceived on the model of the French service industry *hôtels industriels*, the Mario Bellini project on the Via Kuliscioff is a kind of urban intervention new to Italy. This industrial and office complex in the Milan area was undertaken in an effort to re-industrialize the city by the introduction of eleven projects which would offer spaces intended for use as laboratories, offices and storage, but which would allow flexibility to adapt them for other uses if required. The architect's aim was to give an architectural quality to this industrial complex. The plan was highly constrained by internal organizational requirements. It was development as an enveloping fabric which would do more than just wrap the site as a 'package'; it would provide scale, texture, colour, play with light and shadow, proportioning and geometrical coherence. The need to generate these qualities resulted from the location of the complex in a recently urbanized zone to the west of Milan, a context of mixed buildings – residential, office and industrial – deprived of any clear rules of coherence.

The long buildings erected by Bellini present a truly urban, uninterrupted, although asymmetrical, facade. On the north side, the building is characterized by a continuous base

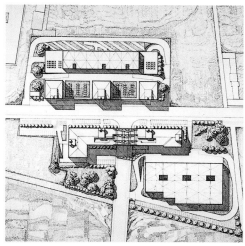

(Opposite, below) Perspective drawing of one of the facades

(Opposite, above) Detail of the facade

(Above right) Perspective drawing of the outdoor corridor

(Far right) Volumetric plan of the site

which carries three 'towers'; the south side presents a solid surface marked only in the centre by a gate suspended from four high metal beams.

The two volumes are unified by a prefabricated reinforced concrete cladding, produced and installed by IPM of Molinella, which is distinguished by a 'refined treatment' of the surface: the joints are smooth, while the internal surfaces are sanded in order to enhance the colour and the granulation of the marble gravel in the concrete. The optical effect is a strong contrast of light that tends, in Bellini's words, to 'ennoble' the appearance of the sheds and to 'reinstate the sculptural values of a non-superficial architecture'. The module of the panels is 120 × 60 cm and covers the height of an entire floor (360 cm), except for the base and the cornice which are 140 cm high. A corner panel hides the open vertical joints, thus re-enforcing the continuity of the cladding. The high quality of the surface of the panelling system was meant to stop any adverse Philistine publicity responses to the enterprise.

Another contributing factor to the architectural quality of the building is the vertical 'breaks' that interrupt the facade, where the coupled cylindrical bodies house the staircases and lifts. This subdivision of the facade helps to form a mental link between the external arrangement of the building and its internal organization, making the complex less formidable and more approachable.

In the final analysis, however, neither the concentration of just one kind of activity nor the introverted character of the complex – both anti-urban attributes – are essentially overcome by the inventive treatment of the facade. Furthermore, the skin of the building is determined more by criteria related to its perception by outside viewers than by the internal requirements of the workplace. Nevertheless, in today's drive for the renewal of cities, such architectural qualities are important for the way in which they improve the quality of life and enrich the cultural wealth of an environment with at least optical comfort. This is something which the Via Kuliscioff project supplies abundantly by means of its indisputably monumental character, a monumentality served by the excellence of the detailing and the machine-based craftsmanship of the panelling system which provide a quality of nobility, to use Bellini's term, for the women and men who work and produce.

Coop Himmelblau
ROOFTOP REMODELLING

(Vienna, Austria)
1983–89

'The law firm of Schuppich, Sporn, Winischofer, Schuppich wished to extend their office, which was situated on the first and second floor of the building at the corner of Falkestrasse and Bilderstrasse, into the attic.' Thus begins the description of the 'scenario' for the 'case' of the rooftop construction by Coop Himmelblau, one of the most intriguing and influential projects of European architecture of the past twenty years and possibly the most idiosyncratic lawyers' office in the world.

This description is intended to provide a 'clue', it is a kind of apocryphal narrative as to what the most significant aspect of the programme was in the genesis of its spatial schema. The clue lies in the name of one of the two streets of the site: Falkestrasse (Falcon Street). A remarkable omen! The authors of the narrative take it back, however: 'We did not, in this case, think of a bird or wings.' And then they change their minds – perhaps: 'although it was hard not to do so.' The figural concept of the project began out of chance and possibility.

The project accommodates a conference room of 90 square metres, three office units, a secretariat, a reception area and adjacent rooms. Provision was also made in the layout for converting the office into an apartment if the need arose. Light from and views of the privileged roof area are controlled by the strategic placement of transparent and opaque roof panels. While the topology of the small facility plan conforms to the ordinary and rather simple requirements of a modest legal consulting workshop, the volumetric layout detonates a poetic fiction about a glass, steel and concrete falcon.

The viewer is initially shocked at confronting what appears to be a 'reversed lightning bolt' breaking up an existing roof, or else a 'taut electric arc', or a realistic silhouette of a strange bird. This first impression swiftly recedes, and what takes its place in the viewer's mind, in a rebus-like fashion, is the abstract representation of either flight or an explosion. Both flying and exploding are instances of conquering space as the result of a sudden release of energy, which involves a displacement of elements. In both flying and exploding, the continuity of the form of the complete figure is broken into snatches of

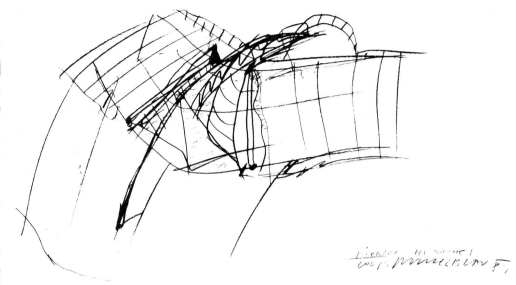

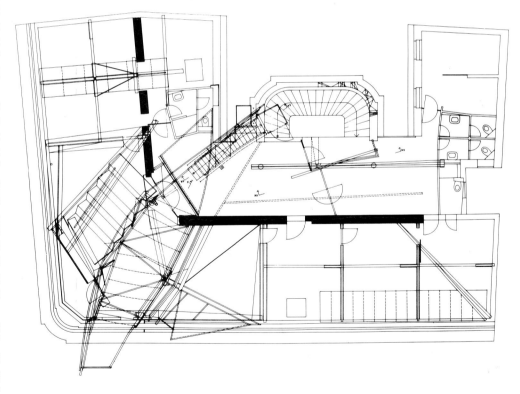

(Above) Design sketch and ground floor plan

(Opposite) Exterior view of the section housing the conference room

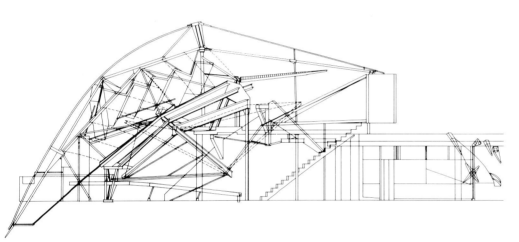

matter. In both cases, the formal characteristics of a closed figure are negated: the geometry of the elements is rectilinear instead of curved; the elements come together at sharp angles and through intersecting lines and planes.

To describe the design we have to proceed through contradictions. While the overall figure approximates a streamlined shape, representing the genesis of form by external forces acting on matter – carving it, sculpting it, rounding it out – the particular pieces that make up this general figure seem unfinished, a representation of the destruction of form by forces from within – detonating, fracturing, dismembering it. There is a duality of containing and contained worlds in the arcane, indeterminate figure, bird or bolt of lightning; but it is also impossible to decide whether the figure on the top corner of Falkestrasse and Bilderstrasse is landing or taking off.

There are, of course, in the history of architecture many precedents of exploding, of displacement, of the breaking up of the conti-

nuity of form. One can cite the Futurists or Constructivists and, closer to home, we see it in the work of the Viennese Hans Hollein, in details such as the emblematic 'cracked' look of the Schullin Jewelry Shop (pp. 72–73).

As in other cases of contemporary architecture – such as Calatrava's Lyon Railway Station for the TGV (pp. 284–85) – Coop Himmelblau's rooftop is to a large extent a study in thinking through architectural means. Both Himmelblau and Calatrava are concerned with movement and flight. Both Calatrava's complex and the general figure of the Coop Himmelblau rooftop appear to be the result of mimesis, as they both outline an airborne silhouette. But any similarities end here.

In Calatrava's structure the streamlined motif of the general figure is repeated in the constituent components. Forms of the same family are embedded in a 'fractal' manner. As a result of his consistent, hierarchical 'nesting' of formal, spatial motifs, there is a continuity without surprises in the unfolding of the total figuration.

In the Coop Himmelblau project, on the other hand, the motif of the arched figure is elaborated on a lower level of the scale in fragments, cracked pieces, shreds, snippets and snatches of matter, which, as previously stated, break the continuity of the form of the overall figure – they negate the figure's formal rules. This negation of the formal rules occurs on two levels: in the geometry of the individual elements (none of which is curved) and in the way they come together. By contrast, on a higher-scale level, there is a general implicit curvilinearity in the intersecting lines and planes at sharp angles of bird-like figures.

At first sight this seeming heap of materials may appear awkwardly assembled: one can find endless 'false' ways of attaching one piece of structure to another and invent interpretations. But there is a studied carelessness that raises questions about structural well-formedness, invites comparisons, provokes thinking. A 'correct' way of construction would not necessarily make one ask deeper questions about form, structure and validity.

(Above) View of the conference room and entrance to the reception area

(Opposite)
(Above left) The conference room, with access to exterior balcony

(Right) View of the office on the Falkestrasse side

(Below left) Section

Especially captivating in the new structure, as it emerges on the top of the traditional Viennese building, is the implicit elective affinity between two kinds of work that are so different. This might be due to the composite, imitative image the two objects suggest, as if they were entangled together in a coital embrace. There is, however, in addition a more abstract, equally fascinating relation between two architectural ways of worldmaking. Both have a long history, and both incorporate cognitive systems for thinking about the world through spatial-iconic categories: the one, the traditional classical canon based on coherence, closure, hierarchy; and the other, the anti-classical canon of incompleteness, openness and chaos.

It is not the first time one encounters such a sophisticated juxtaposition of cognitive systems of organizing space, the classical and the anti-classical. In the music of Arnold Schoenberg, for example, there is a *longue durée* conflict between tonality and dissonance which, in Schoenberg's words, enjoys a special, breathtaking 'renewed strife'. Bringing the products of the two rule systems face to face, or literally superimposing them, has obvious cognitive and aesthetic benefits which result from estrangement and foregrounding. And such a superimposition makes it easier better to capture each system's rules, implicit in the design of each artifact, through comparison and contrast. But one can also unexpectedly read desire, tenderness and passionate consummation in the interplay between these two apparently adversarial systems. And, in the representation of conflict resolution, there is perhaps a hidden motivation to produce an appropriate optimistic emblem for a legal practice.

Otto von Spreckelsen
LA GRANDE ARCHE DE LA DÉFENSE
(Paris, France)
1982–89

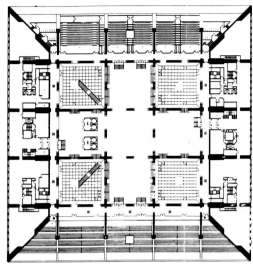

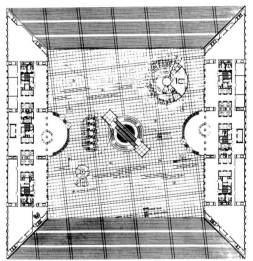

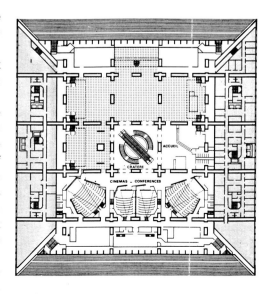

In 1982, 400 entries from more than 40 countries were submitted to the competition for an international communications centre in La Défense, the financial district of Paris located on the north-west edge of the city. After the final choice had been made by President François Mitterand on the basis of the plans submitted, according to the competition organizer Robert Lion, the envelope was opened and Johan Otto von Spreckelsen, a previously unknown Danish architect, was found to be the winner. He had built only his own house and two very small churches in his own country (RSA Journal, August, 1991). This is how one of the most monumental buildings of this century came into existence – a concrete cube measuring 110 metres across, hollowed out in the

centre and dressed in white Carrara marble and glass, accommodating about 150,000 square metres of office space.

The building which seems simple is not. It rests on only twelve pillars, six on each side, a remarkably small number for such a colossal structure. In order to support it, the pillars are 60 square metres in area and their combined weight is twice that of the Eiffel Tower. The structural frame is made out of a solid piece of concrete, which had to be prestressed from every direction and needed suspension cables inside, as the building is in constant motion, in the order of 4 cm. Inclining the walls at a slight angle of 6 degrees helps to stabilize it. The site is crossed by railway tracks and roads, which made it difficult to place the feet of the building in the ground. Another major technical problem was in the construction of the facade. It was like 'a tailor making a suit on someone who kept moving all the time', according to Paul Andreu, Spreckelsen's French collaborator, who explained that this problem was solved by putting metal elements at precise positions in the concrete and then adding a prefabricated element of glass, weighing 3 tons, all at the same time. Certainly, this construction method is an engineering feat but, from a technological point of view, the structure is not necessarily the best that could have been achieved. A steel bearing system with panelling would have been more efficient, and could have had the same visual effect. However, Spreckelsen would consider such a solution architecturally dishonest.

The financing of the building was not simple either. In 1986, President Mitterand lost the elections and the new government of Jacques Chirac decided to put a stop to the project. According to Robert Lion, who was not only organizer of the competition, but also the main administrative planner of the project, the government told him, 'Please continue. Try to build your Arche if you can. But give the government back the money' which it had already paid. 'If you want to put a supermarket on the roof, it would be a good idea because it would recoup our money', the minister suggested. Instead, Lion, who was also chairman of the Société d'Économie Mixte Nationale Tête Défense and director-general of the Caisse des Dépôts et Consignations, the leading institutional investor in France, created a *société d'économie mixte*, or joint company, with very low capital. Of this 45 per cent was provided by the state, 30 per cent by Lion's bank and the rest by public and private insurance companies. In other words, the Arche was paid for not only by the state, but also by private investors. It is, therefore, a mainly privately funded project, very different from President Mitterand's other *Grands Projets*. Furthermore, it is now an office building rather than an international communications centre, and only the roof belongs to the state.

Symbolically too the project was far from simple. The architect could have decided to design the building as a tower, the tradition for financial centres all over the world. Instead, he tried a delicate balancing act between invention and precedent by opting for a modern building in the form of a traditional triumphal arch. This decision resulted in a new hybrid artifact and contributed to the ambiguity of its interpretation as a symbolic, urban object, determined by the site's context. Indeed, the brief called for a building which would terminate one of the most culturally loaded urban axes in the world, leading from the court of the Louvre (where I.M. Pei's Pyramid now stands, see pp. 226–29), through to the adjacent Arc

du Carrousel, from there to the Place de la Concorde and then to the Arc de Triomphe. Spreckelsen himself saw his new arch as a 'window on the world', offering a 'view into the future'.

But another reading was proposed that was equally and, perhaps, even more convincing. As the Spanish architectural historian Juan Antonio Ramirez has pointed out, this axis is also an allegorical representation of 'the political evolution of mankind from the absolutism of the monarchy (Louvre) to the heroism of the Revolution (Concorde, Tuileries) then the grandeur of the empire and the 19th-century bourgeoisie (up the Champs Elysées), winding up at La Défense with the gradual silencing of the state and the triumph of capital'.

Seen from this perspective, the Arche appears as a monument symbolizing the culmination of a long path which, having linked a series of heroic historical events, leads nowhere, standing perhaps for the end of history, a self-deconstructing commentary on the Will to Progress. Such a teleological view of the axis implies a Hegelian belief in an inexorable historical march, although one that, alas, goes in the opposite direction from a 'progressive' one. The same Hegelian belief, when applied to the interpretation of the axis in terms of urban history, reveals the same kind of negative evolution. It suggests that the axis follows a descending path from the lost urban paradise of the past to the technocratic and bureaucratic hell of the present, reflecting the sad history of Paris's urban tissue, from an intricate web of functions and lifestyles, when the court of the Louvre was still occupied by houses and its rooms by workshops, to the highly segregated functional and social organization of La Défense.

Such highly critical interpretations have been triggered by the 'triumphal' associations

implied by an architectural type like the arch. But what if a different historical prototype had been chosen, less loaded with ideas of power and monumentality? What if the prototype, for example, had been the Place Royale, with its traditional harmonious integration of dwellings, workplaces, leisure areas, greenery and art? Then La Défense, no doubt, would have been a truly new way of exploiting the air rights of the Parisian sky, and the project would probably have been more appropriate as a link between the Paris of the past and the Paris of the future, inviting less heroic interpretations perhaps, but also less apocalyptic ones. It would indeed have been a window onto the future in the sense that it would have been a new kind of architecture. It might have been seen, if not as a prototype, then as a laboratory for experiments for a new urban type, leading to a redefinition of the city and urban life on a higher level, literally as well as conceptually and technologically. It would have been a truly daring new vision of an urban architecture, echoing such designs as those of Yona Friedman for Paris in the mid-1960s, expanding the city above the traditional rooftop level, combined with a post-1968 vision of a green, emancipated urbanity, in new, unprecedented, fantastic ways.

(Opposite, left) Exterior view

(Opposite, right) Plans

(Above) View under the Arche

Pei Cobb Freed & Partners Architects
GRAND LOUVRE
(Paris, France)
1981–89

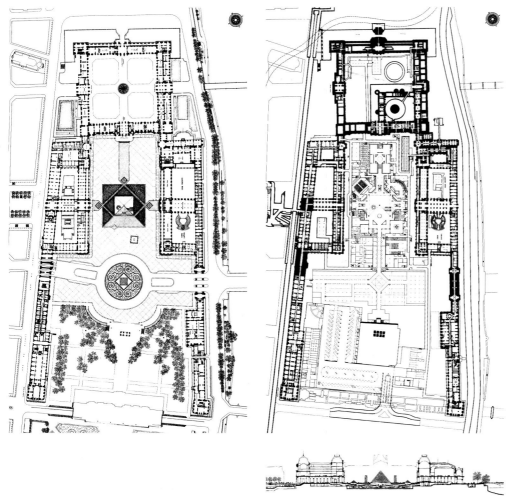

This was the winning entry in the international competition organized directly under the French President François Mitterand. The competition called for an underground expansion of the old Louvre Museum, which would measure well over 46,000 square metres, with a new main entrance to be placed in the centre of the pre-existing U-shaped galleries for more direct access to the museum collections. The final design has increased technical and support facilities and public amenities by 160 per cent and has nearly doubled the exhibition areas. Now, with almost 130,000 square metres of space, the new Grand Louvre is the largest museum in the world and welcomes more than three million visitors a year.

The project also includes a new circulation network for the Cour Carrée, the courtyard of the Louvre. Previously a car park for the Ministry of Finance, which occupied the north wing of the old Louvre, it has been resurfaced with a geometric parterre in which three smaller pyramids and seven triangular reflecting pools have been set, inspired by, according to Pei, and in keeping with the strict geometrical spirit of the existing garden stretching from the Louvre to the Place de la Concorde.

The pyramid, with a base of just over 35 metres, is the project's most significant feature. Serving as the top of the underground building and executed in glass, it is a very effective means of flooding the lower hall with light. At the same time, its inclined transparent walls, tapering to a peak just over 5 metres high, combine maximum visibility for the palace with minimum occupation of the famous Cour Carrée. In Pei's words, the structure has been designed for 'immateriality'. But there is more to it than unobtrusiveness.

The glass pyramid amalgamates the two disparate images of 'glass' and 'pyramid'. The resulting new artifact brings together the two images, 'aggressively throwing into doubt' – to use the expression of Mark Turner about literary metaphor – what we believe we know about each: that weight, robustness and impenetrability are indisputable properties of the pyramid, lightness, fragility and transparency those of glass. The amalgam is in fact a *topos* of classical poetics, an oxymoron that transcends, manipulates and finally invalidates our stereotypes about representation of knowledge. Here, not only is there no conflict between glass and pyramid in the new super-category 'glass pyramid', but we are handed what Turner calls a 'passport through the gates of categorization', a call to use our minds to invent rather than to abide by stereotypes.

The pyramid is made of glass panels which consist of two 10 mm sheets of laminated glass sealed with structural silicone (its first architectural application in France). Each panel is set into an aluminium frame whose minimal mullions, perfectly flush with the glazed surface, have been engineered to preserve the planarity of the crystalline prism. Guided solely by the search for the greatest possible structural lightness, Pei and his engineer from Quebec, Roger Nicolet, chose a hyper-static structure whose bars and members are exceptionally thin, but whose structural geometry is held to be unequalled in the world. All the bolts and articulations associated with 'high-tech' metal constructions have been eliminated. The assembly is connected by handcrafted junctures, or nodes, which were cast by a 'lost-wax' process with a two-phase blasted finish in order to maximize streamlined smoothness. These fittings, like the rods they connect, were produced by a Massachusetts firm that specializes in rigging for America's Cup yachts, where lightness is all important. The glass is as 'white' as possible. The challenge lay in the production of glass in large enough panes of such clarity and absolute flatness as to permit the facades of the Louvre to be seen through them without distortion. The solution required two years of research and the revival of largely abandoned methods of glass production by the French company Saint Gobain. The successful result was hailed as an engineering feat and a symbol of French-American collaboration.

(Right) The pyramid and main entrance seen through the pre-existing building

(Opposite)
(Above left) Ground floor plan

(Above right) Plan of reception and entrance hall level

(Centre) Site section

(Below) Night view of the courtyard

During construction, the pyramid became the subject of much controversy in the press. But when one considers the great weight of the symbolic load borne by the location – perhaps one of the most culturally sensitive areas in Paris – the pyramid, the ultimate expression of 'corporate design' that has become synonymous with the anaesthetic environments of airport terminals and waiting lounges, has succeeded in gaining popular acceptance with remarkable speed. In fact, the pyramid proved to be a virtually flawless piece of public relations.

Despite this success, which guarantees the project a good reception for decades to come, and despite the obvious historic associations of the figure of the pyramid, the question of monumentality still remains unanswered by the scheme. In its rigidity, the pragmatic minimalism of its form, the unalterable harshness of its materials, the work is an exclusively spatial object which excludes the sense or experience of time. This implies a fear of history and, to quote the critic Philip Rahv, suggests unintentionally, 'at bottom, the fear of the hazards of freedom'.

(Above left) View of the pyramid's exterior with water pools

(Top left) Glass surface and construction detail

(Opposite) Interior of the entrance hall and staircase

Aldo and Hannie van Eyck
ESTEC, EUROPEAN SPACE RESEARCH AND TECHNOLOGY CENTRE
(Noordwijk, Holland)
1986–89

ESTEC, the European Space Research and Technology Centre on the Dutch coast at Noordwijk, is Europe's equivalent of NASA. The van Eycks were commissioned to add to the original orthogonal building complex which houses ESTEC's direction and management a conference centre, a restaurant and a technical documentation centre (5000 square metres), together with a series of office towers (7560 square metres).

In its first phase, ESTEC included the biggest space simulator in the world, a vast, vortex-like black box with extremely low-temperature walls and, in its depths, an artificial sun producing extremely high temperatures. This most impressive feat of engineering and creative fantasy is housed, as if imprisoned, in a silent, grim, rectilinear, self-absorbed grid envelope that ignores the surrounding world, its geometry, colours and rhythms. In 1986, Massimo Trella, ESTEC's director, commissioned the van Eycks to free the 'imprisoned' organization and they, accordingly, performed a feat of architectural liberation.

As a result, between the swirling, swelling, tumultuous currents of the North Sea and the lone, stern colossus of the original ESTEC, there sprawls today a fractal-like dragon created by the van Eycks. Indeed, the restaurant and documentation facility, on which we focus here, looks like 'the kind of joke nature plays on mathematicians', to quote Benoit Mandelbrot, the famous French mathematician, originator of fractal geometry. But, concealed in the seeming irregularity and contorted forms of this building, there is a method. Its seeming chaos is contained chaos, its apparent anarchy is based on rules. As in Aldo van Eyck's celebrated Municipal Orphanage in Amsterdam (1957–60), the rules are derived from the classical canon, albeit by systematically negating it! The particular aspect of the canon being negated is the most fundamental one, what Vitruvius called *taxis*: the rule system of spatial partitioning that clearly defines the beginning, middle and end of a composition and its constituent components. *Taxis* is the order that defines boundaries and governs the overall plan of the classical building – columns, piers, walls, doors, windows, down to the smallest ornament. Order also governs ESTEC, but one that in most key respects denies the order of classical *taxis*, by disrupting it locally.

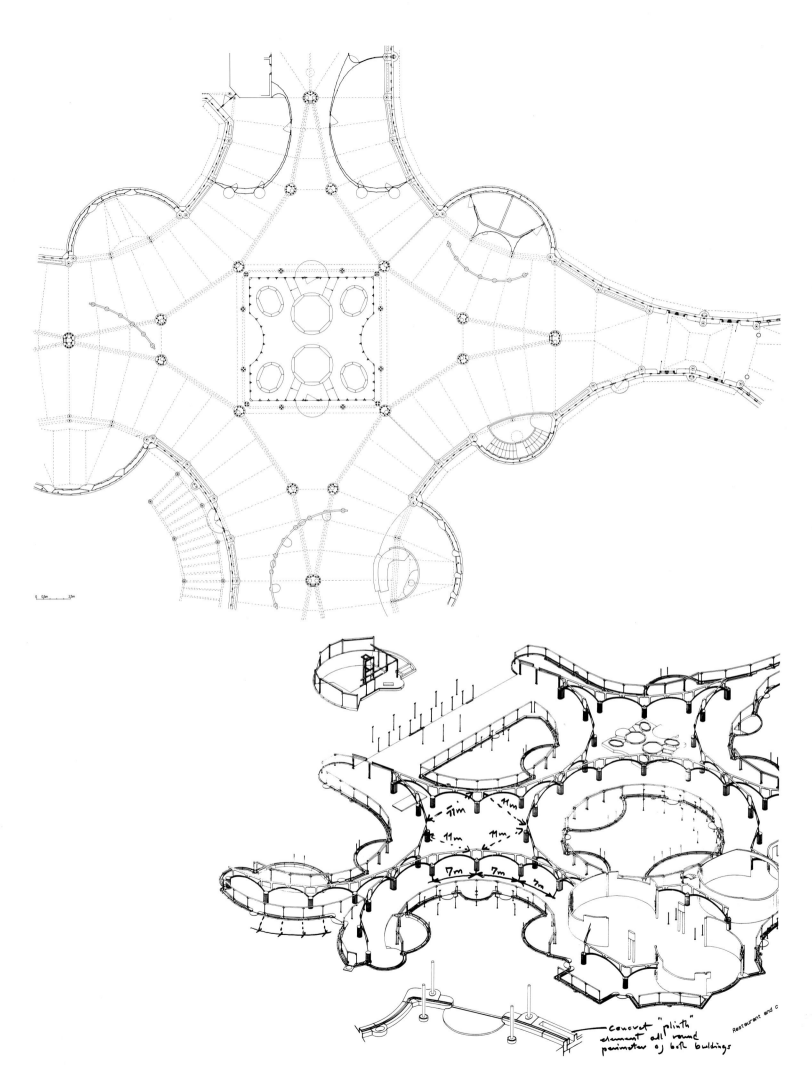

concret "plinth"
element all round
perimeter of both buildings

Restaurant and c

These disruptions of the composition fall into three main categories. First, there are sudden additions to the classical, well-ordered outline which make it exceed its limits, for instance the horn-shaped appendix of the southwest side of the building; second, major elements are displaced, such as the entrance which is shifted at an angle of 45 degrees; and third, shape reversals. The latter is the most frequent type of disruption of *taxis*, both within the building and along its external boundary. Thus, convex is replaced by concave, angular by curved, even by odd. The resulting 'random tremas', to use another term of Mandelbrot's, that is, voids, give rise to a confounding rippling effect of space and an anticipated, pleasant disorientation. Among the disrupting devices of the spatial composition, surely one of the most idiosyncratic inventions in recent architectural history, is the 'hendecagonic column', a composite column 'made out of eleven steel tubes in a ring contained between two steel discs'. This also contributes to the destabilization of the classical *taxis* by making alignments of walls and orthogonal intersections impossible. Thus the user is systematically taken by surprise by agreeable deviations from the expected alignments.

Many of the compositional strategies employed here are complete inventions. Many, on the other hand, are rooted in extraordinary memory and erudition. The dialectic of seeming chaos and underlying rigour encountered at every turn in ESTEC brings to mind the great Baroque masters of the art (and divination) of paradox, Guarino Guarini and Francesco Borro-

mini, the architectural space explorations of the 17th century and the intellectual investigations of fantastic chimerical 'monsters', to borrow Rudolf Wittkower's expression. But, as in its 17th-century predecessors, *commodità* is never neglected for the sake of the image.

In ESTEC, as in their previous works, the van Eycks are concerned with spatial rule making and rule breaking, a delicate balance between rationality and chaos (see pp. 196–97). But ESTEC appears still richer than their other buildings in its results, in the richness of form one finds in organic objects. This is probably because of the finer, more intricate methods of composition employed here. The geometric, spatial effect is enhanced by the colour and the material they have used: phantasmagorically copper clad, 'dragon'-like in its scaly skin of Brazilian oroco wood, shimmering and iridescent in the sun, glaucous and green-tinged in the rain. The complex is, for our time, a rare comment on the poetics of nature and of architecture, a reflection on the structure of the world and the cognitive strategies the human mind uses to understand it. It tries to tame the monstrosity of apparent chaos by resorting to memory and invention, and in its physicality it represents the effort to tame through inquiry.

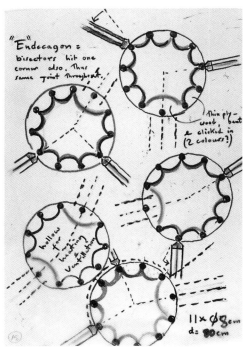

(Top) The restaurant facade

(Above) Conceptual drawings of the columns

(Opposite, above) Construction system of the columns

(Opposite) Interior view and one of the inner courts

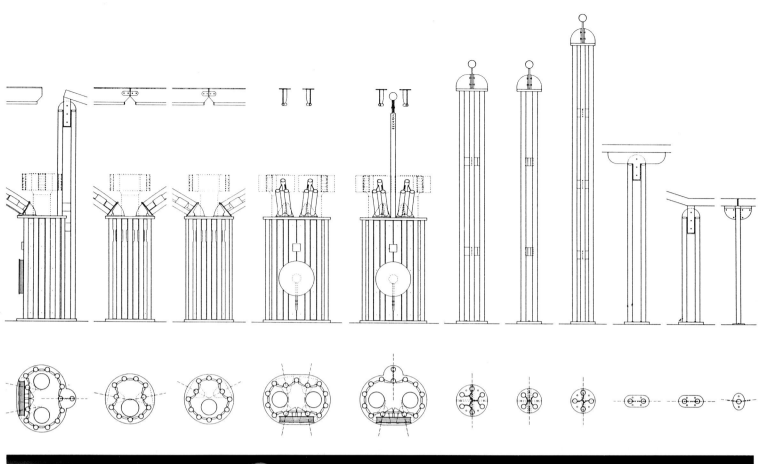

Héctor Fernández Martín/Vetges tu i Mediterrània, Arquitectos
PRODUCTION CENTRE FOR VALENCIAN TELEVISION
(Valencia, Spain)
1986–89

On the plains of Burjassot, close to Valencia's trade fair centre and the university campus, rises the Production Centre of Valencian Television. It is a striking project born on a site typical of the Mediterranean urban periphery, demonstrating negligence, avarice and poverty of ideas, accentuated here by the presence of an exceptional physiognomy of the natural setting.

The complex covers 15,000 square metres and accommodates management and administration facilities, recording studios and a transmission tower. Its programme was determined by the requirements of high technology, as well as the demands of insulation, safety and security. Nevertheless, the Centre is notable for its inventiveness in overcoming conflicts related to meaning and culture, despite the constraints of its programme.

In the midst of scrap heaps and spoilage, the building succeeds in emerging as a memorable image. The coherence of its figure results to a great extent from the robust geometrical primitives employed: the triangle for the floor plan, the curve and the colossal arch counterpoised by the cylindrical glass vortex of the tower encased in a perforated prism. The unique achievement of the Centre is the reappropriation of the fragments of the landscape and their reconstitution into a coherent image through the way the elements of the abstract volumetric composition – triangle, curve, cylinder, parallelepipedes – fit into the sweeps and inflections of the site.

The effect is strengthened by the manner in which the complex of the building and its intricate relation with the contours of the site are recognized through the opportune placement of the elementary, purist volumes that make up the composition. As one approaches gradually from the highway and road, the volumes signal from afar, giving clues for a possible recognition of a well-formed spatial schema developed within severe site constraints. As one enters, the different elements of the building come together to form a unity that confirms this initial perception of a volumetric whole. This sense of unity is further emphasized by the building's detailing.

The composition is in many respects a typical functionalist assemblage, its articulated geometrical organization representing the functional organization contained in the complex. Its spatial structure hints at the paradigm of the Russian Constructivist Ivan Leonidov in the way in which horizontal and vertical components interpenetrate. Yet the building is not a formalistic, nostalgic replay. The basic difference lies in its conjunction with its context. Not only are the deformations of the profile of the site in constant dialogue with the allocation of the regular parts of the building, as in some later paintings by Lucas Samaras (Pace Gallery, November 1991), but the building's construction reflects the deeper character of its surroundings, distinguished by the misery of opportunistic interventions in the Mediterranean landscape. Thus the use of materials, rough industrial elements and the very processes of construction in their harshness do not attempt to obviate and beautify the damage done. They represent it critically, giving to the project a characteristic aura of 'dirty realism'.

(Below) Volumetric plan

(Opposite)
(Top right) The wall, the arch and the screened round tower

(Below right) The screened tower

(Below left) View through the screens

(Above left) Beneath the arch of the wall, looking towards the screened tower

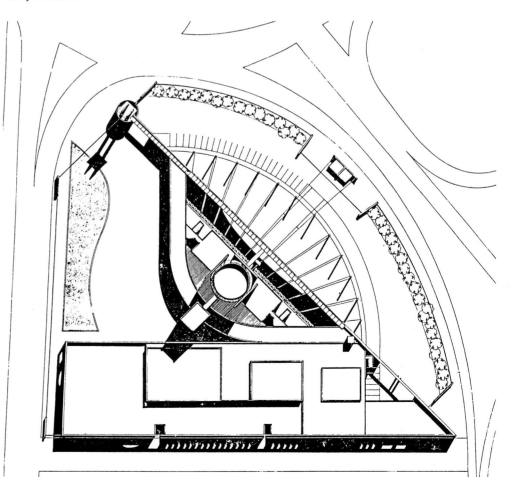

Matthias Sauerbruch and Elias Zenghelis (OMA)
APARTMENT HOUSE AT CHECKPOINT CHARLIE
(Berlin, Germany)
1983–90

Checkpoint Charlie Housing in Berlin is located on what used to be the American-Sector side of the border-crossing between East and West Europe on Friedrichstrasse, an important section of historical Berlin, which was torn apart by the building of the Wall in 1961. The consequences of the Wall for this location were, on the one hand, an urbanistic trauma and a mutilated city anatomy, and, on the other, a deeper functional pathology: that of a way of life involving Berlin's very special 'border activity' – separations, escapes, shoot-ings, the trading of secrets, blackmailing and, last but not least, authoritarian policing, customs and debriefing. This project was intended to facilitate such bureaucratic func-tions. Historians one day will give an account of to what extent other types of 'border activities' went on in the building itself.

Zenghelis believes that 'the programme is the generator of architecture', it 'provides architecture with its visual aesthetic . . . , the action of its plan and section . . . and subsequently with the sensuous materiality of its finish.' Thus, in the midst of a 'void' in a 'landscape of hoardings, sheds, viewing towers, car movement and manning posts', Zenghelis, with the single-mindedness and diligence of a cool dirty realist, designed 'an anti-monumental border facility' with no inten-tion of beautifying or displaying any moralistic message. The whole 'frontier' universe is on ground level: a tarmac, bus concourse, control booth, with all the backstage paraphernalia.

Once above the first level of the complex, the drama and the special services of the building

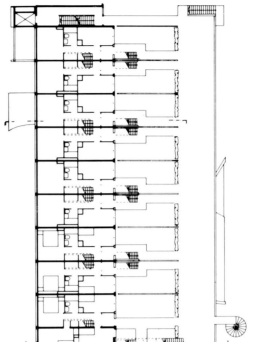

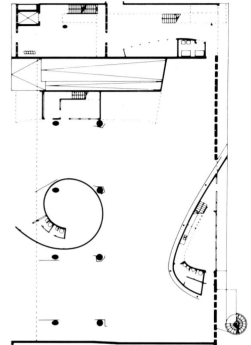

(Opposite, left) The elevation on Friedrichstrasse

(Opposite, right) Interior view of the ground floor

(Above) Rear elevation with gardens

(Right) Typical unit plan

(Far right) Ground floor plan

(Below right) Section

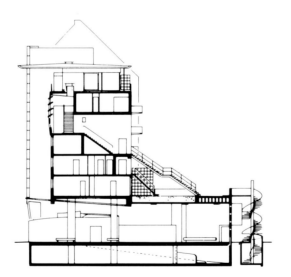

are over. The rest of the project accommodates 'normal life': housing of mixed type in accordance with the city's range of urban dwelling standards. This residential part grows vertically above Checkpoint Charlie, set back from the street and away from the view of the Wall, forming a kind of roof above and beyond its policing functions.

The iconography of the project at ground level transfers American-born, 'Truman-era' roadside structures to an urban setting and reflects the fact that the bare function of the

facility, stripped of its political and social connotations, is ultimately to channel vehicles in and out. Given this fact, the choice of image was easy: 'U.S. Route 1', the only original iconography of highway architecture, which, thanks to Robert Venturi and Denise Scott Brown, is properly codified, at least among architects. It is expressed here in the neon-art 'synthetic night sky' and the arrows pointing to the route to be followed by vehicles, the corrugated aluminium stand and the hovering metal roof clad in polished alloy.

In an ironic vein, Zenghelis conceived that once the cold war ended, 'when the city is no longer divided and the wall is replaced by a leisure zone', the facility would become a supermarket, the memory of the site and its history dissolved and reabsorbed into the market-driven vigour of the new life.

Canyeret is a district of the old historic centre of the Catalonian hill town of Lerida, nestled between the Gothic cathedral and the walled citadel above, and the 19th-century districts along the river Segre below. After decades of abandonment and neglect, deprived of any sort of facilities, Canyeret had become a virtually vacant zone known for drug dealing and delinquency, an impassable barrier isolating the hilltop from the rest of the city.

In 1980, after the fall of Franco and after many years of private speculation, the town found a public-sector client, the Ministry of Justice, whose total contribution to the redevelopment plan so far has been no less that one thousand million pesetas. A competition was organized to rehabilitate the district. Twelve years later, the outcome is one of the most memorable urban experiences of the last two decades in Europe.

The winning design was by a team composed of Domenech, Ramon Puig and Joan Busquets. Over ten years, the team has seen some changes, most notably the departure of Joan Busquets to replace Oriol Bohigas as the director of urbanism for the city of Barcelona.

A remarkable feature of the Canyeret redevelopment is that the court house is the primary focus for the revitalization scheme – a workplace rather than a housing scheme. It is intended to serve as a focus for other new buildings such as the prestigious Collegio de los Arquitectos, a school and housing units. The scheme is strongly inspired by the Italian restoration policies developed during the 1950s for the *centro storico* of the northern

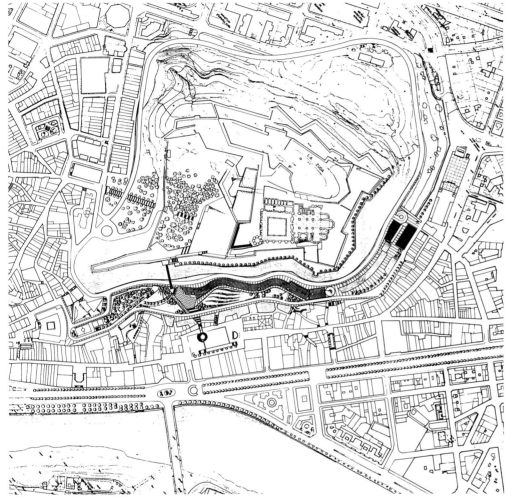

(Opposite, above) Distant view of the Canyeret development

(Opposite, below) The elevator tower and bridge

(Left) Urban plan

(Above) View of the roof top parallel to the promenade, with the elevator tower and bridge in the background

(Below) Entrance floor plan and typical unit floor plan

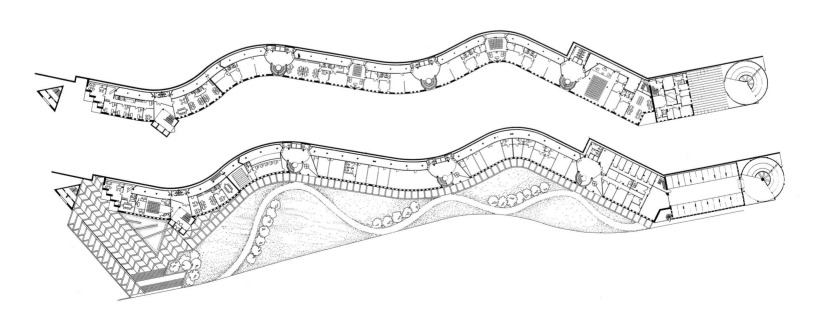

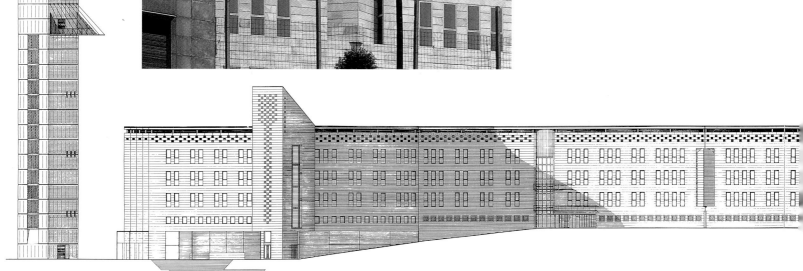

Italian hill towns, and by Giancarlo De Carlo's paradigmatic plan for Urbino, with its emphasis on the problem of inserting new urban fabric into the old and particularly on treating historic hill towns in such a way that the old and the new complement each other.

Another remarkable feature of the new mixed-use urban scheme of Canyeret is the emphasis it places on the provision of an infrastructure to help create pedestrian circulation patterns, public spaces and easy access within the newly created urban continuum. At the time of writing, the streets have been paved and lit, old houses rehabilitated, new open spaces, accesses and public transport provided. The citadel has again become a focus of public life and the river bank has been repopulated. A park is being made and new roads link the court house to the cathedral and the city's commercial centre.

On the formal level, what is architecturally striking about the project is its composition out of two elements: a wall and a tower. These familiar, historical urban types of form are more than picturesque, fabulistic silhouettes raised next to the old centre. They are vessels whose spatial form offers ingenious solutions to practical constraints.

Given the abrupt slope of the hill and its unstable clay soil, a successful radical solution for the building was to give it the form of a wall running along the inflections of the rise – a kind of a concrete screen wall braced with stays tightened from behind, capable of supporting a long, thin, sinuous strip of a building, 250 metres long, 20 metres high and 11 metres deep. The snaking line of its roof offers a fortunate urbanistic opportunity to create a promenade, a *rambla*, that follows the contours of the existing citadel wall, and, at ground level, a generous public space.

The tower, as a type of urban element, satisfies a functional need, like the wall. It is linked to the citadel by a steel bridge and houses a lift which provides an excellent

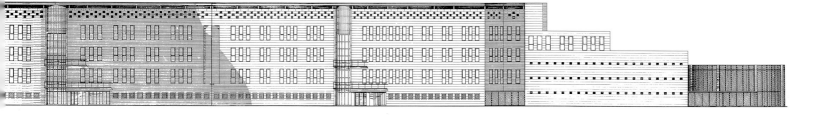

vertical link for pedestrians between the citadel above and the town below.

But both the 'wall', pressed against the flank of the hill whose undulations repeat those of the wavelike form of the fortification above, and the 'tower', juxtaposed with the cathedral tower, serve another purpose in addition to the functional. They are symbolic of the regionalist character of the project.

This type of regionalism is different from the regionalism of the Franco period, which produced hallucinatory, theatrical settings to create replicas of entire towns. This was once the approach used in reconstructing regions devastated by the civil war – the famous *regiones devastadas*. The regionalism of the Barrio del Canyeret is also different from the equally scenographic, commercial kitsch architecture of tourism. It is, however, close to what we call 'critical regionalism': respect for regional elements which are combined with modernist avant-garde themes, compositional *topoi* that recall, as in the case of Valencia's Production Centre for Television (pp. 234–35), Leonidov's spatial experiments, provocatively using stark white cladding instead of the traditional brick. The use of such unexpected devices protects the viewer from the hypnotic use of historical settings and channels memory towards inventive rather than elegiac and regressive nostalgia. This critical regionalist experiment on an urban scale succeeds in endowing the city with what the American urban theoretician Kevin Lynch called 'imageability' and in restoring vital urban functions at a time when the area was threatened by irreparable decay and fragmentation.

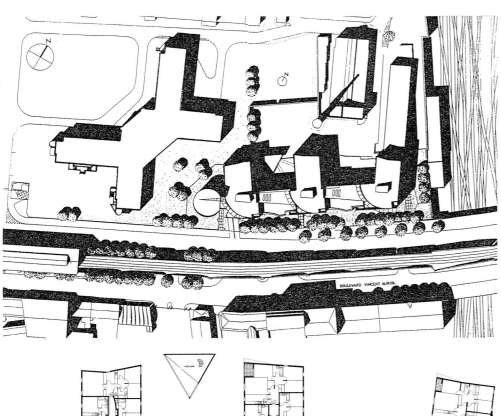

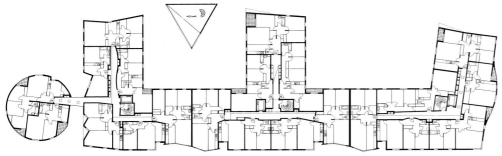

This is a low-budget social housing project for 123 units, subsidized by the City of Paris under its mayor Jacques Chirac. The site is located at the end of the Boulevard Vincent Auriol near the Quai de la Gare road in the 13th arrondissement, a major traffic artery leading out of Paris. Across the river is the warehouse-punctuated landscape of Bercy.

The boulevard, a mainly residential zone traditionally separated from the historic centre of Paris by the Gare d'Austerlitz and the mammoth complex of the Salpêtrière Hospital, had been becoming progressively run down. As is the case with so many commissions given to the younger generation of architects, the site is harsh. More specifically, it is a typically Foucauld landscape composition. It is immediately adjacent to the smoke stacks of the massive Salpêtrière Hospital and to a home for the elderly.

What dominates the area is the 19th-century Métro Aérien (which fascinated Roland Barthes so much), which runs from one end of the boulevard to the other. Its heavy stone and steel structure embodies more than anything else the *genius loci* of the boulevard.

The architect might have chosen to negate the surroundings of the site and to retreat into an idealized world, like the post-modernists of the previous generation, for example Rob Krier and Oswald Matthias Ungers. Instead, Bouchez chose a simple, straightforward option: far from denying the site, he incorporated in a most unexpected way its most dominant unifying element into his own design – the elevated metro. In the architect's words, the choice was made because 'it was the only element to play with'.

Behind the double row of sycamore trees that separate the building from the metro line, the metro is reflected in the building. The facade, broken down into two blocks divided by three inner courts, reproduces the inflexions and rhythm of the metro's stone piers and metallic arches. The three inner courts are 'carved out' at equal intervals along its surface, which helps to distance the apartments from the noise of the traffic. A variation on the theme of cold grey stone and shiny metal, the grey, prefabricated panels of polished concrete that clad the facade, grey on the street side, white on the side facing the inner courts, were produced by IB Morin. They are not only of high visual quality, they also help to reduce the impact of the 40-decibel noise level outside. Visually, they are separated by three horizontal train rails of stainless steel. The irregularly placed openings imply movement through their broken patterns, as if imitating the jerky, staccato cadence of passing metro cars. The

(Opposite, above left) Volumetric plan of the building and site

(Opposite, below) Typical unit floor plan

(Opposite, right) The facade, screened by trees from the Métro Aérien

(Below) The *brise-soleil*

(Bottom) The Métro Aérien in front of the facade

brises-soleil on the southern side of the building, made of two glinting tracks of perforated, galvanized steel that swerve out from the roof of the building into the sky, also refer to the theme of the flying metro. The building, which combines high-quality construction with a very low budget – as the French architectural critic François Lamarre points out – and a good standard of urban livability, also succeeds in grasping in its static form *le mythe moderne*: in Baudelaire's much-quoted phrase, 'the transitory, the fleeing, the contingent'.

SOCIAL HOUSING ON THE BOULEVARD VINCENT AURIOL · 243

For years France's Ministry of Finance was accommodated in the north wing of the Louvre. The design of its new building, perpendicular to and partly straddling the superhighway along the Quai de Bercy to the east of Paris, is the result of an open national competition held in 1982. The winning project, despite its sculptural, volumetric affinities with El Lissitzky's horizontal skyscraper (1923–25), carries the memory of the old classical, conservative spatial layout schema.

As Agnes Vince has remarked, the more innovative aspects of the building are related to its technical construction rather than its spatial organization: not necessarily a drawback. There are virtually inexhaustible possibilities in the classical way of partitioning a building, in its orthogonal grid structure, in its functional differentiation between servant and served, public and private, both differentiations expressed spatially in terms of the simple duality of room and corridor. And as the Ministry's plan shows, this classical formula, implemented through the paratactic ordering of offices along the two sides of a long rectangular prism, the services running down the middle, achieves a very satisfactory balance between efficiency and effectiveness, flexibility and spatial clarity.

It is obvious that, with the workplace units in a row on the two outside walls of the linear skin, the formula easily satisfies needs for natural light, view and natural ventilation. There is a window for every office, incidentally in response to a demand made by the staff stating their aversion to 'introverted' office spaces. It is interesting that the post-May '68 users considered this kind of environmental amenity as their first priority rather than more ideological considerations concerning, for example, the issues of emancipation or 'space appropriation' in the workplace. At the same time, the formula provided an arrangement with a low cost of circulation for the employees and low disturbance. Avoiding the hierarchization of offices in terms of centrality makes any future reorganization of administrative departments relatively easy. Finally, such a linear, tripartite schema is easy to remember and understand, therefore easy to find one's way around.

There are also symbolic benefits to be gained from this kind of traditional, undifferentiated, ordered schema: it can be taken as a representation of egalitarianism, utopianism and the absence of the ritualistic expression of *homo hierarchicus*. The only major exceptions to this flexible spatial organization are the spaces designated for the ministers and their immediate collaborators. These are located strategically at the prow of the bridge-building in a cubic volume whose slight de-axing is oriented towards Notre Dame. A different arrangement is prescribed for the administrative offices as a whole. On all other floors, only the dimensions of the rooms reveal a hierarchy of the employees. Unfortunately, the basic concept gives rise not only to these positive qualities, but also to a prevailing character of bureaucracy and its inevitable corollaries: routine, monotony, impersonality.

The design of the facade of the building stems from technical considerations, but its formal variety results to a great extent from an obvious effort to break away from the severe character of the plan (with some concern for acknowledging the influence of the 'rationalist' motifs of the late 1970s). A facade, however, can be more than a statement of variety and fashion, especially if the building in question not only represents a massive information-processing industry, as any ministry does, but also happens to be a major government building.

The indecisive, and to some extent, unenthusiastic and somewhat banal character of the project is not the result of any lack of inspiration or some new kind of restrictive theory adopted here about architectural inventiveness. It springs rather from the overt absence of a new kind of architectural programme that redefines the role of the workplace, the basic identity of the project, as well as the role of the state, the project client, at a moment when new lifestyles and new world views are emerging in the advanced technological countries at the close of this century.

All the same, when one approaches the building from the road, travelling perpendicularly towards and under it as it soars above one towards the river, its profile is quite exhilarating. Its effect is similar to what one imagines might have been created by El Lissitzky's horizontal skyscraper project, conceived as an elevated propylaeum opening onto the peripheral ring surrounding the centre of Moscow, had it ever been built – an example of 'highway architecture' in the best sense.

(Right) The building stops at the Seine

(Below) The Ministry seen from the Seine

(Opposite) The building straddling the road

(Below right) Volumetric plan of the building within its site

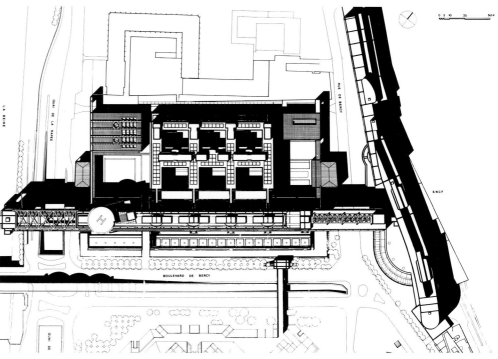

Building Workshop Renzo Piano
S. NICOLA FOOTBALL STADIUM

(Bari, Italy)
1987–90

This structure is an immense white rose, as in Dante's vision of Paradise in the *Divine Comedy*, that emerges out of the unsullied landscape of Puglia. The upper level, consisting of independent segments, rises like a soaring whorl of petals from a cup planted in a verdant mound of land. A roof of luminescent teflon seems to float in the sky above the upper edges of the petals, creating an illusion of pure white light over the white rose. Next to the stadium, Piano has preserved a single *trullo*, a small, traditional, cone-shaped, whitewashed building common in this area; in this context, it conjures up the image of a rose bud.

Piano is no stranger to wild metaphors. One has only to recall the concert chamber in the shape of a gigantic violin which he designed for the performance of the Italian composer Luigi Nonno's *Prometeo* in Milan (1983). But the association here, between a paradisial rose and a football stadium, between exalted purity and a theatre of ritualized violence, is unexpected. It generates a semantic dissonance that lends an aura of absurdity to the activities occurring within the structure.

More closely examined, this fantastic form, in addition to being a statement about an often violent kind of mass-culture, is a shrewd and pragmatic invention. The lower level of seats is carved out of the mounded base, while the upper level consists of 26 independent segments. The gaps between the segments help to separate rival factions among the 60,000 spectators it is designed to hold – a high priority considering the recent history of violence at football matches.

Peter Rice, of Ove Arup Associates, was the structural engineer who turned this metaphor into an engineering feat. Each of the gracefully curved petals uses a minimum of support and is composed of pre-cast barrel staves assem-

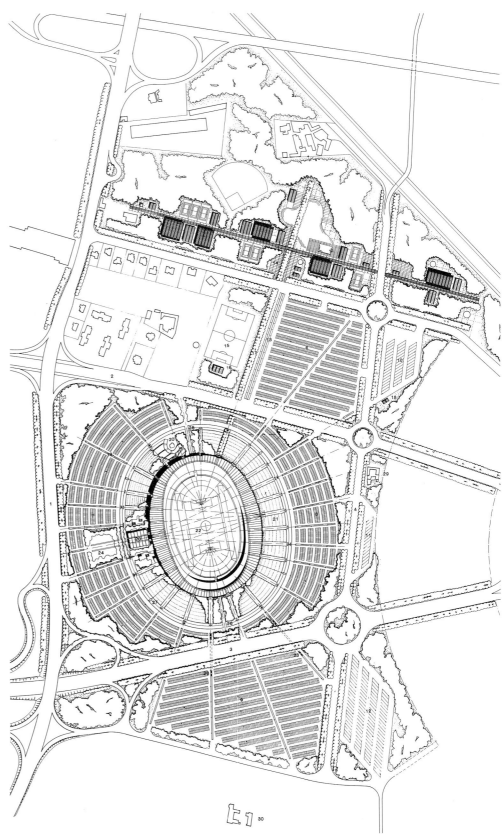

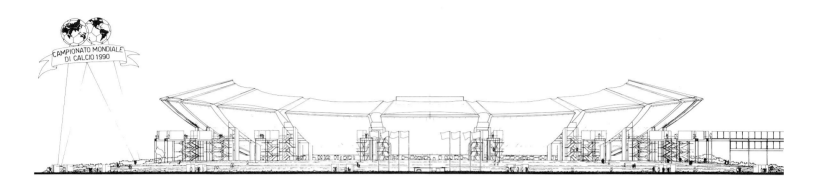

bled on site and held up on internal beams attached to colossal pylons. The roof of metal-braced teflon, which dips on the short sides and rises on the long sides of the oval-shaped field, is supported by steel ribs placed around the upper rim of the seating.

As in most of Piano's architecture, the design is extremely functional. The circulation inside and outside the stadium works very successfully. The route to one's seat is clear. Following the radiating paths from the parking lots to the stairs, one never leaves daylight. Other facilities, such as public lavatories, offices, bars and information desks, are compactly placed under the shaded portico below the stands. Underneath the stands runs an internal route along which are the dressing rooms and four gymnasia; this also gives access to emergency exits. The extensive sloping pine grove that separates the parking areas from the stadium tends to neutralize the negative effects of the overheated asphalt of the car parks and to cool the inside of the stadium, as well as providing an environmental amenity for the spectators – an unusual feature in mass sports facilities.

(Opposite) Urban plan and exterior view

(Above) Elevation

(Centre) Structural detail of canopy

(Right) The stands

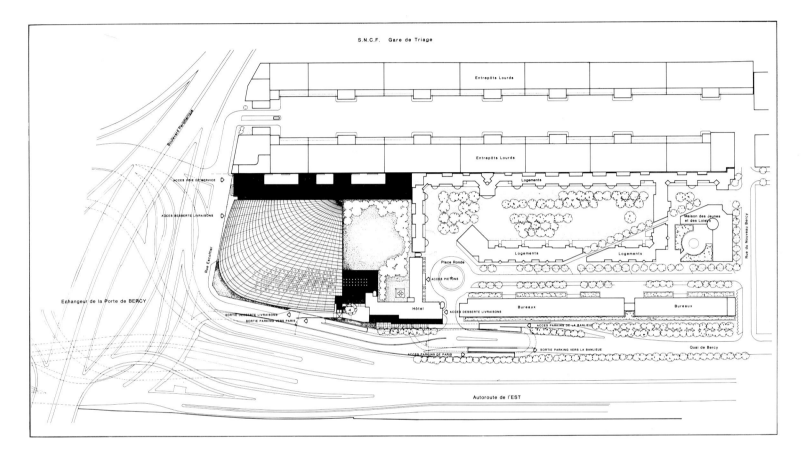

The Bercy II Shopping Centre is located on one of the busiest traffic nodes in the Paris area, at the extreme eastern boundary of the city where the *boulevard péripherique* intersects the A4 highway. With its smooth, curved outer rim and its gleaming surface, this strange megastructure, which contains 100,000 square metres of shops and services, looks like the segment of a hypertrophic car bumper. It is as if the structure were meant, in its reflective capacity, to capture the gaze of the on-coming drivers, offering a car-fetishist culture an astounding, if fleeting, moment of self-awareness.

However extravagant the cultural message of this metaphorically loaded monument of the road, like most of Piano's buildings it employs a highly original and innovative approach in its construction technology. The envelope of the building is composed of three layers: a skeleton of wood-core plywood beams with the purlins following the curved line of the roof; a waterproof membrane of PVC attached to the skeleton; and a permeable membrane made of satinized stainless steel tiles on top of the PVC

membrane. As the architectural critic Jean-Pierre Ménard notes, sophisticated computer modelling generated 34 standard sizes for the 2700 panels, each made of ten stainless steel tiles, to fit the 13,000-square-metre curved roof. The tiles are paradoxically tilted upwards instead of downwards to channel rainfall between them onto the impermeable PVC skin beneath, which has its own draining system. This arrangement is intended to maximize the surface sheen; there is, therefore, a technological rationale behind the paradox. In fact, in what is a typical Piano motif, the skin, instead of being glued onto the body of the structure, is suspended in front of it, a device which has proved highly beneficial for waterproofing.

Once inside the building, the 'high-tech road' look gives way to a grandiose but more intimate, handcrafted impression. The curving purlins are made to look, as Piano has stated, like the wreck of 'the wooden hull of a ship resting gently on the concrete structure at different levels'. This handcrafted quality is complemented by 'shafts of light which come

(Above) Site plan

(Opposite, above) The exterior viewed from a distance

(Opposite) Details of the skin

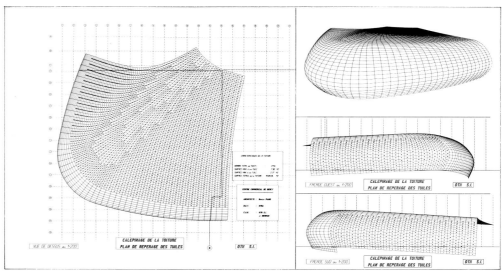

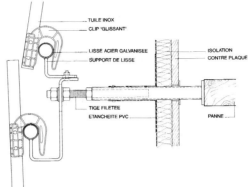

through holes made in the roof that dramatically illuminate the atria and reach the trees in the grove below'.

Bercy II was conceived as a highly functional facility. Priority, from this point of view, was given to aspects of orientation. The plan is divided into parallel strips, each providing shops, a central mall and little boutiques. This clear spatial concept is placed parallel to the Seine in order to enhance even more the awareness of location and reinforce the clarity of what Kevin Lynch called the 'cognitive mapping' of the project in its context. Three atria divide the central mall. The middle is planted with trees, 'like a grove', which adds not only to variety and a sense of nature, but, once again, increases the quality of the plan as an image. Finally, as people arrive by car and enter the shopping area from the underground car park, then take escalators or two panoramic lifts to the upper levels, a kind of map of their location with respect to the complex and its surrounding landscape is revealed to them, thanks to the large, curved roof and the expressiveness of the directionality of its wooden structure.

The geometry of the construction itself is one of the most intriguing aspects of the project, resembling in its meticulousness the soundbox of an enormous stringed instrument. According to Piano, the project's biggest challenge lay in defining the curvilinear form which was achieved during the development of the logic and the method of construction of the exactly divided grid of panels. 'Form, construction and geometry' were, in his words, 'constantly and strictly linked as the project grew up.' 'In a way', he continued, 'the building had first to be determined in an extremely subjec-

tive and visual manner, as for instance, a sculptural piece (all imperative conditions and functional requirements having first been considered); geometry, then, created the skeleton of the form which rose from the combination of three sectors of circles (each one with a different radius) and different lengths of sections. Consequently, the roof had to be constructed with three independent elements: one for the structure, made of wood-core plywood beams (purlins following the curving line of the building); one to form a watertight membrane; and, finally, one of stainless steel sheets held over the membrane.'

Bercy II is a fascinating project, successful in many ways, both on a large scale and, equally, on a very small scale. It is a unique piece of highway architecture, a wonderful artifact of contemporary technology, which brings together many subsystems of construction into one well-tempered synthesis.

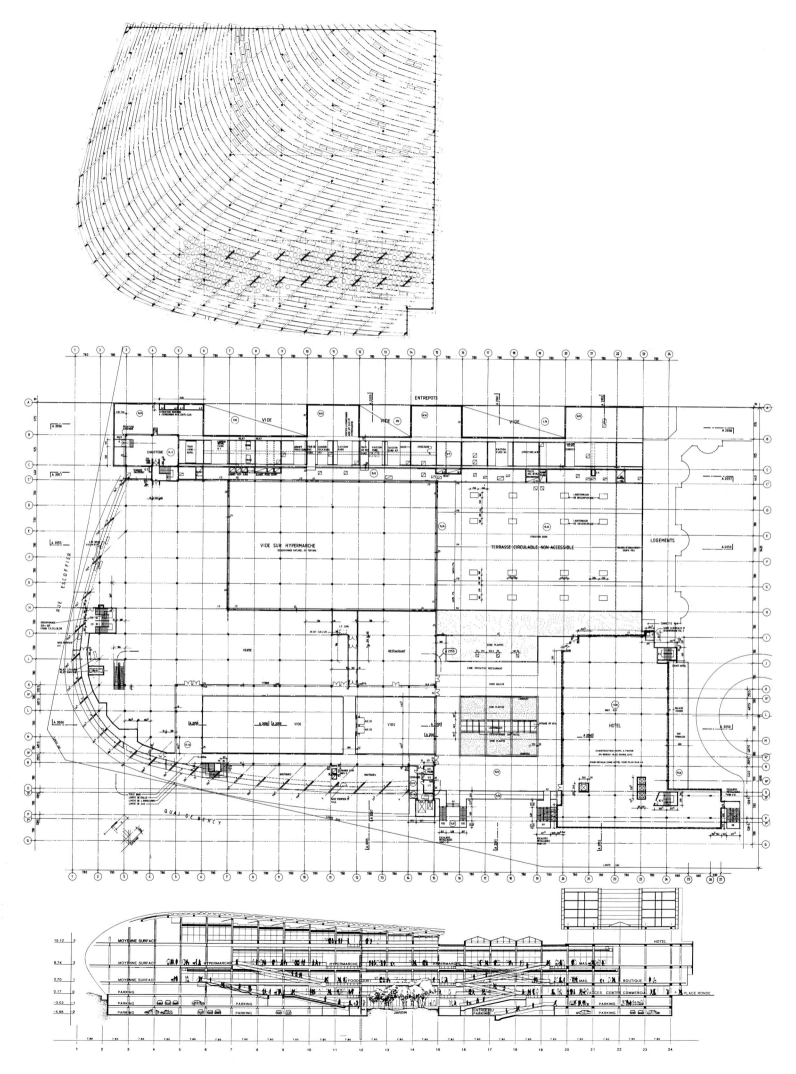

Arata Isozaki & Associates
PALAU D'ESPORTS SANT JORDI
(Barcelona, Spain)
1985–90

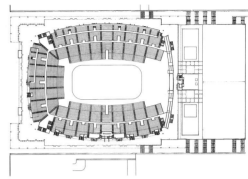

The serene and gently curved roof of the Sant Jordi Sports Palace, the main indoor stadium for the 1992 Barcelona Olympics, rises gracefully, fitting into the contours of the hill of Montjuic overlooking Barcelona. None of the currently fashionable exhibitionist and technophiliac design mannerisms showing off the magnitude or might of construction is applied in this building. The 17,000-seat arena is 14.4 metres below the central plaza from where the spectators approach the stadium. Unobtrusive ramps, local stone and regional ceramic materials dominate the area surrounding the complex, contributing, together with the discreet profile, to the quiet transition between the stadium and its environment.

Once inside the building, the character of the project changes dramatically. Vibrant, reflective, overtly high-tech materials take over. The structural members of the spaceframe of the roof are exposed and foregrounded by the arrangement. Natural light descends from the huge dome through speciàlly installed skylights in the roof and from the fold-lines between the dome and its supporting pendentive ring. By dividing the roof into a dome and a ring, piercing it to let in sunlight that shoots down the great sports hall, Isozaki uses an architectural device with a tradition as old as St Sophia to create a 'sublime' effect of a structure appearing to

float, as if miraculously suspended in space.

Between stadium and service road is a sub-arena, as well as facilities for athletes and officials. For the lighting and ventilation of these inward-looking spaces, Isozaki has employed once more a regional element, the patio. The building is served from a high ring road to the south.

Although the stadium is designed for volleyball, basketball and gymnastics during the Olympics, and can accommodate, with its 200-metre track, indoor field and track sports, it can also be used for other events, such as exhibitions, commercial fairs, conventions and even opera performances, providing multifunctional facilities all the year round.

For all its understated technology, it is here that one of its most important qualities lies. The very process of its construction was, as Ignacio Paricio, professor of engineering in Barcelona, has remarked, a significant learning experience. The dynamic 'pantadome-method' applied in the roof construction consists of five steps: first, parts of the roof and the ring are assembled on the ground independently, using only small cranes. Larger cranes are then introduced to fit together the assembled parts of the roof. During the next stage, a jack placed under the hinges raises the whole roof structure, with the light and acoustic platform suspended from it. This phase com-

pleted, the jack is removed and the space sealed. What we see is a unique cooperation between architectural and structural conception and production techniques.

The combination of sophistication and self-effacement in the use of technology, the integration of a massive structure to a culturally and aesthetically sensitive site and the multi-purpose function of the facility all contribute to the efficiency, but also the urbanity, of the complex. Such features point to the new kind of architecture emerging at the end of this century, an architecture which maximizes the use of innovative technology with clear, unprecedented benefits, while at the same time minimizing unforeseen, negative impacts – an architecture of high intelligence, an expression of what Paricio calls 'the will to do things *well*'.

(Above left) Facade of the complex

(Above) Ground plan

(Opposite)
(Top left) Interior corridor

(Left) Stages of the construction – the pantadome method

(Right) Interior of the roof structure

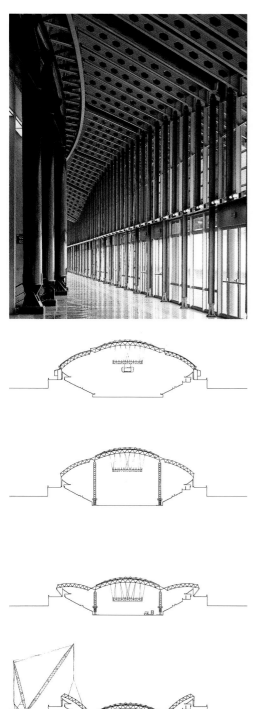

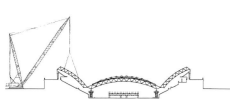

Santiago Calatrava Valls Architecte-Ingenieur S.A.
STADELHOFEN RAILWAY STATION
(Zürich, Switzerland)
1985–90

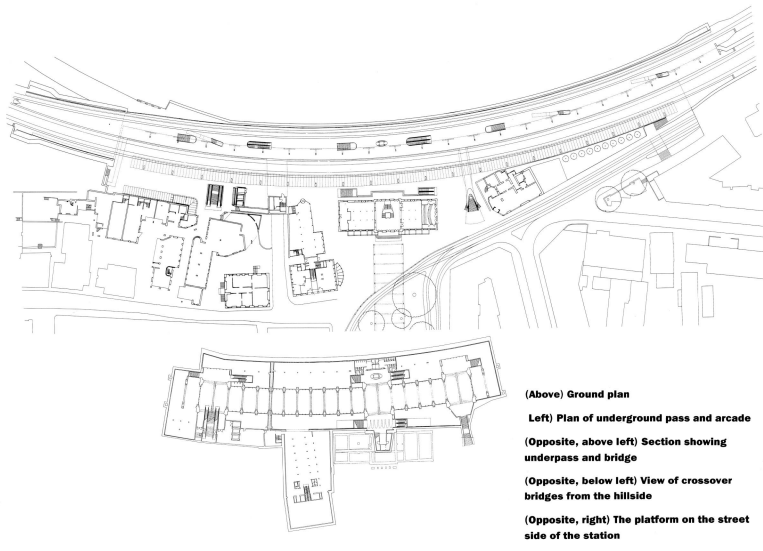

(Above) Ground plan

Left) Plan of underground pass and arcade

(Opposite, above left) Section showing underpass and bridge

(Opposite, below left) View of crossover bridges from the hillside

(Opposite, right) The platform on the street side of the station

The return of interest in the construction aspects of architecture in the mid-1980s – with particular focus on the sculptural elements – is very prominent in the work of Santiago Calatrava, whether in his design of furniture or large-scale engineering projects. The most original and intricate architectural composition by Calatrava is the Stadelhofen Railway Station, part of the local rail network.

With remarkable clarity and veracity, the basic scheme of the station emerges out of an interplay between two kinds of constraints: the topology which is determined by the function of the station, expressing movement and its transportation facility, and topographical considerations defining the available paths and obstacles of the site, which is located at the foot of a park-like hill, once the fortified edge of the city. The site is characterized by the coexistence of two adjacent zones – the hill

contour and the alluvial plain. Within this landscape contour, the train tracks are laid down, curving gracefully at a radius of 400 metres. The station is 270 metres long. Its covered gallery promenade and cantilevered platform roofs conform to the site's gentle shape.

There are three levels: underground, ground and above ground. The ground level is incised by the train tracks and it is bound back by three light steel bridges crossing the hillside and the plain. An underground shopping complex spreads under the tracks, serving as an underpass.

Bridges and platform roofs dominate the composition visually. As in most traditional railway stations, the dominant feature of the project is the cantilevered glass and metal roof. Technical considerations, traditional patterns and patterns derived from fractal geo-

metry are ingeniously combined. This, for example, is manifest in the columns which are triangular in section and spaced at a distance of 6 metres. They branch into a Y-configuration in order to grasp the torsion pipe which, running the entire platform length, stretches out its cantilevered arms to hold up the glass roof. The biomorphic motif of the bridges recurs in the glass and steel platform roof and its supporting light steel structure, and again in the long, arching light steel 'pergolas' sweeping back at 4-metre intervals from the edge of the promenade as one overlooks the tracks from the hill above. The translucent roof held by the 'pergolas' reflects the same motif. Hills, tracks, vine-like and metallic branches, supports, cantilevers and bridges, passing trains, climbing, descending and mingling crowds, all join together into a complex multi-level representation of movement, interaction

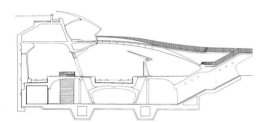

and vitality. The informal, friendly way in which the urban fabric adjoins the station, the immediate proximity of a park, the repeated elements of the structures, interlinking construction elements in steel, ferrovitreous, reinforced concrete, the weaving of paths, passes and passages – not to mention the ease with which the station can be used – all contribute to the *joie de vivre* of the project, reminiscent of the way railway stations were in the last century, before they were replaced in modern times by grim or seedy 'public transportation facilities'. (See also pp. 284–85.)

(Top left and left) The underground arcade

(Above) The middle platform showing the escalator leading to the underground pass and arcade

Foster Associates Ltd
TERMINAL FOR STANSTED AIRPORT
(Stansted, England)
1981–91

Stansted air terminal is unique in having a single internal space 15 metres high and 198 × 162 square metres in surface, with totally transparent walls of glazing. The structure is made of white steel shells floating on top of 36 steel pylons whose spokes open to support the delicate grilles of the curved roof.

Jacques Ferrier, an employee of Foster Associates, has described the construction process in some detail. Various aspects were resolved by several weeks of simulation with a full-sized prototype by Tubeworkers of Clavedon, assisted by Ove Arup Engineers. According to Ferrier, the umbrella solution allows a reduction in the span of the roof beam from 36 to 18 metres because of the 45 degree slope of the spokes. The spokes are pre-stressed and each umbrella has its own internal bracing which enables the spokes to remain in tension. Computer calculations were performed to verify the efficiency of the vertical load transfer. The shaft of the umbrellas (17 × 3.5 × 3.5 metres) also took this constraint into account. Ferrier describes how each spoke was positioned separately and held by temporary cables. Once four spokes were in place and held by the four beams, the eight final cables were fixed at the summit of the pylon and placed in tension. The central bolt, which Ferrier says is the largest ever made in Great Britain, is called a 'Jesus bolt'; it is the key to the stressed node and tightened to 80 tons. The canopy supported by the umbrellas consists of 121 roof panels, each weighing 11 tons.

Foster's design for the terminal was grounded in his perception that the traveller, in other, more conventional airports, has become 'the victim of a complex check-in process, whose most important functions are assumed by the airport building. It is here that the passenger is managed and guided through in

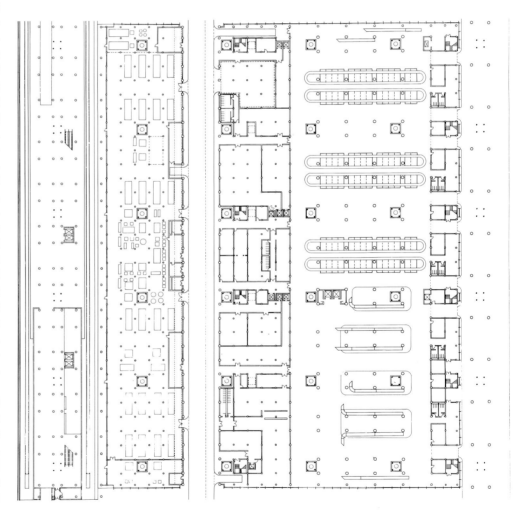

(Left) Exterior view

(Top and above) North-south section and floor plan of the undercroft

(Opposite) Interior perspective view

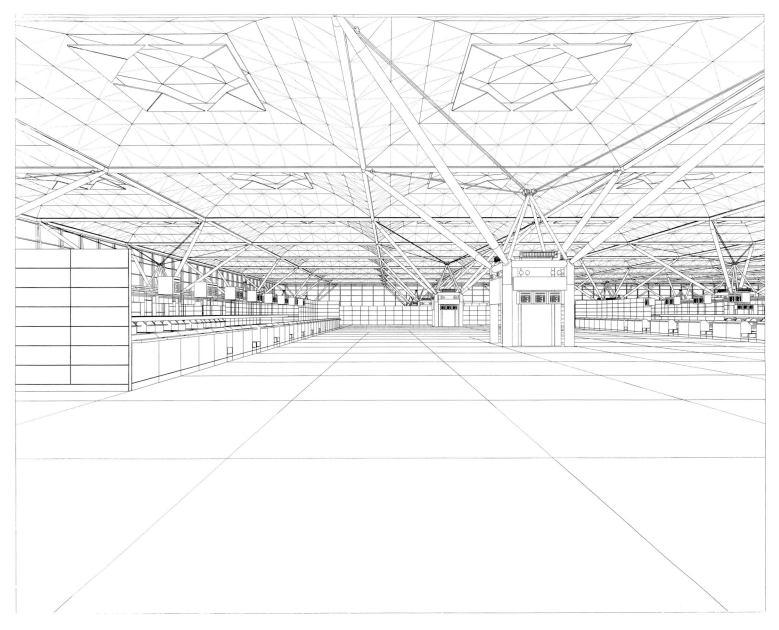

an optimal manner, to achieve an optimal throughput. Controlled by mastering systems, he or she passes through a confusing labyrinth of corridors, stairs, travellators, different floor levels, functional rooms and gates.' As a remedy, Foster attempted to 'restore some of the excitement and clarity of early days of air travel, when waiting aircraft were visible on the tarmac and the logic of the terminal building was easy to comprehend. . . . In the early days of flying, the passenger stood at the edge of an airfield and watched aeroplanes take off and land before he himself set foot on the runway to proceed.'

In order to fulfil this purpose, all public facilities are provided on a single concourse floor in a single universal space, with arrivals and departures side by side, so reducing walking distances for the 15 million passengers a year who are eventually expected to use the airport. Directions are provided by signs. Passengers proceed through a check-in area, security and immigration controls and departure lounge to a tracked transit station on the same level. From there, automatic tracked vehicles transport them to satellite buildings from which they board aircraft. All passenger facilities at concourse level that require enclosure, such as shops, banks, kitchens and lavatories, have been designed as free-standing structures easy to dismantle. The undercroft below the main concourse is intended to service the main concourse and contains the baggage handling system, all the engineering plant for the building, the vehicle servicing area, and storage.

Foster's search for 'clarity' led to the special lighting system. The building is illuminated by natural light that filters into the building through the roof and glazing of the side walls. All artificial light is directed upwards towards the roof from invisible sources. This allows a delicate reflected light to fill the building, enhanced by the grey, white and silver interior, thus turning the building into a gigantic light fixture. After dark, the concourse is lit solely by the artificial light reflected from the internal surface of the roof. The sense of clarity which characterizes the whole terminal is also helped by the 36 pylons, calculated for maximum lightness, which house the services that provide heating, ventilation, air conditioning and lighting.

Foster's aim in the Stansted terminal, to recapture the excitement of the early days of travel facilities, is the same as that of Santiago Calatrava's Stadelhofen Railway Station in Zurich (pp. 254–57) and his Satolas Railway Station in Lyon (pp. 284–85), even though the means by which this is achieved is different.

With Stansted Airport, and through Foster's craftsmanship, the 'universal space', the multi-functional, transparent megacontainer envisaged by Mies and his contemporaries, reaches its anticipated potential.

Miralles Pinós Arquitectos
'LA PISTA' CIVIC CENTRE OF HOSTALETS

(Els Hostalets de Balenya, Spain)
1987–91

A cultural centre housing twenty different functions (including a theatre, a library, studios, a bar and reading room), La Pista makes a clear break from the trend of critical regionalism which has dominated Spanish architecture in the past two decades. Almost nothing could be more different from the sensitive way in which critical regionalist projects, ranging from Rafael Moneo's Bankinter in Madrid (pp. 78–79) to Amado and Domenech's recent courthouse complex in Lerida (pp. 238–41), have been responding to the traditional urban context, preserving its collective memory without falling back on received formulas.

Yet, in its way, La Pista is also contextualist. The apparent difference lies in the context itself. While most other critical regionalist works are to be found in historic centres, this project is located on the 'dirty real' edge of the peripheral road encircling the town of Hostalets, not far from Barcelona. Rather than deny its surroundings, it incorporates the poetics of the 'anti-city' into the new design. This is not to say that the architects simply mimic the environment. On the contrary – and this must be emphasized – like the inner city regionalists, they make the familiar look strange. In so doing, they distance themselves from what Mumford called the anti-city; in other words, they adopt a critical stance.

La Pista defines itself as a boundary. The three-storey building is flat on the street sides, its fortress-like surface reflecting the sloping outline of the road. On the inside, it responds to the fragmentation of the sloping, partially excavated site by itself presenting an image of fragmentation in its sharp, unaligned, triangular floor plans.

The roughness of shapes is coupled with the roughness of the concrete texture. In this, as Josep Maria Montaner, the Catalan architectural critic, has remarked, it has an affinity with the British neo-brutalist roughness of texture – which was, incidentally, associated with the broader cultural manifestation of the 'angry young men' of the 1950s and 1960s.

As is the case in projects such as the Zollhof Media Centre (pp. 286–89) and the Valencia Television Station (pp. 234–35), the influences at work in La Pista can be traced back, ultimately, to the Russian Constructivist architecture of the 1920s in the use of

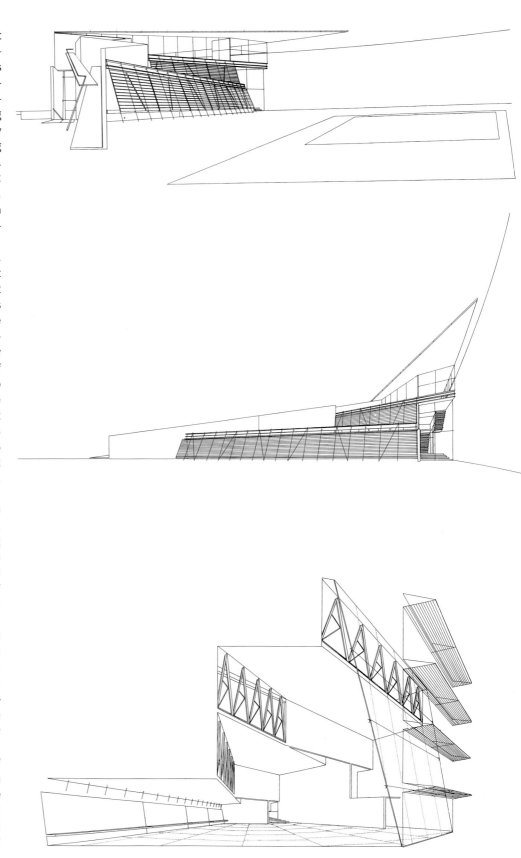

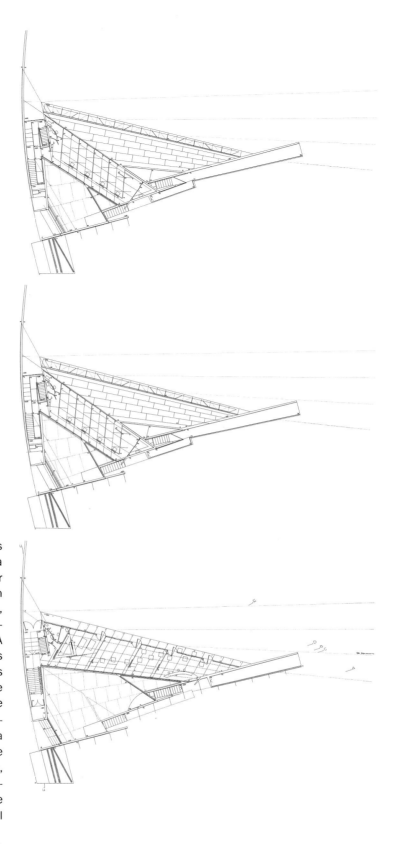

(Opposite, top to bottom)

View of the ramp

The terrace

Perspective drawing of the interior

(This page, top to bottom)

Third floor plan

Second floor plan

First floor plan

Ground floor plan

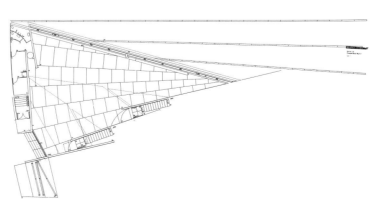

fragmented, anti-classical geometry. Miralles and Pinós themselves acknowledge that a particularly important source of inspiration for their work here is the early work of Konstantin Melnikov who, of the Russian Constructivists, is perhaps the roughest and most industrial-looking in his treatment of surface texture. A clear reference is made to Melnikov's famous USSR Pavilion at the Paris Exposition des Arts Décoratifs of 1925 in La Pista's ramp, in the way its I-beams are exposed. Furthermore, the emphasis on the trusses comes from Melnikov's Leyland Bus Station in Bakmetevskaia Ulitsa in Moscow (1926). Such citations are not for lack of ideas nor inspired by nostalgia, neither is there any irony in them. The architects' intention is to amplify and universalize such ideas in today's historical and cultural context.

A remarkable feature of La Pista is the intentionally 'difficult' system of circulation and the misleading directionality it imparts to the space, which provides contrast. This quality is not, however, intended to create merely an effect of surprise and variety, as is the case in Romantic and even Modernist architecture. Contrast and the jagged motif of the external appearance of the building are its most memorable aspects, forming a microcosmic 'cognitive mapping' of the dislocating forces loose in the outside world of the urban periphery.

Collages by the architects of the interior
space under construction

(Top) Elevations

(Above) Cross section and elevations

(Opposite, top) Typical unit plan

(Opposite) Volumetric site plan

This is no ordinary low-cost, subsidized, pre-fabricated social housing. Each of the 220 apartments, which are broken down into 40 different inventive spaces, has a double exposure. One is onto the street, the other onto the whispy 'cloud of green' formed by the grove of young silver birches planted in the generous, gently sloping inner courtyard (25 × 66 metres).

Each apartment has its own basement, waste disposal unit, entry-phone, ultra-modern thermal control and a brightly lit interior space, thanks to either a terrace, a screened loggia or large glazed openings.

According to the French architectural critic Jean-Pierre Ménard, the building's exceptional formal and functional qualities are in part due to the fact that, rather than being funded by the public sector, it was financed by Mutuelles du Mans, who were willing to invest 6000

French francs per square metre instead of the usual 5000 francs. This allowed Piano relative freedom of manoeuvre in adapting the usual rules and regulations which govern the production of low-cost subsidized housing in France.

As one has come to expect of Renzo Piano in the light of his previous *tours de force*, this is a highly instructive example of technological innovation. Here, in the middle of the famous *ceinture rouge* ('red belt', so-called because of the extensive use of brick) of the popular, traditionally working-class 19th arrondissement of Paris, Piano's concern seems to have been to preserve the memory of the traditional, urban vernacular, but by means of the most advanced, rationally industrialized building techniques, in what amounts to a critical regionalist vein.

Piano's use for the costly extension of IRCAM of a skin of prefabricated panels made of

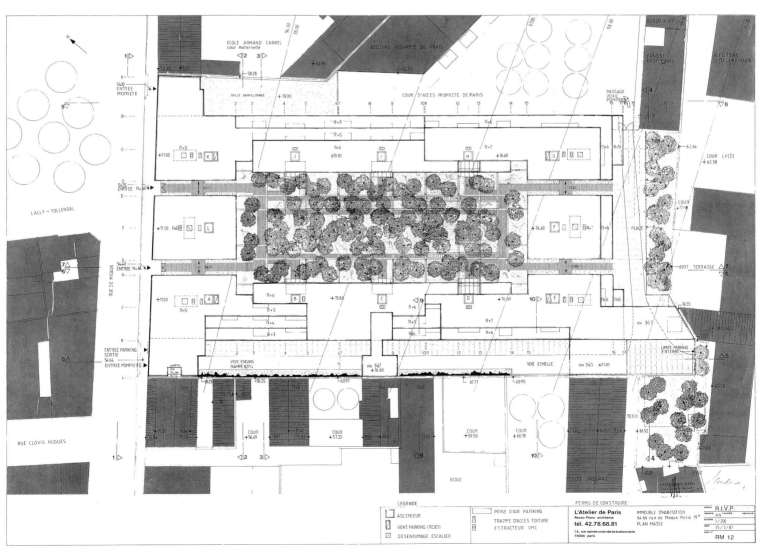

bricks encased in stainless steel frames could not be repeated here for budgetary reasons. In a much less expensive variation on the same theme, however, he opted for terracotta tiles, instead of bricks, and prefabricated panels of fibreglass-reinforced concrete, instead of steel, thus conferring on the project a character which *Le Monde* referred to as an economical version of IRCAM. Fibreglass-reinforced concrete can be as finely sculpted as steel but it has the added advantage of being much cheaper, as Jean-Pierre Ménard has pointed out. This technique was still at an experimental stage when the building was conceived. The combination of glass and cement is normally ruled out because the former is attacked by the alkaline components of the latter. Working with the Betsinor company, two types of panels were developed: one a 'shell' for the solid walls; the other a 'lattice' for the transparent ones. These are attached by metal brackets sealed into the structural cement. The terracotta tiles, specially moulded to interlock with each other once in place, are not plastered onto the surface, but hung from

snub-nosed supports projecting from the surface of the shell modules. This building shares a common trait with other Piano buildings: it is at the cutting edge of new construction technology, and it could not have been built previously.

It is to the credit of the Régie Immobilière de la Ville de Paris that it had the foresight to commission the Renzo Piano team for this project, and to the credit of the uniquely versatile Renzo Piano team that it applied the same enlightened rationality and technological invention to this modest social project as it has in the past when working on higher 'prestige' profiles.

(This page and opposite) Views of the units from the interior court

(Opposite, below left) Detail of the ceramic-tile exterior of the wall showing the suspension method used

Frank Gehry and Associates
VITRA DESIGN MUSEUM
(Basel, Switzerland)
1987–89

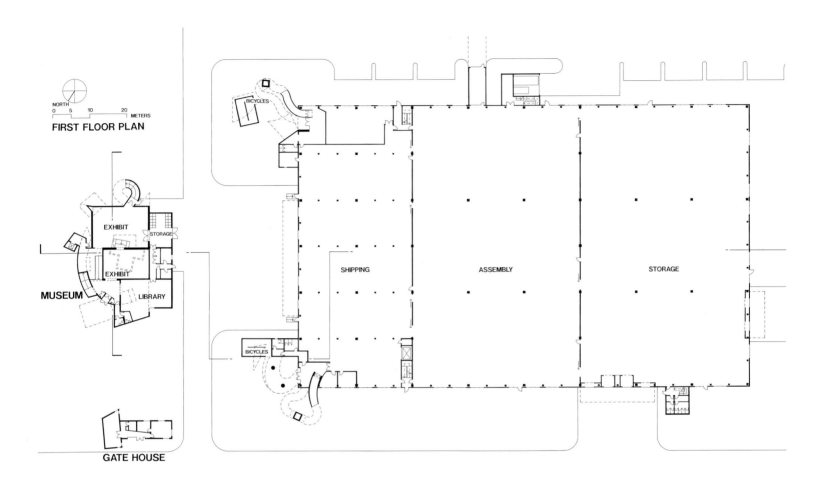

NORTH
0 5 10   20   METERS
FIRST FLOOR PLAN

EXHIBIT
STORAGE
EXHIBIT
MUSEUM
LIBRARY

BICYCLES

SHIPPING   ASSEMBLY   STORAGE

BICYCLES

GATE HOUSE

Frank Gehry is, in one sense, the creator of 'dirty realist' architecture. He has had the most wide-ranging influence on forming the new sensitivity in the profession over the last decade. His studio for Ron Davis in Malibu (1970–72) was the first building to introduce elements from the harsh urban and industrial realities into design (which is what we mean by 'dirty realism'): materials such as corrugated and sheet-metal siding in steel, zinc or copper; chain-link fence, exposed and often oversized girders treated with a propensity for wilful neglect, roughness and *non-finito*. The origin of this sensitivity is the sculpture of the 1970s, in particular that of Gehry's friend and occasional collaborator Richard Serra.

The Vitra Museum contains a foyer, a cafeteria and conference rooms arranged round two exhibition halls that extend upwards the full height of the building. It was supposed to be a lot rougher than it actually is. Originally, the outer cladding was to be in sheet steel, in

Gehry's words, 'like an old oil-can'. But the client of this prestige building was most insistent that it should have a 'finish'. As a result of a 'heated intercontinental fax discussion', a compromise was reached, and the building was finally executed in grey titanium zinc sheeting and white plaster, with 'sheet steel wherever it gets rained on', according to the executive architect of the project, Günter Pfeifer (Martin Filler and Olivier Boissière, *Frank Gehry: Vitra Design Museum*, 1990). As a result, the building does indeed look like an old oil-can, but one which has exploded, then been lavishly detailed and painted white. The deliberately nondescript entrance looks more like an entrance to a bus depot than to a museum; the forms of the building seem to be derived from industrial plant ramps.

The museum houses Vitra owner Rolf Fehlbaum's collection of industrial chairs dating from the 19th century to the present which are significant for their function, form, construc-

tion or material. The building is located across the car park from a complex made up of a factory building by Nicholas Grimshaw and the extension to the production unit for the Vitra furniture design company, also designed by Gehry. The Vitra factory stands in a vast industrial area in the Rhine valley, a once agricultural landscape now scarred by factories, where smokestacks compete with church towers and massive production plants with vineyards.

In this unsettled, 'dynamic' environment where a dislocated, technological, global *genius loci* has encroached upon the traditional agrarian, regional one, the building takes its 'dirty real' revenge by appearing to be more disarrayed, jumbled and disjunct than anything around it, even when compared with the expressionist buildings of the region. It looks like a Ronchamp gone wild, in a state of convulsion, or a Goetheanum caught in a tornado.

This chaos in the building's form is only seeming, however. In fact, the thunderous, mighty volumes are measured, balanced and in dialogue with each other; there is as much mass and space as the whole requires; the runaway curves are encountered and counter-pointed by broken up-prisms. The result has a sense of balance and variety.

More importantly, once inside the museum, one's impression is the reverse of disorder. Not only is the atmosphere solemn, the light acting as a unifier of the polymorphy of the interiors of these highly fragmented volumes, but there is also a serenity of total harmony between form and goal. As in a medieval cathedral, all the arcane contortions of shape are there for the purpose of modulating light. These interiors are also highly individualized spatial frames to accommodate the display of objects.

It is as if the building's essential form were its interior, a space as if sculpted out of thickened air, each room leading to the next

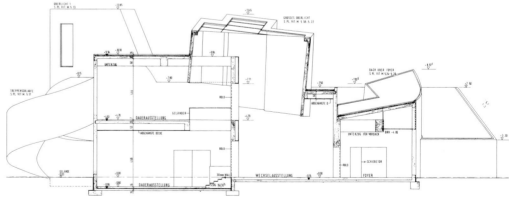

with a lightness superior to the atmosphere surrounding it, an architecture of 'pure space' as imagined by Hans Hollein in diagrams of his early years and, to some degree, a spatial composition which has certain affinities with the Action Architecture movement of the late 1950s.

(Opposite) Ground plan showing the relationship of the Vitra Design Museum to the rest of the site

(Above) Exterior view and cross section

(Opposite, top) Night view of the exterior

(Above) Exterior view

(Opposite and right) Views of the interior

Venturi, Scott Brown & Associates, Inc.
THE NATIONAL GALLERY, SAINSBURY WING
(London, England)
1986–91

Few buildings have generated so much controversy and passionate writing as the Sainsbury Wing of London's National Gallery by the American architectural firm of Venturi, Scott Brown and Associates. This is understandable because of the unfavourable conditions attending the building's birth – 'wicked' problems which invited solutions that had to be debated at each step of the design.

Trafalgar Square, fraught with 'complexity and contradiction', is a difficult site. A vast, untamed 'camp' rather than a square, it has a long architectural history which still begs for some definition. The specific site, just west of the National Gallery – a quiet, felicitous, careful and rather undemanding building of the 1830s by William Wilkins – has been associated in its recent past with uninspiring if practical uses: before the War it was occupied by a furniture store; then it was left a bombed out hole until it became a car park. Across from it stands what Ludwig Wittgenstein deemed the most stupid building in the world, the superficially classical Canada House. To add to the difficulties of the variety of the area, Trafalgar Square also contains a masterpiece – Gibbs' St-Martin-in-the-Fields – along with, at its very heart, a disaster – the 19th-century, indisputably State-kitsch monument, Nelson's Column.

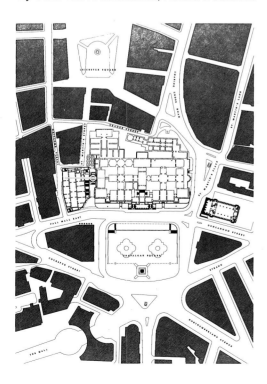

The government acquired the site for the museum extension in 1959 and a saga of conflict and frustration began as soon as plans took shape. The first competition was won by the British architects Ahrends, Burton & Koralek, whose project was described by the Prince of Wales as 'a monstrous carbuncle on the face of a much-loved and elegant friend', a stunning characterization for a rather unastonishing project. The phrase became legendary and was adopted as a war cry by anti-modernists, especially in the UK. It left many victims in its wake, including Richard Rogers' proposal for the site which was both fascinating and also popular with the public.

Despite the troublesome competition for the architectural design of the extension, finances for its realization had not yet been secured, since the government was not prepared to spend any money on the extension of the National Gallery of Great Britain. While this unwillingness would have been inconceivable in most other countries in Europe, it followed the doctrines of the Thatcher era about the need for self-reliance by all, including national institutions. Finally, in 1985, Sainsbury Brothers, Sir John, Simon and Timothy, offered to fund the project with an unquestionably generous donation which did not stipulate the creation of rentable office space above the extension, as the previous scheme had done. The estimated £35 million budget and the 10,000 square metres of usable space were modest by the standard of other contemporary international and European comparable institutions. Thus, one more degree of difficulty was added to a problem already made difficult by the awkward configuration of the site, the super-demanding programme, the number of 'masterpieces' that had to be accommodated and the formidable size of the crowds expected to use the facility.

In 1986, in a reversal of the open procedures followed up to then, Robert Venturi and his associates were chosen from among six other architectural firms after a worldwide search. Not much was disclosed about the underlying reasons for the selection of an American firm in a city and a country where projects by foreign architects have tended to be rare. Obviously, this decision contributed even more twists to an already tangled knot.

This situation was not made any simpler by the fact that one of the chosen architects, Robert Venturi, author of what is probably the most influential architectural book of the past twenty-five years, *Complexity and Contradiction in Architecture* (1966), is one of the most complex and contradiction-loving theoreticians and practitioners today, and this at a time when architectural practice as a whole is going through a phase notorious for a generalized lack of simplicity.

It is difficult to imagine how all this could have resulted in anything but controversy, a controversy that contributed, with few exceptions, to the general lack of understanding of the solution offered by Venturi. Such lack of understanding, and indeed misunderstandings, about the Sainsbury Wing have led, for instance, to the impression that its design is dominated by historicist motifs whimsically posing merely to tease the passer-by, pretending to offer a polite gesture to the building of William Wilkins, while a few metres away proceeding to disintegrate into a jocular banality of commercial brick surfaces: and all this without any relation to the structure, function or purpose of the building which remain suppressed behind a farcical facade.

A more careful inspection of the building leads, however, to an altogether different set of conclusions. To begin with, the National Gallery extension is a highly functional building dedicated to satisfying the basic operational, programmatic needs of a contemporary museum. It is a major contribution to a unique collection of cultural institutions located in a unique metropolis. With great skill, the project fulfils the programme requirements in the way it interweaves and interlinks spaces. The route the visitors take through the galleries and the secondary facilities of the museum is perfectly clear. This is the result of a simple, hard-headed choice. Instead of ignoring the problems of circulation, or inventing an idiosyncratic network, an ordinary, traditional path-pattern has been rediscovered which possesses the qualities of directionality, memorable organization and flexibility. The setting it offers for the display of paintings, the sequencing, the approach to each gallery, the architectural framing of the objects, the vistas it opens, the entry, dimensioning, proportion-

ing, and the scale of each exhibition area are quite simply stunning. The internal spaces are related to the outside through strategically inserted openings across the visitor's path, thus overcoming the difficult problem of disorientation so frequent in contemporary museums because of their great demands for controlled environments. At the same time, the spaces do not disrupt the degree of concentration expected by modern audiences. A superb quality of lighting is achieved by clerestory windows framed in wood with acid-etched glazing to diffuse daylight, located at the upper perimeters of the galleries. The allocation of activities within the building perfectly balances the conflicting requirements of space occupation and the demands of accessibility of services – conference rooms, special exhibitions, shop, brasserie, coffee bar, a computer interactive facility and galleries. Functionally, therefore, the building is one of the most successful accommodations for a museum in the last two decades, a period massively characterized by museum production.

Far from disregarding technology, the Sainsbury Wing offers a highly intelligent solution to the technical problems posed by the programme and the site. From the point of view of construction, there were many difficulties posed by the clay sub-soil, the high environmental demands of the enveloped space, the tight schedule of implementation. An innovative 'top-down' method was followed, in which a perimeter wall was erected before excavation. Formed by a dense row of secant piles, it was braced by the concrete slab on top of which grew the concrete shell of the building. Certainly, the collaboration with the engineering firm of Arup and Partners was crucial to the success.

These observations demonstrate Venturi's commitment to what the building does, as distinct from what it looks like it is doing. Operational and technical requirements were satisfied as separate concerns and not glossed over by visual-spatial, semantic aspects of the building. Venturi's theory of architecture and his design method are founded on the idea that architecture involves

(Opposite) Site plan at the level of the extension's main floor

(Above) Facade

complex, multi-level cognition, and that architectural products are complex, multi-aspect objects which cannot be reduced to simplistic, monist design worlds without tremendous impoverishment of functional as well as cultural qualities. Transforming Mies's dictum of 'less is more' into 'less is less', Venturi singled out Mies's post-war architecture as an example of reductive monism and a mere simulacrum of function. Against it, he juxtaposed Alvar Aalto's and Louis Kahn's more multivalent, intricate and inclusive designs.

These were ideas demonstrated at the very beginning of Venturi's career, then amplified later through his collaboration with Denise Scott Brown. This enlargement of scope led to

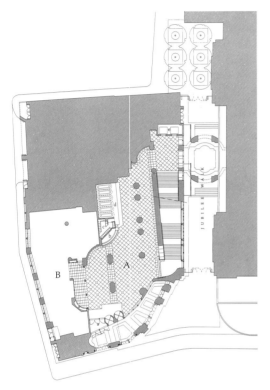 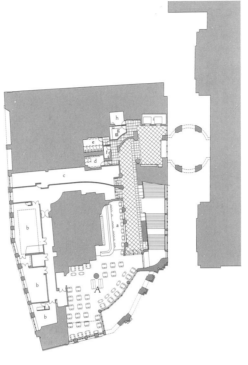 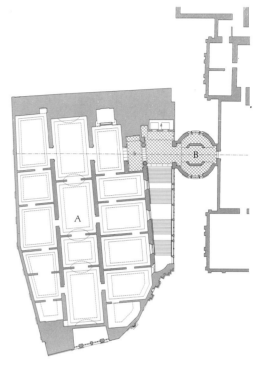

the acceptance of the casinos of Las Vegas and the emporia of Main Street, USA, as prototypes for the directness with which they confronted and solved contemporary problems.

On the other hand, this sort of demanding credo of truth as opposed to verisimilitude, of virtue as opposed to moralism, made Venturi and Scott Brown's work difficult to understand. Their oeuvre never did quite fit into the simplistic 'blackboard diagrams', to use the phrase of American art critic Harold Rosenberg, of postwar architectural history. Taken out of context, some of the characteristics of their work have led critics to classify Venturi and Scott Brown as anti-modern and anti-intellectual. And this has been the case, to a great extent, with Venturi's Sainsbury Wing.

Hence the incomprehension with regard to the exterior of the building, with its way of presenting 'a different face at each of its edges' being taken as failure to 'show' the interior subdivisions and functions or 'the way the building is constructed' – a criticism which is irrelevant since, according to Venturi, these are issues which were not supposed to be addressed by the visual organization of the building.

Equally misguided has been the claim that the facade of the building is a mere mirroring of the strongly contrasted surrounding site, a downgrading of the building's intent to one of simple contextualism – hardly a significant performance for an architectural work aspiring to be a significant work of art. In fact, the exterior of the building is trying to do something else and something more. Of course, it uses as a motif the Corinthian mode, overtly taken from the Wilkins building. Using techniques of formal transformation, echoing Michelangelo's methods, or Guarini's, as well as Aalto's, the Corinthian motif is varied until it fades into a brick wall, another motif taken from the surroundings, to dissolve later into a plain, screen-like wall on which, in huge letters, the name of the building emerges – in true cinematic fashion.

The handling of the Corinthian motif of Wilkins' building is not just a pastiche or an ironic citation, or even a sympathetic effort to integrate the new with the old. This, as well as the use of the banal motif of the brick wall, comes closer to the kind of picking up, transforming and incorporating of 'found objects' that Pop art makes – a school of thought not alien to Venturi.

Thus, here, the found objects, such as the Corinthian motif, the brick wall, are only as important as plot is in a novel: a fabrication to carry a deeper literary message. Such objects, as Harold Rosenberg has remarked in writing about Pop art, are 'not real things but pictures of things', representations rather than presences, and their use, beyond the mimetic or the shocking, is cognitive. In the Sainsbury Wing, the bringing together of these heteroclite, contradictory motifs serves as a device for answering questions about 'well-formedness' and for coping with constraints in 'world-making' when multiple possible worlds which are inconsistent with each other must, nevertheless, communicate and co-exist. The building is, therefore, a multi-faceted object, at once a shelter and a structure whose visual organization can be read as an essay in built form about epistemological and moral problems. The problem it addresses through architectural, iconic means is that of communication and co-existence within the framework of numerous incommeasurable worlds, one of the major issues in the philosophy of mind today, not to mention in contemporary life.

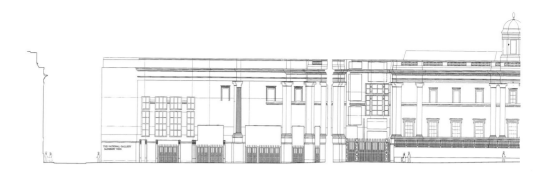

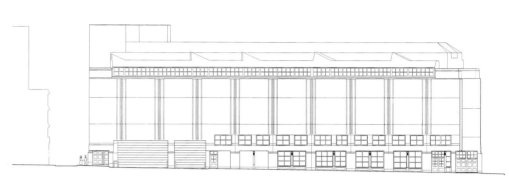

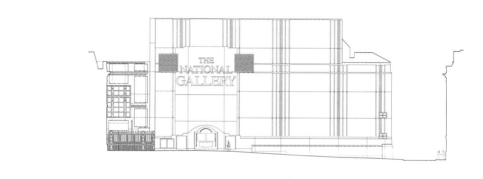

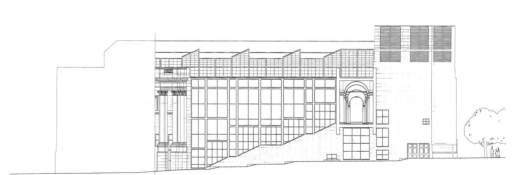

(Opposite)
(Top left) Transverse section

(Centre, left) Ground floor plan of the
Sainsbury Wing: A = entrance foyer;
B = gallery shop; a = vestibule;
b = information desk; c = parcels storage;
d = cloaks; e = lifts

(Centre) First floor plan: A = restaurant;
a = coffee bar; b = conference suite;
d–g = toilets and infants' room; h = first
aid room, i = lifts

(Centre, right) Main floor plan: A = Early
Renaissance and Northern European
galleries; B = bridge to pre-existing galleries;
a = lifts; b = introduction

(This page)
(Above, top left) Conceptual drawing of the
exhibition space

(Above left) Looking up the main staircase

(Above, top to bottom) Extended south
elevation; west, north and east elevations

Hans Hollein
THE SALZBURG GUGGENHEIM MUSEUM
(Salzburg, Austria)
1989–

Salzburg, one of the cultural capitals of Europe, will be celebrating the millennium of its foundation in 1995. For this occasion, its mayor, Joseph Reschen, has planned an annex to the Guggenheim Museum which will house a part of its immense collection, 90 per cent of which is not at present on view to the public. The greatest problem Salzburg faces today is its dense urban mass and a mountainous belt girding the city that impedes new construction.

The new museum will be sited in the Monchsberg mountain dominating the city walls.

Hans Hollein was selected as the architect of the project after an international competition which also included Jean Nouvel. Turning the geological odds to his advantage, Hollein opted to convert the caverns concealed in the mountain into exhibition areas. The visitor climbs laterally up the cliff to an excavation 20 metres wide and 40 metres high, illuminated

from above. Stairs lead first to halls inside the caverns, then to the large exhibition spaces, inundated by light, on the upper side. The interplay of contrasting dark and light areas thus becomes the predominant theme of the museum's architecture, reflecting perhaps the same contrasts and sublime effects as in Mozart's *The Magic Flute*.

In attempting to define spatial configurations, Hollein's writings, exhibitions, actual and utopian designs throughout his career, have always been in search of an architecture of 'pure space', emancipated from the constraints imposed by physical necessities. In the Guggenheim Museum, given the happy coincidence of the programme, site, technology, as well as the brief of his clients, Hollein seems closer than ever before to realizing this ambition.

(Left) Model of interior

(Below left) Section

(Opposite) Bird's-eye view – section of the mountain-top museum complex with surroundings

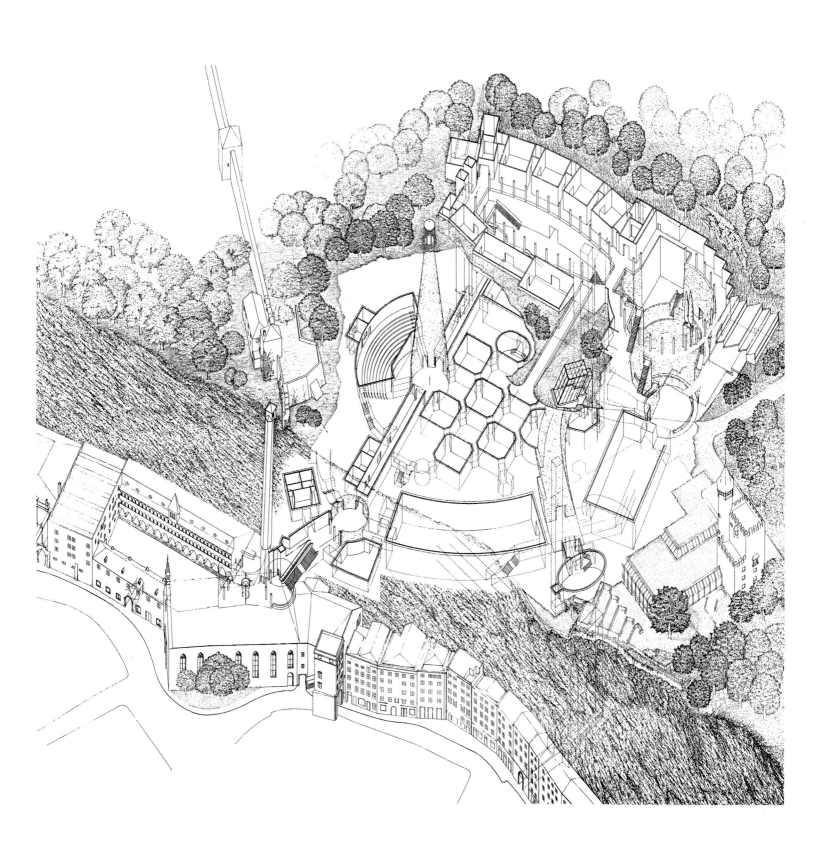

Tadao Ando Architect & Associates
JAPAN PAVILION EXPO '92
(Seville, Spain)
1989–91

The Japanese Pavilion at the Seville Expo '92 is one of the largest wooden constructions in the world, 25 metres high and with four levels, each with a surface 60 metres by 40 metres. The upper part is covered by a roof of translucent film made of teflon. The exterior is finished in warped lap siding wood.

Technologically, the project therefore combines a most traditional material with the most advanced construction techniques that stretch the potential of wood to its limit. Functionally, the organization is clear. Visitors are brought to the heart of the building, to a high point from where they descend through the various display areas. But, more than the displays, what is presented throughout their journey is the building itself and the way it is constructed.

The material used is different from most of the previous works of Ando, which are based on exposed reinforced concrete. In addition, while in most of his previous projects the solids of the building, despite their massiveness, are dematerialized by downplaying their structural identity through what Ando has called abstraction, and by foregrounding their pure geometrical configuration, in the Seville Pavilion the technology of the structure and details – an up-to-date technology drawn from all over the world – is exhibited explicitly.

This collection of technologies in one structure, traditional and modern, Japanese and international, was a conscious choice following the directives of the programme of the building: to present the idea of 'the past, present and future of Japan' participating simultaneously in a world of local traditions and one of modern globalism. At the same time, the building is meant as a celebration of the idea of discovery; the Expo's theme is *The Age of*

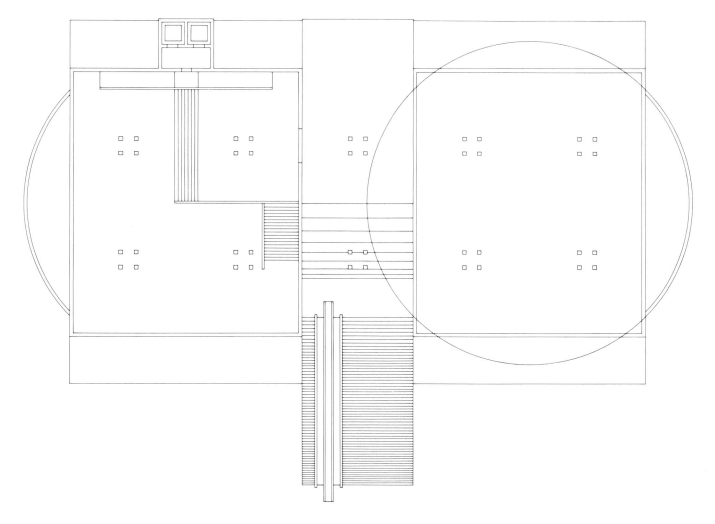

(Opposite) Views of the model of the pavilion

(Above) Plan

Discovery. Discovery refers, more concretely, to that of America by Columbus 500 years before in 1492; the discovery by Europe of its unity in 1992; and, in the specific case of this pavilion, the discovery of Japan by the world.

There is, however, more to the pavilion than its pragmatic display of its programmatic message, in fulfilment of the requirements of being part of an international exposition; more, too, than its unique size, operational clarity and technological intricacy. The building is also an intricate poetic object.

In his poetics, here as in his previous work, Ando relies on minimal geometric elements in his spatial compositions. The Seville Pavilion, however, overcomes his previous Euclidean elementarism of straight lines, circles, orthogonal prisms and simple intersections between them. Instead, the spatial elements have a freer configuration. Still, self-con-

tained, their shape suggests what in Japanese painting is called *fude no chikara*, the strength of the hand at the moment the brush applies a stroke to a two-dimensional surface, here translated into built form. The pavilion is in fact an enormous ideogram, created fundamentally from two *kanji*, or written characters: a single curved stroke forming a pathway, and a number of straight strokes enclosing a space. The two elements are opposed to each other, convex bridge to concave facade. Yet, in their opposition, the two characters interpenetrate and become enmeshed as an inseparable whole. The curved stroke of the arched bridge, 11 metres in height, is one of the most striking features of the project. By climbing up through it, the visitor enters the pavilion. An archaic Japanese symbol, this traditional arched bridge, or *taikobashi*, originally represented the passage from this world to the other. In the

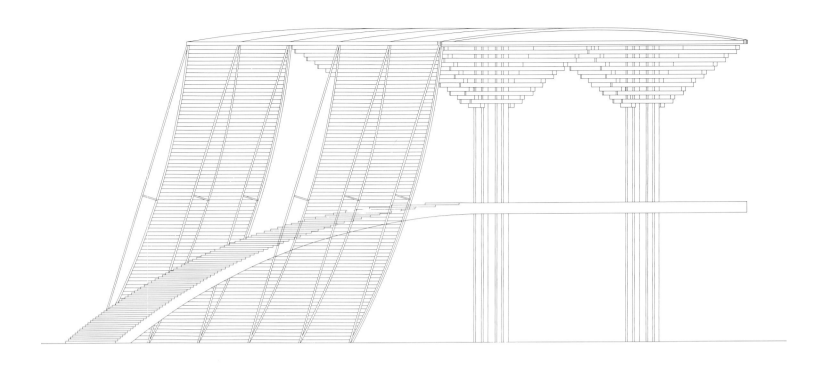

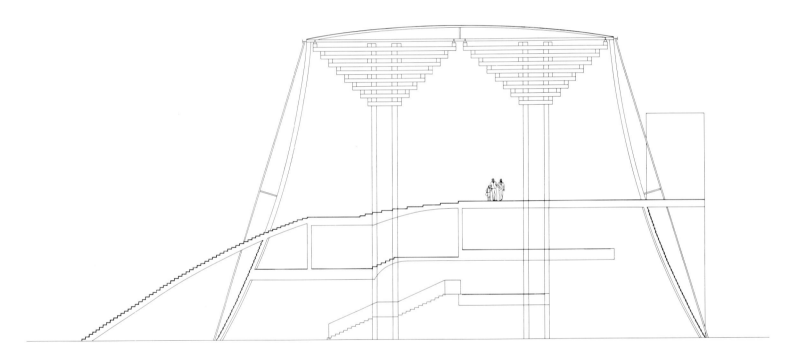

pavilion, the *taikobashi* is used as a double metaphor to symbolize the crossing from the realities of life into the world of imagination, as well as the bridging of knowledge between East and West.

Representational and poetic functions are not confined to the visual structure of the building. Ando conceives spatial organization and use to be interwoven with meaning: as in all traditional Japanese ritual, so in this pavilion ceremonial architecture, formal structure and process are one. 'I pursue precisely that vital union of abstract geometrical form and daily human activity'; 'abstract existence [is] meeting with concreteness', Ando remarks in his statement for the catalogue of his major exhibition at the Museum of Modern Art in New York, in Autumn 1991.

In this space-event complex, visitors, after their ascent through the bridge, enter a gallery, a huge open space. From here, they proceed downwards, passing through each of the exhibition rooms. And as they descend inside the great open space of the gallery, with its 17-metre-high ceiling, they turn to the plain wooden columns and beams, which together form a configuration washed by the light they sense streaming through the transparent teflon film above. As the visitors actively experience this visual-kinetic process, navigating through the architecture and being guided by it, they will 'be able to feel the historical movement of Japan'; the whole building will become for them a bridge of international exchange and understanding, just as the programme required. But even more than this,

the pavilion is born as an architectural space of ideogram-ritual which incorporates the concepts of evolution and encounter merged into one, and offers a cognitive synthesis through an experience of space in which the whole body participates.

(Above) Axonometric drawing and section

(Opposite) Conceptual drawing

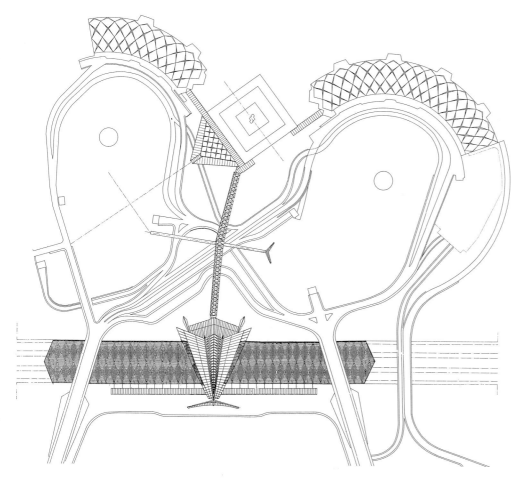

The result of a competition, the TGV railway station for Lyon-Satolas is the most ambitious of Calatrava's projects to date and, in many respects, gives the clearest indication of the direction of his investigations towards a poetics of construction (see also pp. 254–57).

The project consists of the main station building, the platforms and a passageway connecting the station to the nearby airport. Contextual aspects were important in determining the composition. The existing air terminal has been respected and used as a reference object dictating the massing and the orientation of the new buildings. The axis of the station is placed almost as an extension of the diagonal of the air terminal and the complete bilateral symmetry of the new building echoes the airport's symmetrical shape.

Orientation is a key determinant of the design of the building. Space has been sculpted in order to give cues about circulation. Passengers are informed through a clear differentiation of the volumes about where they are and how to find their destination. Venturi would no doubt have dismissed this kind of solution, which bends architectural form in order to fulfil functional requirements, as an architectural 'duck'.

But there is more to Calatrava's spatial-plastic solution than facile functionalism. He has used architecture as a means of making the activity of travelling an exciting and memorable event rather than dreary, utilitarian and drudgery-filled, and has tried to make the collective and ritualistic aspects of using public transport essential ingredients of the building. In order to do this, a symbolic image was needed which would be instantly recognizable by the travellers, fulfil their expectations as they arrived, and offer a memorable impression as they departed. He chose that of speed and flight. The 'symbol' Calatrava tried to evoke was one that 'embodies the idea of flight and passage'.

The metaphorical representation of flight in architectural terms can be of two kinds: first, when the geometry of the volumes mimetically 'describes' flying organisms or those parts of the anatomy of such organisms that are used for flight – pinions, wings, feathers – or when it presents abstracted, streamlined figures; and second, when the configuration of the building 'describes', still more abstractly, what we might call aviational actions – taking off, landing, soaring. Coop Himmelblau, for example, would have chosen the second – and carried it out on a small scale (see pp. 220–23). Calatrava, in his choice of 'a broadly spreading roof that unfolds its wings longitudinally over the platforms like a bird taking flight', has clearly opted for the first. There is also an implication of movement in the stream-lined curving of the structural members of the roof of the platforms.

In this choice Calatrava appears to have taken a path characteristically different from Foster's at Stansted Airport (pp. 258–59), where the building is a universal volume, its roof spreading calmly like a second vast sky beneath the sky; where the users' sense of direction is strengthened by relating their progress directly to views of the outside; and where the serene architecture expresses the idea of rest – but not without excitement and intrigue – between changing modes of transportation. Calatrava's path seems, instead, to follow the one opened up by Eero Saarinen three decades ago with his design for Dulles Airport for Washington DC, and, in particular, the mimetically simulated eagle of the TWA building in New York.

Calatrava's buildings have certainly benefited from the technological advances and experience that have occurred since Saarinen's designs were built in the early 1960s. He is, furthermore, more daring and, one might say, more obsessed. This explains no doubt why the specifics of the shapes created in Lyon-Satolas and the individual use of a varied but continuous geometry in its overall configuration are so original.

This is not the first time Calatrava has tried to capture movement in a design. Most of his projects are attempts to do just that. When he is not picturing flight, then he is picturing growth, that slow movement in time which

increases the volume of organic form. He does so through the application of a fractal geometry at all levels of scale.

Of course, buildings do not move. Neither are they shaped by movement. Although Calatrava's buildings are metaphorical representations of movement, they can also be seen as suggesting the paradox that architecture's striving for permanence in space is always achieved in time and through time. These general reflections become happily appropriate as his specific projects have tended to be related structures meant to serve movement, such as bridges and stations, as is the case with the Lyon-Satolas station.

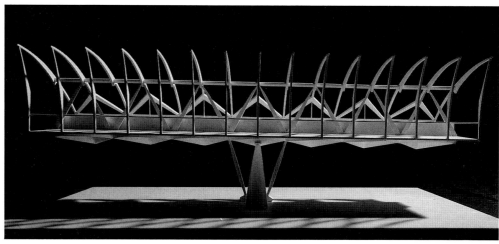

(Opposite) Plan

(Above) View of the model

(Right) The model showing canopy construction

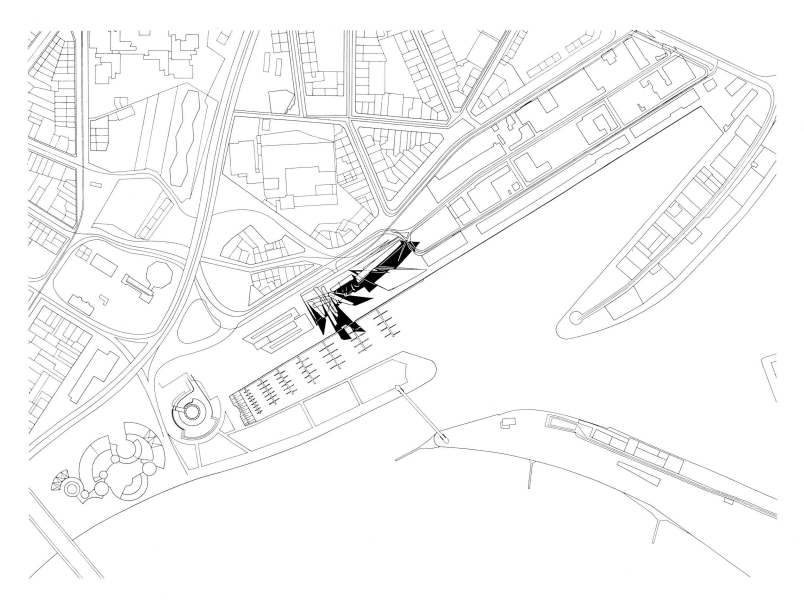

Like so many of the sites that the younger generation of European architects are increasingly being commissioned to build on, this one, in the once thriving but now declining and desolate dockland area of Düsseldorf, is full of abandoned warehouses and industrial buildings. As with other projects of the 1980s by prominent architects, Zaha Hadid's Media Centre was 'chosen to act as an impetus' for the transformation of the whole area into a 'new enterprise zone', in the words of the brief.

The programme of this redevelopment is the accommodation of advertising companies and communications businesses along with commercial, cultural and leisure activities. Situated between a major traffic artery and a river, the building scheme is defined by the distinctive quality of its relationship to both. On the road side, the building is plain and solid, an assertive wall against the traffic; it houses studios and offices. On its ground level are sited the more public-related functions (galleries and showrooms) and above are those areas which require quietness. The river bank is considered the active part of the site, animated with sport and other leisure pursuits, and this is where the explosive character of the scheme emerges. Here the building is 'open', the walls 'break free', and the use of a number of slabs provides the advantage of 'generating a variety of different spatial conditions inside', in contrast to the traditional uniformity of

(Opposite) Site plan

(Right) View from the city

(Below right) Conceptual drawing

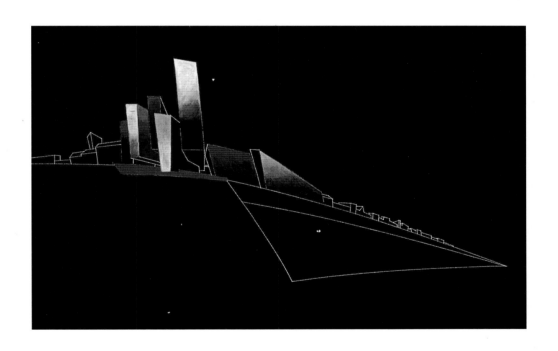

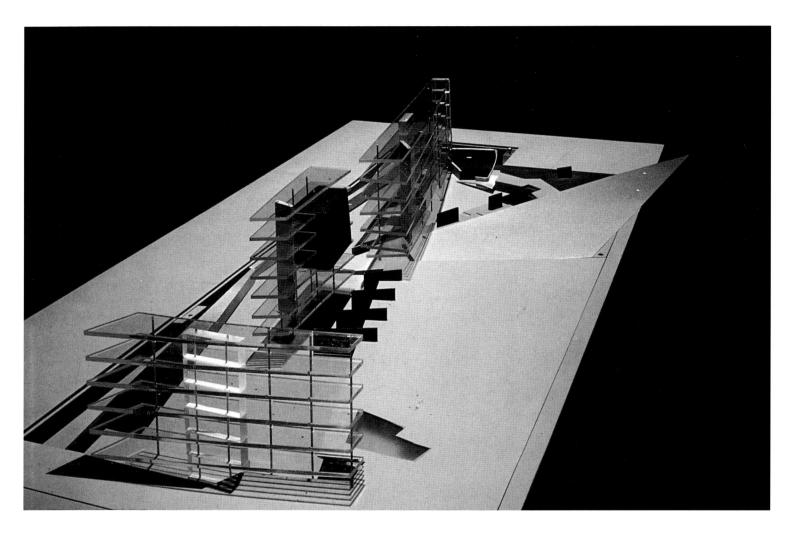

office space. At the points of intersection between the skewed slabs, Hadid places big spaces for meetings, the ordinary functions of the programme. The walls are as if cracked and 'articulated in relief'. Floors vary in depth and are also skewed. This spatial system of disengaged planes and detached volumes consistently implemented throughout the composition serves practical requirements such as providing the individual conditions for each activity, varying light, ventilation and contact with the outside.

The dynamic, askance, fragmented forms are determined by a robust, internal formal rule-system. Hadid has remarked that two visionaries of a new way of living – the Suprematist Malevich and the later Russian Constructivist Leonidov – have inspired and informed her work. And indeed this project is characterized by the anti-classicism of these two precursors in its systematic and radical infractions of the rules of orthogonality, hierarchy, symmetry – all those rules that Vitruvius and the entire classical tradition after him equated with the classical poetics of order. The Media Centre is a prodigiously rich, formal exploitation of Suprematist and Constructivist poetics; there is nevertheless a feeling of tension between the formal avant-gardism of the project and its programmatic ordinariness – an example, perhaps, of 'recuperated' adversarial critical culture, where the language of invention has been transformed into one of accommodation. For some, there is also in this work an underlying irony, a sense of utopia shattered, a sense of the impatience which Hadid expressed when she said (on a different occasion), 'Nobody has made a statement . . . about a new way of living.'

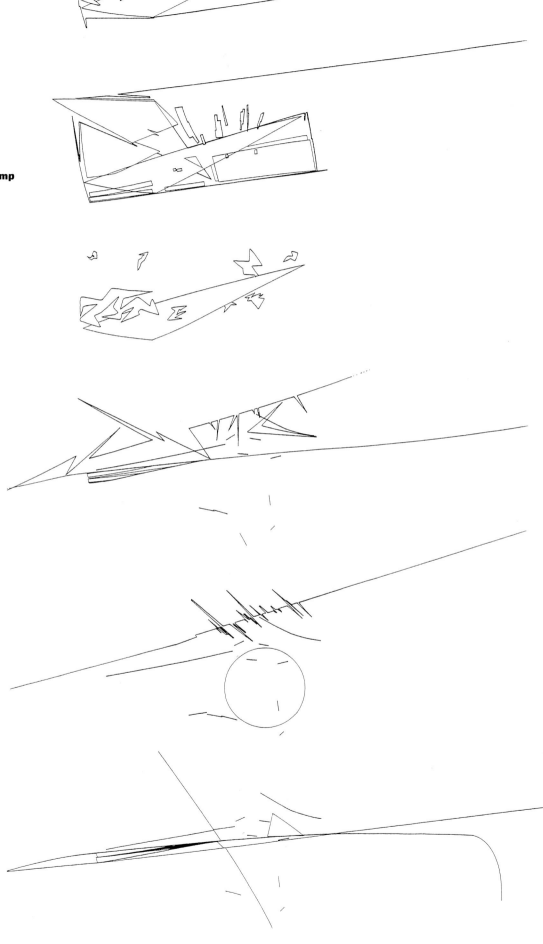

(Opposite) Model of the building

(Right, top to bottom) Sketch studies
Shops and semi-public elements

Mid-level shops and parking access ramp

Public ground elements

Ground slab openings

Divisions and streetscape

Entrance ramp

Daniel Libeskind Architekturbüro
EXTENSION OF THE BERLIN MUSEUM WITH THE DEPARTMENT JEWISH MUSEUM
(Berlin, Germany)
1989–

At the intersection of Wilhelmstrasse, Friedrichstrasse and Lindenstrasse, in an area where empty bomb sites from the Second World War are still unfilled, an extension to the Berlin Museum is intended to house the Jewish Museum, a combined archive and memorial occupying more than 1000 square metres. After a competition held in 1988, Daniel Libeskind, the Polish-born, internationally renowned architect, was selected. The programme for the extension to the Berlin Museum required that there should not be a separate, isolated Jewish museum, but that the new building should reconnect the German and Jewish 'experience' and completely integrate it into the other museum collections of the city. Libeskind accepted the validity of this objective. In his design, no visitor to one building can avoid the second, nor can a Jewish visitor withdraw to a separate wing surrounded by the Jewish past alone.

About twenty years before, two architects had offered diametrically opposed solutions in an effort to bring architecture out of what was generally acknowledged to be an impasse at that time. At '*La Mémé*', the Medical Faculty of the University of Louvain (pp. 44–47), Lucien Kroll tried to construct an architecture that would be completely new, spontaneously generated by the users of the building working in collaboration with the architects. It would not have to submit to any design preconceptions, and there would be hardly any previously established institutional constraints – which would have given the architect a free hand in making design decisions independently of the building's users, as had happened in the past. Aldo Rossi, in the Cemetery of San Cataldo in Modena (pp. 56–59), attempted to reconstruct an architecture relying on a building typology, a number of prototypes of architectural forms and an institutional framework within which architects could practise autonomously.

Two decades later, neither of those clear-cut approaches seemed satisfactory. For the extension of the Berlin Museum, Libeskind worked alone, without the participation of users and without following any established typology.

As a museum, the new building could have been conceived in conventional terms, archiv-

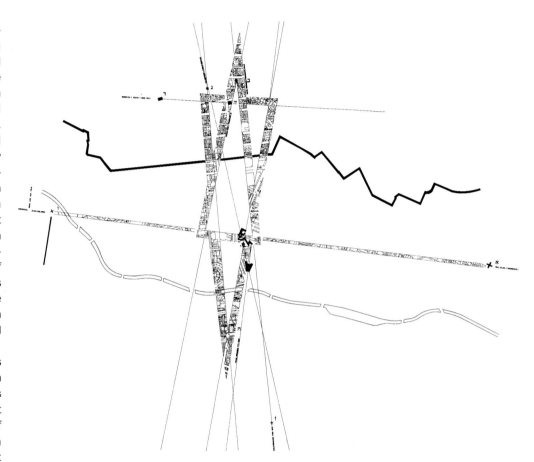

ing, conserving, receiving, supplying and displaying facts about the past, on request. As a monument *in memoriam* of the dead, the building could have been conceived symbolically, representing past facts. It was the latter way which Libeskind chose. No comparable structures quite of this kind existed, no tried solution for a building meant to represent this particular kind of memory. Feelings of absence, pain and bafflement and images of fire and incineration were the only materials he had to work with. There were also some facts, but they were isolated single points, fragments, single names and addresses. The architect could go through the archived and documented evidence to try and detect some suggestive patterns. He did. He located the home and work addresses on the map of Europe of certain prominent Jews, 'someone like Rachel Varnhagen', Friedrich Schleiermacher, Paul Celan, Mies van der Rohe. The points on the map were plotted and, as in any work of detection, possible links were tried.

Lines were drawn between the points, connections were made between 'figures of Germans and Jews', lines were crossed. 'An irrational matrix' was plotted. And patterns began to emerge: 'Some reference to the emblematics of a compressed and distorted star; the yellow star that was so frequently worn on this very site . . . a particular urban and cultural constellation of Universal History.'

(Above) Site analysis

(Opposite, above) Museum model seen from above

(Opposite) Site plan and volumetric plan showing the connection between the two buildings

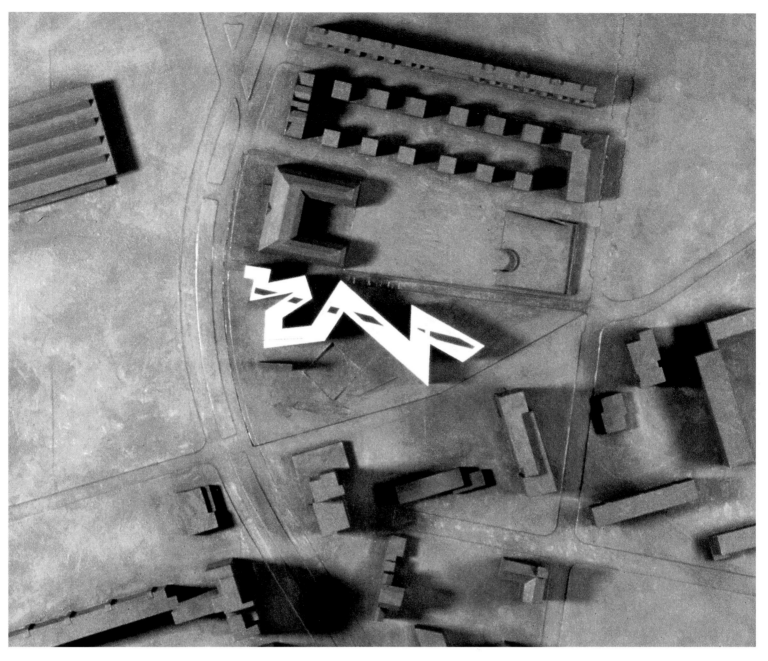

Four more 'aspects' of the Jewish experience were incorporated: Arnold Schoenberg's *Moses and Aaron*, an allegorical opera 'whose subject', according to the writer and pianist Charles Rosen, 'is the impossibility of realizing an artistic vision'; two large volumes called the *Gedenkbuch* (The Book of Commemoration), just names, locations and dates of birth, deportation and murder during the Holocaust; and Walter Benjamin's *One Way Street*. These became the four orientating 'aspects of the project', together with the existing building of the Berlin Museum to which its extension had to be tied, inseparably, 'in depth' through an underground connection. Libeskind made up clues, created cues, reached for handles to give shape to an unformalizable form. These were constraints, 'invisible', 'elliptical', as Libeskind calls such background material, significant but not sufficient to define a plan. The search continued.

One day a plan was drawn and simulated in a model. 'To put it simply,' Libeskind said, 'the museum is a zig-zag with a structural rib, which is the void of the Jewish Museum running across it.' Another element is an underground passage which 'crisscrosses' the existing building and binds the old museum to the new, under the surface, while from the outside, the two buildings appear separate. How did this plan come about? What did it mean?

The 'structural rib', consisting of empty space which the architect calls voids, stands for the vacuum left in Berlin by the disappearance of Jews during the Holocaust. The city's Jewish population, which was about 185,000 before the War, is about 8,500 today. The 'zig-zag' schema indicates search. It ultimately defines the project. It testifies, for Libeskind, to the patient hunt through the site and the city, through culture, literature and political events which lead only to a search path, a path connecting 'nodes' down a 'search tree' – a diagram for representing the process of problem solving in contemporary science, of decision making, remarkably similar to medieval kabbalistic images of the process of emanation out of the *Serifot* chart. But the search path here is only the palindromic road of an unravelled labyrinth without an end point, the trail of a tortuous passage. What is suggested by this schema, therefore, is that the search initiated with the competition programme did not arrive at a solution, a point of rest. This open figure tracing a search without a discovery reflects perhaps what most characterizes the 20th century as it nears its end: giving up hope of a 'meta-narrative' which would make chronicles comprehensible, so they can be turned into history and 'cognitive structures' through which madness can be interpreted.

Thus the idea – if there ever was such an idea of designing a memorial in the Grand Tradition, a Monument, a well-formed, coherent structure symbolizing a historical event as well as the idea of remembering a significant act of the past, is not at all what Libeskind had in mind. Although that tradition survived until recently, not only as an academic tradition, but also in the modern idiom in works such as Georges-Henri Pingusson's *Mémorial à la Déportation* in the Ile de la Cité (1962), it seemed to Libeskind to be out of place today. Instead of designing the building as a vessel and as a representation of memory, he turned out a petrified description of a shattered mind which succeeds in accumulating names and places and events and in distributing them along lists, planes and niches, but which refuses to structure them into any meaningful order.

Besides the representation of the unspeakableness of the Holocaust and 'Berlin's twisted history', there is another way of interpreting Libeskind's choice of a zig-zag configuration, a schema which is hard to represent spatially and which may well lie deeply in his Hebrew cultural identity. In a celebrated study on *Hebrew Thought Compared with Greek*, Thorlief Boman has pointed out that in the language of the Bible, objects are not described in terms of their appearance; they are conveyed instead through descriptions of their process of 'construction', since the making of objects is a process, in temporal rather than spatial terms, which results in the 'restful harmonious unity in the beauty of whose lines the eyes find joy'. This may be one of the determinants of the zig-zag line which, although hard to capture through spatial concepts, is easy to see as a representation of process. Consequently the appropriate way of describing this building is by describing the process of its creation and by using words such as bending, turning, switching, rather than geometrical-spatial ones.

This was not the first time that Libeskind had used the zig-zag figure. He had already conceived it in his installation *Line of Fire* for the Centre d'Art Contemporain in Geneva, commissioned by its director, Adelina von Fürstenberg. To refer to Libeskind's own explanation of his way of working, as revealed in his interview with Vittorio Magnago Lampugnani in *Domus* (November 1991), the figure was a 'framework' about which he had already been thinking. It existed prior to the museum competition, 'self-generated', resting in his 'creative thought', 'without a name', with an 'unstated' function, and subsequently found in a 'political and public programme' a way to be instantiated.

This oblique, wry, winding, broken-line spatial pattern has fascinated for a long time because of its geometry, which is notoriously hard to describe, and because of its associations – a crack caused by a sharp blow, splitting a hard substance unexpectedly, the revelation of the inner structure of an object as a result of 'force acted upon it', the erratic eruption of a striking thunderbolt, the wrathful incoherent spittle of fire, the catastrophic, but also the dynamic, as the Book of the Prophet Micah describes the divine, its affinity with energy, power, destruction, an emblem of formlessness, the form of the unanswerable.

Thus, far from being original here, the zig-zag pattern has a history of at least five centuries in architecture and the visual arts. The Mannerist designer Wendel Dietterlin, the Baroque architects of the Churriguera family, the visionary Piranesi, can easily be cited in this respect. But no architect before Libeskind has ever attempted such an extreme identification of an entire building with the broken figure. And in no period other than ours could the broken line seem more appropriate as an image of an epoch, a reflection on and questioning of the intractability and incoherence of a world which is characterized not only by the failure to understand, but by the still greater failure to uphold moral responsibility towards the 'Other'.

At the date of this writing, construction has been officially delayed for one year.

(Opposite, top to bottom) General plan; two elevations of the facades; section of the old and new buildings; longitudinal section

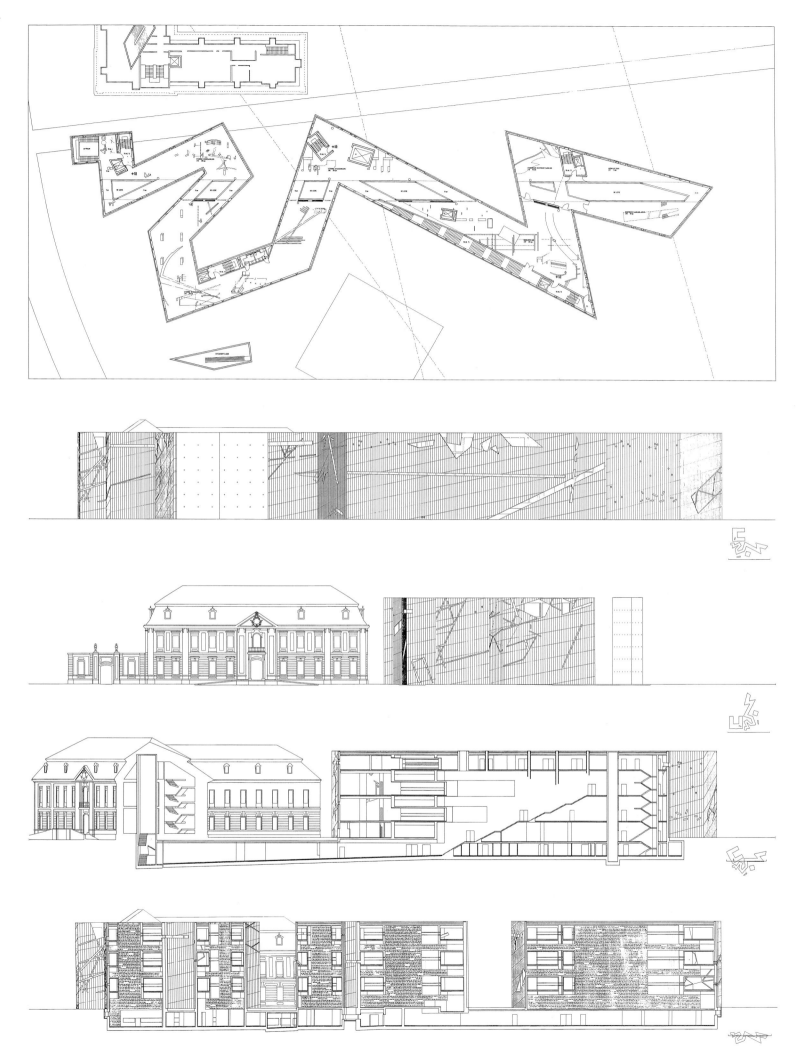

Documentation: architects' biographies, project specifications and select bibliographies

Arranged alphabetically by architect.

Roser Amado Cercos and Lluis Domenech Gibau

Amado: b. Barcelona, Spain, 1944. Degree in architecture from the Escuela Tecnica Superior de Arquitectura de Barcelona (1968). She has worked in collaboration with Lluis Domenech since 1974.

Domenech: b. Barcelona, 1940. Received degree in architecture from the Escuela Tecnica Superior de Arquitectura de Barcelona (1964), and later his doctorate. Since 1965, has been a professor there. Has worked in collaboration with Roser Amado since 1974.

Project specifications

Barrio del Canyeret (Lerida, Spain), 1982–90, pp. 238–41

Client: Gobierno Autonomico de Cataluna; Ayuntamiento de Lerida; Ministerio de Justicia.
Built area: 2.8 ha (park), 15,000 m² built.
Design team: J. Busquets, R. Puig (architects). J. Jimenez, A. Garcia-Pozuelo, E. Alonso, J. Casanovas (civil engineers). R. Brufau, A. Obiol (structural engineers). F. Labastida, J.G. Asociados (installation). P. Armadas, T. Alsina (architects), R. Domenech (equipment).
Construction company: Cubiertas Y MZOV S.A./OCISA.
Key materials: concrete, machael marble.
Technology of interest: permanent anchors in the wall.
Budget: 1000 million pesetas.
Site characteristics: intermediary zone between the cathedral and the civic-commercial axis of the city.

Bibliography
El Croquis, no. 46, 1991
Architecture, Mouvement, Continuité, no. 20, 1991
Lleida, nova activitat per a un centre antic, Lerida, 1991

Tadao Ando

b. Osaka, Japan, 1941. Self-educated in architecture. In 1969, established Tadao Ando Architect & Associates. Awards include the Annual Prize, Architectural Institute of Japan (1979); the Japanese Cultural Design Prize (1983); Alvar Aalto Medal (1985); Annual Award, Japanese Ministry of Education (1986); Mainichi Art Prize (1987); Isoya Yoshida Award (1988); Gold Medal of Architecture, French Academy of Architecture (1989); Osaka Art Prize (1990).

Project specifications

Japan Pavilion Expo '92 (Seville, Spain), 1989–91, pp. 280–83
Client: Government of Japan.
Area built: 5660.3 m².
Design team: J.C. Theilacker Pons, J.F. Chico Contijoch, J.M Marco Cardona, J. Martines Calzon, Pedro Ibanez.
Construction company: Takenaka España.
Key materials: glue laminated wood.

Bibliography
GA Architect, Tokyo (A.D.A. Edita), 1987
Architectural Monographs 14, London (Academy Editions), New York (St Martin Press) 1990

Antonio Barrionuevo Ferrer

b. Seville, Spain, 1947. Graduated from the Escuela Tecnica Superior de Arquitectura de Barcelona in 1973.

Project specifications

Housing Block in Pino Montano (Seville, Spain), 1981–83, pp. 114–15
Client: Patronato Municipal de la Vivienda.
Design team: Javier Ruiz Recco.
Construction company: Dragados y Construcciones, S.A.

Bibliography
Barrionuevo Ferrer, A., *Arquitectura y Vivienda*, no. 3 , 1985, pp. 54–57
Arquitectura Español 1950–1980, Madrid (Ministerio de Obras Publicas y Urbanismo. Direccion General de Arquitectura), 1987

Mario Bellini

Degree in architecture from the Politecnico of Milan (1959). Directed the Milan Triennale exhibitions 'Il progetto domestico' (1986) and 'Le città del mondo e il futuro delle Metropoli' (1988). Twenty-five of his works are in the permanent design collection of the Museum of Modern Art, New York. Since 1986, he has been the director of the monthly review *Domus*.

Project specifications

Industrial and Office Complex on the Via Kuliscioff (Milan, Italy), 1982–88, pp. 218–19
Client: Scotti Immobiliare s.p.a.
Design team: G. Origlia (architect); C. Pedrazini (engineer); O. De Luca (architect); L. Morandi (geom.).
Construction company: for the structure, Cattaneo Costruzioni Bergamo, s.p.a.; for the panels, IPM s.r.e., Molinella.
Key materials: prefabricated panels of cement and granulated pink marble; the 4 steel trusses from which are suspended the portions of the slabs related to the vault.
Budget: 13,000 million lire.
Site characteristics: a mixed zone, made up of residential and industrial units.

Bibliography
Ranzini, E. (ed.), *Mario Bellini, Architettura*, Milan (Electa), 1988

Ricardo Bofill

b. Barcelona, Spain, 1939. Studied at the School of Architecture in Geneva, Switzerland. In 1963 founded the Taller de Arquitectura, his design firm.

Project specifications

La Muralla Roja (Alicante, Spain), 1969–72, pp. 52–53
Client: Manuel Palomar Llovet.
Built area: 3650 m².
Design team: Manolo Nunez Yanowsky.
Construction firm: Emilio Bofill S.A.
Key materials: brick, concrete.
Budget: 50 million pesetas.
Site characteristics: rocky coast above the sea.

Les Colonnes de Saint Christophe (Cergy-Pontoise, Paris, France), 1981–86, pp. 144–47
Client: Foyer du fonctionnaire et de la famille.
Built area: 31,000 m².
Design team: Ramon Collado, Patrick Genard, Peter Hodgkinson, Rogelio Jimenez, José-Maria Rocias, Bernard Torchinsky. Realization team – Ramon Collado, J.M. Dominguez, Hilario Pareja, I. Ducloux.
Construction firm: Bouygues S.A., Clamart.
Key materials: precast architectural concrete with white portland.
Technology of interest: in situ casting of architectural concrete.
Budget: standard French housing budget – 2789 FF per m².
Site characteristics: flat platform on hilltop.

Bibliography
Bofill, Ricardo, *L'Architecture d'un homme*, Paris (Editions Arthaud), 1978

——, *Los Espacios de Abraxas, El palacio, El teatro, El arco*, Paris (Editions L'Equerre), 1981

——, *Projets Français 1978–81. La Cité: Histoire et Technologie*, Paris (Editions L'Equerre), 1981

Holz Kay, J., 'Developing Superscale Housing', *The Christian Science Monitor*, 2 Sept. 1983, p. 11

Ricardo Bofill Taller de Arquitectura, Global Architecture, Tokyo, 1985

Ricardo Bofill Taller de Arquitectura: Buildings and Projects 1960–84, New York (Rizzoli International), 1988

Bofill, Ricardo, *Espaces d'une vie*, Paris (Odile Jacob Editions), 1989

Mario Botta
b. Mendrisio, Switzerland, 1943. From the age of 15 to 18, apprenticed as a building draughtsman in the architectural office of Carloni and Camenisch in Lugano. From 1964 to 1969, attended the Istituto Universitario di Architettura in Venice, then, in 1965, did practical work with Le Corbusier in Venice and Paris. Collaborated on setting up the exhibition of Louis Kahn in Venice in 1969, the same year he formed his own architectural practice. Has been Visiting Professor at Yale. In 1986 his work was exhibited at the Museum of Modern Art, New York.

Project specifications
House at Riva San Vitale (Ticino, Switzerland), 1971–73, pp. 64–67
Client: Carlo and Leontina Bianchi.
Built area: *c.* 220 m².
Design team: Sandro Cantoni.
Key material: cement blocks.

Bibliography
Mario Botta. Architettura e progetti degli anni '70, Milan (Electa), 1979
Frampton, Kenneth, *Modern Architecture, A Critical History*, London (Thames and Hudson), 1985

Gilles Bouchez
b. 1940. Received his architecture degree in 1967. In private practice since 1970.

Project specifications
Social Housing on the Boulevard Vincent Auriol (Paris, France), 1987–90, pp. 242–43
Client: Société de Gérance d'Immeubles Municipaux; Assistance Publique (City of Paris).
Built area: 17,100 m².
Design team: Marcio Uehara.
Construction company: Revert S.A.
Metal work: SOMEAL.
Key materials: concrete structure poured on site, facades of panels of polished concrete and aluminium.
Technology of interest: polished concrete and aluminium panels.
Cost: 720 million FF.
Site characteristics: located between the back

of the Salpêtrière Hospital and the Métro Aérien in the 13th arrondissement.

Bibliography
Lamarre, F. 'Boogey Woogey urbain', *Revue d'Architectures*, no. 10, Nov. 1990, pp. 12–13
Edelman, F., 'La ville laboratoire', *Le Monde*, 30 Apr. 1991, p. 19

Neave Brown
b. Utica, New York, 1929. Graduated from the Architectural Association in London (1956). From 1965–78 Senior Architect for the London Borough of Camden, during which time the Alexandra Road housing scheme was built. Since 1986 has been in private practice with David Porter.

Project specifications
Alexandra Road Housing (London, England), 1968–78, pp. 96–99
Client: London Borough of Camden.
Built area: unmeasured. Includes 520 dwellings, school for handicapped children, public park, community centre, building department depot, shops, youth club, play centre, supplementary car park.
Design team: Gordon Benson, Lynn Cohen, Alan Forsythe, Graeme Frost, Geoff Griffiths, Ophir Kolker, David Toppin, David Webb, Julian Feary (architects); Anthony Hunt Associates (structural engineers); Max Fordham and Partners (services engineers); Monk & Dunctone, Mahon and Sceers (quantity surveyors); Janet Jack (landscape).
Construction company: Thomas McInerny & Sons Ltd.
Key materials: white in situ reinforced concrete, cast in rough sawn-timber faced steel shutters. Special secondary elements – steel balustrades, door frames, etc., and prefabricated plywood stairs.
Technology of interest: integral wall heating, noise and vibration reduction from adjoining mainline railway. Special foundations – deep-sleeved piles, trough-ground beams, anti-vibration steel interleaved bearing pads, precast concrete starter beams.
Budget: £20 million.
Site characteristics: low-lying old riverbed site – many layers of unreliable clay – including Victorian main sewer crossing site. Adjoining mainline railway – 95–100 dba frequent.
Programmatic aims: integration of high-density social housing, and public buildings, into existing fabric, with regard for physical, social and cultural continuity. At 220 persons per acre, this is the highest (allowable) urban density scheme in London (except for one special Thames-side scheme in Chelsea). The 'plan' anticipated high-rise apartments. It was the architect's intention to produce a street.

Bibliography
Brown, Neave, 'Housing, Alexandra Road, London NW8', *Architectural Design*, no. 39, 1969
Maxwell, Robert, 'Housing, School and Community Centre, Alexandra Road', *Architectural Review*, no. 166, 1979
Brown, Neave, 'A general article on my work in housing', *A + U*, Nov. 1980

Santiago Calatrava Valls
b. Valencia, Spain, 1951. From 1959–60 attended evening courses at the local School for Arts and Crafts, then Art School in the same city. In 1979, received his degree in civil engineering at the ETH, Zürich, and in 1981 his doctorate in the Department of Architecture. After teaching at the same institution, opened his private practice in 1981 in Zürich. Among his awards are the Auguste Perret UIA Prize (1987); the Art Prize of the City of Barcelona (1988); the Fritz Schumacher Prize (1988); Fazlur Rahman Khan International Fellowship for Architecture in Engineering (1988); the Médaille d'Argent de la Recherche et de la Technique (1990); and the European Holzleimbau-Preis (1991).

Project specifications
Stadelhofen Railway Station (Zürich, Switzerland), 1985–90, pp. 254–57
Client: Schweizerische Bundesbahnen (SBB).
Area built: 10,000 m².
Design team: Arnold Amsler, Werner Rueger.
Construction company: Fietz & Leuthold AG, ARGE Stahl (Schneider AG, Geilinger AG, Metabau AG, Tobler + Co., ZWA).
Key materials: concrete, steel, glass, granite.
Budget: 50 million SF.
Site characteristics: urban.

TGV Railway Station of Lyon-Satolas (Lyon, France), 1989–92, pp. 284–85
Client: Région-Rhône Alpes, SNCF.
Design team: Hans-Pieter Mueller, J.C. Grosso, Chris Bartz, Nandy Gurprasad, Victor Fientes, Sebastien Memet, Frank Lorind.
Construction company: Entreprise Industrielle.
Key materials: concrete, steel, glass.
Budget: 500 million FF.
Site characteristics: generally flat terrain, existing airport & related buildings.

Bibliography
Archithèse, no. 2, 1990 (monograph on Calatrava, Stadelhofen)
El Croquis, no. 20, 1990 (monograph on Calatrava)
Blaser, W. (ed.), *Santiago Calatrava*, Basel (Birkhauser), 1990
Harbison, R., *Creatures from the Mind of the Engineer. The Architecture of Santiago Calatrava*, Zürich (Artemis), 1992

Philippe Chaix and Jean Paul Morel
Chaix and Morel were born in 1949 and have been associated since 1983.

Project specifications
Zenith of Montpellier (Montpellier, France), 1985–86, pp. 164–65
Client: City of Montpellier.
Area built: 7400 m².

Design team: Remy van Nieuwenhove. ARCORA (structure).
Construction firm: SITRABA.
Budget: 48,626,000 FF.

Bibliography
Concert, Le Zenith, Milan (Motta), 1988

Paul Chemetov and Borja Huidobro

Chemetov: b. Paris, France, 1928. Studied at the École Nationale Supérieure des Beaux-Arts with Lurçat, Vivien, Lagneau and Gillet. Graduated in 1959. Between 1968–72, Professor at the Architecture School of Strasbourg; from 1977–89, Professor at the École des Ponts et Chaussées in Paris. Since 1973, has been associated with Borja Huidobro. He is Chevalier de la Légion d'Honneur, Chevalier de l'Ordre du Mérite and Officier des Arts et des Lettres.

Huidobro: b. Santiago, Chile, 1936. Studied architecture at the Catholic University in Santiago. In 1970–71, he was Professor at the Architecture Faculty of the University of Havana, Cuba. In 1983, became the associate of Paul Chemetov. He is Chevalier de la Légion d'Honneur and Chevalier des Arts et Lettres.

Project specifications
Ministry of Economy, Finance and Budget (Paris, France) 1982–90, pp. 244–45
Client: French Ministry of Economics.
Area built: 225,000 m².
Design team: Emile Duhart-Harosteguy, Yves Lietara, Roberto Benavente, Herve Chanson, Gerard Chauvelin, Louison Gorgiard, Jean-Pierre Degraef, Jean Chantalat (architects). Alexandre Chemetoff, with assistant Catherine Pierlet (landscaping); Marc Mimram, Sam Baruch, Pierre Diaz Pedregal, Jean Pierre Barille (engineers); Andrée Putman (interior design for ministers' offices).
Construction firm: SERETE.
Mechanical engineers: SETEC (electricity), SGTE (Fluides), Sechaud et Bossuyt (structure), Technip SERI Construction.
Key materials: stone, polished concrete slabs, curtain wall.
Budget: 1.845 million FF.

Bibliography
Chemetov, P., 'Big is beautiful', *Techniques et Architecture'*, no. 351, Dec. 1983–84

Lluis Clotet and Ignacio Paricio

Clotet: b. Barcelona, Spain, 1941. Received his degree in architecture from the Escuela Tecnica Superior de Arquitectura de Barcelona (1965), where he was Professor of Drawing between 1977 and 1984. In 1964 founded Studio PER with Pep Bonet, Cristian Cirici and Oscar Tusquets, which was dissolved in 1983. He collaborated in the 15th Milan Triennale (1973); 'Transformations in Modern Architecture' at the Museum of Modern Art, New York (1979); the Venice Biennale (1980); 'Lluis Clotet' in Frankfurt (1986); and 'Contempor-

ary Spanish Architecture' at the Architecture League of New York (1986). Since 1983, he has been working in association with Ignacio Paricio.

Paricio: architecture degree from the Escuela Tecnica Superior de Arquitectura de Barcelona (1969). Chair of Construction since 1981. Has been an editor at Editorial Gustavo Gili since 1980. In 1981 won the FAD prize for the best restoration project of the year (for his work on Gaudí's Park Guell). Since 1983, has been associated with Lluis Clotet.
(*See also* Oscar Tusquets.)

Project specifications
Belvedere Georgina (Gerona, Spain), 1972, pp. 54–55
Architectural firm: Studio Arquitectos PER (Clotet & Tusquets).
Client: Regas family.
Banco de España Headquarters (Gerona, Spain), 1982–85, pp. 132–33
Architectural firm: Clotet, Paricio & Assoc., S.A.
Client: Banco de España.
Area built: 1100 m².
Design team: Joan Sabate (associate architect); Jesus Jimenez, Alfonso Garcia (engineers); Maribel Correa, Edgardo Manino, Dolors Andreu, Angel Orbananos, Jordi Ruiz, Pilar Carceles (architects).
Construction firm: AGROMAN.
Key material: structural brickwork.
Technology of interest: combination of traditional craftsmanship and modern techniques. Brick arches with stainless steel skeleton.
Budget: 712 million pesetas.

Bibliographies
Belvedere Georgina
'Introducir una vivienda funcional en un Belvedere Palladino', *Domus*, Milan, no. 522, 1973
El Croquis, no. 23 (undated)
Banco de España Headquarters
'Clotet-Paricio & Assoc., S.A.', *Documentos de Arquitectura*, no. 13. Colegio Oficial de Arquitectos de Andalucia Oriental

Coop Himmelblau

Coop Himmelblau is the name of the office established in 1968 by Wolf Prix (b. Vienna, 1942) and Helmut Swiczinsky (b. Poznan, Poland, 1944). They have been working on a series of study and building projects in architecture, design and fine arts. They established a second office in Los Angeles in 1988. In spring 1990, Wolf Prix became Professor of the Master Class of Architecture at the Akademie für Angewandte Kunst, Vienna. Their work has been shown on many occasions, including 'The Dissipation of Our Bodies in the City' exhibition at the Storefront Galerie in New York (1988); 'Deconstructivist Architecture' at the Museum of Modern Art, New York (1988); and 'Architect's Art' at the Gallery of Functional Art,

Los Angeles (1990). Among their awards are the Berliner Forderungenspreis für Baukunst (1982); the Bauherrenpreis der Zentralvereinigung des Architekten Österreichs (1985); the City of Vienna Prize for Architecture (1988); the Progressive Architecture Award (1989, 1990).

Project specifications
Rooftop Remodelling (Vienna, Austria), 1983–89, pp. 220–23
Client: Dr Walter Schuppich, Dr Werner Sporn, Dr Michael Winischhofer, Dr Martin Schuppich, Lawyers.
Built area: 400 m².
Design team: Dieter Helml, Max Pauly, Markus Pillhofer, Franz Sam, Michael Spies, Sepp Weichenberger.
Construction firm: Metallbau Treiber, Fa. Uniprojekt/Innenbau GesmbH, Fa. Baumann-Glas.
Key material: glass.
Technology of interest: a delicate system of reinforced concrete and steel is arranged to allow the distribution of structural loads into the existing building, while circumventing the transfer of concentrated vertical and lateral loads into the unreinforced main brick walls between the chimneys. The main truss forms the visual and structural spine of the construction. The spatially slanted and laterally supported prestressed 'Gerber cantilever' truss transgresses the existing roof lines and encloses the conference room by spanning the rooftop. The side trusses define and differentiate the glazed canopy spatially and structurally. Structural glazing of clear thermal glass is spatially curved to form the main glass plane. Louvred blinds control sunlight, and folding and sliding windows regulate ventilation.

Additional statement: (poem by Coop Himmelblau, 1989)

When we speak of ships,
others think of ship wreckage.
We, however, think of wind-inflated
white sails.

When we speak of eagles,
the others think of a bird.
We, however, are talking about the wing span.

When we speak of black panthers,
the others think of predatory animals.
We, however, think of the untamed
dangerousness of architecture.

When we speak of leaping whales,
Others think of saurians.
We, however, think of 30 tons of flying weight.
We won't find architecture in an encyclopedia.
Our architecture can be found where thoughts
*   move faster than hands to grasp it.*

Bibliography
Wigley, M., *Deconstructivist Architecture*, New York (Museum of Modern Art), 1988

Antonio Cruz Villalon and Antonio Ortiz Garcia

b. Seville, Spain, in 1948 and 1947 respectively. They graduated from the Escuela Tecnica Superior de Madrid in 1971 and 1974. Among their awards are the National Prize for Urbanism (1981) and the Architectural Prize awarded by the City Hall of Madrid (1989). They have been Professors of Design at the Escuela Tecnica Superior de Sevilla (1974–75), and Visiting Professors at the Polytechnic School in Zürich (1987–89) and the Graduate School of Design at Harvard (1989–90).

Project specifications
Housing Block on Doña Maria Coronel Street (Seville, Spain), 1974–76, pp. 82–83
Area built: 1765 m².
Key material: brick.
Budget: 14,027,000 pesetas.

Bibliography
Quaderns, Barcelona, no. 160, Jan./Feb./ Mar. 1984
Lefaivre, L., and A. Tzonis, 'El regionalismo critico y la arquitectura española actual', *A&V*, Madrid, no. 3, 1985, pp. 4–19
El Croquis, Madrid, no. 24, Apr. 1986

Giancarlo De Carlo

b. Genoa, Italy, 1919. Studied at the Politecnico of Milan and the Istituto Universitario d'Architettura in Venice, then established himself as an architect in Milan in 1950. Appointed Professor of Town Planning at the Architectural School in Venice in 1955. A member of CIAM from 1952 to 1960, then of Team X from its inception. His first important and most influential commission, which went on to become prototypical of inserting new buildings into a traditional urban fabric, was the Students' Residence in Urbino (1962–66). From 1970 to 1983 he was Professor at the University of Venice and since 1983, Professor at the Architecture School in Genoa. He has been Visiting Professor at Yale, MIT, Cornell and the University of California at Berkeley. Founded the Laboratorio Internazionale di Architettura e Urbanistica (ILAUD) in 1976 and has been its director since. Also director of the architectural review *Spazio e Società* ('Space and Society'). Among his honours and awards: Cittadino Onorario della Città di Urbino; the Wolf Prize (1988); the Fritz Schumacher Prize (1990).

Project specifications
Mazzorbo Housing Project (Venice, Italy), 1980–85, pp. 198–201
Client: Istituto Autonomo delle Case Popolare della Provincia di Venezia.
Built area: 2600 m².
Design team: Alberto Cecchetto, Daniele Pini, Connie Occhialini, Paolo Marotto, Renato Trotta.
Programme: 36 housing units.

Bibliography
De Carlo, G. *Tra Acqua e Aria*, Genoa (Sagep), 1989

Lluis Domenech: *see* Roser Amado

Raymond Erith: *see* Quinlan Terry

Ralph Erskine

b. London, 1914; moved to Sweden in 1939. Educated at the Friends School, Saffron Walden, Essex, 1920–32, and at the Regent Street Polytechnic, 1932–37. Since 1936 has been in private practice in Sweden. Has been a guest professor at the Polytechnic of Zürich (1964–65) and at McGill University, Montreal (1967–8). He has won many prizes, including the award of the Union International des Architectes (1980); Litteris et Artibus Royal Gold Medal, Sweden (1980); Gold Medal, Royal Architectural Institute of Canada (1982); Wolf Foundation Prize, Israel (1984); the Fritz Schumacher Medal (1984); and the Prince of Wales Prize (1988).

Project specifications
Byker Wall (Newcastle upon Tyne, England), 1968–74, pp. 68–71
Client: Newcastle upon Tyne Metropolitan District Council Housing Committee.
Built area: (a) Pilot scheme – total area of buildings, including dwellings, public and private circulation areas, calorifer station etc., 3500 m²; 20 car parking spaces. (b) Perimeter block, phase 1 – total area of buildings, including dwellings, public circulation areas, public and landlords' stores, etc., 13,850 m²; 244 car parking spaces. (c) Grace Street. Perimeter block – total area of buildings including dwellings, public and private circulation areas, including storage, etc., 8123 m². Tail block, 2027 m². Car parking spaces for both blocks – 196. (d) Kendal Street. Low-rise and link blocks – total area of buildings, including dwellings, public and private circulation areas, 15,829 m². (e) Grace Street low-rise/Gordon Road, 16,640 m².
Design team: Vernon Gracie, Bengt Ahlquist, Mike Drage, Bettan Gateson, Por Gustafsson, Per Helderus, Dave Hill, Ken McKay, Arne Nilsson, Tony Smith, Roger Tillison.
Consultants: Gardiner & Theobald (quantity surveyors); White-Young & Partners (structural and civil engineers); National Industrial Fuel Efficiency Services (service engineers).
Key materials and special techniques of construction: structure. (1) In-situ concrete cross-wall – perimeter block (stage 1), Grace Street (perimeter block). Perimeter block – concrete strip foundations to each cross-wall with ground beams to support external walls. Precast cantilever brackets cast into cross-walls. Steel shuttering and tabling system used and rapid-hardening cement. Grace Street 3-storey perimeter block – in-situ concrete cross-walls with precast wide slab floor units. Precast cantilevers for balconies and access decks built into cross-walls. (2) Block work cross-wall with precast concrete flooring units – Kendal Street and Grace Street (low-rise) link blocks. Kendal Street and Grace Street (low-rise) link blocks – cross-walls in high-density thermalite blocks with party floors in precast flooring units. Floors within maisonettes of timber construction. Precast cantilevers for balconies and access decks built into cross-walls. (3) Low-rise housing – standard timber frame.
Budget: total, £197,688 (as fixed tender, July 1970).
Site characteristics: 1 mile east of the centre of Newcastle, with view of the Tyne valley.

Bibliography
Architectural Review, no. 155, 1974, pp. 346–62

Aldo van Eyck

b. Driebergen, the Netherlands, 1918. Received his architectural education at the ETH, Zürich, graduating in 1942. Opened his practice in 1952. Was associated with Theo Bosch (1971–82) and (since 1983) Hannie van Eyck. Was Professor at the Technological University at Delft from 1967–84, and Paul Philippe Cret Professor of Architecure at the University of Pennsylvania from 1978–83. Was co-editor of the Dutch architectural periodical *Forum* (1959–63) and a member of Team X since 1953 and De 8 en Opbouw. Represented Holland at the CIAM (Congrès Internationaux d'Architecture Moderne) from 1947. Among his many awards and prizes is the RIBA's Royal Gold Medal for Architecture (1989).

Project specifications
Hubertus (Amsterdam, Holland), 1982–87, pp. 196–97
Architect: Aldo van Eyck.
Area built: 1704 m².
Budget: 3,202,850 DFL.

ESTEC, European Space Research and Technology Centre (Noordwijk, Holland), 1986–89, pp. 230–33
Architects: Aldo and Hannie van Eyck.
Client: European Space Research and Technology Centre.
Area built: 5000 m².
Construction firm: De Nijs.
Key materials: exterior facades and window frames – untreated iroko, narrow coloured glass panes in spandrils. Semicircular spaces around the perimeter – overlapping waterproof panelling painted light grey with, along with the overlap, vertical coloured lines in spectral sequence. Sills and base elements all around – precast concrete. Roofs – PVC. Trimmings – copper. Interior – steel structure painted in rainbow sequence. All partitions and ceilings – Oregon pine plywood self-colour. Floor – burl-

ington black with mosaic inlay in two blues and carpet in same shade.

Budget: 12.1 million DFL.

Programme: large conference room for 180 people, small meeting room for future video-conferences, staff restaurant for 550 people, 3 dedicated lunch corners with a capacity of 20 people each for working lunches, large technical documentation centre (570 m²).

Bibliographies

Hubertus

Eyck, A. van, *Hubertushuis*, Amsterdam (Van Loghum Staterus), 1982

ESTEC, European Space Research and Technology Centre

Lefaivre, L., and A. Tzonis, 'Dragon in the Dunes', *A + U*, no. 247, Apr. 1991, pp. 70–74

Hannie van Eyck: *see* Aldo van Eyck

Adrien Fainsilber

Studied at the Royal Academy of Architecture, Copenhagen (1958), and received his architecture degree from the École Nationale des Beaux-Arts (1960). Is a member of the Order of the Architects of France, of the French Association of Town Planners and of the International Academy of Architecture.

Project specifications

Cité des Sciences et de l'Industrie, Parc de la Villette (Paris, France), 1980–86, pp. 172–73

Client: Établissement Public du Parc de la Villette.

Built area: 164,966 m².

Design team: Sylvain Mersier (architect); SABOTA (engineers, concrete structure); S.G.T.E. (engineers, services); ALGOE (project management); Themis Constantinidis (steel structure); Rice Francis Ritchie (glazing and cupolas); BETEB (quantity surveyor).

Construction firm: G.T.M. B.T.P.

Key materials: concrete, steel, glass. Finishing in granite and stainless steel.

Technology of interest: bioclimatic facades and rotating cupolas.

Budget: 838 million FF.

Programme: transformation of a slaughterhouse complex into the world's largest science museum containing a permanent exhibition, temporary exhibits, lobby and shops, multi-media shops, multi-media library, discovery room, current events, planetarium, convention centre (2000 seats), Omnimax cinema (360 seats).

Bibliography

Techniques et Architecture, Paris, no. 332, 1980

Le Moniteur, Paris, no. 46, 1980

Archi-Crée, Paris, no. 212, Jul. 1986

Fainsilber, Adrien, *La Virtualité de l'Espace. Projets et Architecture 1962–1988*, Paris (Electron), 1988

Wilkes Encyclopedia of Architecture, New York

(Wiley), vol. 5, 1988, pp. 556–58

Héctor Fernández Martín / Vetges tu i Mediterrània, Arquitectos

Vetges tu i Mediterrània: founded in 1974 in Valencia, Spain, this is the architectural office of Victor Bernal Calderon, Alfredo Fouz Fernandez, Amando Llopis Alonso, Angel Martinez Baldo, Juan Moreno Segui, Javier Munoz Guillen, Antonio Picazo Cordoba and Miguel Arraiz Cid. They were born between 1949 and 1953 and all graduated from the Escuela Superior Tecnica de Valencia between 1975 and 1977. They began their collaboration in 1974 at school in the context of a seminar on Urban, Rural and Leisure Sociology offered by Mario Gaviria. Among their prizes are the Primer Premio Concorso Ejecucion Tramos del Jardin del Turia (1985); special mention in the COACV-85 and in the Arquitectura y Urbanismo Region de Murcia (1988); Third Prize in the Casa Cultura de Tavernes competition (1989); Mejores Urbanistas de la CV (1989); Joven Arquitectura Española (1990); and special mention in the Premios Arquitectura COAV-89–90.

Fernández Martín: b. Argentina, 1945. Graduated from the National University of Rosario (1971) and from the ETSAV (1976). Since 1982 he has been professor at the Escola Massana of Barcelona. Collaborated with Vetges tu on the Valencian Television project.

Project specifications

Production Centre for Valencian Television (Valencia, Spain), 1986–89, pp. 234–35

Client: Generalitat Valenciana.

Built area: 14,300 m².

Design team: M. Garcia Cabrera, Stella Delmonte (collaborators).

Direction of the work: Union Temporal de Empresas Cast-Telling.

Electrical engineering: Telling S.A. (dir. Luis Sanz).

Civil engineer: Cast S.A. (dir. Eduardo Franco).

Construction firm: DICTEVA (UT/Dragados y Construcciones y Cubiertas and MZOV).

Programme: the centre contains two groups of buildings clearly differentiated. The first contains the services of programming and managing. It consists of two buildings: one rectangular and the other cylindrical that contains commercial activities and a centre for calculation. The second group consists of a trapezoidal building that houses studios and another, curved building containing screening rooms, technical services, etc.

Bibliography

Bonet, Correa, A., 'Vetges tu i Mediterrània o el empeno de construir una auténtica ciudad', *On 112*, Barcelona, 1990

Llopis, T., and P. Insausti, *Arquitectura Valenciana. La decada de los Ochenta*, Valencia (IVAM), 1991

Norman Foster

b. Manchester, England, 1935. Studied at the University of Manchester, then at Yale University in 1963. After graduating, worked briefly at Buckminster Fuller's office. Back in London, he founded 'Team 4' with Wendy Foster, Su Rogers and Richard Rogers, and in 1967 Foster Associates. Since its formation, the firm has received 46 awards and commendations from the Royal Institute of British Architects, the American Institute of Architects, the Constructa-European Award Programme and several other organizations. Norman Foster is an Associate of the Royal Academy, Honorary Fellow of the American Institute of Architects, a Royal Designer for Industry, an Honorary Member of the Bund Deutscher Architekten and a member of the International Academy of Architecture, Sofia. In 1989 the Akademie des Kunste of Berlin presented him with the Grosser Kunstpreis. He received the Queen's Gold Medal in 1983; was knighted in 1990.

Project specifications

Willis, Faber & Dumas Head Office (Ipswich, England), 1970–75, pp. 74–77

Client: Willis, Faber & Dumas Ltd.

Area built: 21,000 m².

Design team: D. Bailey, R. Bradley, L. Billar, L. Butt, A. Branthwaite, C. Chhabra, R. Fleetwood, N. Foster, W. Foster, B. Hawards, M. Hopkins, J. Kaplicky, D. Johns, T. Ovrum, T. Prichard, K. Shuttleworth, M. Sutcliffe, J. Yates.

Construction firm: Bovis Construction Ltd.

Key materials: glass cladding, exposed concrete frame, reflective aluminium ceilings.

Technology of interest: glass walls suspended from roof. Low profile shape, low proportion of glass to floor area, high efficiency glare-free lighting and exceptional insulation created by roof landscaping result in effective control of energy consumption.

Budget: £4 million.

Site characteristics: medieval market town, narrow streets, low-rise surrounding buildings.

Renault Parts Distribution Centre (Swindon, England), 1980–83, pp. 116–19

Client: Renault UK Ltd.

Area built: 24,250 m².

Design team: N. Bailey, L. Butt, C. Chhabra, R. Fleetwood, N. Foster, W. Foster, P. Jones, D. Morley, I. Simpson, M. Stacey.

Construction firm: Bovis Construction Ltd.

Key materials: steel frame, aluminium cladding, planar glazing cladding, concrete slab.

Technology of interest: despite many penetrations for structure, the roof cover consists of one continuous solvent welded PVC membrane of reinforced trocal 'S' flexible fascia linking roof to walls. Accommodates *c.* 75 mm vertically and *c.* 30 mm horizontally with neoprene nylon fabric originally developed for hovercraft skirts, together with spring fasteners used to hold down truck trailer covers.

Budget: £7.5 million.
Site characteristics: green fields site, irregular slope, about 6½ ha, existing road system on 3 sides. Building placed so that expansion is possible in one direction.

Terminal for Stansted Airport (Stansted, England), 1981–91, pp. 258–59
Client: British Airport Authority.
Area built: 85,700 m².
Design team: A. Ahronov, A. Branthwaite, C. Chhabra, S. de Grey, C. Eisner, M. Elkan, N. Foster, E. Hutchison, M. Haste, P. Kalhoven, M. Majidi, S. Martin, W. Shu, J. Silver, I. Small, A. Reid, A. Thomson, M. Thum.
Construction firm: Laing Management Contracting.
Key materials: steel structure, concrete slab and floors, glass and aluminium cladding, granite and carpet floor finishes.
Technology of interest: all services contained in undercroft feeding up to concourse level through structural trees at 36 m centres and distributed under the floor. Ceiling shells reflect artificial up-lighters from top of pods (structural trees). Natural light enters from rooflights diffused through suspended reflectors.
Budget: £200 million. Terminal £400 million – total terminal zone.
Site characteristics: green fields site along existing runway, opposite terminal buildings. Surrounding countryside low and flat with maximum tree height of 12 m to be respected.

Bibliographies
Willis, Faber & Dumas Head Office
Architecture d'Aujourd'hui, Dec. 1972/Jan. 1973
Baumeister, no. 10, 1975
Architectural Design, Mar. 1976
Bauen und Wohnen, no. 2/3, 1976
Architecture and Urbanism, Feb. 1981
Renault Parts Distribution Centre
Knobel, Lance, *Architectural Review*, Jan. 1982, p. 72
Emery, Marc, *Architecture d'Aujourd'hui*, Jun. 1982, p. 14
Fruiter, Louis, *Techniques et Architecture*, no. 342, Jun. 1982, p. 104
Pawley, Martin, 'Renault Inspection', *Architects' Journal*, 15 Jun. 1983, p. 20
Sugimura, Kenji, *Architecture & Urbanism*, Oct. 1983, p. 27
Terminal for Stansted Airport
New Scientist, 22 Jan. 1981
Architectural Review, Jun. 1986
Waters, Brian, *Building*, 'Jesus nuts & teapot castings', 11 Sept. 1987, pp. 46–52
Architectural Record, Sept. 1987, pp. 126–27
Architecture d'Aujourd'hui, Apr. 1988
Architektur und Wettbewerbe, Jun. 1988
Techniques et Architecture, no. 382, Feb.-Mar. 1989
Architectural Review, 14 Dec. 1989
Daedalos, 15 Sept. 1991

Aurelio Galfetti
b. Lugano, Switzerland, 1936. Worked at the architectural firm of Tito Carloni in Lugano before graduating from the ETH in Zürich in 1960, when he opened an architectural office in Lugano, and later in Bellinzona (1976). In 1984 he was Visiting Professor at the Polytechnic of Lausanne and in 1987 at UP8 in Paris.

Project specifications
Public Tennis Club (Bellinzona, Switzerland), 1982–85, pp. 142–43
Client: Municipio di Bellinzona.
Design team: Piero Cesera, Walther Buchler. Sergio Cattaneo, Elisabetta Sternheim, Claudio Andina, Roland Delarue, Markus Heggli, Carlo Antognini, Giano Bernasconi (collaborators).
Construction firm: Antonini & Ghidossi, SA.
Budget: 3 million SF.

Bibliography
Zardini, M. (ed.), *Aurelio Galfetti*, Milan (Electa), 1989
Brown-Manrique, G., *The Ticino Guide*, Princeton (Princeton Architectural Press), 1989

Frank Gehry
b. Toronto, Canada, 1929. Educated at the University of Southern California, Los Angeles (1954), and at the Graduate School of Design at Harvard University (1956–57). After working in the firms of Victor Gruen, Hideo Sasaki and William Pereira, he opened his private practice in Los Angeles in 1962 – Frank Gehry and Associates. Has been a Visiting Critic at the University of California at Los Angeles (1977 and 1979), Charlotte Davenport Professor of Architecture (1982) at Yale University, and Eliot Noyes Professor, Harvard University (1984). Among his awards are the Special Award, American Institute of Architects, 1975; Honor Award 1975 (twice), 1976 and 1978; the Architectural Design Award 1981 and Special Merit Award 1983, California Coastal Commission; Arnold W. Brunner Memorial Prize, American Academy and Institute of Arts and Letters, 1983; and the Pritzker Prize, 1988.

Project specifications
Vitra Design Museum (Basel, Switzerland), 1987–89, pp. 268–71
Client: Vitra International (Rolf Fehlbaum).
Built area: factory 9000 m²; museum 800 m².
Design team: Robert Hale, C. Gregory Walsh, Berthold Penkhues, Liza Hansen, with Edwin Chan and C.J. Bonura; Günter Pfeifer, Roland Mayer (associate architects).

Bibliography
A&V, no. 25, 1990
Boissière, O., and M. Filler, *Frank Gehry Vitra Design Museum*, London (Thames and Hudson), 1990
Archithèse, Zürich, no. 1, 1991

Vittorio Gregotti
b. Novara, Italy, 1927. Architecture degree from the Politecnico of Milan (1952). In 1974 founded Gregotti Associati International in Milan. He was architectural consultant for La Rinascente Stores group in Milan (1968–71) and director of the visual arts section of the Venice Biennale (1974–76). Has been Professor of Architectural Composition at the Politecnico of Milan since 1964 and at the School of Architecture in Venice since 1978. He was Ernesto Rogers' Associate Editor at *Casabella* (1952–60). Since then, his editorial positions have included editor for Edilizia Moderna, monographs, Milan (1962–64); architectural editor of *Il Verri*, Milan (1963–65); co-editor *Lotus*, Venice (1974–82); director of *Rassegna* magazine since 1979; and of *Casabella* since 1982. Among his awards are the Grand Prize of the Milan Triennale (1963); the Compasso d'Oro Milan (1968); first prize, IACP housing development competition, Palermo (1970); first prize, University of Florence competition (1971); and first prize at the University of Calabria competition (1973).

Project specifications
University of Palermo Science Departments (Palermo, Italy), 1969–88, pp. 204–07
Client: Università degli Studi, Palermo.
Built area: 235,000 m².
Design team: Gino Pollini, with Spartaco Azzola, Hiromichi Matsui, Renzo Brandolini, Christina Calligaris, Camilla Fronzoni, Giovanna Passardi, Carlo Pirola; Antonio Cangemi Leto (direction of the work); Calogero Benedetti (structure).
Technology of interest: anti-seismic structure.

Bibliography
Gregotti, V., *Il territorio dell'architettura*, Milan (Electa), 1966
Tafuri, M., *Vittorio Gregotti*, Milan (Electa), 1982
Gregotti Associati 1973–1988, Milan (Electa), 1989

Nicholas Grimshaw
Graduated from the Architectural Association in London (1965). Has been in private practice since, and his present firm of Nicholas Grimshaw and Partners Ltd was set up in 1980. Among the awards and commendations he has received are those of the Civic Trust, the Department of the Environment, the RIBA and Royal Fine Art Commission.

Project specifications
Sports Hall for IBM (Hampshire, England), 1980, pp. 104–05
Client: IBM.
Design team: Mark Goldstein, Simon Bean. Consultants – Felix J. Samuely & Partners (structural engineers); Ronald Hurst Associ-

ates (services engineers); Michael Edwards & Associates (quantity surveyors).

Bibliography
Winter, J., 'Criticism', *The Architectural Review*, vol. CLXXI, no. 1021, Mar. 1982, pp. 34–41

Zaha Hadid
Earned a BSC in mathematics at the American University in Beirut, the Lebanon (1971), and her architectural degree at the Architectural Association in London (1977). Between 1977–87 she was Unit Master at the A.A. In 1986 she was Visiting Professor at Harvard University, in 1987 at Columbia University. Entered private practice in 1978 with the Office for Metropolitan Architecture with Rem Koolhaas and Elias Zenghelis; opened her own firm in 1979. She has received many awards and prizes, among them first prize for the Peak Competition, Hong Kong (1982); Gold Medal Architectural Design, British Architecture Award (1982); first prize, Kurfurstendamm Office Building (1986); first prize in the competition for the Media Park, Zollhof 3, Düsseldorf. Her work has been exhibited at the Milan Triennale (1985); the Paris Biennale at the Centre Pompidou (1985); the G.A. Gallery, Tokyo (1985); National Gallery of Art, Kyoto (1986); Grey Art Gallery, New York (1986); Max Protech Gallery, New York (1987); 'Deconstructivist Architecture' at the Museum of Modern Art, New York (1988); Aedes Gallery, Berlin (1988); 'Wild and Uncertain Times', Institut Français d'Architecture, Paris (1989); 'New Berlin 2000' for Frankfurter Allgemeine and the Architektur Museum, Frankfurt (1991).

Project specifications
Zollhof 3 Media Centre (Düsseldorf, Germany), 1989–92, pp. 286–89
Client: Thomas Rempen.
Design team: Michael Wolfson with Nicola Cousins, Ed Gaskin, Ursula Gonsior, Edgar Gonzalez, Craig Kiner, Bryan Langlands, Urit Luden, Vincent Marol, Yuko Moriyama, Patrick Schumacher. Ursula Gonsior, Craig Kiner, Graeme Little, Antony Owen, Maria Rossi, Oliver Sorg, Christina Verissimo (design development). Günter Pfeifer & Associates (co-architect); Ove Arup & Partners (structural engineer); Loren Butt Consultancies (service engineer).
Built area: 21,100 m².

Bibliography
Wigley, M., *Deconstructivist Architecture*, New York (Museum of Modern Art), 1988

Herman Hertzberger
b. Amsterdam, the Netherlands, 1932. Graduated from the Technical University of Delft (1958). Opened his own office in 1958 and became editor (until 1963) of *Forum* magazine with Aldo van Eyck, Bakema and others. Has been Professor at the T.U. Delft since 1970 and Chairman of the Berlage Institute in Amsterdam since 1990.

Project specifications
Centraal Beheer Office Building (Apeldoorn, Holland), 1968–72, pp. 48–51
Client: Centraal Beheer.
Construction firm: Nederlandse Aannemings Maatschappij, NEDAM N.V.
Budget: 21,493,000 DFL.
Programme: 'An office building as a "work space" for 1000 people designed as a single articulated unit, consisting of 60 tower-like cubes connected on each floor by overpasses. The extensive central street area, in which the space is equally developed in vertical and horizontal direction, calls to mind the street pattern of medieval towns. Also the materials of the glass-roofed inner space evoke an outdoor atmosphere. In each corner there is a place to have coffee, to relax or to hold meetings. The illumination throughout is an integral part of the architecture, in this case conceived in terms of street lighting. The transparency and lightness of the metal stairs together with the glass-brick fillings create a harmonious contrast with the heavily dimensioned main structure of the building. We try to arrive at a wealth of formal expression by using simple, sober means, to create a feeling of spaciousness even when working on a small scale.'

Bibliography
Hertzberger, H., *Lessons for students in architecture*, Rotterdam (010), 1991
Reinink, W., *Herman Hertzberger Architect*, Rotterdam (010), 1991
A + U (extra edition on the work of Hertzberger, 1959–90), 1991

Hans Hollein
b. Vienna, 1934. Educated at the Department of Civil Engineering, Bundesgewerbeschule, Vienna (1949–56); Illinois Institute of Technology, Chicago (1958–59); University of California, Berkeley (1959–60). Since 1964 in private practice in Vienna. Since 1979, has been head of the School and Institute of Design at the Academy of Fine Arts in Vienna. He received the Pritzker Prize in 1985.

Project specifications
Schullin Jewelry (Vienna, Austria), 1972–74, pp. 72–73
Data unavailable from the architect's firm.
Städtisches Museum (Mönchengladbach, Germany), 1972–82, pp. 112–13
Design team: Thomas von den Valentyn, Jurgen Bertisch.
Project management: Architekturbüro M. Gandke, Architekt H.P. Jensen.
Engineer: H. Dederich, H. Schnock.
Lighting: Lichtdesign GmbH, Hans T. von Malotki, H. Kramer.
Structural calculations: K.H. Grabusch, M. Jahnsen.

Neues Haas Haus (Vienna, Austria), 1985–90, pp. 194–95
Design team: Dieter Blaich, Andrezj Kapuscik.
Consultants: Marchart Moebius & Partner.
The Salzburg Guggenheim Museum (Salzburg, Austria), 1989–, pp. 276–79
Data unavailable from the architect's firm.

Bibliography
Pettena, G., *Hans Hollein*, Milan (Idea Books), 1987
Arquitectura Viva, May/Jun. 1990, p. 71
Architecture d'Aujourd'hui, Feb. 1992

Michael Hopkins
b. Dorset, England, 1935. Qualified at the Architectural Association, London (1962). Partner at Foster Associates Ltd, 1969–75. Founded Michael Hopkins & Partners in 1975. Awarded CBE for Services to Architecture in 1989. Is a commissioner with the Royal Fine Art Commission and a member of the London Advisory Committee to English Heritage. Awards for his buildings include RIBA National Awards in 1977, 1980, 1988, 1989; Civic Trust Awards in 1979, 1986, 1988, 1989, 1990; *Financial Times* Industrial Architecture Award 1980, 1985, 1989; Structural Steel Design Awards in 1980, 1988, 1990; BBC Design Award 1987, 1990.

Project specifications
Research Laboratories for Schlumberger (Cambridge, England), 1984, pp. 124–25
Client: Schlumberger Cambridge Research.
Built area: 6000 m².
Design team: Michael Hopkins, John Pringle, Robin Snell, Chris Williamson, Nic Bewick, John Eger.
Construction firm: Bovis Construction Ltd.
Key materials: steel, glass, teflon-coated fabric.
Technology of interest: tensioned teflon-coated membrane roof.
Budget: £4.1 million.

Borja Huidobro: *see* Paul Chemetov

Arata Isozaki
b. Oita City, Japan, 1931. Graduated from the Architectural Faculty of the University of Tokyo (1954). Worked at the office of Kenzo Tange from 1954–63; established his own firm in 1963. In 1969 he won the Artists' Newcomer Prize, Ministry of Culture; in 1975 the Annual Prize, Architectural Institute of Japan; in 1983 the Mainichi Art Award; in 1986 the RIBA's Gold Medal for Architecture; in 1988 the Arnold Brunner Award; in 1988 the Asahi Award of the Asahi Shimbun; and in 1990 the Chicago Architecture Award.

Project specifications
Palau d'Esports Sant Jordi (Barcelona, Spain), 1985–90, pp. 252–53
Client: Ayuntamiento y Diputacion de Barcelona.

Design team: Toshiaki Tange (coordinator). M. Kawaguchi, J. Martinez Calzon, T. Yanagisawa, O. Nakamura, N. Lletos (structure). J.M. Millan, F. Labastida, INYPSA, A. Delgado y Sarrate (installations).

Construction firm: Comsa, Folcra, Dragados, Orona and Texsa.

Bibliography

Stewart, David Butler, *The Making of a Modern Japanese Architecture – 1868 to the Present*, Tokyo and New York (Kodansha International), 1987

Paricio, I., 'Sant Jordi y la virtud', *Arquitectura Viva*, Mar. 1991, pp. 18–25

Klaus Kada

b. 1940. Graduated from the Technical University of Graz in 1971. Founded his own firm in 1971. In 1986 he won the Styrian Award.

Project specifications

Glasmuseum (Bärnbach, Austria), 1988, pp. 208–09

Client: Stadt Bärnbach und Landesregierung Steiermark.

Area built: 1512 m².

Design team: G. Mitterberger, E. Steiner, J. Reiterer, J. Abner, G. Gebhardt.

Construction firm: Probst & Schmidt.

Key materials: glass, steel, ferro-concrete.

Technology of interest: detached glass wall; different variants of glass roofs; steel construction hall; glass brick facade.

Budget: 12.5 million OS.

Site characteristics: industrial area – glassworks, coal mining.

Bibliography

Werk, Bauen + Wohnen, 1 Feb. 1989

Techniques et Architecture, Apr./May 1989

Architecture d'Aujourd'hui, Sept. 1989

Architectural Review, Nov. 1989

Bauwelt, no. 32, 1990

Hans Kollhoff

b. Lobenstein (Thur.), West Germany, 1946. Graduated from the Technical University at Karlsruhe (1975). Between 1975 and 1978 held the DAAD scholarship at Cornell University. From 1978–85 was Teaching Assistant at the Technical University, Berlin. Since 1990, -has been Professor at the ETH in Zürich.

Project specifications

Luisenplatz Housing Project (Charlottenburg, Berlin, Germany), 1982–88, pp. 210–13

Client: AVM Allgemeine Bau-, Verwaltungs und Management-GmbH & Co., KapHag Fonds Viersehn.

Design team: Helga Timmermann, Thomas Dietsch, Mathias Essig.

Construction company: Gruppe 80, Wohnungs-und Industriebau Ingenieurgesellschaft mbH.

Key materials: blue industrial clinkers. Owing to the unfavourable ground conditions, part of the building was constructed on piers of up to 12 m in length. The glass facade consists of simple safety-glass windows in 40 mm steel frames between steel girders fixed at each floor at the ceiling fronts.

Budget: 16.5 million DM.

Programme: 65 housing units (20 with 2 rooms, 34 with 3–4 rooms, 11 with 4–5 rooms), with 9 studios, 3 commercial spaces and an underground garage for 10 cars.

Bibliography

'Wohnbebauung Luisenplatz', *Bauwelt*, no. 26, 1988

'Wohnen am Berlin-Museum Baumeister 9/ 88, Wohnbebauung Luisenplatz', *Quaderns d'Arquitectura i Urbanisme*, no. 176, 1988

Neumeyer, F., *Hans Kollhoff*, Barcelona (Gili), 1991

Rem Koolhaas

b. Rotterdam, 1944. Lived in Indonesia, 1950–56. Between 1964–68 he was a journalist and scriptwriter in Amsterdam. Graduated from the Architectural Association in London in 1972. In 1972 he received a Harkness Fellowship for an extended stay in the USA. Studied at Cornell University in 1972–3. In 1974, he won the Progressive Architecture Award for the design of a 'House in Miami' with Laurinda Spear. In 1975, he founded Office for Metropolitan Architecture (OMA) with Elias and Zoe Zenghelis and Madelon Vriesendorp. In 1978 he published *Delirious New York* (New York, London and Paris), coinciding with the exhibition 'The Sparkling Metropolis' at the Guggenheim Museum. In 1980 he opened OMA's Rotterdam office. Since 1990, he has been a Visiting Professor at Harvard University's Graduate School of Design.

Project specifications

The Netherlands Dance Theatre (The Hague, Holland), 1984–87, pp. 182–85

Client: Carel Birnie, Director of the Nederlands Danstheater.

Built area: 54,000 m³ plus 4000 m³ extension.

Design team: Jeroen Thomas, Willem-Jan Neutelings, Frank Roodbeen, Jaap van Heest, Ron Steiner, Dirk Hendriks, Frans Vogelaar, Wim Kloosterboer. Interior – Franz Vogelaar, Petra Blaisse, Boa Contractors (bars, furniture), Hans Werlemann (light). Engineers – Polonyi und Finck, van Toorenburg, Stakebrand. Mural – Madelon Vriesendorp.

Construction company: Bouwcombinatie SPUI.

Key materials: corrugated metal 'wave' roof, 13–metre span with stress beam support (acoustically advantageous in theatre).

Budget: 15 million DFL.

Programme: auditorium, rehearsal facilities, lobby, offices, cafeteria, restaurant.

Bibliography

Koolhaas, R., *Delirious New York*, New York, 1978

——, *Rem Koolhaas: Urban Projects 1985– 1990*, Barcelona (Colegio de Arquitectes de Catalunya), 1990

Lefaivre, L., 'Dirty Realism in European Architecture', *Archithèse*, Jan. 1990 (special edition edited by L. Lefaivre, entitled 'Dirty Realism')

Lucan, J. (ed.), *OMA – Rem Koolhaas*, Cambridge, MA (MIT Press), 1991

Rob Krier

b. Grevenmacher, Luxemburg, 1938. Educated at the Technical University of Munich (1959–64). From 1976 has been Professor at the Technical University of Vienna, where he was Dean of Architecture and Interior Design from 1979–81.

Project specifications

Schinkelplatz Housing Project (Berlin, Germany), 1983–87, pp. 186–87

Client: Klingbell-Gruppe.

Design team: Klaus Kamman.

Key materials: brick walls, 50 cm thick outside.

Budget: 400 DM per m³.

Site characteristics: area bombed in World War II close to the former Berlin Wall.

Bibliography

Architektur + Wettbewerbe, 'Schinkelplatz', Stuttgart, no. 106, Jun. 1981

Casabella, 'Schinkelplatz', Milan, no. 492, Jun. 1983

Bauwelt, 'Schinkelplatz (Ritterstrasse-Nord)', Berlin, no. 42, Nov. 1983

Techniques et Architecture, 'Schinkelplatz', Paris, no. 351, Dec. 1983, Jan. 1984

Architectural Design, 'Rob Krier', London, no. 55, 1985

Lucien Kroll

b. Brussels, Belgium, 1927. Received his architectural degree from the Institut Supérieur d'Urbanisme de la Cambre in Brussels and taught at the Institut Supérieur d'Urbanisme in Brussels. In 1957, established his private practice in its present form.

Project specifications

The Medical Faculty at Woluwe-Saint Lambert, 'La Mémé' (Louvain, Belgium), 1968– 72, pp. 44–47

Client: Catholic University of Louvain.

Built area: 20,000 m².

Design team: They 'have all dispersed' (i.e the students of the Medical Faculty).

Construction company: Engema S.A.

Key materials: 'all of them'.

Technology of interest: use of the SAR method developed by Habraken in Eindhoven.

Budget: 7000 BF per m².

ZUP Perseigne (Alençon, France), 1978, pp. 92–95

Client: City of Alençon, SEMIAVA, HLM.

Construction firm: Lucien Kroll claims, 'I have forgotten his name. It was the same contractor who had built the prefabricated buildings in the first place!'

Key materials: 'all of them'.

Budget: typical 'Papulos' budget for rehabilitations – 'cannot remember the exact cost'.

Bibliography

Pehnt, W., *Lucien Kroll*, Stuttgart (Hatje), 1987

Daniel Libeskind

b. Poland, 1946. Studied music in Israel; received his B. Arch. at the Cooper Union, New York, and post-graduate degree in History and Theory of Architecture at Essex University, England. Has taught and lectured at many universities in North America, Europe and Japan and was head of the department of Architecture at Cranbrook Academy of Art from 1978–85. Has been appointed Distinguished Visiting Professor at Harvard University, the Danish Academy of Art in Copenhagen, the University of Naples, the Lee Chair at UCLA and in 1991 the Bannister Fletcher Professorship at the University of London. From 1986–89, he was the founder and director of Architecture Intermundium in Milan, Italy. He has been invited by the John Paul Getty Foundation to become a Senior Scholar. Has exhibited extensively in Europe, Japan and the United States, and was one of the seven international architects selected for the 'Deconstructivist Architecture' exhibition (1989) at the Museum of Modern Art, New York. He has been awarded the National Endowment for the Arts Award; the Senior Fulbright-Hayes Fellowship; the Graham Foundation Fellowship; the Getty Center Visiting Fellowship; first prize of the Leone di Pietra at the Venice Biennale (1985).

Project specifications

Extension of the Berlin Museum with the Department Jewish Museum (Berlin, Germany) 1989–, pp. 290–93

Client: *Land* of Berlin, represented by the Administration for Construction and Housing.

Built area: 15,507,000 m².

Design team: Bernhard von Hammerstein, Martin Buchner, Hannes Peter Freudenreich, Robert Choeff, Miller Stevens.

Construction firm: subject to bidding.

Key materials: facade in zinc panels with various directions of orientation; windows will have various and irregular shapes and will be constructed flush with the interior walls.

Budget: 120 million DM.

Site characteristics: 'The site is located in the district of Kreuzberg in an area characterized by various urban developments. The new building is to be constructed directly to the south and adjacent to the existing Berlin Museum, which was built by Philip Gerlach in 1734. The new building will be accessed via an underground connection from the old building.'

Bibliography

Libeskind, D., *Line of Fire*, Milan (Electa), 1988 (catalogue published in conjunction with the exhibition 'Daniel Libeskind: Line of Fire', organized by the Centre d'Art Contemporain, Geneva)

Archithèse, Zürich, 1989, pp. 5–89

Deconstruction II, Architectural Design, 'Daniel Libeskind, Selected Writings and Projects', London, vol. 58, no. 1/2, 1989

Daniel Libeskind. Countersign, London (Academy Editions, Architectural Monographs no. 16), 1991

Tagliabue, J., *International Herald Tribune*, 10–11 Aug. 1991, p. 6

A + U, Tokyo, Sept. 1991 (special issue on Libeskind)

'Daniel Libeskind between the Lines', *Assemblage*, Cambridge, MA (MIT Press), vol. 12, pp. 29–51

Richard Meier

b. in Newark, New Jersey, 1934. Architectural degree from Cornell University, 1957. Established own practice in New York, 1963. In 1973 he was Resident Architect at the American Academy in Rome. In 1974 and 1977 he was William Henry Bishop Visiting Professor of Architecture at Yale University, in 1977 Visiting Professor of Architecture at Harvard University and in 1980 Eliot Noyes Visiting Critic in Architecture at Harvard University. His work has been exhibited, among other places, at the ETH, Zürich (1982), and the Whitney Museum of American Art (1982, 1985). His awards include the Arnold Brunner Memorial Prize (1972); the American Institute of Architects' National Honor Award (1974); the Pritzker Prize (1984); the Royal Gold Medal from the RIBA (1988).

Project specifications

Museum for the Decorative Arts (Frankfurt-am-Main, Germany), 1979–85, pp. 136–37

Client: City of Frankfurt-am-Main.

Built area: 10,197 m².

Design team: Günter R. Standke, Michael Palladino. Project partner – Günter R. Standke. Collaborators – Hans Goedeking, John Eisler, Manfred Fischer, David Diamond, Margaret Bemiss, Geoffrey Wooding.

Construction company: F.A.A.G., Frankfurt.

Key materials: structure – reinforced concrete (frame); reinforced concrete, masonry (walls); reinforced concrete (floors); reinforced concrete (roof). Surface – porcelain enamelled metal panels and stucco (exterior wall); plaster (interior walls); gypsum board (ceiling); white oak, Sarizzo granite, carpet (floor).

Budget: 43 million DM.

Bibliography

Lampugnani, Vittorio Magnago, 'The Jewel with all Qualities', *Lotus International*, 28, 1980, pp. 34–38

Frampton, Kenneth, 'Il Museo come Mesco-lanza', *Casabella*, Jul./Aug. 1985, pp. 11–17

Cook, Peter, 'White Magic', *Interiors*, Jul. 1985, pp. 202–05, 217–18, 231

Papadakis, Andreas (ed.), 'Richard Meier: A Personal Manifesto'; 'Museum for the Decorative Arts, Frankfurt, West Germany', *Architectural Design*, vol. 55, no. 1/2, 1985, pp. 56, 58–69

Enric Miralles and Carme Pinós

Miralles: b. Barcelona, 1955. Received architectural degree from the Escuela Tecnica Superior de Arquitectura de Barcelona (1978). In 1980 he was a Visiting Scholar at Columbia University in New York and won a Fulbright Scholarship. He received his doctorate from the ETSAB in 1988, where he has been teaching since 1983. He was Visiting Professor at Columbia University in 1989.

Pinós: received her degree from ETSAB in 1979. In 1983 founded a private practice with Miralles. Among their awards and prizes are the FAD prize (1983, 1987).

Project specifications

'La Pista' Civic Centre of Hostalets (Els Hostalets de Balenya, Spain), 1987–91, pp. 260–63

Client: Servei de Cooperacio, Diputacio Barcelona.

Built area: 900 m².

Design team: Arienja (eng.), Edecto S.A., Se Doch, Eva Prats; Moya-Brufau-Obiol (engineers); Edecto S.A. (quantity surveyors).

Construction firm: Constructadora San José.

Key materials: concrete, metal trusses, wood finishing.

Technology of interest: at the time of assembling, the use of the beams as part of the scaffolding.

Budget: 125 million pesetas.

Site characteristics: it was necessary to destroy an existing building on the site in order to keep the trees. It is on the periphery of a very small town.

Bibliography

The Architecture of Enric Miralles and Carme Pinós, New York (Sites Lumen Books), 1990. Texts by Peter Buchanan, Dennis Dollens, Lauren Kogod, Josep Maria Montaner.

Archithèse, Zürich, Jan. 1990 (special edition on 'Dirty Realism', ed. L. Lefaivre)

Buchanan, P., *Arquitectura Viva*, no. 13, Jul. 1990

El Croquis, no. 49–50. 1991

Rafael Moneo

b. Spain, 1937. Received from the Escuela Tecnica Superior de Arquitectura de Madrid architecture degree (1961) and doctorate (1963). From 1980–84 was Professor of Composition, again at the ETSAM, and from 1985–90 Chairman of the Department of Architecture, Harvard University. Since 1990, he has returned to private practice in Madrid but retains a professorship at Harvard.

Project specifications

Bankinter (Madrid, Spain), 1973–76, pp. 78–79
Client: Bankinter.
Design team: Roman Bescos, Francisco Gonzalez Peiro; Oficina Tecnica FOCSA (engineering).
Construction firm: FOCSA.
Key materials: brick, travertine, olive wood.

Museo Nacional de Arte Romano (Merida, Spain), 1980–86, pp. 148–51
Client: Ministry of Culture.
Built area: 10,380 m².
Design team: Nieves Laroche, Juan José Echeverria, Enrique de Teresa, Francisco Gonzalez Peiro, Georges Mylon, Charles Meyer, Stanley Allen, Pedro Feduchi; Jesus Jimenez Canas, Alfonso Garcia Pozuelo (engineering).
Construction firm: Cubiertas y M.Z.O.V. S.A.; Manuel Jaen Garcia.
Key material: brick.
Budget: 450 million pesetas.

Bibliography

La obra arquitectonica de Rafael Moneo, 1962–74, Nueva Forma no. 108, Jan. 1975
Moneo, R., 'On typology', *Oppositions*, no. 13, summer 1978, pp. 23–45
——, 'Kahn. Padre Comun.', *Arquitecturas BIS*, no. 41–42, Jan./Jun. 1982, pp. 46–50
'Il progetto di Rafael Moneo per il Museo Arqueológico di Merida', *Lotus International*, no. 35, II, 1982, pp. 86–92
'Rafael Moneo', *El Croquis*, no. 20, Apr. 1985
José Rafael Moneo, Obras y Proyectos, 1981–1986, Monografias de arquitectura contemporanea, no. 1, Madrid (Ed. Idea Diseño), 1986

Oscar Niemeyer Soares Filho

b. Rio de Janeiro, Brazil, 1907. His name, he maintains, could 'really have been Oscar de Almeida Soares'. His ancestry is 'predominantly Portuguese: Ribeiro de Almeida on the maternal side and Soares on the father's. Much more distant are the Niemeyers of Hanover.' His education began under Herminia Lyra, in Laranjeiras, in primary school – the only teacher he acknowledges in his curriculum vitae. He graduated from the Escola Nacional de Belas Artes in 1934. In 1936 he was a member of the design team for the Ministry of Education and Health under Le Corbusier. His prolific career is marked mainly by his projects in Brasilia between 1957 and 1979. Among his many international awards and honours are: membership of the American Academy of Arts and Sciences (1949); Medalha do Trabalho (1959); the Lenin Prize (1963); the Premio Benito Juarez to celebrate the centenary of the Mexican Revolution (1964); Médaille Joliot-Curie (1965); Légion d'Honneur (1970); the Lorenzo il Magnifico Prize of the Accademia Internazionale Medicea

(1980); honorary member of the Academy of Arts of the USSR (1983); the Pritzker Prize (1988); gold medal, awarded by the Colegio de Arquitectos de Barcelona (1990); Cavaliero Comendador da Ordem de Sao Gregorio Magno, granted by Pope John Paul II (1990).

Project specifications

Communist Party Headquarters (Paris, France), 1965–1980, pp. 106–09
Data unavailable from the architect's firm.

Bibliography

Niemeyer, O. *Mensia Experiência em Brasilia*, Rio de Janeiro (Civilisação Brasiliera), 1960
——, *Quase Memorias, tempos de entusiasmo e revolta*, Rio de Janeiro (Civilisação Brasiliera), 1966
——, *A Forma na Arquitetura*, Rio de Janeiro (Avenir), 1978
La maison du Parti Communiste à Paris, Paris (Imprimerie du Lion), 1981
Niemeyer, O., *Oscar Niemeyer*, São Paolo (Editora Almed), 1985
——, *Como se faz Arquitetura*, Rio de Janeiro (Editora Voces), 1986

Jean Nouvel

b. Fumel, France, 1945. Ranked first in the entrance examination to the École des Beaux-Arts, graduated from there in 1971. Is co-founder of the movement of French architects called 'Mars 1976' and co-founder of the Syndicat de l'Architecture. Chevalier de l'Ordre du Mérite and Chevalier des Arts et Lettres (1983). Received the Médaille d'Argent de l'Académie d'Architecture and is a doctor *honoris causa* of the University of Buenos Aires. Has received the Grand Prix de l'Architecture (1987); a special mention for the Aga Khan Prize (1987); the Équerre d'Argent (1987); and the Architectural Record Prize (1990).

Project specifications

Institut du Monde Arabe (Paris, France), 1983–87, pp. 174–77
Architects: Jean Nouvel, Gilbert Lezènes, Pierre Soria, Architecture Studio.
Client: Institut du Monde Arabe.
Design team: M. Robain, J.F. Galmache, R. Tisnado, J.F. Bonne, J.J. Raynaud, A. Robain, A. Rispal, P. Debard, J.L. Besnard. J. le Marquet and F. Seigneur (consultant for scenography-interiors). Fruitet (engineer). ARCORA (structure). P.M. Jacot (serigraphy on the northern facade).

Némausus (Nîmes, France), 1985–87, pp. 178–81
Client: City of Nîmes.
Architect: Jean Nouvel et Associés.
Built area: 10,300 m².
Design team: J.M. Ibos, Jean-Remy Negre, Frédéric Chambon, Arnault de Bussière, Anne Forgia. Polychromy – Sabine Rosant (facades and parking); artists – Daniel Buren, Anne Fremy, François Seigneur.

Construction firm: UTEAC.
Budget: 36.5 million FF.
Profile: 'Who lives in Némausus? Mostly young people. 80 per cent of the tenants are under 35 years old, the oldest is 51. Many single-parent households. Unemployed: 20 per cent; few worker households (3 per cent), more employed (22 per cent), white-collar workers (31 per cent) and 19 per cent students. 50 per cent have a junior college degree.'

Bibliography

Powell, N., 'An Institute Built on Arab History', *Wall Street Journal*, 8 Jan. 1987
Duroy, L., 'Nîmes, le Quartier Némausus', *Architecture d'Aujourd'hui*, no. 247, Sept. 1987, pp. 2–10
'Jean Nouvel', *A&V*, no. 31, 1991
Lucan, J., 'Jean Nouvel', *Quaderns*, no. 181–82 (undated), pp. 174–81

Antonio Ortiz: *see* Antonio Cruz Villalon

Ignacio Paricio: *see* Lluis Clotet

Ieoh Ming Pei

b. Canton, China, 1917. Emigrated to the USA, 1935. Received his B. Arch from the Massachusetts Institute of Technology (1940) and his M. Arch from the Graduate School of Design of Harvard University (1946). Instructor, then Assistant Professor, there from 1945–48. Established his private practice in 1955. Among his many awards are the Arnold Brunner Award (1961); the Thomas Jefferson Memorial Medal for Architecture (1976); Gold Medal, the American Institute of Architects (1979); La Grande Médaille d'Or of the Académie d'Architecture, France (1981); the Pritzker Prize (1983); the Medal of Liberty (1986); Chevalier de la Légion d'Honneur (1988); the National Medal of Art (1988); the Praemium Imperiale for lifetime achievement in architecture (Japan, 1989); and the UCLA Medal (1990).

Project specifications

Grand Louvre (Paris, France), 1981–89, pp. 226–229
Client: Établissement Public du Grand Louvre.
Built area: public spaces (total), 17,639 m²; technical space and support, 8801 m².
Design team: project direction – I.M. Pei (partner in charge), Leonard Jacobson, Yann Weymouth, C.C. Pei. New York office – Norman Jackson, Arnaud Puvis de Chavannes, Beatrice Lehman, Chris Rand, Andrezej Gorczynski, Steven Rustow, Masakazu Bokura, Vincent Wormser, Robert Crepet, Claude Lauter, Ion Ghika, Svein Edvardsen, François Boillat, Elizabeth Cordoliani, Caroline Voss, Steven Elmets. Mihai Radu, Roland Nomikossoff, Elizabeth Mahon, Margaret Sobieski, Kristof Pujdak, Rijk Rietveld, Marco Penanhoat. Architectes en charge du Louvre – Georges Duval, Guy Nicot. Consultants – pyramid structure design con-

cept – Nicolet Chartrand Knoll Ltd.; pyramid construction – Rice Francis Ritchie; fountains – S.E.P.T. and Jacques Labyt; lighting – Claude E. Engle; safety exit grilles prototype – MATRA transport. Technical consultants – SEGELERG (structural); SERETE (mechanical and electrical); SEEE for Dumez (structural).

Construction firm: Quillery, Dumez, C.F.E.M. Industries, St. Gobain, NAVTEC, I.C. Entreprise, FORCLUM, Central du Granit et Granitière du Seine, Croiseau, Otis, ERCO, Delattre.

Budget: 620 million FF (Cour Napoléon) and 1.1 million FF (Grand Louvre, including partial conversion of Ministry of Finance wing, reconstruction of Cour Carrée, and underground connections to existing Louvre).

Key materials: colourless glass, concrete, aluminium, stainless steel, French marble.

Technology of interest: cast-in-place reinforced concrete mat with soldier beams and rock-anchor tie-backs. Post-tensioned and normal cast-in-place reinforced concrete with columns and coffered slabs. Stainless steel bar and cable support frame for pyramid. Colourless laminated glass, flush aluminium mullions with organic coat of lead grey colour.

Bibliography

Allain-Dupré, E., *Architecture d'Aujourd'hui*, no. 253, Oct. 1987, pp. 63–69

Weatherhead, Peter, 'Crystal Palace Connection', *Building*, 8 Apr. 1988, pp. 49–52

Russel, James S., 'There and Not There', *Architectural Record*, May 1988, pp. 142–49

Vigezzi, Marie-Jeanne, 'Musée du Louvre: un Chantier d'Exception', *Cahiers Techniques du Bâtiment*, Sept. 1988, pp. 45 ff.

Gustav Peichl

b. Vienna, 1928. Graduated from the Akademie der Bildenden Kunste, Vienna, 1953. Since 1973 has been professor there, and from 1987–88, its rector. Has been awarded the Prize of the City of Vienna (1969); the Grosser Österreichischer Staatspreis (1971); the Reynolds Memorial Award (1975); the Steirischer Architekturpreis (1984); the Mies van der Rohe Prize (1986); and the Berliner Architekturpreis (1989).

Project specifications
ORF-Studio (Graz, Austria), 1978–81, pp. 110–11

Client: ORF-Österr. Rundfunk.

Design team: R. Just, R. Weber, P. Nigst, W. Rudolf. Wolfdietrich Ziesel (structure); Architekturbüro Haidvogel-Oratsch-Andree (project management).

Bibliography

Davey, P., 'Austrian Nautical', *Architectural Review*, no. 173, Feb. 1983, pp. 23–28

Scalvini, M.L., 'Medium and Message', *Domus*, no. 626, 1992, pp. 8–13

Dominique Perrault

b. Clermont-Ferrand, France, 1953. Graduated from the Unité Pédagogique 6, Paris, in 1978 and received a certificate of advanced studies in urbanism from the École Nationale des Ponts et Chaussées, Paris, 1979. In 1980, he earned a Master's degree in Historical Studies at the École des Hautes Études, Paris. Among his awards and prizes are first prize for 'Architecture et lieu du travail' (1990) and the Équerre d'Argent (1990).

Project specifications
ÉSIÉÉ, École d'Ingénieurs en Électronique et Électrotechnique (Cité Descartes, Marne-la-Vallée, France), 1985–87, pp. 188–89

Client: Chambre de Commerce et d'Industrie de Paris.

Built area: 25,000 m².

Design team: B. Ropa, A. Lauriot-Prevost (assistants); F. Jacquiod, Ph. Merle, G.G. Roquelaure, Y. Bour, J. Read, M. Alluin, Ch. Legillon, P.Y. Schultz (collaborators). Engineers – M. Mimram, D. Allaire, J.P. Boitel; BEFS SA. Coordination – Setec-Planitec. Control – Veritas.

Construction firms: Dumez (TP construction). Barbot (roof, metal structure). Chamebel (facades in glass). Weisrock (gymnasium). VSO (roofs). CRSM (flooring). CGEE (electricity). TNEE (heating). Giffard (carpentry). SPR (paint). La Manutention (elevators). Remag (kitchens).

Key materials: polyester panels (Barbot), glazing (Saint-Gobain and Solar-Siv); Alucobond coverings; PVC sheets, Taraflex.

Budget: 160,000 FF.

Programme: library, amphitheatres, restaurant, teaching units, administration offices, 350 parking spaces.

Bibliography

Chaslin, F., 'L'atmosphère est à la pluie de météores', *Architecture d'Aujourd'hui*, no. 11, 1987, pp. 77–78

Meede, N., 'Flight of Science', *Architects' Journal*, 21 Sept. 1988, pp. 43–53

Perrault, D., *École Supérieure d'Ingénieurs en Électrotechnique et Électronique*, Paris (Demi-Cercle), 1990

Renzo Piano

b. Genoa, Italy, 1937, into a builders' family. Graduated from the Politecnico of Milan in 1964, then worked with his father in Genoa. From 1962–64, worked with Franco Albini, from 1965–70 with Louis Kahn and Z.S. Makowsky in London. His collaboration with Richard Rogers dates from 1971, with Peter Rice from 1977, and with Richard Fitzgerald in Houston from 1980. He is now associated in Genoa with Shunjii Ishida and Flavio Marano, in Paris with Bernard Plattner, in Osaka with Noriaki Okabe. Has been a Visiting Professor at Columbia University, the University of Pennsylvania and the Architectural Association in London. In 1984 was awarded Commandeur des Arts et des Lettres, in 1985 the Légion d'Honneur. In 1981 he was awarded the Compasso d'Oro and an AIA Honorary Fellowship; in 1986, the RIBA Honorary Fellowship in London; and in 1989, the RIBA Gold Medal.

Project specifications
Centre Culturel d'Art Georges Pompidou

(Paris, France), 1971–77, pp. 84–89

Architect: Renzo Piano & Richard Rogers.

Client: Centre National d'Art et de Culture Georges Pompidou.

Area built: each of the major floors is 170 m by 48 m by 7 m high. 5 large open-plan floors.

Design team: Walter Zbinden with Hans-Peter Bysaeth, Johanna Lohse, Peter Merz, Philippe Dupont, Laurie Smith with Shunjii Ishida, Hiroshi Naruse, Hiroyuki Takahashi, Eric Holt with Michael Davies, Jan Sircus, Gianfranco Franchini, Alan Stanton with Michael Dowd, William Dowd, William Logan, Noriaki Okabe, Rainer Verbizh, Cuno Brullman, Bruno Plattner. Engineers – Ove Arup & Partners with Peter Rice, Lenart Grut, Rob Pierce (structure), Tom Baker, Bernard Legrand, Bryan James (air conditioning), Alain Bigan, Vincent Randozzo (electricity), Daniel Lyonnet (plumbing), Cabinet Trouvin (consultant), Marc Espinoza, Denis Stone (cost control), Frazer MacIntosh, Malek Grundberg, Michael Sargent (transportation), Harry Saridjin (project planning).

Construction firm: G.T.M. (Grands Travaux de Marseilles). Main firms – Krupp, Pont & Mousson, Pohlig (structure), CEEM (facades), Otis (lifts and escalators), Voyer (secondary structure), Industrielle de Chauffage (services), Saunier Duval (services), Alsthom (service equipment), CETEK (fluorescent lighting), Concord (museum lighting systems).

Key materials: main cladding of the building is formed from a series of 7-metre-high suspended curtains, each fixed to the edge of the floor above. The curtain consists of external steel lattice mullions and transoms which are designed to accept a wide range of infill materials. Infills include clear single or double glazing, fire-resistant glazing, insulating metal sandwich panels and metal-faced, fire-resistant solid panels.

Technology of interest: the structural concept of the building is that of two principal main structural planes 50 m apart, which support a series of free-span decks between them. Each deck provides an uninterrupted clear space. The flanking structural blades carry all vertical and horizontal circulation, one blade being dedicated to people-movement systems and the other to services support. The foundations are a series of 28 diaphragm wall sections of 12 to 20 m depth, each carrying two vertical loads of 5000 tons compressed and 1000 tons in tension on two column lines. A 13-bay, 6-floor-high superstructure is constructed of 16,000 tons of cast and fabricated steel with reinforced concrete floor sections. The two main structural support planes comprise a series of 800mm-diameter spun steel hollow columns, each of which supports a 10-ton cast rocker beam known as a gerberette. The toe of each gerberette is connected to an outer tension column and its heel supports a 48-metre-span lattice beam. All main joints are pin or free joints, the stability of the building being gained by diagonal bracing in the long facades and by stabilized end frames on the cross-section ends of the building, to which lateral wind loads are transferred by the composite reinforced concrete and fabricated steel floor plates. The 7-metre-wide zone provided by the gerberettes in the main structural framework is occupied on the piazza facade of the building by lifts, horizontal walkways, escape stairs and entrance zones. Suspended from the outer skin of the framework is a 150-metre-long multiple escalator system, climbing diagonally up the facade and serving all levels at a peak rate of over 3000 people per hour.

Budget: the Centre was built in six years, on time and at a budget of $100 million, with an average attendance of approximately 7 million people per year.

Schlumberger Industrial Site (Paris, France), 1981–84, pp. 120–23
Architect: Building Workshop Renzo Piano.
Client: Schlumberger Ltd.
Built area: 79,000 m².
Design team: N. Okabe, B. Plattner, M. Dowd. Assistants – A. Alluyn, S. Ishiba, T. Hartman, J.F. Schmit, J. Lohse, G. Petit, G. Petit, G. Saint-Jean, Ch. Susstrunk. Engineer – Peter Rice (for the distended structure), assisted by H. Bardsley. Landscape design – Alexandre Chemetoff, M. Massot, C. Pierdet.
Construction company: GEC, GTM, Albaric, Bateg, Roc, Rontaix.
Technology of interest: skin of the structure – teflon.

S. Nicola Football Stadium (Bari, Italy), 1987–90, pp. 246–47
Architect: Building Workshop Renzo Piano.
Client: City of Bari.
Design team: S. Ishida, F. Marano, O. di Blasi, L. Pellini. Landscape architect – M. Desvigne. Structures – Peter Rice and T. Carfrae of Ove Arup & Partners.
Construction firm: Bari 90 s.r.l.

Bercy II Shopping Centre (Paris, France), 1987–90, pp. 248–51
Architect: Building Workshop Renzo Piano.
Client: G.R.C. Ermin, Jean Renault.
Built area: 104,740 m².
Design team: Alain Vincent, associate engineer. Architects – Noriake Okabe (associate), Jean François Blassel (chief architect), Bernard Plattner (associate), with Maria Salerno, Renaud Roland, Susan Dunne, Marie Henry, Nicolas Westphal, Ken McBryde, Anna O'Carroll, Djenina Illoul, Marco Bojovic, Patrick

Senne. Interior – Crighton Design Management. Landscape – Michel Desvigne. Structures – J.L. Sarf. Roofing – Robert Jan van Santen, Peter Rice, A. Lenczner of Ove Arup & Partners. Computer work on the roof – Oth S.I., J. Herman.
Construction firm: Tondela Nord-France, Cosylva, E.I., S.P.P.R., Unimarbre, Richou-Simon-Remere, C.M.S., AFfa, Baumert, Ascinter Otis, Kone, C.N.I.M., Bohnert, Walther, C.G.C.D./ I.N.E.S./Genin, S.G.T.E.
Key materials: reinforced and prestressed concrete; wood; PVC and polyurethane; satinized stainless steel tiles.
Programme: a hypermarket, 10 medium-size shops, 120 boutiques, 1 restaurant, 2000 parking units.

Housing, rue de Meaux (Paris, France), 1988–91, pp. 264–67
Architect: Building Workshop Renzo Piano.
Client: Les Mutuelles du Mans.
Built area: 15,600 m².
Design team: Bernard Plattner, associate architects, Florence Canal, Ulrike Hautch, Joanna Lhose, Robert Jan van Santen, Jean-François Schmidt, Catherine Clarisse, Tom Hartman. Engineering collaboration – GEC Ingénierie, Paris. Study – Dumez France. Site management – Cabinet Durand. Prefabrication – Betsinor. Terracotta – Woestland. Plumbing and ventilation – Cochet. Electricity – M2 E. Blinds – Le Store Français.
Cost: 115,742,230 FF.
Key materials: terracotta tiles, fibreglass reinforced concrete.

Bibliographies
Centre Culturel d'Art Georges Pompidou
Architectural Design, vol. 47, no. 2, 1977

Schlumberger Industrial Site
Le Moniteur, no. 40, 30 Sept. 1983, pp. 60–67
Architecture d'Aujourd'hui, no. 233, Jun. 1984, pp. 14–23
Techniques et Architecture, no. 359, Apr./May 1985, pp. 42–53
Baumeister, Jun. 1986, pp. 37–43

S. Nicola Football Stadium
Architects' Journal, vol. 191, no. 23, 6 Jun. 1990, pp. 50–53
Moniteur Architecture AMC, no. 12, Jun. 1990, pp. 32–39

Bercy II Shopping Centre
Le Moniteur, no. 4469, 21 Jul. 1989, pp. 42–45
Techniques et Architecture, no. 386, Oct./Nov. 1989, pp. 114–19
Architectural Review, no. 1112, Oct. 1989, pp. 70–73
Architecture d'Aujourd'hui, no. 269, Jun. 1990, pp. 162–66
Arquitectura y Vivienda – Monograph, 199a, no. 23, 1980–90, pp. 52–57

Housing, rue de Meaux
Le Monde, 13 Apr. 1991, p. 19

Le Moniteur AMC, no. 21, May 1991, pp. 55–61

Raili and Reima Pietilä
Raili Pietilä: b. 1926. She was educated at the Institute of Technology, Helsinki (1955) and at the Architectural Association in London. Worked at the Atelier Alvar Aalto; has been in private practice with Reima Pietilä since 1960.
Reima Pietilä: b. Turku, Finland, 1923. He was educated at the Institute of Technology, Helsinki (1953). Has been Professor of Architecture since 1973 and Dean of the Department of Architecture since 1978 at the University of Oulu, Finland.

Project specifications
Tampere Main Library (Tampere, Finland), 1978–86, pp. 152–55
Client: Tampere City.
Area built: 11,230 m².
Design team: A-Insinoorit Ky (structural engineer). Inststo Erkki Leskinen (mechanical engineer). M. Nappila Ltd (electrical engineer).
Construction firm: Tampere City, Housing Construction Department.
Key materials: concrete in situ structure with element ribbing and infill areas cast in situ. External walls sheathed in copper with rough-hewn granite base, black felt roofing, wooden window mullions with copper outside. Foundations – reinforced concrete piling.
Expansion joints: the building is divided into 4 expansion joint areas. Basement floors – these are mainly of in situ reinforced concrete. The projecting parts in the main library area are of prestressed concrete. Upper floors – constructed according to conventional construction methods together with some special arch and dome structures. The main hall roof is arched with a ribbed membrane construction of prefabricated arch units and in situ concrete vaulting envelopes. The main foyer hall dome is constructed of small inner circumferential ring beam and a larger circumferential ring beam. Between these two beams are 24 sectors consisting of dome segmental units made of reinforced concrete. The dome is thus framed by the conjunction of two in situ circumferential beams with the prefabricated units between. Roof construction: roofing materials are bitumen felt and copper sheeting. On the flat roofs the insulation is generally of thermal chippings and water-resistant bitumen felt. The arch and other roofing areas are insulated with mineral wool and wind-resistant sheeting. Water insulation is achieved through a normal timber cavity substructure and also copper flashing for various arched sections of roofing and the dome. Exterior walls: interior skin is mainly of reinforced concrete, with a mineral-wool layer for insulation and the elevation material of either natural stone or copper.

Budget: *c*. 80 million FMK.

Site characteristics: a sculptural harmony of exterior shapes and materials with the immediate surrounding park trees and foliage.

Programme: main lending and reference library, school lending library, reading rooms, lecture facilities, language laboratory, cafés and kitchen facilities. Natural science museum, exhibition spaces, children's department, hobby rooms, puppet theatre and administrative area.

Bibliography

Stevens, Wallace, 'Thirteen ways of looking at a Blackbird', *Collected Poems*, 1954

Pietilä, R., *Intermediate Zones in Modern Architecture*, Helsinki (Alvar Aalto Museum), 1985

Connah, R., *Writing Architecture: Fantomas Fragments Fiction*, Cambridge, MA (MIT Press), 1990

Carme Pinós: *see* Enric Miralles

Christian de Portzamparc

b. Rennes, France, 1944. Graduated from the École Nationale Supérieure des Beaux-Arts, Paris, 1969. Has been painting and drawing regularly since 1960.

Project specifications

Cité de la Musique (Paris, France), 1984–90, pp. 190–93

Client: École Nationale Supérieure de la Musique.

Built area: 40,000 m².

Design team: Bertrand Beau, François Chochon, Jean-François Limet, Francis Barberot, Benoit Juret, Pascal Boutet. Acoustics – Commins. Scenography – Dubreuil.

Construction firm: Sodeteg, Sogelerg. Contractor, TPI.

Budget: 207 million FF.

Bibliography

Lucan, J. *A+U*, no. 255, Dec. 1991, pp. 60–133

Richard Rogers

b. Italy, 1933. Graduated from the Architectural Association and received an M. Arch from Yale University, where he was a Fulbright, Edward Stone and Yale Scholar. Has taught at the A.A., Cambridge, Yale, Princeton, Harvard, Cornell and the University of California at Los Angeles and Berkeley. Among his main prizes and awards are the Royal Gold Medal for Architecture (1985); Chevalier, l'Ordre Nationale de la Légion d'Honneur (1986); Chairman of the Board, Tate Gallery; and the Arnold Brunner Prize. His work has been exhibited at the Museum of Modern Art, New York; the Louvre; and the Institute of Contemporary Arts, London, etc.

Project specifications

Centre Culturel d'Art Georges Pompidou: *see* Renzo Piano

Lloyd's of London (London, England), 1978–86, pp. 156–59

Client: Lloyd's.

Design team: John Young, Marco Goldschmied, Mike Davies. Project administrator – Richard Marzec. Analysis – Laurie Abbott, Ian Davidson, Malcolm Last, John McAslan, Michael McAslan, Michael McGarry, Henrietta Salvesen, Kiyo Sawoaka, Richard Soundy. Main cladding and external works – Stephen Le Roith with Graham Fairley, Ivan Harbour, Elizabeth Post, Niki van Oosten. Consultants – Ove Arup & Partners (structural and services engineers); Monk Dunstone Associates (quantity surveyors); Bovis (management contractor).

Construction firms: substructure – Costain Construction Ltd; superstructure – M.J. Gleeson. Precast concrete – Anglian Building Products Ltd, Trent Concrete Structures Ltd. Roof plantroom steelwork – S.W. Farmer & Son Ltd. Atrium steelwork – Tubeworkers Ltd. Plant supports and secondary steelwork – Nusteel Structures Ltd. Lift steelwork – Tubeworkers Ltd.

Bibliography

Rogers, R., *Architecture: A Modern View*, London (Thames and Hudson), 1990

Aldo Rossi

b. Milan, 1931. In 1949 he registered at the Politecnico of Milan. In 1955 was the delegate of the Unione Internazionale Studenti in Rome. Then moved to Prague and the Soviet Union for study and cultural encounters. Invited by Ernesto Rogers to be a collaborator of *Casabella-Continuità*, where he remained until 1964. In 1956, he began work at the office of Ignazio Gardella, then Marco Zanuso. In 1959, graduated from the Politecnico; in 1965, became a Professor there. In 1971, began his association with Gianni Braghieri. In 1972, appointed professor at the ETH, Zürich, where he stayed three years. In 1975, appointed Professor at the University of Venice. In 1980, was Visiting Professor at Yale University. In 1983, appointed director of the architecture section at the Venice Biennale. In 1990, he won the Pritzker Prize. His work was the subject of a major exhibition at the Centre Pompidou in 1991.

Project specifications

San Cataldo Cemetery (Modena, Italy), 1971–73, pp. 56–59

Client: Commune of Modena.

Design team: Gianni Braghieri.

Key materials: concrete, plaster, steel, Porfido paving stone.

Technology of interest: concrete frame, steel trusses and roofs. Steel columns, metal grate galleries and stairs in columbarium interior.

Site: a rectangular compound occupying approximately 1.5 ha, adjacent to Costa's Neo-classical cemetery of 1858.

Gallaratese Housing Project (Milan, Italy), 1969–73, pp. 60–63

Data unavailable from the architect's firm.

Bibliography

Rossi, A., 'Emil Kaufman e l'architettura dell' illuminismo', *Casabella-Continuità*, no. 222, 1957

——, *L'Architettura della città*, Padua, 1965

——, 'Il pasticciaccio socialdemocratico', *Nuova società*, no. 69, 1975

——, 'Une éducation réaliste', *Archithèse*, no. 19, 1976

——, *A Scientific Autobiography*, Cambridge, MA (MIT Press), 1981

Braghieri, G. (ed.), *Aldo Rossi*, Milan (Zanichelli), 1981

Rossi, A., 'Il convento de la Tourette de Le Corbusier', *Casabella-Continuità*, no. 246

Francisco Javier Saenz de Oiza

b. Madrid, 1918. Received his degree from the Escuela Tecnica Superior de Arquitectura de Madrid; has been in private practice since 1946.

Project specifications

Banco de Bilbao (Madrid, Spain), 1971–78, pp. 100–03

Client: Banco de Bilbao.

Design team: Velles, Valdes, Alonso, Azofra. Engineers – Fernandez Casado and J. Manterda.

Bibliography

El Croquis, 32/33, 1988

Alain Sarfati

b. 1937, educated at the École Nationale Supérieure des Beaux-Arts, Paris, and in the studio of Tony Garnier. He is Chevalier de l'Ordre National du Mérite and Professor at the École d'Architecture de Paris-Conflans. He founded the review *AMC* in 1967. In 1969 with Philippe Boudon, Bernard Hamburger and Jean-Louis Venard founded a private firm which would engage in research and practice, the AREA (Atelier de Recherche et d'Études d'Amenagement).

Project specifications

88 Housing Units in Savigny-le-Temple (Ville Nouvelle de Melun-Sénart, France), 1982–86, pp. 166–67

Client: Office Public d'Habitations à Loyer Modéré (OPHLM) de Seine et Marne.

Area built: 6567 m².

Design team: Michel Ferrand, Christian Laquerrière.

Construction firm: Drouet.

Key materials: concrete, red brick, slate.

Budget: 28,269,515 FF.

Bibliography

Alain Sarfati, Paris (Editions du Moniteur), 1990

Matthias Sauerbruch: *see* Elias Zenghelis

Alvaro Siza

b. Matosinhos, Portugal, 1933. Between 1949–55, studied at the School of Architecture, University of Porto. Taught at the School of Architecture from 1966–69; appointed Professor of Construction in 1976. Was awarded the prize for architecture by the Portuguese Department of the International Association of Art Critics and an award from the Portuguese Architects Association (1987). In 1988, was awarded a Gold Medal by the Colegio de Arquitectos of Spain; a Gold Medal from the Alvar Aalto Foundation; the Prince of Wales Prize; and the European Award of Architecture from the Economic European Community/Mies van der Rohe Foundation of Barcelona.

Project specifications

Bouça Social Housing (Porto, Portugal), 1973–77, pp. 90–91

Client: Dwellers' Association of Bouça.

Design team: Antonio Madudeira, Francisco Guedes Carvalho, Adalberto Dias, Miguel Guedes Carvalho, Eduardo Souto Moura, Manuela Sambade, Nuno Ribeiro Lopes, José Paulo Santos.

Key materials: load-bearing blockwork walls with concrete bracing.

Bibliography

Cassirer, Brigitte, 'Die Operation SAAL in Porto', *Bauergerbeteiligung in Portugal*, Berlin, 1984

Celani, Mara, and Paulo D'Ugo, 'La vicenda di Bouça e Malagueira: Alvaro Siza', *Spazio e Società*, Sept./Dec. 1985

'Alvaro Siza 1954–1988', *A+U*, Jun. 1989

Luigi Snozzi

b. Mendrisio, Switzerland, 1932. Graduated from the ETH, Zürich, in 1957; started a private practice in 1958 with Livio Vacchini. His work has been exhibited at the Festival d'Automne (1983); the Milan Triennale (1987); and the Hochschule für Angewandte Kunst, Vienna.

Project specifications

Casa Kalman (Locarno, Switzerland), 1974–76, pp. 80–81

Client: Dr Paula Kalman.

Area built: 500 m².

Design team: Walter von Euw.

Construction company: Impresa Ing. D. Scaffetta & Co.

Budget: 280,000 SF.

Bibliography

Ackerman, James, *The Villa*, London (Thames and Hudson), 1990

Werner, F., *Neue Tessiner Architektur*, Berlin (DVA), p. 17

Alejandro de la Sota

b. Pontevedra, Galicia, 1913, where he finished his schooling before going on to study mathematics for two years at the University of Santiago de Compostela. In 1941, graduated as an architect from the Escuela Superior de Madrid, which awarded him his doctorate in 1965 and where he worked as a teacher from 1965–72. Among his principal awards are the Premio Nacional de Arquitectura; the Medalla d'Oro al Merito en Telecommunicaciones (1985); the Medalla d'Oro al Merito en las Bellas Artes (1986); the Medalla d'Oro de la Arquitectura del Consejo Superior de Arquitectos de España (1988).

Project specifications

Post Office and Telecommunications Building (León, Spain), 1985, pp. 138–41

Client: Direccion General de Correos y Telecommunicaciones.

Built area: 10,595 m².

Design team: Alejandro de la Sota.

Construction firm: Fomento de Obras y Construcciones S.A.

Key materials: metal structures and Robertson panels.

Budget: 480 million pesetas.

Site characteristics: located in a transition zone between the old city and the modern district called *ensanche* in Spanish.

Bibliography

'Monográfico Alejandro de la Sota', *Quaderns d'Arquitectura i Urbanisme*, no. 152, May/Jun. 1982, pp. 14–43

'Centro de Telecommunicaciones en León', *El Croquis*, no. 19, Jan. 1985, pp. 30–41

Sota, Alejandro de la, *Alejandro de la Sota*, Madrid (Ed. Pronaos), 1989

Otto von Spreckelsen

b. Denmark, 1929. Educated at the Royal Academy of Fine Arts, Copenhagen, where he was director at the time of his death in 1987.

Project specifications

La Grande Arche de la Défense (Paris, France), 1982–89, pp. 224–25

Data unavailable from the architect's firm.

Bibliography

Architecture d'Aujourd'hui, no. 252, Sept. 1987, pp. 68–71

Ramirez, J.A., 'New Ritual Buildings', *A&V*, no. 17, 1989, pp. 8–12

Chaslin, F., 'Paris, Capital of the Republic of Pharaohs', *A&V*, 17, 1989, pp. 4–8

James Stirling

b. Glasgow, 1926. Architecture degree from the Liverpool School of Architecture (1945–50). Has been in private practice since 1956, first with James Gowan, then with Michael Wilford (since 1971). Taught at the Architectural Association in London (1957), Cambridge University (1961), Yale University (1960, 1962).

Project specifications

New State Gallery (Stuttgart, Germany), 1977–84, pp. 126–31

Client: Land Baden-Württemberg, Staatliche Hochverwaltung.

Built area: 15,300 m².

Design team: Ulrich Schaad, Russell Bevington, Peter Ray, Alexis Pontvik, John Tuomey, John Cannon, Markus Geiger, Paul Keogh, John Cairns, Ulrike Wilke, Alfred Munkenbeck, Peter Schaad, Shinichi Tomoe, Chris Macdonald. Stuttgart Office – Siegfried Wernick, Tommi Tafel, Rudolf Schwartz, Pia Riegert, Laszlo Glaser, Jochen Bub, Heribert Hamann, Christian Ohm. Consultants – Staatliches Hochbauamt 1 and Davis, Belfield and Everest (quantity surveyors); Boll and Partner in conjunction with Ove Arup & Partners (structural engineers); Eser Dittman Nehring and Partner in conjunction with Ove Arup & Partners (mechanical and electronic engineers). Building physics and acoustics consultants – Oskar Gerber and Partner. Site management – Staatliches Hochbauamt 1 Stuttgart (Leader) Klaus Wilkens and Hermann Reichnecker. Bauleiter – Hans Eckenreiter.

Cost: 89 million DM.

Programme: new building for the State Gallery, New Chamber Theatre, extension to the Music School.

Bibliography

Architectural Design, vol. 47, no. 9/10, 1977

Architectural Design, vol. 49, no. 8/9, 1979

Architectural Design, vol. 51, no. 3/4, 1981

Stirling, J., *James Stirling, Michael Wilford & Associates*, London (Academy Editions), 1990

Studio PER: *see* Lluis Clotet *and* Oscar Tusquets

Quinlan Terry

b. London, 1937. Studied at the Architectural Association. In 1962 joined Raymond Erith; for the next eleven years they worked together developing the classical tradition on a number of buildings. After Erith's death in 1973, Terry continued in the classical tradition.

Project specifications

Richmond Riverside (Richmond, England), 1985–88, pp. 202–03

Client: Haslemere Estates PLC.

Built area: 1.6 ha.

Design team: Quinlan Terry.

Construction company: Sir Robert McAlpine & Sons Ltd.

Key materials: solid load-bearing brick construction in lime mortar without expansion joints or cavities.

Bibliography

Architectural Design, vol. 58, no. 1/2, 1988 (profile)

Peters, P., 'Brentwood, Baroque and the Bible man', *Evening Standard*, 3 June 1991, p. 19

Oscar Tusquets

b. Barcelona, 1941. Architecture degree from the Escuela Tecnica Superior de Arquitectura de Barcelona in 1965. Founded Studio PER with Pep Bonet, Cristian Cirici and Lluis Clotet. In 1975, he points out, he designed the Mae West Room in the Salvador Dali Museum of Figueras and remained a close friend of Dali's. He collaborated in the Milan Triennale (1973, 1983, 1985); in the Venice Biennale (1980); in 'Transformations in Modern Architecture' at the Museum of Modern Art, New York (1979); Europalia in Brussels (1985); and Documenta in Kassel (1987). Among his awards are the National Design Prize (1988); FAD prize (1965, 1972, 1979, 1983); and the Iberdiseño '90 Prize for the best Spanish design of the 1980s. (*See* also Lluis Clotet.)

Project specifications and bibliography
Belvedere Georgina: *see* Lluis Clotet

Oswald Matthias Ungers

b. Kaiseresch, Eifel, Germany, 1926. Received his architectural diploma from the Technical University of Karlsruhe and established private practice in Cologne in 1950. In 1963, appointed Professor at the Technical University in Berlin with the Chair in Urban Design. In 1965 and 1967, was Visiting Critic at Cornell University and was appointed Dean of the Faculty of Architecture and Senator of the Technical University in Berlin. From 1969–75 was Chairman of the Department of Architecture at Cornell University. Since 1986 has been Professor of Architecture at the Kunstakademie in Düsseldorf.

Project specifications
Architectural Museum (Frankfurt-am-Main, Germany), 1981–84, pp. 134–35
Client: City of Frankfurt.
Design team: K.L. Dietzch, Barbara Taha, Kathrin Napel.
Construction firm: Aufbau AG. Hochbauamt Frankfurt, Roland Burgard.
Budget: 11.4 million DM.

Bibliography
Niemeyer, F., et al., *Oswald Matthias Ungers: Architektur 1951–1990*, Berlin (DVA), 1991

Robert Venturi

b. Philadelphia, USA. Bachelor of Arts (1947) and Master of Fine Arts (1950) from Princeton University. As recipient of the Rome Prize in Architecture was in residence at the American Academy in Rome from 1954–56, returning there in 1966 as Architect-in-Residence. During his early career worked for Louis Kahn and Eero Saarinen, was a faculty member at the University of Pennsylvania and was named Charlotte Shepherd Davenport Professor of Architecture at Yale University. Among his prizes and awards are Commendatore of the Order of Merit, Republic of Italy (1986); the President's Medal, the Architectural League of New York (1985); Arnold Brunner Award (1973); and the Pritzker Prize (1991).

Projects specifications
The National Gallery, Sainsbury Wing (London, England), 1986–91, pp. 272–75
Client: N.G. Services Ltd., a charitable company formed to administer the project and directed by representatives of the National Gallery Trustees and the Donors.
Area built: 11,150 m².
Design team: Robert Venturi (principal in charge); David Vaughan (project director); Denise Scott Brown, John Rauch, Steven Izenous, William Algie, Ed Barnhart, Britt Brewer, Andrew Erstad, Steve Glascock, James Kolker, Jeff Krieger, Perry Kulper, Brian LaBau, Robert Marker, Richard Mohler, Tom Purdy, Nancy Rogo Trainer, George Ross, Mark Schlenker, Carreth Schuh, David Singer, Rich Stokes, Maurice Weintraub, Mark Wieand (project architects); Sheppard Robson Architects (associated UK architect). Principal consultants – Ove Arup & Partners (structural engineers); Ove Arup & Partners with Jaros, Baum and Bolles (services engineers); Gardiner and Theobald (quantity surveyors); Mott, Green and Wall (services quantity surveyors).
Construction firm: Sir Robert McAlpine Construction Management Ltd (construction manager). Over 45 separate trade contractors.
Key materials: the structure is primarily reinforced concrete, with structural steelwork used for the glazed wall of the east facade and the upper portion of the top floor, including the roof and rooflights. Foundations employ bored piles, with the basement perimeter wall of interlocking secant pile construction. Interior basement construction was of top-down sequence concurrent with construction of the superstructure. Structural acoustic isolation is used to separate the loading bay from public functions below. Exterior materials include Portland stone and brick; aluminium rooflights, window wall, windows, louvres and doors; cast aluminium decorative colonettes; oak entry doors; granite and yorkstone paving; laser-cut painted steel grates; and specially selected and trimmed plane trees. Interior materials include Chamesson limestone, pietra serena stone, Cold Spring granite, burlington slate, fumed oak flooring, oak panelling and interior windows and doors, painted hardwood trim, lacquered hardwood counters, veneer plaster over plasterboard, cast fibrous plaster profiled sections, metal and fibrous acoustic ceiling panels, ceramic tile, carpet, stainless steel railings, display cases and revolving door housings, bronze gallery guard rails, and cast aluminium colonettes.
Technology of interest: tight control of gallery environment for constant temperature and humidity. Control of amount and direction of UV-filtered natural light through sensor-operated system of louvre blinds, before its indirect admission to the galleries through high clerestories. Coordinated control and colour balance of artificial light to augment the changing daylight. All these systems are automatically operated by an electronic building management system. Natural and artificial lighting systems were developed, tested and revised using both a 1:5 and full-scale gallery mock-up. An extensive electronic security system is integrated with that of the old building.
Programme: brief required provision of the following functions (a) primarily, new day-lit galleries for the early Renaissance collection, to be contiguous to the existing galleries; (b) suite of galleries for changing temporary exhibitions and an adjacent cinema for film/video presentations; (c) lecture theatre for various media presentations to a public of 350; (d) restaurant/coffee bar; (e) gallery shop; (f) series of conference rooms; (g) computerized art information room for the public; (h) series of support functions, including loading bays (one structure), a picture storage vault, exhibition packing and preparation spaces, and an entrance foyer.

Bibliography
Venturi, R., *Complexity and Contradiction in Architecture*, New York (Museum of Modern Art), 1966
——, and Denise Scott Brown, *Learning from Las Vegas*, Cambridge, MA (MIT Press), 1972

Vetges tu i Mediterrània: *see* Héctor Fernández Martín / Vetges tu i Mediterrània, Arquitectos

---

Myrto Vitart

b. 1955; received architectural degree in 1984. Between 1985 and 1989 she was a founding member of Jean Nouvel et Associés. In 1989 she went into private practice in association with Jean-Marc Ibos. Her work has been exhibited at the Institut Français d'Architecture in Paris; the Salon International de l'Architecture de la Villette, Paris (1988–90); the Tepia Building in Tokyo; Gallery 9H, London; the Venice Biennale (1991).

Project specifications
ONYX Cultural Centre (Saint Herblain, France), 1987–88, pp. 214–17
Client: City of Saint Herblain.
Built area: 4000 m².
Design team: Myrto Vitart for Jean Nouvel et Associés. Frédérique Montanel (main architect). Jacques le Marquet (scenography), B & C Barto (artists).
Construction firm: SOGEA ATLANTIQUE.
Key materials: concrete structure, metallic skeleton. Floors – granite, rubber, polished concrete; walls – perforated PVC, galvanized tin.
Technology of interest in the operation of the building: the void.
Budget: 17 million FF, plus 7 million FF (for the scenography).

Site characteristics: ONYX is located on a 10-hectare-parking lot on the edge of important commercial facilities, overlooking a water retention pool.

Additional information: 'The parking lot was under construction when we won the commission. We obtained from the city hall of Saint Herblain the right to prolong it in the form of a point submerged in the water retention pool'.

Bibliography
Architecture d'Aujourd'hui, no. 263, Jun 1989
Arquitectura Viva, no. 13, Jul./Aug. 1990

Weber, Brandt and Partners

Jurgen Kurz was responsible for the design of the Medical Faculty of the Technical University of Aachen. B. Hessia (Federal Republic of Germany), 1944, he studied at the Technical University of North-Rhine-Westphalia in Aachen (1968). There have been exhibitions including his works in Paris (Septième Biennale de Paris, and at the Centre Pompidou in 1987); and Aachen (1980).

Project specifications

New Medical Faculty, Technical University of Aachen (Aachen, Germany), 1968–86, pp. 168–71

Client: Government of North Rhine-Westphalia.
Area built: 200,000 m² floor area, base area 38,000 m², volume 1 million m³.
Design team: Jurgen Kurz with P. Troger and W. Weber.
Construction company: Ph. Holzmann and others.
Key materials: main structure – prefabricated concrete, mostly prestressed. Auxiliary constructions – steel and aluminium. Ceilings – fire-protected sandwich constructions of steel plates.
Technology of interest: complete separation between structural and finishing works to allow for alterations. Extremely comprehensive means for safety, especially fire protection.

Project budget: 2000 million DM.
Site characteristics: situated in an expansion area of the university near the Dutch border, but just ten minutes from the city centre.

Bibliography
Buchanan, P., 'Appraisal', *Architectural Review*, London, no. 1076, Oct. 1986, pp. 96–101

Elias Zenghelis and Matthias Sauerbruch

Zenghelis: b. Athens, 1937. Graduated from the Architectural Association, London (1961). In 1975, he went into partnership with Rem Koolhaas and founded OMA (Office for Metropolitan Architecture) in London. From 1980–85 was a partner of OMA Rotterdam and senior partner in charge of OMA London. In 1982, he was founder of OMA Athens. In 1985, he went into partnership with Eleni Gigantes and founded the firm Gigantes Zenghelis Architects in Athens and London. He is currently partner at Gigantes Zenghelis Architects (Athens, London) and sole partner of OMA Athens. Has been Visiting Professor at Princeton, Columbia and Syracuse Universities and Unit Master at the A.A., London.

Sauerbruch: b. Konstanz, Germany, 1955. Architecture degrees from the A.A. (1984) and the Hochschule der Kunste (1984). Worked at OMA London, 1984–1988. Unit Master at the A.A., 1985–1990. Among his awards are the Eternity Prize for European Architecture, 1990; finalist, Mies van der Rohe Award, 1990.

Project specifications

Apartment House at Checkpoint Charlie (Berlin, Germany), 1983–90, pp.236–37
Client: Berliner Eigenhaimbau GmbH.
Area built: residential part, 1850 m²; Allies' part, including underground garage, 19,000 m².
Design team: Dirk Alten, Barbara Burren, Eleni Gigantes, Reni Keller, Alex Wall. Polonyi & Fink (engineers).

Construction firm: main concrete contractor, Voigt GmbH. Different companies for different trades.
Key materials: main structure of reinforced concrete slabs. Sheer walls and facades (all load-bearing) which come down on 4 pairs of columns only.
Budget: approx. 8 million DM.
Site characteristics: 'Checkpoint Charlie!'

Bibliography
Zenghelis, E., 'The Aesthetics of the Present', in A. Papadakis et al. (eds), *Deconstruction*, London (Academy Editions), 1989, pp. 239–43

Peter Zumthor

b. Basel, 1943. Studied furniture design; graduated from the Schule für Gestaltung, Basel (1963) and the Pratt Institute, New York, in Architecture and Interior Design (1966). Set up private practice in Haldestein, Graubunden. Has been Visiting Professor at the Southern California Institute of Architecture (1988) and at the Technische Universitat in Munich (1989). Received the Heinrich Tessenov-Médaille in Hanover in 1989.

Project specifications

Protection Shed over Roman Ruins (Chur, Switzerland), 1985–86, pp. 160–63
Client: AMT für Bundesbauten, Lugano.
Design team: Reto Schaufelbuhl and Jurg Buchli.
Key materials: wood. Structure of members, glue-lam. technique. Exterior screen, larch.
Technology of interest: building functions as an open shelter. Inside and outside climate are the same. The wind breezes through.
Budget: 1.15 million SF.
Site characteristics: periphery of the old city, site of Roman excavations.

Bibliography
Wang, W., 'On the work of Peter Zumthor', *Ottagono*, Milan, no. 97, pp. 50–61

Photographic acknowledgments

Key: *t*=top, *c*=centre, *b*=bottom, *l*=left, *r*=right. References are to page numbers.

Tadao Ando Architect & Associates 280, 281, 282; Architectural Press 68*bl*, 69, 71; Sina Baniahmad 195, 276, 279*t*; Barrionuevo office 114, 115; Ch. Bastin & J. Evraert 45, 46, 47; Bauwelt Verlag, Berlin 31*b*; Bellini office 218, 219; Berlin: Bauhausarchiv 27; Berlin Museum 24, 28*ct*; Quentin Bertoux/Pavillon de l'Arsenal 32, 33, 34, 35; Bofill office 52, 53, 144-45*t*, 145*b*; Bohigas, Martorell and Mackay office 19; Nicolas Borel 191, 192, 193; Botta office 65, 66*bl*; Richard Bryant 38*b*, 85, 89, 127*t*, 129, 131; Calatrava office 285; De Carlo office 198, 199, 200, 201; Lluís Casals 132, 133, 150, 151; F. Català-Roca 78*r*; Martin Charles 96, 97; Chicago: Art Institute 28*cb*, 30*ct*; Michel Claus 236, 237*l*; Clotet, Paricio & Assoc. office 132*cr*, 132*br*; Roberto Collova 91; Coop Himmelblau 220, 222*b*; Stephane Couturier 16*c*, 164, 165*b*; Hans Danuser, Zürich 161, 163; Marliese Darsow 113*t*;

Richard Davies 117, 118, 119*c*, 258*l*; Michel Denancé 266, 267*t*, 267*br*; Design Quarterly 30*cb*; Deutscher Kunstverlag, Berlin 28*t*; Willem Diepraan 51; Günther Domenig office 21*t*; Dover Books on Architecture 26*c*; Dumage Studio 39*tl*; ESTEC 230; Van Eyck office 197, 232, 233*b*; Terry Farrell office 12*b*; Foster Associates 74, 75, 76*bl*, 76*br*, 77*b*, 116*tl*, 116*bl*, 119*t*, 258*tr*, 258*br*, 259; Gianni B. Gardin 250*l*; Gehry office 268, 269*b*; Giorgio Grassi office 13; Gregotti office 204*r*, 206, 207; Nicholas Grimshaw & Partners Ltd 104, 105; Hadid office 288; Hectic Pictures, Werleman/ Scagliola 182, 183*bl*, 183*br*, 184*r*, 185; Hertzberger office 11*b*, 48, 49*bl*, 50; Eduard Hueber 80, 81, 142*r*, 143; Hundertwasser 20*t*; Imagination 39*r*; Yasuhiro Ishimoto 252*l*, 253*tl*, 253*r*; Kada office 209; Kienhold 49*t*, 49*br*; Ken Kirkwood 77*t*; Kollhoff office 210*l*, 211, 212; Krier office 186, 187; Margherita Krischanitz 16*b*; Kroll office 93; Ian Lambot 40*tr*; Dieter Leistner 135*b*; Lucien Levy, Berlin 26*t*; Libeskind office 290, 291, 293; Peter Loerakker 15*t*; Duccio

Malagamba 82, 83; Peter Mauss 255, 256, 257; Vittorio Mazzucconi 12*t*; Meier office 136, 137*t*; Claude Mercier 203*tr*; Enric Miralles 260, 261, 262, 263; Miralles and Pinós office 21*b*; Max Missmann, Berlin 25*t*; Michel Moch 107, 108; Moneo office 78*l*, 78*c*, 79, 149; Rudolf Mosse Buchverlag, Berlin 30*t*; Studio Ivan Nemec 213; New York: Museum of Modern Art 28*b*, 31*t*, 31*c*; Oscar Niemeyer office 16*t*; OMA, Rotterdam 30*b*; Ove Arup & Partners 37, 38*t*, 38*ct*, 38*cb*, 39*bl*, 116*r*; Pantheon Books, New York 25*b*; Pei Cobb Freed & Partners 226*tl*, 226*tr*; Peichl office 110, 111; J.L. Perales y Altar Photo 235; Perrault office 189*l*; Piano office 122*b*, 123*b*, 246, 247, 248, 249*b*, 250*r*, 251, 264, 265, 267*bl*; Pietilä office 153, 154, 155; Christian de Portzamparc 11*t*, 190; Quaderns, Barcelona 26*b*; Uwe Rau 210*r*; RFR, Paris 39*cl*; Richard Rogers Partnership 84, 87, 88, 156, 157; Aldo Rossi 56, 57, 59, 60, 61, 63; Philippe Ruault 214*l*, 215*t*, 217, 249*t*; Deidi Von Schaewen 120, 121, 122*t*, 123*t*, 125, 145*c*, 146, 147, 172, 173*t*, 175, 176, 177, 178, 180, 181, 188, 189*tc*, 189*tr*, 189*br*, 224, 225, 226*b*, 227, 228, 229, 242*r*, 243, 244, 245*l*,

245*tr*, 269*t*, 270, 271; De la Sota office 138, 140, 141; Stirling office 126, 127*b*, 128, 130; Ezra Stoller 137*b*; Tim Street Porter 76*tl*; Studio PER 54, 55; Dahliette Sucheyre 166*t*, 167*t*, 167*bl*; Jerzy Surwillo 72, 73; Suzuki 100, 101, 102*t*, 238*b*, 239*tr*, 240*t*, 241*t*; Szyszkowitz and Kowalski office 20*b*; Ungers office 134, 135*t*; Francesco Venezia 12*c*; Venturi, Rauch and Scott Brown and Associates 274, 275; Versuchanstalt für Wasserbau und Schiffbau, Berlin 14; Matt Wargo 273; Wasmuth Verlag, Berlin 29*b*; Weber & Brandt office 169, 170, 171; Shadrach Woods 10; Yale University Press, Newhaven and London 25*c*; Alo Zanetta 67; Takis Zenetos 15*b*; Gerald Zugmann 221, 222*tl*, 222*tr*, 223.

Index

A

Aalto, Alvar 75, 78, 90, 152, 273
Ackerman, James 64, 65
Action Architecture 269
Adorno, Theodor 10, 58
Ahrends, Burton & Koralek 272
Alexander, Christopher 166
alienation 200
Alofsin, Anthony 23
Althusser Louis, 12
Amado, Roser 17, 238–41
Amourgis, Spiros 23
Ando, Tadao 280–83
Andrault, Michel 32, 176
Andreu, Paul 225
anti-authoritarianism, *see* populism
anti-classical 20, 110, 194, 208, 212, 223, 260, 288
anti-elitism, *see* populism
anti-functionalism, *see* populism
apartment house, *see* residential facilities
Archigram 84, 168
Architecture, Mouvement, Continuité 10, 166
Arup Associates 122, 158, 172, 246, 258, 273
auditorium facility 164
Aulenti, Gae 86
autonomy 12, 56–59, 60–62, 290
Auzelle, Robert 34
Aymonino, Carlo 32

B

Baluschek, Hans 24
Banham, Reyner 74, 84–88, 156
banks 78–79, 100–03, 132–33
Bar Boo, José 19
Barrionuevo Ferrer, Antonio 19, 114–15
Barthes, Roland 176
Battisti, Eugenio 20
Beaudoin, Laurent 35
Belgiojoso, Lodovico 18
Bellini, Mario 16, 218–19
Bentham, Jan 15
Berger, Patrick 33
Berlage, Petrus 156
bien-fini, *see* well-formedness
Bill, Max 138
bird image 21, 152–55, 220–22, 284–85
Bloc, André 34
Bofill, Ricardo 54–55, 144–47
Bohigas, Oriol 19, 238
Boman, Thorlief 292
Bordaz, Robert 86
Borel, Frédéric 33
Borie, Henri-Jules 30
Botta, Mario 19, 64–65, 80, 142
Bouchez, Gilles 15, 22, 242–43
Boudon, Philippe 166
Breuer, Marcel 138
brises-soleil 15, 100–03, 178–81, 242–43, 260–63
Brown, Neave 96–99
Brunelleschi 29
Buffi, Jean-Pierre 33
Buford, William 22
Buijs, J.W.E., and J.B. Lursen 86

Burckhardt, Lucius 23
Busquets, Joan 238

C

Cabrero, Francisco 78
Cagan, Michel 33
Calatrava, Santiago 15, 122, 222, 254–57, 259, 284–85
Calder, Alexander 185
Campos Michelena, Pascuala 19
Candilis, Georges 32
Cano Lasso, Julio 78, 138
Capitel, Anton 55
Le Carré Bleu 10, 23
Chaix, Philippe 164–65
chaos 19–21, 110–11, 194–95, 208–09, 220–23, 232, 286–89, 290–93
Chareau, Pierre 176
Charles, Prince of Wales 203, 272
Chemetoff, Alexandre 122
Chemetov, Paul 12, 33, 206, 244–45
Chermayeff, Serge 15, 32, 84, 124, 168
Chirac, Jacques 225, 242
Ciriani, Henri 32
Citroen, Paul 27
City Beautiful 186
city centre rehabilitation 82–83, 84–89, 186–87, 194–95, 210–11, 238–41
cityscape 29
civic centre 260–61
civic image 56–59, 60–63, 128, 136–37, 157, 186–87
classical architecture 20, 60, 62, 76, 110, 113, 131, 138, 144, 146, 148, 197, 203, 208, 212, 223, 226, 230, 244
Clotet 11, 19, 54–55, 128, 132–33
cognition, architectural 10, 13, 20, 22, 23
'cognitive mapping' 14, 20, 117, 248–51, 261
cognitive structure of space 20, 131, 148–51, 195, 197, 220–23, 272–75, 280–83, 290–93
Cohen, Jean-Louis 23, 186
Cohn-Bendit, Daniel 10
collage city 210
Collins, Peter 20
Colonna, Francesco 11
colour 52, 196, 200, 268
commercial 72–73, 116–19, 194–95, 216, 248–51
community 17, 70, 114, 146, 156, 198
complexity 272
computers 38–40, 95
Condorcet, Marquis de 10, 47
Congrès Internationaux d'Architecture (CIAM) 186
Constructivism 20, 84, 260, 288
consumption 52, 73
contextualism 136–37, 182, 195, 198, 204, 216, 260, 274
Coop Himmelblau 22, 122, 208, 220–23
court house 238–41
Crevel, Édouard 34
critical architecture 10, 18, 52, 58, 65, 73, 82, 94, 181, 195, 216
critical regionalism, *see* regionalism, critical
Crouwel, Mels 15
Cruz, Antonio 22, 82–83

D

de-alienation, *see* alienation
De Carlo, Giancarlo 11, 17, 19, 56, 114, 198–201, 240
'decorated shed' 160–63; *see also* Venturi
defamiliarization 18, 52–53, 54–55, 81, 148–51, 197, 216, 220–23, 272–75
de-institutionalization, *see* populism
Devillers, Christian 33, 34
dirty realism, *see* realism *and* realism, dirty

Domenech, Luis 17, 238–41
Domenig, Günther 21, 208
Duchamp, Marcel 110
'duck', architectural 15, 284
Duiker, Johannes 197
Duroy, Lionel 178
Dusapin, Fabrice 33
Dvorak, Max 162

E

Eames, Charles and Ray 104, 116, 138, 178
ecological issue 37, 42–43
Eesteren, Cornelis van 196
energy control 76, 172
Enlightenment 47, 84, 88
Erith, *see* Terry
Erskine, Ralph 11, 68–71
Eyck, Aldo and Hannie van 19, 21, 153, 196–97, 230–33

F

fabulism 21, 72–73, 112–13, 152–55, 194–95, 240
Fainsilber, Adrien 16, 172–73
Farrell, Terry 12, 104, 202–03
Fathy, Hassan 164
Fehlbaum, Rolf 268
Fellini, Federico 56
Fernandez Alba, Antonio 78
Fernandez Martín, Héctor, *see* Vetges tu i Mediterrània
Ferreri, Marco 52
Ferrier, Jacques 258
Filler, Martin 268
flexibility 46, 108, 156, 164, 272
Flores, Antonio 138
Follina, Antonio 19
Foroughi, Mohsen 34
Foster, Norman 16, 74–77, 116–19, 122, 258–59
Foucauld, Michel 242
fractal geometry 222, 230
Frampton, Kenneth 23, 65, 142
Friedman, Yona 84, 225
Fuller, Buckminster 16, 74, 84, 116, 125, 156, 178
functionalism 15, 60, 73, 154, 272
Fürstenberg, Adelina von 292
futurism 88, 158, 222

G

Gabetti, Roberto 19
Galfetti, Aurelio 16, 142–43
Galilei, Galileo 14
Gaudin, Henri 16, 33, 34, 35
Gehry, Frank 20, 268–71
genius loci 17, 19, 80, 152, 242, 268
Gesamtkunstwerk 73
Ghiai, Hedar 34
Giedeon, Sigfried 20
Gleick, James 19
globalism 280
Goethe 17
Goetheanum 268
Goff, Bruce 110
Gracie, Vernon 70
Gramsci, Antonio 56
Grassi, Giorgio 12, 56
Gregotti, Vittorio 204–07
grid system 48, 75, 116, 137, 148, 168, 205, 208, 244
Grimshaw, Nicholas 104–05, 268
Gropius, Walter 138
Guarini, Guarino 197, 232, 274
Guichard, Olivier 32
'guy' principle 116; *see also* rigorism, structural

H

Habraken, Nicolaas John 11, 46
Hadid, Zaha 20, 286–89

Hamburger, Bernard 23, 166
Harvard University 78
Hertzberger, Herman 11, 15, 48–50, 52, 56, 60, 74, 200
Herzog, Jacques 16
Hilberseimer, Ludwig 28
historicism 128, 149, 202, 228
Hollein, Hans 19, 72–73, 112–13, 194–95, 222, 276–79
Hopkins, Michael 15, 17, 124–25
Horta, Victor 47
hospital 34, 168
Huet, Bernard 32
Huidobro, Borja, *see* Chemetov, Paul
Hundertwasser 20

I

iconic aspects 73; *see also* bird image *and* fabulism
'imageability' 241
incommeasurable worlds 274
incremental planning 196
infill 196
Interbau 186
International Architecture Exhibition, Berlin 1987 (IBA) 186, 210
Isola, Aimaro 19
Isozaki, Arata 15, 252–53

J

Jacquot, P.M. 176
Jencks, Charles 22
Johnson, Philip 86
Jourda, Françoise-Hélène 35
Judd, Donald 162

K

Kada, Klaus 20, 110, 208–09
Kahn, Albert 84
Kahn, Louis 15, 48, 74, 84, 132, 156, 273
Kant, Immanuel 22
Kay, Jane Holtz 145
Kétoff, Maxime 33
Klerk, Michel de 70
Klose, Friedrich 28
Klotz, Heinrich 135, 187
Kollhoff, Hans 22, 107, 210–13
Koolhaas, Rem 21, 29, 30, 107, 182–85
Kowalski, Karla 20, 208
Kramer, Hilton 14
Krier, Leon 12
Krier, Rob 12, 186–87
Kroll, Lucien 11, 19, 44–47, 48, 56, 60, 92–95, 107, 200, 203, 290
Kropotkin 47

L

Lamarre, François 243
Lampugnani, Vittorio Magnano 292
Lang, Fritz 30
Lang, Jack 164
Laugier, Abbé 160
Leclerc, François 33
Le Corbusier 15, 32, 33, 62, 76, 96, 108, 142, 180, 192, 197, 210
Lefaivre, Liane 23
Lefebvre, Henri 10, 11
Léger, Fernand 14, 116
Leo, Ludwig 14
Leonidov, Ivan 234, 241, 288
Libeskind, Daniel 23, 290–93
library 152
lighting 273
Lion, Robert 224
Lissitzky, El 244
Lodoli, Carlo 13–14
Lods, Marcel 32
Loerakker, Peter 15
Loos, Adolf 110
Lopez, Raymond 34

Lucan, Jacques 181
Lukács, Gyorgy 13, 58
Lurçat, André 47, 200
Lynch, Kevin 166, 241, 250; see also imageability and cognitive mapping

M

MacCormac, Richard 198
Mackay, David 19
Mackovecz, Imre 18, 152
McLuhan, Marshall 84
magical realism 54, 132–33; see also realism
Malevich 288
Mandelbrot, Benoit 230
Marcuse, Herbert 10
Marin de Terán, Luis 17, 18
Maurios, Georges 33
May, Ernst 18
May 1968 impact 10, 21, 50, 68, 86, 106, 244
Mazzucconi, Vittorio 12
medical facilities 168–71
megastructure 32, 84–89, 168–71, 204–07
Meier, Richard 136–37, 150
Melnikov, Konstantin 261
Ménard, Jean-Pierre 264
Mendelsohn, Erich 30
Menzel, Adolf 24
metaphor 16, 20, 246, 248, 284; see also bird image
Meuron, Pierre de 16
Mèyer, Hannes 102, 138, 168
Michelangelo 20, 274
Mies van der Rohe, Ludwig 16, 28–29, 74, 76, 101, 104, 113, 125, 150, 259, 273
minimalism 162, 228
Miralles, Enric 15, 21, 22, 260–63
Mitterand, François 164, 190, 224, 226
modernity 24
Moneo, Rafael 18, 19, 22, 78–79, 82, 113, 148–51, 260
Montaner, Josep Maria 260
monumentality 44–47, 56, 60–63, 106, 133, 148–51, 164, 210, 219, 224, 226, 236, 290–93
Moore, Charles 134
morality 23
Morel, Jean Paul, see Chaix
Morin, I.B. 242
movement, see time
Mumford, Lewis 18, 21, 120, 260
Muratori, Saverio 58
museums 84–89, 112–13, 126–31, 134–35, 136–37, 148–51, 172–73, 174–77, 190–93, 208–09, 226–29, 268–71, 272–75, 276–79, 290–93
Muzio, Giovanni 62

N

narrative architecture 112, 194–95; see also iconic means
neo-brutalism 32, 96, 260–63
neo-realism 22, 206
Neumeyer, Fritz 23
Neutra, Richard 138
new abstraction 134
Nicolet, Robert 227
Niemeyer, Oscar 16, 106–09
Nochlin, Linda 22
'non-finito' 22, 268
Nono, Luigi 246
Nouvel, Jean 15, 174–77, 178–81, 276

O

OMA, see Koolhaas
'open' system 74, 84–89, 124, 168–71
organic pattern 75, 232, 254
Ortiz, Antonio, see Cruz
over-aesthetization 53

P

Palacios, Antonio 138
Palladianism 55, 62; see also classical architecture
Parat, Pierre 176
Parent, Claude 20, 131
Paricio, Ignacio 128, 132–33, 252
Pavel, Thomas 150
Pei, I.M. 188, 225, 226–29
Peichl, Gustav 20, 110–11, 208
Peressutti, Enrico 18
performing arts 84–89, 164–65, 173, 182–85, 190–93, 214–17
periphery 21, 33, 174, 180, 182, 214, 218, 234, 248, 260
Perrault, Dominique 188–89
Perrausin, Gilles 35
perspective 25
Petit, Marie 33
Piano, Renzo 11, 14, 16, 17, 84–89, 120–23, 124, 246–47, 248–51, 264–67
Picturesque 17, 20, 81, 104
Pietilä, Raili and Reima 18, 152–55
Pingusson, Georges-Henri 32, 292
Pinós, Carme, see Miralles
Pompidou 84–89
Pop Art 274
populism 10, 11, 20, 45, 52, 56, 58, 60, 62, 69, 76, 82–88, 90, 92, 198
Portzamparc, Christian de 11, 107, 190–93
post-modernism 22, 31
Pound, Ezra 62
Pozo, Aurelio del 17, 18
programmatic innovation 14, 84–88, 146, 236
proportion system 136–37
Proust, Marcel 187
Prouvé, Jean 16, 86, 104, 106, 116, 176, 178
Puig, Ramon 238
pure space 277
purism 162

Q

Quaroni, Lodovico 206

R

Rahv, Philip 228
Ramirez, Juan Antonio 225
rappel à l'ordre 11–13
realism 21, 138, 166, 174, 206, 216, 234, 236
realism, dirty 21–22, 174–77, 178–81, 182–85, 214–17, 234–35, 236–37, 242–43, 260–63, 268, 272–75
regionalism 17, 55, 65, 78, 80, 82, 94, 100, 115, 132, 142–43, 150, 152, 166, 196, 198, 204, 212, 252, 260
regionalism, critical 17–19, 64–67, 78–79, 81, 82–83, 92–95, 114–15, 132–33, 148–51, 152–55, 198–201, 238–41, 264
Renaudie, Jean 20, 32
residential facilities 44–47, 52–53, 54–55, 60–63, 64–67, 80–81, 82–83, 90–91, 92–95, 96–99, 114–15, 144–47, 166–67, 178–81, 186–87, 196–97, 198–201, 236–37, 242–45, 264–67
re-use 120–23, 196
Riboulet, Pierre 33, 34
Rice, Peter 23, 125, 172, 246
Ridolfi, Mario 206
rigorism 13–17, 62, 108, 142, 160, 168, 234
rigorism, skin 15–17, 62, 100–03, 106–09, 124, 160–65, 172–73, 248–53
rigorism, structural 14–15, 84–89, 116–19, 168–71, 146–47, 254–57, 284–85
Rogers, Carl 196

Rogers, Ernesto 18, 206
Rogers, Richard 11, 14, 74, 84–89, 116, 120, 124, 156–59, 203, 214
Rosen, Charles 292
Rosenberg, Harold 127, 274
Rossi, Aldo 12, 19, 56–59, 60–63, 107, 200, 203, 290
Rousseau, Jean Jacques 10, 47, 80
Rowe, Colin 210

S

Saarinen, Eero 15, 152, 284
Saenz de Oiza, Francisco Javier 15, 16, 100–03
Samaras, Lucas 234
Sarfati, Alain 23, 166–67
Sauerbruch, Matthias, see Zenghelis
Scheffler, Karl 27
Schiller, Johann Christoph Friedrich von 47
Schinkel, Karl Friedrich 28, 138, 210
Schklovsky, Victor 18, 22; see also defamiliarization
Schoenberg, Arnold 223, 292
Scott Brown, Denise, see Venturi
Scully, Vincent 12
Seigneur, François 180
Sennett, Richard 126
Serlio, Sebastiano 25, 26
Serra, Richard 268
'servant' and 'served' spatial structure 15, 48, 74, 124, 156, 205, 244; see also Kahn, Louis
Silver, Nathan 22
Simounet, Roland 33
Siza, Alvaro 70, 82, 90–91, 114
skin rigorism, see rigorism, skin
Smithson, Alison and Peter 23
Snozzi, Luigi 19, 80–81, 142
social housing 60–63, 68–71, 80–83, 90–91, 92–95, 96–99, 144–47, 166–67, 178–81, 186–87, 198–201, 242–43, 264–67
Sota, Alejandro de la 15, 22, 78, 138–41
Speer, Albert 144, 186
sports facility 142–43, 246–47, 252–53
Spreckelsen, Otto von 224–25
Stalinist architecture 18, 186
Stella, Frank 39–40
Stevens, Wallace 154
Stirling, James 12, 18, 22, 91, 113, 126–31
Strauss, Richard 194
structural rigorism, see rigorism, structural
Stübben, Joseph 26
Studio PER, see Clotet
Sullivan, Louis 78
suprematism 288
syncretism 78, 84
Szyszkowitz, Michael 20, 208

T

Taba, Beno 18, 152
Tafuri, Manfredo 32, 206
Taillibert, Roger 32, 34
Taut, Bruno 18, 90
Team X 124, 153, 168, 200
technology transfer 157
terminals, see transportation facilities
Terry, Quinlan 12, 202–03
Thurnauer, Gérard 34
time, aspect in architecture 22, 126–31, 148–51, 220–23, 229, 242–43, 254–57, 284–85, 290–93
transparency 75, 197, 258–59
transportation facilities 254–57, 258–59, 284–85
Trella, Massimo 230
Trilling, Lionel 143
Tschumi, Bernard 34
Turrell, James 216
Tusquets, Oscar, see Clotet
typology 12, 13, 56, 58, 62, 134, 290
Tzonis, Alexander 23

U

Ungers, O.M. 12, 134–35
universal space 104, 164, 190, 258–59
university 44–47, 168–71, 204–07
urbanity 25, 126, 132, 187
utopia 10, 44, 64

V

Velez, Antonio 19
Venezia, Francesco 12
Venice Biennale 33
Venturi, Robert 15, 18, 22, 73, 104, 112, 150, 160, 166, 182, 237, 272–75, 284
vernacular architecture 15, 50, 80
Vetges tu i Mediterrània 234–35
Vince, Agnes 244
Virilio, Paul 181
Vitart, Myrto 21, 214–17
Vriesendorp, Madelon 185

W

Wagner, Otto 27
Watkin, David 202
Weber, Brandt & Partners 14, 124, 168–71, 172, 204
well-formedness 22, 73, 274
Wenders, Wim 22, 214
Wilkins, William 272
Wilson, Robert 216
Winter, John 104
Wittgenstein, Ludwig 20, 272
Wittkower, Rudolf 232
Woods, Shadrach 168
workplace 40, 51, 74–75, 78–79, 100–03, 106–09, 110–11, 124–25, 138–41, 156–59, 218–19, 220, 230, 234, 244–45
Wright, Frank Lloyd 16, 50, 101, 156

Z

Zenetos, Takis 15
Zenghelis, Elias 21, 236–37
zero-degree architecture 26, 182
zig-zag motif 94, 292
Zumthor, Peter 16, 160–63